D1649164

Redefining Sexual Ethics

REDEFINING SEXUAL ETHICS

A Sourcebook of Essays, Stories, and Poems

Edited by

Susan E. Davies
Eleanor H. Haney

THE PILGRIM PRESS   CLEVELAND, OHIO

Copyright © 1991 by The Pilgrim Press

All rights reserved. Except for brief quotations used in critical articles or reviews, no part of this book may be reproduced, stored in a retrieval system, or transmitted by any means without the prior written permission of the publisher.

Scripture quotations are from the New Revised Standard Version Bible, copyright 1989, Division of Christian Education of the National Council of the Churches of Christ in the United States of America, and are used by permission.

Book design by Jim Gerhard.
Cover design by Jim Gerhard.

Library of Congress Cataloging-in-Publication Data

Redefining sexual ethics : a sourcebook of essays, stories, and poems
    / edited by Susan E. Davies, Eleanor H. Haney.
      p. cm.
    Includes bibliographical references.
    ISBN 0-8298-0912-0 (acid-free paper)
      1. Sexual ethics. 2. Sex in literature. 3. Sex—Religious
aspects. 4. Sex role. I. Davies, Susan E. II. Haney, Eleanor
Humes.
    HQ32.R43 1991
    305.3–dc20   91-33864
                                                          CIP

This book is printed on acid-free paper.

Printed in the United States of America.

10 9 8 7 6 5 4 3 2 1

The Pilgrim Press, Cleveland, Ohio

Contents

Religious Community, Theology, and Sexuality

Social Structures and Sexuality

PART TWO: THE LAND WE SEEK

Personal Statements

Introduction

Eleanor H. Haney

Redefining Sexual Ethics locates the exploration of sexuality and sexual ethics in the context of contemporary, multicultural movements for liberation. It explores two questions: How do we understand our human sexuality in the light of the ethics of liberation from oppressions based on race, gender, age, class, sexual orientation, disability, and the human exploitation of the natural world? Who defines a new ethic, a new way of being sexual, a liberated sexuality?

THE NEED FOR A NEW STARTING POINT

These questions indicate the need for a new starting point for a fruitful discussion. The question of how we understand our sexual being and action recognizes that human sexuality as we know it is primarily a social construct, not simply a biological given. People in positions of power and authority in the West have, over centuries, shaped present-day understanding and experience of embodiedness, of what it means to have a physical body. Certain expectations, values, and beliefs have been given to our physical selves, and those characteristics vary according to the social categories we fall into, for example, straight, white, young, affluent, male; old, white, female. Further, institutions have been designed in which those characteristics are reproduced from generation to generation and which order the expression of our embodiedness. The major institution in Western culture is, of course, marriage. The critique offered in this book is that much of the construction of sexuality in regard to marriage is oppressive to individuals and supports other, equally oppressive institutions and conventions such as racial supremacy; economic elitism; patriarchy; the human domination of nature; and disapproval of gay and lesbian people, the old, and the disabled.

The question whether any one individual or group has the authority to speak for all on sexual ethics in relation to God's will or the natural law reveals the editors' deep awareness of the oppressiveness that has resulted from an elite group speaking for the many. We believe that a first step toward creating a new ethic, new constructions of sexuality, is to listen, to listen to a diversity of voices, speaking, singing, crying, screaming out of their own experiences and perceptions.

This belief means that the resources for formulating sexual ethics today must be multicultural and feminist. They must reflect the experiences and perspectives of all who have been controlled, devalued, rendered powerless, and hurt, if not destroyed, by the dominant social construction and by individuals who have ordered their lives by that construction. Such ethics must also reflect the experiences of those who have been dominant and privileged and who are struggling against their advantageous socioeconomic position. The struggles of each group illumine dimensions of the social construction of sexuality and its connection to oppression.

Further, and equally important, the struggles and insights of each group are located within a particularity of history and experience. This concreteness means that the issues identified by each group have their own authority and pain and should not be dismissed by others as somehow invalid, insignificant, or inadequate. This particularity also helps protect us against the temptation to formulate some kind of universal sexual ethics that abstracts from the historicity of people's lives. Normative sexual ethics may be intrinsically and profoundly pluralistic and "contextual," a concept that has to be redefined.

There is no literature — either a single work or a collection — that currently offers that perspective. This book seeks to meet the need for it by bringing together writings by women and men struggling with issues of, or celebrating, sexuality from a diversity of views. It includes contributions by and about old people, white people, people of color, gay and straight people, and people in relation to the rest of the natural world. Further, this diversity is built into each phase of understanding and ethical construction. The stories of our lives are diverse, the analyses of the social context and construction are diverse, and the attempts to envision and formulate alternatives are diverse.

The forms of these contributions are also diverse. They include poems, songs, essays, and stories. They speak to the cognitive, emotional, intuitive, and expressive dimensions of our selves.

The idea for such a book arose during an annual gathering of feminist ethicists. Each year, a group of East Coast feminist scholars and activists concerned with feminist liberation ethical theory and practice meets to share work in progress and areas of common concern. On one occasion, several of us had identified the absence of readily available material that approaches issues of sexuality from the perspectives of the many groups in the United States that are struggling for liberation and integrity — women and men of color, those addressing issues of age and disability, those advocating an end to the exploitation of nature, as well as those largely white authors challenging sexism and heterosexism. At the same time, we all recognized that to formulate a new ethic ethically, we needed those perspectives; we needed to work within the framework of an ongoing, culturally diverse conversation.

The conclusion we drew from that discussion was inevitable. We should create such a resource. This book is the result.

VALUES AND BELIEFS SHAPING THIS BOOK

Redefining Sexual Ethics reflects certain values and ethical convictions of its editors. We believe, for instance, that ethical reflection about sexuality must be grounded in a person's experiences. That conviction means that one should be aware of her or his own sexuality, that one should be cognizant of how membership in a particular group, whether dominant or subordinate, shapes one's sexuality, and that one should be aware of the diversity of sexual understandings and experiences.

Related to this conviction about grounding in experience is a second belief — that experiential realities are to be understood as resources or perspectives, not as problems. Thus, for instance, the sexual identities and concerns of "disabled" people are not ethical problems, to be solved primarily by "abled" ethicists; rather, the experiences of the disabled are necessary resources and perspectives for understanding the way sexuality has been constructed in the United States and our common existence as sexual beings. Certainly there are specific issues to be addressed, but the first task is to understand the ways in which the dominant culture has created many of the problems that disabled people face with respect to their sexuality. Then we can address both the common and distinct issues we face as individuals and members of oppressed or privileged groups.

A third conviction of the editors is that normative ethics moves between the poles of analysis of what exists and construction of what might be and that both the analysis and the construction are political as well as personal. Sexual ethics is intrinsically political.

The analysis represented in the book is of two kinds: it includes an analysis of religious and social patterns that have negatively, oppressively shaped our sexuality; it also seeks to identify some of the alternatives hidden within those patterns that can be resources for change. Further, both kinds of analyses are made of the traditions of the dominant and the traditions of the oppressed. We have all internalized oppression, and our sexuality bears the scars of our lives. At the same time, we believe there are resources to be found in all traditions.

As a normative sexual ethic is rooted in analysis, so it is also rooted in constructive ideas, both evocative and reflective, both theoretical and practical. Ethical construction includes visions and images of something "better" than what currently exists, something more just, more satisfying, less destructive, something good. It includes principles and values underlying and shaping those visions. It includes policies and perhaps even rules of personal and social action. And it includes the actual struggles to transform the personal and social status quo toward that goodness.

Finally, the book is an invitation. We believe that identifying and constructing an ethic is an ongoing endeavor. It requires the insights, resources, and questions of all of us who are committed to creating a more just and peaceful universe. There should not be and really cannot any longer be "experts" who hand to others an ethical answer book.

ORGANIZATION OF THIS BOOK

The book is organized in the light of two principles. The first is rhythm. It begins with poetry and ends with poetry. The analytical material is contained within the boundary posts of the more expressive writings and, we hope, is accountable to the latter. Further, the beginning is in adolescence — a painful time for many of us. It ends in joy. That ending may reflect the editors' hope as much as present reality. The next-to-last piece, "Eudora," is an excerpt from Audre Lorde's biomythography, *Zami: A New Spelling of My Name*. It is there in a place of honor because so many of us have learned so much from Audre Lorde, and we wish to thank her. It is there also because it includes — and in a sense, therefore, concludes — so many themes in the book, and it does so transformatively. Heterosexism, racism, and ableism are all challenged, and, for the time being, overcome in a love that is painful, joyful, and ultimately nurturing.

Within those boundary posts there are much pain and violence. There are also resistance, survival, and challenge to find and live in more just and healthy patterns.

The second organizing principle is based on our conviction that feminist ethics moves between the two poles of analysis and construction. Following that principle, we divided the selections into two parts. Part One, "The Ground We Walk On," deals with the present; it contains analyses of what is wrong and also of some of the resources for constructing an alternative ethic and society. It is subdivided into three areas.

The first, "The Days of Our Lives," contains vignettes, or samples, of what it means to be sexual in the United States today. The material ranges over an individual's life from adolescence to old age. It also ranges across racial, cultural, and gender lines. The material is allusive, illustrative, and provocative. To it should be added the stories and experiences of readers and class members, if this book is being used as a text. All of us provide the resources for understanding and creation.

The second and third subsections of Part One are analyses of religion and society. They reflect aspects of the structures of oppression that define our sexual being and activity. The material examines issues of power and powerlessness, control and violence, pain and terror, and some of the connections among the different forms of oppression and domination. Some of the selections, indeed, say very little about our sexuality but help illumine what is meant by "structures of oppression." Class members should be encouraged to draw their own conclusions.

Part Two, "The Land We Seek," deals with the future; it includes material that envisions alternatives, explores moving toward those alternatives, and suggests dimensions of a normative ethic. And, of course, once again, readers should be encouraged to develop and test their own ethical perspectives and determine what the tests are for a valid or "good" ethic.

Some of the contributions contain material relevant to the themes of several subsections. Eleanor Haney's article, "Sexual Burden," for instance, includes a theological analysis that could profitably be read in connection with the other analytical material in Part One. Since its focus, however, is on constructive ethics, it is located in Part Two.

The book concludes with a section "For the Classroom," which suggests a variety of ways of using the selections in a classroom situation. It contains several principles of feminist pedagogy with examples of how they might be applied. It also contains an author-by-author series of questions and exercises designed to deepen both the cognitive and intuitive exploration of the material and one's own sexuality, the ability to relate personal dimensions of sexuality to social and structural ones, and the construction of a normative ethic and new society.

THEMES OF THIS BOOK

A number of major themes are reflected or addressed in the selections. One is the relative absence of theoretical attention to love — either the emotions of romantic love or love as an ethical value. The absence was not intentional on the editors' part. We did not set out to select material that ignored love, and the reasons for its absence are unclear. Perhaps there is simply a drawing back from the assumed connection between sex and love that has prevailed both popularly and theologically. Perhaps it is coincidence. Perhaps it is related to an uneasiness about the way in which the language of love has masked abusive relationships.

At the same time, there are strong expressions of many kinds of love. The selection by Audre Lorde is an eloquent and moving account of a loving encounter between two women, one of whom has had a mastectomy. The poems by Gina Masur are brief poetic evocations of sexual passion. Sharon Hashimoto and Nellie Wong write of intergenerational love, Deborah Carney of the love of God, and Redwing Wilderbrook of the love of nature.

A second theme concerns the ambiguity and complexity of sexual experience. There are pain, terror, and violence in sex; incest and rape thread their way through the selections. Confusion and guilt about sexual identity abound. Sex is used to support racism and ableism and militarism. It is a commodity and a tool for survival. Communion and ecstasy seem to be rare phenomena for many.

A third theme is the many-sided connection between religion and sexuality. Susan Davies traces theological and liturgical connections to sexual abuse. Emilie Townes and James Evans reflect on the black church and issues of justice; Davies and Carney bear witness to the pain and hope of lesbian clergy. Haney and Carter Heyward explore oppressive dimensions of Western theological traditions. And Paula Roper powerfully relates traditional Christian imagery to oppression.

A fourth theme is that of the connections between social structure and sexual oppression. Heyward traces a connection between sexism and heterosexism, and Debra Connors traces some connections between ableism and sexual oppression. Carolyn Merchant traces historically some of the connections among patriarchy and exploitation of nature. Other selections explore the impact of racism, violence, and capitalism on sexuality.

John Stoltenberg, James Nelson, and Roberto Mendoza, from radically different cultural and racial contexts, explore something of what it means to be male in American society and share some of the struggle to attain an ethical manhood, a sixth theme of the book.

Ways to go about formulating normative sexual ethics is a seventh theme. Many writers explore methodological questions. James Evans, for instance, locates black theology in the full black community, a community that includes women as well as men. Paula Gunn Allen explores resources in Native American cultures for developing an alternative ethic.

Gloria Anzaldúa explores the borderlands between cultures as a starting point for normative reflection.

Several of the essays and poetry reflect other efforts to develop normative ethical perspectives. Haney pursues a structural approach. Evans identifies areas in black theology that must be revised and some of the resources for the task. Stoltenberg and Nelson identify new starting points for redefining male sexual identity and activity. Judith Plaskow suggests directions for a new Jewish theology of sexuality. Carney, Lucy Hitchcock, Haney, and Wilderbrook all in somewhat different ways seek to redefine and revalue white women's bodily existence and integrity. And Roper's poetry images a powerful sacramental role for women.

A number of selections address or identify specific norms for sexual activity, an eighth theme. For Haney, they include justice, healing, survival, respect, and nurturance. Similarly, Plaskow seeks an integration of sexuality and spirituality.

A ninth theme concerns the relationship between a sexual ethic and other ethics. Many of the authors assume or state explicitly that there is no special ethic of sexuality; it is part of a larger social-personal ethic. As such, therefore, it is a social ethic as well as a personal one. Structural issues in society must be addressed as well as interpersonal ones.

The last theme is ceremony. Our lives and their passages need ceremonies that liberate, that are just. These ceremonies may be transformations of older ones; they may be new. Mary Hunt and Vicki Hollander explore such possibilities. Readers may want to create some of their own.

Finally, a few specific sexual personal-social issues are addressed. They include prostitution, pornography, the ethics of monogamy and marriage, and sado-masochism, among others. They are not, however, addressed in any comprehensive way, and readers may want to explore any of these or others much more fully than the treatment given them here. The purpose of this book is not so much to explore such issues in depth as to suggest the diversity of perspectives from which any issue must be addressed.

ELEANOR H. HANEY

Redefining Sexual Ethics

PART ONE
THE GROUND WE WALK ON

The Days of Our Lives

Adolescence

Vickie Sears

In peddlepusher days
I'd stand in front of the mirror
nipple pinching
pulling them to encourage growth
envied classmates with burgeoning blossoms and
evidence of training bras
barely shadowed beneath their blouses
snapped by boys amid laughed whispers.
oh well
I'd content myself with pubic hairs
all of ten or so
and wondered if anyone knew what was happening to my body.

it took forever to convince mother that
one of stepfather's white sunday churchshirts
worn only at funeral mass or easter
was a necessity to match
rolled-up bluejeans and penny-crested loafers.
dad said I was like a greenbay packer and that was
the best someone who looked like me could hope for.
I'd adjust my glasses with a humph
bury hurt
leave to play baseball
where I was invincible in running
fast as spit splitting the wind.
if there wasn't a game,

"Adolescence" by Vickie Sears is reprinted from *Gathering Ground: New Writing and Art by Northwest Women of Color* (Seattle: Seal Press, 1984). Copyright © by Vickie Sears. Used by permission.

I'd run in the hot of the day awhile,
mom wanted me in the sun,
then make my way through the window of
my room
where waited all the secrets of the world.

there were movie magazines about people from the
1920's through the 1950's
pill bottles filled with bugs so I could be a scientist
a backless panda bear where treasures were hidden
prayer books with rosary beads for the time I wanted to be a nun
secrets of my body to explore
despite the threat of wart-covered fingers
so I could be a woman
and cosmopolitan and seventeen
which assured me of what I needed to know of
how to catch and love a husband
because just having a man was wicked.
there was paper and pencils
to weave a life where it was
alright to be a girl and not a linebacker.
poems spilled from a midnight pen
scratching by flashlight under the covers.
there I was Dickinson, Brontë or Woolf
good and powerful
true to whoever I was
knowing I was lovely.
I took all the magazine tests on
how you got along with your husband
I always did well.
then came the curse or
riding the white bunny
as my mother euphemistically called it.
it interfered with baseball.
brought sweetsmiles from mom's friends with
chimings about being a young lady and
not letting anyone touch me
lectures from dad which presumed I'd be somehow bad
and his nickname of basketball boobs.
I hated it
I loved it
there was a secret everyone knew

but only I could feel
it promised other worlds to which a cosmopolitan prince
would whisk me.
did it show?
sing the treasure of itself?
powerful gift
bringer of admonitions
secret weapon
for what I never knew.
what an awesome event
that's what ladies home journal called it all
participant in a miracle
I waited to get pregnant
but nothing happened.
oh yes,
the problem was
I didn't have a husband.

Then Green

Gina Masur

For one rub of your cheek
I'd leave my nest
of a bed, the cat's frost-
muttered purr, I'd go out
morning or night, (would the stars
be beating their light-
song? or the sun
sliding between
the firs?) just for one
slow caught kiss, I'd offer
myself to the snow
heart first — then green
would leap the synapse
between body and soil, snow melt,
seeds flower, webs
of leaves spread sudden

•

    kissing, with tongues
entering each other's mouths
    that new place
       is this how a leaf feels
giving itself to the sky?
•

A Native American's Experience with Feminism

Roberto Mendoza

While growing up in rural Oklahoma, among my people, the Musco-gee Creeks, I first became aware of the difference in men's and women's roles and power. My people and our culture had been all but destroyed. My people had endured the Trail of Tears (forced removal from ances-tral lands in Georgia and Alabama) in the nineteenth century and forced termination of our sovereignty by the formation of the State of Ok-lahoma from our national territory in 1907. In addition, the cultural genocide practiced by the United States government and the missionar-ies had nearly stamped out our traditional Green Corn religion. Southern Baptist white patriarchy lay heavily on my oppressed people, creating a hi-erarchy of power, status, and economic strength that benefited the men at the expense of the women.

GROWING UP IN OKLAHOMA

My own grandfather was a minister in the Creek Indian Baptist Church. He was not a bad man, but he took for granted that women would stay home with the children and serve their husbands and that children could be physically punished for disobedience. My stepfather, a Creek veteran of World War II, was cast in the same mold. He expected my mother to do all the cooking and housecleaning. He ab-solutely forbade her to work outside the home. During the war, before she was married, my mother had been a riveter at Douglas Aircraft and had fond memories of being self-reliant and earning her own money.

In addition, my stepfather suffered from the expectations of him as a man. When his father died, he became the head of the household and had to drop out of school and go to work in his early teens. That experi-ence and the experience of World War II hardened and embittered him.

The loss of a relatively well-paying union job during a drawn-out strike further undermined his self-esteem. He took to arguing about money with my mother, became possessive and suspicious of her, and often sat on the porch, brooding and isolated.

I remember being angry at my stepfather's treatment of my mother, but I also remember my mother subtly favoring the boys in the family. As my older sister reached puberty and tried to rebel against sex roles, my mother became more fierce in her efforts to keep her daughter under control.

In addition to the sexism I saw as a child, all of us experienced the overt racism prevalent in Oklahoma in the 1950s, but it wasn't until I went to college in the 1960s and read Marx, Upton Sinclair, and John Steinbeck that I began to understand the connection between racism and classism. As my awareness grew, I became increasingly angry at the American capitalist system and became a Marxist.

PREPARING IN NEW YORK AND SAN FRANCISCO

Then, when I reached New York City in the mid-1960s, I began to understand the significance of what I had experienced as a child — the oppressiveness of sexism. I started going with a woman, a non-Indian, who was reading books such as Betty Friedan's *The Feminine Mystique* and Simone de Beauvoir's *The Second Sex*. She began to see why she had so much trouble breaking into theater, even though she was an excellent actress and playwright (she didn't have the "right" looks). She demanded that I get rid of my sexist conditioning — expecting her to do all the housework, for instance. At first I was defensive and apprehensive. But since, as a Marxist, I had already made a commitment to human liberation, I adapted to the equal-housework situation quickly. I also remembered that my mother did not mind us doing housework and even taught us how to cook and to wash and iron clothes. In another area, however, I was unable to meet my friend's expectations. I found it very difficult to share long-buried feelings, and I still tended to stuff away those that made me feel weak, feelings of jealousy and low self-esteem.

We moved to San Francisco and began trying out drugs, communal living, "free love," and all the experiments in lifestyle that went with that tumultuous time. My main goal was preparing for what I and a lot of other people thought was an armed revolution that would overthrow all existing bourgeois institutions, especially the hated United States government (the Vietnam War was at its height then). We added Lenin and Mao to our reading of Marx, bought weapons, and devoured manuals on guerrilla warfare.

TAKING AN ACTIVE PART
IN THE AMERICAN INDIAN MOVEMENT

My life took another turn in 1969 when Alcatraz Island was occupied by a group of Native Americans from all over the continent. This event, the first national action by Native Americans in modern times, galvanized many young people and led to a new sense of pride in our history and culture. I plunged into the movement with renewed fervor, which soon became tempered with the reality of the movement's contradictions.

The early phases of the movement were led by charismatic, usually male leaders, who advocated bold, often armed actions that captured the attention of the media. The media focused on these leaders and ignored quieter, more thoughtful leaders, especially women. Women in the Native American movement were expected to remain in the background, supporting the men by doing "women's work" such as cleaning up, typing, and cooking.

Some male leaders also treated the more attractive young women as sex objects. This was especially true of male leaders who grew up in cities and spent time in prisons. Away from the reservations, they were more deeply influenced by white patriarchal society. In this respect they were similar to some black male leaders who grew up in ghettos and who led the Black Power movements of that time.

Men such as Thomas Banyacya, a Hopi spokesman, and John Mohawk, a Seneca editor of *Akwasasne Notes,* who grew up on more traditional reservations, tended to be quieter, more thoughtful, and less inclined to violent, confrontational tactics. Mohawk's culture valued women's leadership, and Banyacya, as a Hopi, was steeped in a spiritual tradition of nonviolence. *Hopi* means "peaceful people." Their approach reflected a positive style of male leadership and made a deep impression on me.

The macho posture of the early American Indian Movement (AIM) leaders was difficult for me to accept. Their competing for leadership and for recognition by the media, as well as their sexist treatment of women, were contrary to my own growing values and commitments. But there were tremendous pressures to go along for the sake of unity. They were putting their lives on the line, suffering prison, assassination attempts, and even death. Yet the more I saw the damage done by uncontested sexism, substance abuse, and playing to the media, the more I became convinced that this style of leadership would ultimately undermine, if not destroy, our movement from within. They were hurting themselves, they were dividing members of the movement, and they were denying women a leadership role.

I co-chaired one West Coast AIM chapter with a mixed-blood Native American woman, and we struggled to confront sexism in our ranks. We encouraged women's leadership, welcomed gay and lesbian Native Americans into our chapter, and encouraged criticism and self-criticism in our leadership. We were, of course, attacked by the macho AIM leaders as being "not traditional," "communists," "not Indian enough," and "letting queers in."

GAINING UNDERSTANDING AND CONTINUING THE STRUGGLE

I moved to a reservation in the East, married, and started to raise a family. I also tried to organize the young people who were beginning to be attracted to the American Indian Movement, or Native movement. One of the strongest young leaders there was a lesbian, who did not hide her identity from her peers. Consequently she suffered a lot of rejection from some of the males on the reservation. This rejection fed her negative feelings toward men but did not end her attempts to work with them and for all her people.

As I struggled with all these issues, trying to understand what was happening within the Native movement and in myself, as well as in the dominant, non-Indian society, I eventually gained insight into the reality and destructive power of internalized oppression. This is the message of the dominant society that oppressed people came to accept as true. Racism, sexism, and homophobia infect our people, just as they do non-Indians. We internalize messages about ourselves and others. As a result, we live with low self-esteem as well as with the realities of poverty, lack of education, and racism directed at us. Putting down gays, lesbians, and women was one way for Native men to feel better than someone else.

Internalized oppression also has the effect of directing our hurt and anger against one another. Native leaders fight other Native leaders, straight Native people fight gay and lesbian Native people, Native men fight Native women. Thus we remain divided and powerless.

Homophobia and sexism among our men and internalized sexism among our women are still a problem in our communities and our movement. Leaders of AIM have not come out clearly and publicly against this oppression in our ranks. But all is not bleak. Increasingly the quieter, more thoughtful leaders, both male and female, are eschewing sexism and homophobia. Two books, *The Sacred Hoop,* by Paula Gunn Allen, and *I Am Woman,* by Lee Maracle, offer good information and positive thinking on these subjects. Native American women such as Janet McCloud and Winona LaDuke are organizing women in groups, for example, the Indigenous Women's Network, which foster economic and political empowerment for Native women in North America. Some of the strongest leaders in this current period are older Dine women, as well as younger ones, such as Pauline Whitesinger and Roberta Blackgoat, from the Big Mountain struggle in Arizona.

I am now active in the Green and Bioregional movements, as well as in the ongoing Native American struggle for sovereignty. The analysis by eco-feminists in the first two movements of the connection between the oppression of the Earth and the oppression of women rings true to me. I believe that patriarchy must be ended if humans and the earth are to achieve their liberation. For there to be a balance between human life and all other life on this planet, we must end the seeking of *power over,* which characterizes patriarchy, and seek *power with* the natural world and one another.

Partings

Sharon Hashimoto

My grandmother speaks my name
slowly, an exotic taste
new on her tongue; asks
again if I have forgotten
anything. I shake my head no,

feeling the heat of the day
bead on my forehead, bake
my skin brown in the silence
that follows. Cool in a sweater,
she watches her hands fold

into a temple on her lap,
remembers in a voice leathery
with sun, of how my father
loved the taste of papaya,
how the juice dripped

from his mouth, made his chin
sticky and sweet. I breathe
the damp smell of Oahu
she sighs into the air. Soon,
I will be gone, pulled away

like the tide from the sand
and she will begin anew

"Partings" by Sharon Hashimoto is reprinted from *Gathering Ground: New Writing and Art by Northwest Women of Color* (Seattle: Seal Press, 1984). Used by permission.

her waiting of long days
swirling into night. She tells
me she will pray until I am safe

in Seattle and I can see her
kneeling, legs bent beneath
the blue print dress, chanting
a sutra as thick as the incense
she will burn. When she rises

her legs will ache until she cups
the muscles between her hands.
Now we embrace, her arms twining
like leis around my neck, fingers
linked in a gentle clasp

and I am afraid to let go
for she will crumble, then I will
forget how for this moment
she is soft as a plumeria blossom,
small as a child.

Mean Old Woman Blues

Susan Savell

I've been a good girl all my life,
Let me tell you, it's been boring,
And I've paid a price —
Never getting what I really want for me.
I've never shown you just how mean I can be,
But tonight there's no "making nice" in me,
And, darlin', I'm not just asking, no!
I'm telling you, you listen carefully
When I let you know what I want for me —
I've got the mean, I'm gonna be a mean old woman blues.

CHORUS:
I'm gonna be a mean old woman
Someday before I die!
I'm gonna be a mean old woman,
Someday before I cry anymore!
I'm gonna scream, shout, let the ugly out —
And you're gonna feel what demanding's about —
When I sing the mean old woman blues.

Now I see how bad I've been treating myself,
Let me tell you, it's been awful,
The way I've lost my health —
Working so hard to keep it all inside of me.
I've been so sweet and nice and understanding of everybody
    but myself,

"Mean Old Woman Blues" by Susan Savell, ASCAP. Copyright © by Ritual Music Publishing Co. Used by permission.

But lookout, darlin', tonight I'm not just aching, no!
I'm taking me back home to California shores,
Gonna get me some sunshine, and maybe more!
I've got the mean, I've got the mean old woman blues.

The Death of Long Steam Lady

Nellie Wong

If Paisley Chan had her way, she would not go to Long Steam Lady's funeral. But of course she must. If she didn't go, she couldn't forgive herself. Besides, she loved Long Steam Lady and she missed seeing the old woman sitting in the sun in Portsmouth Square. Long Steam Lady with her plastic shopping bag filled with bock choy, carrots and sometimes a roll or two of pressed crab apples. Long Steam Lady with her painted eyebrows and fat red lips which even made them thicker, more sensuous than Paisley thought she should have colored them. But who was she, Paisley Chan, to say, to judge how Long Steam Lady dressed, how Long Steam Lady decorated herself? Even in an old flowered nylon dress and a tattered wool coat, Long Steam Lady looked elegant, with her eyes closed, letting the sun beat down on her unlined face, her unwrinkled hands.

Paisley dressed herself slowly and deliberately. What to wear to a Chinese funeral these days? Though Paisley was not a blood relative, she would wear sensible navy blue, or perhaps her coffee-brown pantsuit and her beige polyester blouse, the one she could tie into a puffy bow. Yes, she'd look tailored, dignified, and she would not wear lipstick. Yes, she'd walk into Gum Moon Funeral Parlor at the edge of Portsmouth Square, and no one would know her. Paisley Chan, thirty-six years old. Paisley Chan, who worked as a telephone receptionist in the Financial District for nineteen years. Paisley Chan, who discovered Long Steam Lady looking grand in a frayed purple cloche in Portsmouth Square, who found herself having lunch with a talkative old woman for the past three months, who found it refreshing to leave her office every day at lunch, a reprieve from

"The Death of Long Steam Lady" by Nellie Wong is reprinted from *The Death of Long Steam Lady* by Nellie Wong (Los Angeles: West End Press, 1986). Copyright © 1984 by Nellie Wong. Used by permission.

the enforced sterility of saying, "Good morning, J & C Enterprises," as if she were a machine.

Paisley ran a tortoise comb through her thick curly hair. Then she grabbed an Afro comb and separated several stubborn strands, letting them curl away from her scalp, then watched the hair form commas, curving into each other like a chorus line of dancers in a dream. Long Steam Lady had told Paisley that she had been a dancer, a dancer at Imperial City, which was now a disco. Whether that was true Paisley didn't know and she didn't care. She loved sitting in Portsmouth Square listening to Long Steam Lady spin her stories of how she slithered in sequined gowns, how she danced in top hats and tails, how she tap danced, how she tangoed with her lover-partner, Alexander Hing, and how she never rose from bed until one o'clock in the afternoon after an exhausting performance.

One day when Paisley was nibbling on hom foon and getting her fingers all sticky, she asked Long Steam Lady how she got her name. Long Steam, *cheong hay,* a talker, a blabbermouth. "Why are you called *Cheong Hay Poa?*" Paisley had asked, licking her fingers and relishing the grease from the filled rice noodles. Several pigeons clustered at Paisley's and Long Steam Lady's feet, pecking at seeds that Long Steam Lady spread lovingly on the ground as she pantomimed a folk dance of planting rice for the autumn harvest.

Paisley had watched the old woman with wonder, with awe. "Well, aren't you ever going to tell me your real name?" Paisley had asked impatiently. "I really want to know. It is Estelle, Miranda, Sylvia?" The old woman closed her eyes for a moment, ignoring the beautiful names that her young companion had tossed at her like newly burst fireworks. "Ah, *Nu,* that doesn't matter. No names matter, don't you know that? I am Long Steam Lady. I am *Cheong Hay Poa* because I talk too much. I talk so much that no one ever listens to me, and no one listens to me because they can't make sense of what I say. Who has time?" She shrugged her shoulders. "I talk about everything, this and that about love, not just worrying where my body will be laid to rest, whether it will be pointed in the right direction of heaven's blessing. Ah, no, life is too short to worry about dying when all one has to do is to love. No name, child, just Long Steam Lady, just *Cheong Hay Poa.* That is enough."

Long Steam Lady had refused to continue the discussion any longer. She had begun to spread more seeds on the ground, and more pigeons clustered around her feet, pecking around her worn shoes, not Dr. Scholl's that were high laced, not in somber black leather, but silver sandals that she had danced in when she was young. The heels were badly worn and in need of repair, but somehow Long Steam Lady's legs were still slender, a dancer's legs with strength and vitality. Long Steam Lady had told Paisley she never married. She had only loved Alexander Hing. Yes, Alexander Hing who danced circles around Fred Astaire. Yes, Alexander Hing. Long Steam Lady's eyes got misty, but Alexander Hing already had a wife.

Paisley slipped on her pantyhose and cursed as she had slipped them on backwards. She removed them and began again. She stared out her apartment window and watched the leaves of a pink camellia bush glisten in the sunlight. She watched the nylon panels move lightly in the breeze. Autumn was her favorite season, Halloween, Thanksgiving, homemade oxtail stew and chrysanthemums. Yes, she'd visit Long Steam Lady with her spider chrysanthemums though she wasn't sure whether Long Steam Lady would be cremated or buried at Ning Yeong Cemetery at Colma.

Paisley didn't know whether Long Steam Lady had any relatives. Long Steam Lady had mentioned once a sister who lived in New York City. Perhaps Paisley would meet that sister today at the funeral, but Paisley didn't even know her last name. Whom would she ask for? Would she yell out, "Yoo hoo, is Long Steam Lady's sister here from New York City? Long Steam Lady, *Cheong Hay Poa,* the dancer, the old woman who died all alone?" Why that would be downright embarrassing for someone whose name she didn't even know. And if she did find the sister, then what? How would she describe her friendship with the old woman? Lunch friends, companions? Philosophers, sisters? Grandmother, granddaughter?

Paisley sighed, again wishing she didn't have to go to the funeral. She didn't want to see Long Steam Lady lying in her coffin, lifeless, painted grotesquely by morticians who knew nothing about her, morticians who would over-rouge her cheeks, morticians who would redesign her with no creativity, no imagination. If Paisley had her way, she would dress Long Steam Lady in a black gown of airy silk crepe, satin spaghetti straps, with a huge sunburst of rhinestones pinned on one shoulder, with a red silk rose tucked into her bunned hair. But no, the morticians would probably dress her in a wool suit of salt-and-pepper tweed, or in a housedress with droopy lavender flowers, or worse yet, in an old coat sweater with large pockets and military buttons. The mourners would never know Long Steam Lady, the dancer. The mourners would never know, would never see the silver sandals that Long Steam Lady wore daily to the park. They would shake their heads. Women would weep and sniff into their handkerchiefs, and Paisley would hear them say, "Long Steam Lady was a good woman, she never harmed anyone." And she would hear them say, "Ai yah, too bad she never married, never had any sons to look after her in her old age."

Paisley had never heard Long Steam Lady complain about not getting married, about not having sons. Sometimes Long Steam Lady wandered in her conversations. Sometimes she jumped from talking about dancing at Imperial City to looking for a letter written to her from her village in Toishan. But always, Paisley remembered, Long Steam Lady's eyes sparkled, her eyes grew large and luminous as she fell into lapses of memory, smiling as if she harbored the most delicious secret in the world.

And then Long Steam Lady was no more. For the past week Paisley had gone looking for her at the bench nearest the elevator in Portsmouth Square. Paisley took roast beef sandwiches and Bireley's orange drinks as if those items would seduce Long Steam Lady's appearance from the dark. Even the pigeons clustered closer to Paisley as she searched for the slender old woman among the crowds of men huddled in their games, among children laughing and running from their mothers, among the men who exercised Tai Chi Chuan, among the shoppers who spilled out into the park.

Paisley kicked herself for not knowing where Long Steam Lady lived. It had to be somewhere in Chinatown, perhaps at Ping Yuen, perhaps up Jackson or Washington Street, or Mason near the cable car barn. But Long Steam Lady, as talkative as she was, never revealed where she slept, never revealed whether she had any relatives looking in on her. But that was what attracted Paisley in the first place. Long Steam Lady's elegance, her dignity, her independence. Though Long Steam Lady must have been at least seventy-five, she never walked dragging her feet. She never hunched. She had moved with the agility of a younger person, younger perhaps than Paisley herself. Funny how Long Steam Lady used to call her "Pessalee" instead of Paisley, speaking to her in a mixture of English and Sze Yip dialect, in a language familiar and warm and endurably American. "Hah, hah," Long Steam Lady had laughed, "you have to learn how to jom the cow meat the right way. See, like this, not like that," and she had begun to move her hands in quick vertical rhythms, showing Paisley how to jom cow meat. "See, it's all in the way how you jom. Jomming, it's the best secret."

Of course, Long Steam Lady had to have a name. How else could relatives have arranged the funeral at Gum Moon? How else could mourners order wreaths of carnations and marigolds streaming with white ribbons, with Long Steam Lady's name brushed in black ink? Although Mr. Eng, the florist, had told Paisley that Long Steam Lady's funeral was Saturday, he never said Long Steam Lady's name. He had said he read her obituary in the *Gold Mountain Times*. Paisley rose from her vanity and searched through a stack of *Chronicles* on her hall table. It had never occurred to her to look through the obituaries in the *Chronicle,* but if there were services for Long Steam Lady, it had to be in the *Chronicle* too. Paisley flipped through the last three days' papers. Nothing on Long Steam Lady, nothing on names such as Wong, SooHoo, Young, Lee, Fong, Chin. Nothing on former dancers at Imperial City, on old women who fed pigeons in Portsmouth Square. On old men who died alone in their rooms. Not that Chinese people didn't die, not that waiters, laundrymen, seamstresses, dishwashers didn't die. Paisley lingered over an article on the death of a philanthropist, a member of the Pacific Union Club, a world-wide traveler, a grandfather of twelve, a civil servant. And if an obituary had appeared in the *Chronicle* on Long Steam Lady, would they have identified her as a talkative crazy old lady who fed pigeons in the park? Would they have described her silver sandals?

Well, she'd go to the funeral, she owed Long Steam Lady that. It didn't matter to Paisley that she wouldn't know any of Long Steam Lady's relatives. Who knows? Perhaps Alexander Hing might be there, an old Alexander Hing in his tapdancing shoes, an old Alexander Hing whose hair might still be black and shiny as Long Steam Lady had described him, whose pencil-thin mustache tickled Long Steam Lady as they kissed? Paisley smiled and pushed her bangs out of her eyes. Long Steam Lady and she sitting together in Portsmouth Square, laughing and talking loudly. Long Steam Lady and she devouring custard tarts as if they were gold. Long Steam Lady and she scolding panhandlers away from their pink boxes of cha siu bow and hah gow and hom foon.

In the sunlight Paisley walked up Washington Street to Gum Moon Funeral Parlor. She cast her eyes across Portsmouth Square, at the bench where she and Long Steam Lady spent many lunch hours together. She saw pigeons pecking near the garbage can. She saw felt hats, grey suits, plaid shirts. She saw beer cans roll across the pathway. Paisley shifted her gaze and began to daydream about silver sandals. At thirty-six perhaps it was not too late to sign up for dancing lessons.

A Hispanic Garden in a Foreign Land

Ada María Isasi-Díaz

After twenty-six years of being away from my mother's garden, I returned to Cuba for a visit in January 1987. For two very special weeks, with the greatest of intentionality, I walked around *la tierra que me vió nacer* (the land that witnessed my birth), the land I have missed so very much. I tried to notice everything around me. My senses were constantly on alert, trying to imbibe every single detail, trying to sear into my heart the sights, sounds, smells of that beautiful island from which I have been gone for over half my life. The beauty of its majestic palm trees, the striking combination of green fields and white sand, the calm blue waters of the tropical sea, the immense variety of the colorful tropical plants and flowers, the exciting rhythms of its music, my Cuban sisters and brothers — no wonder Columbus said, when he landed there in 1492, "This is the most beautiful land human eyes have ever seen."

CAUGHT BETWEEN TWO WORLDS*

Every minute of the two weeks I was in Cuba I reminded myself I was only visiting; I was going to have to leave in a very short time. There I felt the same as I feel in the United States: a foreigner. I am caught between two worlds, neither of which is fully mine, both of which are partially mine. I do not belong in the Cuba of today; I do not belong in the States. I am repeating the history of my mother and of her mother. Grandma came to Cuba as a young woman in search of a brother who had left their home in the small village of Tineo in northern Spain and had never even written to his family. Once in Cuba she was never to

* Heads have been added.

"A Hispanic Garden in a Foreign Land" by Ada María Isasi-Díaz is reprinted from *Inheriting Our Mothers' Gardens: Feminist Theology in Third World Perspective*, ed. Letty M. Russell, Kwok Pui-lan, Ada María Isasi-Díaz, and Katie Geneva Cannon (Philadelphia: Westminster/John Knox Press, 1988). Copyright © 1988 Letty M. Russell. Reprinted by permission of Westminster/John Knox Press.

go back to her native land. My mother was forty-eight when we came
to live in the United States because of the political situation in Cuba.
She has never gone back and now, at the age of seventy-three, has little
hope of seeing Cuba again.

As a foreigner in an alien land, I have not inherited a garden from my
mother but rather a bunch of cuttings. Beautiful but rootless flowering
plants — that is my inheritance. Rooting and replanting them requires
extra work on the part of the gardener; it requires much believing in
myself to make my life flourish away from the tropical sun of Cuba.
Some of the flowers I have inherited from my mother help me to deal
with this situation; others at times can hinder me.

One of my ongoing gardening tasks is to find a place to plant the
flowers I have inherited from my mother. At the age of eighteen I was
uprooted from my country. What I thought would be a hiatus turned
into twenty-six years. I am beginning to suspect it might well become
the rest of my life. For many different reasons I have had no choice but
to try to plant my garden in the United States. But belonging to the
culture of one of the "minority groups" has meant that the plants in
my garden have been seen as weeds or exotica; they are either plucked
up or treated as a rarity. In general they are not accepted as part of the
common garden of the dominant U.S. culture.

Most people think I should not find it too difficult to adapt my flowers
and my gardening style — my cultural inheritance — to a new situation.
After all, culture is always changing; it is dynamic. The fact is, however, that by belonging to a minority culture within another culture,
the changing dynamic of my culture becomes a nonorganic force. The
changes taking place in the Hispanic culture in the United States do not
start from within but are imposed from without. These inorganic changes
do not enhance the culture but rather negate it. Forced changes bring
not flourishing but wilting and dying. A culture forced to change by
outside forces suffers violence; its values begin to deteriorate. A culture
that is not valued, whether by being ignored or by being commercially
exploited, is in danger of losing little by little its will to live.[1]

This is what happens to Hispanic culture in the United States. It is
sacked and raped every time we are told that our children cannot learn
in Spanish in school, when our customs are ridiculed, when our cultural artifacts — typical dress, music, etc. — are commercialized. The
intergenerational crisis among Hispanics goes beyond the usual differences between youth and older people. This crisis is directly connected
to the lack of importance and significance given to Hispanic culture by
the dominant culture. On top of the identity crisis that all young people
suffer as they search for their own worth and a way to be themselves,

Hispanic youths suffer from the violence against our culture in this society. No wonder they try to hide their *abuelitas,* anglicize their names, and join the world of drugs in order to have the money they think will bring recognition. No wonder I have never been able to plant my garden successfully in this society.

TRYING TO PLANT MY GARDEN

In the 1960s I tried to plant my garden in the convent. The enormous value given to family and community in my culture seemed to me to be the very core of this style of life. But, at least in the time when I was there, the restrictions on personal relationships that were part of life in the convent made true community life impossible. The emotional intensity of my Cuban culture was also out of place in the convent. The very poor and oppressed of Peru, among whom I worked for three years, taught me *too much,* and I could not maintain a lifestyle in which people talked about poverty while living a privileged life. Finally, my unwillingness to repress my spontaneity and passion led me to realize that my garden could not flourish within the convent walls.

If not in the convent, as a Roman Catholic woman, where could I make bloom the flower of my commitment to the poor and the oppressed? The search led me to the feminist movement. I was born a feminist on Thanksgiving weekend, 1975, when over one thousand Roman Catholic women met to insist on the right of women to be ordained to a renewed priestly ministry in our church. Failing, as the overwhelming majority of humans do, to remember my bodily birth, I am privileged to remember every detail of this birth to the struggle for liberation. But the process of "giving birth to myself"[2] was not an all-of-a-sudden experience; in many ways the process had started years before.

I spent the early part of my life in Cuba, where I belonged to the dominant race and the middle class. Growing up in the 1950s, I did not notice the oppressive structures of sexism operative in my country. But I was always attracted to struggling along with those "who had less than I did" — as I thought of the oppressed then. As a matter of fact, it was precisely that attraction which made me come to understand my vocation to the ministry. It was that attraction, which I now understand as the seed of my commitment to the struggle for liberation.

At age eighteen I entered the convent, a protected way of life that used to carry with it much prestige and privilege. Therefore, the few times I came into contact with the broader society during the first eight years of my adulthood, I was treated with deference, respect, and even reverence. My life within the convent walls was very difficult, and at the time I did not have the lenses needed to understand ethnic prejudice.

I was greatly misunderstood and suffered much because of it, but I did not have a good analysis of what was happening to me and how I was being treated by the other nuns.

By 1975, therefore, the only oppression I was aware of was the one I suffer within the church simply because I am a woman. It is no surprise, then, that it was in relation to church teaching and practice that I came to understand the dynamics of oppression and joined the struggle for liberation. The 1975 Women's Ordination Conference was such an intense experience that when I emerged from the hotel where we had held the three-day conference, I realized I was perceiving the world in a different way. It took a few months before I realized what the difference was that I was seeing. My eyes had been opened to the reality of sexism. My whole life had been affected; how I saw myself and what I was to do with my life had changed radically.

The struggle against sexism in the Roman Catholic Church has been the school where I have learned about feminism, as well as the main arena in which I have carried out my struggle for liberation during the last twelve years. I rejoice in the sisterhood in whose creation I have participated and am grateful for all that I have learned from the women involved in the Womanchurch movement. This became my home. Soon I proceeded to plant my own garden there; however, that brought conflict into the sisterhood. As long as I toiled in the garden of Anglo feminism, I was welcomed. But as I started to claim a space in the garden to plant my own flowers, the ethnic/racist prejudice prevalent in society reared its head within the Womanchurch movement.

The issue was and is power.[3] Somewhat naively I had thought that together we would decide not only how to garden but what the garden was to look like, what it would be. But the Anglo feminists, being part of the dominant culture, deal with Hispanic women — and other racial/ethnic women — differently from the way they deal with each other. They take for granted that feminism in the United States is *their* garden, and therefore they will decide what manner of work racial/ethnic women will do there.

By the time I began to experience all this, I had learned much about the dynamics of oppression and prejudice and I could understand what was going on. However, what took me totally by surprise was the inability or unwillingness of the Anglo feminists to acknowledge their prejudice. Most feminists "believe that because they are feminists, they cannot be racists." Anglo feminists, like all liberals, sooner or later, have come to the point at which they are willing to "acknowledge that racism exists, reluctantly of course, but nobody admits to being a racist."[4] While whitewashing their personal sins of racism/ethnic prejudice — pun intended — in the restful waters of guilt, they continue to control access to power within the movement. Anglo feminists need to understand that as long as they refuse to recognize that power-over is an intrinsic element of their racism/ethnic prejudice, they will continue to do violence to feminism. As a liberative praxis, feminism has to do with radically changing the patriarchal understandings of power, which are operative even in the feminist movement. Anglo feminists need to remember that, in order to undo patriarchy, we must create societies in which people can be self-defining and self-determining. To achieve that, power has to be transformed and shared.

True sharing of power leads to mutuality, and that is what we Hispanic feminists ask of Anglo feminists. It is not a matter of their allowing us to share in what they define as good. Nor is it only a matter of each one of us respecting what the other says and defending her right to say it. Mutuality asks us to give serious consideration to what the other is saying, not only to respect it but to be willing to accept it as good for all. Hispanic feminists' understandings must be included in what is normative for all feminists. Our priorities must be considered to be just as important as the priorities of the Anglo feminists. All feminists must work together on deciding the priorities for the movement. This is the only thing that will allow me to continue to believe that the feminist movement "is one of the few parties left in town where we can all come together for the larger common cause. But if we're really going to boogie, power has to be shared."[5]

One of the easiest ways to understand the structure of power in society and within the feminist movement is to look at how we both construct and express what we think. Let us, therefore, look at language. For example, the fact that the word "women" refers only to middle- and upper-strata white women shows who decides what is normative. All the rest of us, in order not to be totally invisible, have to add adjectives to the word: *poor* women, *Black* women,[*] *Hispanic* women. *Poor* women means white, underemployed, or unemployed women. Black women means poor *Black* women; Black women who are not poor are called *educated* Black women. Women *of color* in reality refers only to Black women, with the rest of us racial/ethnic women being added as an afterthought — if we are given any thought at all. *Salvadoran* women, *Guatemalan* women — at present they command the attention of our liberal communities. After all, what we need to help change are their countries, not the United States! *Hispanic* women refers to poor women, usually Puerto Ricans, Dominicans, Mexicans, and Mexican Americans.

[*] Black is upper cased by the author's preference.

Then there are *Cuban* women — those middle- and upper-class women down there in Miami who vote conservative. Since heterosexuality is normative in society, that meaning is also included in the words "feminists" or "women." The "others" have to be qualified: *lesbian* women, *bisexual* women.

As these examples show, power always rests with those who define the norm. Language offers us a very important tool for understanding the power dynamics in society and in the feminist movement. It clearly points out to me, at least, where I will not be able to plant my own garden and in which gardens I will never be anything but a hired hand at the very best. The net result of all this, I believe, is an impoverishment of the feminist movement, which in turn arrests its effectiveness and contribution as a liberation movement. As long as Anglo feminists do not share power within the movement with Hispanic, Black, and other racial/ethnic women, the movement will only be capable of bringing about a liberalization of those who control and oppress. Under these circumstances, the feminist movement might moderate patriarchy but it will not do away with it.

MY MOTHER'S BOUQUET

As I go about trying to find a place to plant my mother's flowers, I have to look critically at this inheritance. Some of her flowers are of immense beauty and value. The one my mother values the most stands for her faith in God. *Tener fe* for my mother is to be aware of the ongoing presence of God with her and with those she loves. Faith for her is a deep conviction that God is intrinsic to her life and takes care of her. Her faith in God translates into the common everyday practice of giving credit to God for the good things that happen to her and the family. That has made her come to see that, to a certain degree, what one believes is secondary to the kind of life one leads. In my life this translates into the centrality of orthopraxis instead of worrying about orthodoxy. It is indeed from my mother that I learned we must be about doing the work of God.

A second flower my mother has given me is the understanding *La vida es la lucha* — the struggle is life. For over half my life I thought my task was to struggle and then one day I would enjoy the fruits of my labor. This is the kind of resignation and expectation of being rewarded in the next life that the Roman Catholic Church has taught for centuries. Then I began to reflect on what my mother often tells the family: "All we need to ask of God is to have health and strength to struggle. As long as we have what we need to struggle in life, we need ask for nothing else." This understanding gives me much strength in my everyday life. It has allowed me to be realistic — to understand that, for the vast majority of women, life is an ongoing struggle. But above all it has made me realize that I can and should relish the struggle. The struggle is my life; my dedication to the struggle is one of the main driving forces in my life.

A third flower in my mother's bouquet is her deep commitment to the family. While growing up she knew only a very small portion of her family, since both of her parents had emigrated from Spain with only a few members of their families. Out of this dearth of relatives came a great need to be close to the family she birthed. My mother often says that if all of us, her children and grandchildren and other members of her family, are not with her in heaven — well, it just will not be heaven! For her there is no way to have a good time if it does not involve a major number of us. Her involvement in our lives is continuous and intense. She expects each one of us to be just as involved as she is. For her, love has to be shown with words and action.

My mother's deep understanding of and need for family has given birth to my deep commitment to community and friendship.[6] Like her, I believe that apart from community we cannot be about the work of God — which for me is the work of justice. And the measuring rod for community is how it enables and provides sustenance for friendships. But community, like family, does not just happen. It requires intense, continuous work which must be given priority in the feminist movement, especially across racial/ethnic lines. I believe the building of a new order of relationships based in mutuality is at the core of feminism. And this new order of relationship must start among ourselves as feminists. That conviction is indeed based on my mother's commitment to family.

But not all of my mother's bouquet is necessarily flowers. There are also some weeds. Often, when I disagree with my mother, she gets upset, because she thinks I do not value her way of thinking and the way she has lived. But that is not true. To see things differently, and even to think that the way my mother has acted in certain situations is not the way I would act, is in no way a judgment of her. I have a different perspective and have had very different experiences. As a matter of fact, I think the difference exists in part because what she has told me and the way she has lived have pushed me a few steps farther. I believe we must take time to explain this to our older sisters in the feminist movement. We build on what they have wrought. If we only maintain what they have built, the feminist movement will retreat instead of advancing. Our older sisters in the movement must be told time and again that if we can see farther than they do it is because we stand on their giant shoulders and capitalize on what they have accomplished.

My mother has lived all her life in the private arena of the family. She has never had to work outside her home and has lived for twenty-five years in the United States without speaking English and understanding it only in a limited way. This has led her, I believe, to a lack of understanding and a distrust of those who are different from her, be it because of class, race, sexual preference, or culture. Her lack of personal dealings with people different from herself, coupled with her own personal story of having gone beyond a severely limited economic situation, has resulted in a lack of systemic analysis. For her, people are poor because they are lazy, because they do not try hard the way her mother did to give her and her sister what they needed. My mother's greatest prejudice is against those who do not have an education. She even severely criticizes people in the middle economic strata who have not studied beyond high school.

Because I grew up surrounded by this idea that people were personally responsible for the difficulties in their lives, and because of the privilege due to race, class, and social status that I enjoyed for the first twenty-seven years of my life and as a nun, I have had to struggle to make myself understand the need for systemic analysis. Three things have helped me mightily in this endeavor. The first thing was the immersion experience I had when I lived among the very poor in Peru. I often talk about those years as an exodus experience — an experience that radically changed my life. Those three years gave me the opportunity of being reborn; they made me understand what the gospel message of justice and preferential option for the poor was all about. The second thing that has been most helpful in understanding the need for systemic analysis and has given me some tools to do it has been the opportunity for study. Courses in economics, history, ethics, and anthropology have given me the tools to understand systemic conditions that made personal liberation impossible. Third, some wonderful foremothers have taught me what solidarity is all about by the way they have lived their lives. To join the liberative praxis of the oppressed, and to have personal relationships with them, has enabled me to understand systemic oppression and to go beyond thinking, as my mother does, that persons are oppressed because they do not try hard enough to overcome the limitations of their situations.

The second weed I see in my mother's bouquet is related to the first one and has to do with an inability or unwillingness to see sexism in the private sphere and to change radically in our own personal world the way we relate and operate. As the mother of six daughters who have had to struggle in the public sphere for all their lives, my mother understands and denounces the sexism she sees us struggling against in the workplace. Though many times she feels uncomfortable about my criticism and denunciation of the sexism in the church, she can deal even with that as long as it is not very public. But when it comes to the domestic sphere, she finds it very difficult to criticize the sexist behavior she sees there. This goes beyond the sense that we all have of protecting our own. What she finds difficult is not only criticizing her family but also seeing the oppression of women in any domestic sphere. I believe that what is at work here is internalized oppression; the domestic sphere has been her world, and she has come to see what happens to women in it as our proper role.

A SIEGE MENTALITY AND THE STRUGGLE

There is no way I can communicate adequately to my mother how much I have learned in our sometimes heated discussions about this issue. I have come to understand how much I have internalized my own oppression, not only in the private sphere but also in my role in the church — which until very recently was for me mainly an extension of the family. When internalized oppression moves from the private sphere to the public one, it becomes an element of a "siege mentality."

As a Hispanic I belong to a marginalized group in this society and have had to struggle to understand and deal with the siege mentality we suffer. The need to protect ourselves against discrimination is such an integral part of our lives that we are unable or unwilling to critique ourselves. It is difficult to see criticism as constructive when we are not valued by society. Those of us who as feminists criticize sexism in the Hispanic culture are often belittled and accused of selling out to the Anglo women. But Anglo feminists call into question our integrity and praxis as Hispanic feminists when we are not willing to criticize Hispanic men and culture in public. I would like to suggest that this kind of horizontal violence is linked to both internalized oppression and the siege mentality.

The challenge that lies before me has many different facets. I must struggle to convince myself and other Hispanics that our goal has to be liberation and not participation in oppressive situations and societies. We must not give in to internalized oppression and a siege mentality. We must be willing to look at ourselves and examine our experiences in view of our liberation and continue to insist, no matter where we are, on being included in setting the norm of the feminist movement. Then I have to find renewed strength and commitment to struggle with Anglo feminists over the issue of sharing power with all feminists, unless their goal is to replace one oppressor with another. Finally, I have to challenge myself and others to understand that, as feminists, the changes we are advocating will change the world radically and that we need to begin to live out those changes so they can become a reality.[7] The only way we can move ahead is by living the reality we envision. Our preferred future as feminists will only flower if we allow it to be firmly rooted in

us and among us. It is up to us to change our lives radically if we want
our world to change.

I plow ahead, aware that I must not idealize what I have inherited
from my mother — especially because we have been transplanted and in
that process have lost some of our roots and have not always correctly
reinvented them. I must be careful because as transplants we often have
to defend ourselves, and that can easily distort the truth. What I have
received from my mother, as well as what I have gained on my own,
must be subjected to the critical lens of liberation; that is the only way
I can be faithful to myself and to other Hispanic women and men. The
task is not easy, but the community of my family provides for me a safety
net — it gives me an immense sense of security. This is one of the main
reasons why, for me, hope is guaranteed and I always see possibilities.
That is why I keep trying to plant my garden. That it has been uprooted
several times does not keep me from trying again. Though often it is a
painful struggle, I believe the feminist struggle is the best of struggles,
and this is why that struggle is my life. *¡La vida es la lucha!*

Enero de 1988

Mi querida Alexandra,

Ya tienes 19 meses y empiezas a demostrar ser una niña-mujer llena de vida y de un carácter bien fuerte. Qué bueno! Espero que el mundo siga cambiando para que cuando te toque luchar en esta vida no tengas tantas dificultades como tenemos hoy en día las mujeres. Fíjate, Alex, no te deseo una vida fácil. Pero sí te deseo una vida en la cual la posibilidad de un mundo justo sea más grande de lo que es hoy día.

Eres, mi querida Alex, una mujer de muchos mundos. Tus appellidos, Surasky e Isasi, lo proclaman a los cuatro vientos. No puedo menos que desearte que las experiencias en tu vida sean tan ricas y variadas como la sangre que corre por tus venas. Pero debes también saber que integrar esa variedad, esa multiplicidad de culturas que has heredado no es fácil. Posiblemente siempre sientas tensiones — pero no consideres eso negativo. Lo mejor de la vida es llegar a balancear sin destruir los diferentes elementos presentes en nuestras vidas y en nuestro mundo.

Para mí, Alex, lo más difícil ha sido el permanecer fiel a quien soy. Ser fiel a uno mismo a la vez que tratamos de crecer — de luchar en forma responsable por lo que creemos — eso, Alex del alma, es lo más difícil. Lo que la mayoría de la gente quiere es definirnos y controlarnos — y contra eso tenemos que luchar.

Complica todo esto grandemente el ser mujer... al igual que el hecho de que yo he tenido que venir a vivir y tú has nacido en un país que cree ser el mejor del mundo y que se considera ejemplar. Porque tienes sangre cubana y americana, judía y cristiana yo espero comprendas a edad temprana que si vemos a los demás como mejor o peor que nosotras, nunca habrá paz. Tenemos que estar dispuestas, Alex, a examinar los valores, ideas y costumbres de los demás y ver si las podemos incorporar en nuestras vidas sin dejar de ser quienes somos. Eso es lo que quiere decir el aceptar a los demás... sólo entonces dejaremos de trater de hacer que sean como nosotras; sólo entonces dejaremos de sentirnos amenazadas por otras personas y otros paises; y sólo entonces habrá justicia y paz en nuestro mundo.

Tienes que ser tu propia persona, Alex. Pero nunca creas que lo tienes que lograr sola. Siempre busca apoyo, consejo, ayuda de los que te quieren. Entre ellos estoy yo, Alex... y siempre estaré. Y como tu madrina te bendigo una y mil veces deseándote fuerzas para la lucha y un deseo insaciable de SHALOM.

Te quiere,
Ada María...

The Ninth Hour

Paula Lorraine Roper

He travels alone mostly
but now and again
He leads her to Golgotha

She, like the one before her,
carries a cross
too heavy for simple neck adornment

Mostly, he travels alone
but from time to time
he carries tools
nails, saw, hammer
and charms her to Golgotha

where he strokes her hair
with thorns
where he kisses her wrists
with nails

Time and again, he travels alone
but ever so often
he lulls her to Golgotha

where her blood is
turned to wine
on an altar far too fine
to pass-over ...

Religious Community, Theology, and Sexuality

Let Us Bless Our Angels
A Feminist-Gay-Male-Liberation View of Sodom

Robin Gorsline

Being gay and living that way in the United States requires confrontation with well-developed heterosexist structures of social control whose maintenance and continued vitality require the denial — if not the elimination — of homosexuality. The dominant religions in this nation — Christianity and Judaism — are integral elements of these heterosexist power structures. Because these religions retain considerable power to determine moral values by framing the limits of socially acceptable sexual behavior, they provide powerful support for heterosexist ideology.

Within Christianity and Judaism — as within the larger American culture — the Bible has awesome power to frame the debate surrounding sexual morality. The Hebrew scriptures for both Christians and Jews and the New Testament for Christians form powerful proof texts, against which anyone deviating from socially normative heterosexuality must contend. Nor is it only adherents of these religions who must contend with biblical sexual morality; the entire American culture is permeated with the mythic structures embedded in the scriptures. Anyone challenging dominant structures of morality sooner rather than later must overcome biblical "truths."[1]

I propose here that gay men — feminist, gay men committed to the liberation of all oppressed people — must develop hermeneutical lenses in order to focus a critical gaze on texts contributing to our oppression. We must rob these texts of their power to terrorize us.

To that end, I propose five principles of feminist-gay-male liberation as a normative framework undergirding our efforts to uncover resistance and liberation among traditionally oppressive texts.[2]

After a brief discussion of these principles, I will examine a biblical passage — Genesis 19:1–14, the destruction of Sodom — which more than any other has been used to oppress gay men. Finally, I will offer a

new reading of the Sodom story, a reading based on the reality of gay
men's lives.

A fundamental question is being raised here: Is the Bible, in this instance the Hebrew scripture, a source for normative ethical behavior? I
will make clear my biases at the outset. I read this text, indeed the entire
biblical record, as a white, North American, middle-class, well-educated
gay man whose faith commitments have in the past encompassed Christian elements but who is now engaged in a more freewheeling search
for a spiritual "home." At this writing, I am finding spiritual sustenance among the Radical Faeries, a loose-knit gathering of feminist, gay
men (and sometimes women) who explore and expand our connections
with one another and the world through play, ritual, and political action, as well as within the relative openness of the Unitarian Universalist
tradition.

Such a social orientation makes my reading of scripture contrary to
that of the dominant circles of scriptural interpretation. My reading is a
hermeneutic of resistance. I hope the reader will find sufficient encouragement here to move more fully into his or her own particularity for
the sake of liberation. Together, we make a difference. Together, we keep
resistance — and hope — alive.

FIVE PRINCIPLES OF FEMINIST-GAY-MALE LIBERATION

1. **The liberation project begins with self-affirming, gay men
committed to the struggle of all oppressed people for justice.**
The struggle for justice for gay men begins with the struggle within
each of us to proclaim that we are gay. The heterosexist ideology dominating American culture causes us to doubt ourselves, to doubt the erotic
stirrings that urge us toward other men. Our individual stories differ, but
for most of us, overcoming the fear of "coming out" is the centerpiece.
After coming out, we look back and see that the process leading up to
it appears to be an almost inevitable chain of events. We do not forget,
however, that the struggle was difficult — and essential to our well-being.

After coming out the first few times — coming out in a homophobic
society is a process and not a one-time event — we find we must join with
other gay men, not only for our own support but also to press forward
the larger movement for gay liberation. As we march in the streets, form
organizations, speak in city halls and state capitols, appear on television
and radio talk shows, write letters to the editor, and undertake other
more mundane tasks, others are emboldened to come forward.

In the early 1970s gay liberation made common cause with women,
racial minorities, the poor, and the antiwar movement. Open, self-
identified, gay men joined the struggles for justice then moving America,

and often gay men were assumed to be politically left of center. In the later years of the decade and into the 1980s, sharp rifts appeared in the ranks.[3] In the age of Ronald Reagan and George Bush, the equation gay = left is less certain, in part because many white gay men discovered that there were less militant ways to be "out" and still be upwardly mobile.

Against this trend, feminist-gay-male liberation understands that male privilege, the focus of the dominant heterosexist ideology, is not erased by gayness. Being a man still counts for much in American society; being gay need not necessarily prevent business or professional success, especially in competition with a woman or a person of color.

But these divisions have not put out the fires carefully breathed into life and patiently tended by lonely pioneers in the 1950s and 1960s, fires that were fanned into a blaze in June 1969 by Stonewall Rebellion in Greenwich Village. Participants in today's rallies for racial justice, an end to United States imperialism, abortion rights, nuclear disarmament, and a host of other progressive causes nearly always include a contingent of gay men (usually in conjunction with a group of lesbians).

These activities form the feminist-gay-male liberation movement today. We have struggled out of our closets. We have discovered that we must struggle each day not only to stay out of the closet but also to move farther away from it. We have discovered that women, blacks, Hispanic Americans, Asians, Native American peoples, the poor, and the differently abled are struggling to move forward, too. We are not alone. We will not be free until all are free. We struggle to act faithfully within our commitment to the liberation of others, and we are learning to ask sisters and brothers in that struggle to share our struggle, as well. Liberation begins by naming ourselves. The struggle begins in self-affirmation.

2. The oppression—and liberation—of women is no less important than the oppression and liberation of gay men.

Analysis of the pervasive structures of sexual and gender oppression demonstrates that heterosexism operates to keep women in place, on the bottom, by keeping men in place, on top. As a hierarchical structure of domination, heterosexism links with racism and classism to create strata of society descending from the highest to the lowest. Those at the top are served by myths and structures that prevent those closer to or at the bottom from discovering their common enterprise in overcoming the myths and structures.

Analyzing biblical stories in order to liberate gay men without a concomitant commitment to women's liberation will ultimately liberate neither group. Not until being a gay man is no longer associated with being "a woman" *and* being a women is no longer associated with "being on the bottom" will liberation be a reality for gay men, lesbians, and all women. Not until women's sexuality is taken as seriously as that of men will gay men also be taken seriously as legitimately embodied sexual beings.[4]

Feminist-gay-male liberation must insist that biblical textual criticism and interpretation scrutinize scripture to unmask and disentangle every deeply embedded strand of violence against, and subjugation of, women. The authority of scripture must be judged critically in light of women's oppression, both within the text and within social structures whose ideologies rest on heterosexist biblical views of women. Further, texts that reveal women's resistance must be appropriated in ways that draw attention to the moral agency of women in all ages.[5] Only in this way can the liberative task overcome the historic misogyny inherent in heterosexist culture.

3. Bodily integrity is central to the liberation struggle.

> Kenneth Dover draws attention to an ancient practice, namely that human societies at many times and in many regions have subjected strangers, newcomers and trespassers to homosexual [i.e., same-sex] anal violation as a way of reminding them of their subordinate status.[6]

Such practices were and are degrading to men, not because such practices *"turn men into women"* but because the bodily integrity of men is violated.

Within the gay-liberation movement, as within the feminist community, rape is violent sexual activity. If sexuality is valued as a relational expression of mutually desired intimacy, then rape is devoid of sexuality. Rape is violation; rape is violence against the victim. The concept that sexual activity means that someone must be on the bottom and someone on top is not based on biological necessity, or "nature," but on a socially constructed ideology designed to maintain the heterosexist power structure. Consequently, those who are subordinate can be forced to serve those who are dominant.

The victims of bodily violation in American society are many and are characterized by a lack of social power. Children, women, "pretty boy" young men in prisons (and on the streets), the physically and mentally differently abled, racial minorities, and others are primary pawns for men on violent power trips. Moreover, gay men of all shapes and sizes and ages and status are constantly subject to the perversions of angry, macho, nongay men. As in the stories of Sodom (Genesis 19) and Gibeah (Judges 19), there always seem to be some who must violate the bodily integrity of those they view as different, as "other," as being without the fundamental human dignity of an inviolable body.

Men and women of color, all other women, and gay men bring special sensitivity to issues of embodiment. We are considered somehow not quite "right" because of our bodies' pigmentation or genitalia or because of what we do with our genitalia. Feminist-gay-male liberation requires a commitment to the bodily integrity of all because our integrity is shaped by the struggle to bring our lives into harmony with our bodily desires for life companions and lovers whose basic anatomy is identical to our own.

We insist that the authority of scripture be viewed critically and that the numerous texts that undermine bodily integrity be unmasked and disentangled in order to overcome their gruesome effects.

4. We must name our oppression and our oppressors.

The stories of Sodom and Gibeah, among other culturally powerful stories, are stories that link gay men, lesbians, other women, and all those who because of their difference from the dominant groups occupy the lower spaces of heterosexist social structures. That linkage, however, will remain a force for oppression as long as the evil in these stories continues to be misnamed by heterosexist powers. Only when gay men and women name the evils perpetrated against them and identify their oppressors will these stories become litanies for liberation. Claiming these stories as our own, as stories of what heterosexist structures and ideology have done and continue to do to us throughout history, robs them of their power to terrorize us.

Gay men have not been recognizable in the mainstream historical record. "Gay" men became asexual in the history books. Until very recently, awareness of our gay ancestors came through word-of-mouth stories, passed along the gay grapevine. These stories kept us connected to a wider gay world. In the secret compartments of our lives we held on to the stories as a way of holding on to life.

Now, we are engaged in the effort to name publicly what has been done to us and to name who has done it. We are learning not only to tell the stories that keep us alive, at the margin of society, but to challenge the oppressive structures that keep us from the center. Often that means retelling old stories, such as the saga of Sodom, in new ways.

5. We must name our own liberation and assume responsibility for the struggle to achieve it.

Feminist-gay-male liberation supports the struggle for lesbian and gay civil rights but has a much broader vision of liberation than gaining acceptance into an unreconstructed and unjust society. Our struggle is to transform the very society of which we are a part and which at the same time rejects us. Very often, middle-class, white, gay men — men whose only marginalization is that they are gay — fall into the trap of believing that liberation means being able legally to marry their life partners or to have full visiting rights in the hospital or at the funeral home or simply to be out — fully out — anywhere and everywhere.

These goals are important and laudable. Opponents of gay liberation recognize, however, that more is at stake than simply making some adjustments in social customs and ending legal discrimination. The Christian Far Right, for example, understands that if society really affirms gay relationships, the entire structure of heterosexism, on which the Far Rights's power to regulate private morality depends, will crumble. Moreover, the fundamental connections between heterosexism, sexism, racism, and classism — what it calls by various names, such as "God's will" or "the American Way" — mean that with the fall of one piece of the structure, others will come tumbling down as well. Thus, the Far Right views the threat of gay liberation very seriously, often according it more power than we ourselves do.

We must not allow our opponents to determine the nature of our liberation so that they may then deny us what they say we want. Liberation is the work of the oppressed. What we really want is a new social order in which all the marginalized are not only affirmed but also participate as full partners at the center of the social order, determining with all others the priorities of an egalitarian and open society.

Naming our liberation is our task, as is assuming the responsibility for achieving it. We cannot rail against the Bible and the religious bigots unless we are willing to do the hard work of writing our own stories and opening the closets for our own spirits to fly free. The Bible is not keeping us in its rigid enclosure of patriarchal morality; we are choosing to stay there as much as we are being forced to remain. The churches and synagogues are not our only oppressors; we are complicit in our own spiritual oppression by giving them power to name the value of our lives. The power to name is the among the most potent power of all, and we have the power to take it back. Taking back the power to name begins with talking back, with interrupting the monologue about us and changing it into a dialogue with us and with all who are committed to liberation.[7]

One example of false naming comes from the story of the destruction of Sodom in Genesis 19:1–14. This story has resulted in labeling gay men as "sodomites." The truth for us is actually quite different. We are not the Sodomites but actually their victims — the victims of angry, uptight patriarchs who commit phallic aggression against those who are different. The motif is a familiar one for gay men — being the victim and then also being blamed for the crime.

We need not remain victims; we have the power to write our own stories and to rewrite the ones written about us.

LIBERATING OURSELVES — AND THE SACRED TEXTS

A feminist-gay-male-liberation reading of the Bible is shaped by the experience of the lesbian-gay community, as outlined in the principles above. Gay liberation is deeply suspicious of attempts, however well intentioned, to address the issue of homosexuality in the Bible. The issue is not one of homosexuality and whether the Bible sustains, condemns, or is neutral about it. *Neither canonical testament carries any authority for gay liberation on the subject of homosexuality.* Gay liberation interprets scripture, not the other way around.

The issue is not homosexuality but heterosexism. This hermeneutical principle carries significant implications for biblical reflection and demands a highly suspicious reading of the text. Moreover, the gay-liberation struggle maintains a fundamental attention to what the text reveals not only about the status of women but also about men and their participation in, and resistance to, heterosexist structures of domination.

Resistance, by women and men, is the key to unlocking the heterosexist secret compartments of biblical meaning. The lesbian, feminist theologian Carter Heyward, speaking of the link between sexism and heterosexism, points to this resistance:

> Understanding the link between sexism and heterosexism may help illuminate also why so many openly gay, self-affirming men are feminists — and why so many frightened and ashamed homosexual men are not. A gay man who understands the sexist character of his own oppression knows that those who govern the structures of patriarchal capitalism are determined to use his body to enforce the sexual control of women's lives. He is able to comprehend his homosexuality not simply as a "private orientation" or "preference" but rather as a form of resistance to sexism, not necessarily "chosen," but a form of resistance nonetheless.[8]

As women have begun the arduous process of reclaiming their biblical history and naming what is left out, so feminist-gay-male liberationists must examine the Bible for the stories of what men have done to women *and* what powerful men have done to powerless men. We also must search for those instances of resistance to oppression and claim the resistors as our people. And when there is no story of resistance, we must dig below the record to recover it. For we know by our own survival, and by the spirit that moves us forward, that there always has been resistance.

I began this essay wondering if it was possible to recover pieces of our liberation history from a biblical story that has given its name as an epithet used against gay men. Is it possible to find liberative elements, or at least glimpses of resistance, in the tale of Sodom's destruction? Can we, called sodomites for so long, find any heroes in the sad saga of this city? Out of Sodom's ashes can we, as gay men, find evidence to sustain us for the liberation struggle?

A word about the choice of this particular text is in order. Gay men understand this text as an example of "gay bashing." It has been used endlessly to portray the evil of our sexual activities, indeed, of our very lives. *This text has been used to kill men.* Their deaths have often been at the hands of angry mobs and small gangs of marauding youths. This text and its heterosexist interpretation, however, also have been enshrined in the laws of many nations, laws even prescribing the death penalty for a single act of male-to-male "sodomy."[9]

To confront this text requires strength and courage. Gay men have been told over and over, for two thousand years, that we are the violent men of Sodom. Despite our best intentions and our deepest desires to affirm ourselves, we feel ashamed when we encounter this text. This shame is not because what we do or who we are is inherently wrong. Rather, this story is the foundational myth sustaining the homophobia, that is, hatred toward gay men and lesbians by others and the self-hatred of gay men and lesbians. The visual images produced by the story of the attempted "sodomizing" of the two men, angels of God, has been appropriated as a powerful weapon in the arsenal of homophobia. Of course, the story's homophobia is deeply linked with its misogyny.

Although it is true that several present-day biblical scholars and ethicists have identified the central issue in this story as a violation of the ancient codes of hospitality rather than the alleged sin of homosexuality, few have identified what the gay-male liberationist finds most sinister: the violation of personhood through violence committed, or attempted, against the body.[10] The central issue in this story from a gay-liberation perspective is not a denial of hospitality or sex, although both are present, but rape, the violation of another through the medium of sexuality distorted by violence. In the parallel story in Judges, the violence is not only attempted but actually carried out to a gruesome extreme.

The issue of violence, bodily violation of another, contradicts the gay liberation struggle at its core. We who are violated because of our embodied sexuality are fundamentally alienated by *any* suggestion that bodily violation is normal. Most commentators agree that a small group of biblical texts forms the entire body of problematic texts regarding homosexuality. Such agreement is predicated on finding those texts that explicitly condemn same-sex acts and relationships and those texts, such as Genesis 19, that have traditionally been interpreted as conveying condemnation. The gay-liberation struggle demands additionally that texts that explicitly or implicitly condone bodily violation by persons of greater power against persons of lesser power be viewed as clearly heterosexist. When viewed in the context of ancient Greek and Hebrew culture, the victims of such violation are either women or subordinate men. The present-day social situation of gay men and lesbians draws us into solidarity with those victims, and we understand that we ourselves are also under attack. This suggests the breadth and depth of the gay-liberation critique of the Bible required by the liberation movement.

The story of Sodom has been recast here as a modern tale of what it means to be a gay male, always subject to the greater power and violence of "straight" men. This rendering of Genesis 19 significantly alters the more usual interpretation in a number of ways, but perhaps chief among them is the labeling of the visitors (the angels of Genesis 18 described as two men in chapter 19) as "queers" or "faggots" — at least in the eyes of the crowd of angry men. Reading the text through gay liberation eyes turns the story upside down and assists in identifying the heterosexist elements. Unmasking the heterosexist structure allows traditionally neglected elements, including the story's misogyny, to be highlighted.

TWO MEN IN SODOM — A MODERN TALE

The two men arrived in the city. Although they were hot and tired, they retained their handsome appearance. In fact, sweat made their skin gleam, burnishing its various hues. Their clothes stuck tightly to their frames, highlighting the definition of their bodies. Their eyes glowed with the satisfaction of a journey well begun; their hair shone with sweat and from days in the sun. They had no place to stay, but they planned to find a resting place on the street or in the park.

As they walked they were greeted by a man who recognized them as travelers. He was kind and invited them to rest at his home. He seemed not to fear them, even though they were strangers. He was unlike others whom the travelers had encountered in the city — men who looked at them with hostility, suspicion, and anger; women whose eyes were downcast and whose bodies were heavy with burdens.

The visitors at first refused his invitation, not sure what to make of this one man who acted with natural graciousness and hospitality. But he persisted. The two men, weary from their journey and eager for baths, good food, and comfortable beds, relented.

Indeed, their needs were amply met by their kind host and the women and slaves who bustled to do the master's bidding of providing hospitality for the strangers. Despite their worries about the other residents of the city, they began to relax. Their host's amiable conversation and easy manner reassured them.

And then there came a loud commotion outside. Heavy knocks fell on the door of their host's home. He excused himself. "I must answer the door," he said. His words were no longer gentle; there was fear in his voice, in his eyes, in the nervous movements of his body.

He opened the door, and before him stood a multitude of angry men of the city. The crowd filled the street in front of the house. Many shouted at him, "Who are these men in your house?" Others derided him for sheltering "queers" and "faggots." One said, "We saw the way they walked, hips swaying like women." Another said, "The big one, who is lighter, dominates the smaller, darker one." All demanded that he send the visitors out to them.

The kind host shrunk back at the violence of their words, but he quietly refused their demand.

One of the leaders of the crowd said, "You, too, are different; you are not of us, you are a stranger among us. You have no right to refuse us. Bring out these men that we may give them a taste of their own medicine! We will do unto them as they do unto each other. We will show them how disgusting they are!"

A great cheer arose throughout the crowd, and there was much murmuring and agreement with the leader's words.

But the quiet, kind host again refused. Desperate not to turn his guests over to the violence of the mob, he said to the leader, "Take my daughters, my virgin daughters, and do with them as you will." His stomach turned at his own words, but still he spoke them. He felt strongly about keeping the bond of hospitality with his male guests.

The crowd jeered him, and many voices again demanded the two men. Several even began to demand the body of the host. They began to call him "queer," too. He was, after all, a stranger, not one of their own people.

The man cowered outside his door. Inside, the two visitors cursed him for betraying his daughters. Suddenly, the door opened. The man was pulled inside and the door slammed shut. The two visitors then opened the door again, went out, and sprayed a vile stinking gas into the crowd. The gas burned the eyes of the angry townsmen, and they staggered about, choking and falling down. Their curses were reduced to shocked gasps and inarticulate coughing. The cloud of horrible gas hung in their midst, and they began running in all directions, hoping to escape the sting and stench.

The two visitors, who had returned into the house as quickly as they had left it, watched the crowd disperse. "We will be safe tonight, for a little while," they said. They turned to their host and the members of the household who had gathered around and said, "But our safety — and yours — will not last long. We must prepare to leave quickly. This is no place for any men — or women — of peace and justice to live. The men of this city are so afraid of themselves they do evil to all who are different. Surely, this is an evil place. It will be destroyed by its own will." The words sent a chill of apprehension through the host, for they resounded with the cold fury of righteous judgment.

The father spoke to the young men who were to marry his daughters and urged them to leave the city with them. These men, who were not strangers in the city, laughed at him. They too had felt fierce anger at the visitors. They were angry at the father for offering their women to the crowd.

The visitors persisted in urging their host and his wife and their daughters to leave, and when their host hesitated, the visitors pulled them along. "Do not look back," they said. "There is nothing there for you. Soon there will be nothing there at all." They spoke with authority, as if they had a vision of an event that had not yet occurred. They urged their host to flee into the hills around the city, but he wished to go with his family to the nearest small town. As they turned in that direction, the visitors said, "Hurry."

The wife looked back. She did not wish to return to the evil city, the scene of so much violence toward her and her daughters. But she was troubled; she did not wish to go with her husband, the man who had offered her daughters to the evil townsmen. When she looked back, certain that there was no place of safety for her and her daughters, her heart was hardened and her feet remained stuck on the spot where she stood. Never again did she laugh. Never again did she cry. Her cries of anguish died in her throat.

The man and his daughters later learned that indeed the city had burned in a great conflagration. The cause was unknown. Nothing remained but rubble. They never again saw the two visitors who saved their lives. Often they wondered if these two gentle, strong men had been messengers from God. They gave thanks to God for their survival and for the man's brother, the daughter's uncle, and his family who had chosen not to settle in the city with them. Out of all of them and their offspring the family would continue.

EPILOGUE

Gay-male liberationists recently observed the twentieth anniversary of the Stonewall Rebellion — three nights in gay history when Greenwich Village drag queens and transvestites fought back against the routine, macho violence of the New York Police Department. For many of us, that moment of resistance was when the violence of the Sodomites several millennia ago began to lose its power.

Never again do we need to return to the streets of Sodom filled with shame. After Stonewall, we began to find pride. Of course, even before Stonewall, gay men and lesbians were beginning the process of renaming and reclaiming our lives. That there has always been resistance is now clear.

Fortunately, what we also are beginning to know is that there always have been angels, in the form of men and women, sent from God or the Goddess, and they are our own people. We are grateful for the angels in Sodom, as we are grateful for the angels at the Stonewall. Let us bless the angels among us, let us dance with our gentle warriors, and let us be strong.

Reflections on the Theological Roots of Abusive Behavior

Susan E. Davies

Orthodox Christian theology has historically seen God as the Other, the One who has ultimate power over all things in the universe, who stands at the top of the pyramid of reality. As the Wholly Other, God has been seen as the One who is transcendent to human beings, totally beyond our ken. This divine being is understood as the One who has the power to define who or what human beings most truly are because the divine is the One who has created us for purposes that are not our own. Human beings are thus only fully, completely human insofar as we participate in that reality for which the divine has created us.

While orthodoxy has stressed the otherness of God, it has at the same time utilized another strand in Christian tradition, based upon Genesis 1, which declares that human beings are made in the image of God, that there is a likeness between the divine and the human. Christian theology has teetered between these two claims about the human relationship with the divine, now insisting that our likeness with the divine is our glory, now declaring that we are so far from God as to be, and deserve to be, in the darkness.

According to the dominant traditions, humans have valid being as humans only insofar as we participate in the definition of us given us by the Other. We have no being in and of ourselves that exists in its own right. Our nature is wholly derivative, wholly created, as is the potter's vessel. Our completeness as human beings moves from potential to actual as we move toward becoming that for which we were created. Insofar as we deviate from the purposes of the Other, that is, insofar as we fall short of the glory of God, the true nature that is designed for us by God, then we are that much less than fully human.

There are two problems here, both of them intertwined in the reflections that follow. The first is the commonly understood nature of the divine Being as the omnipotent, omniscient, omnipresent Ruler, Maker, and Enforcer at the top of the pyramid.

The second, and more fundamental, problem is the very principle that one being may be defined by another. It does not take much translating of the terms of classic Christian theology to comprehend the bases of abuse within it. If one — the Other — has ultimate power and the right, nay, the duty, to define the purposes for which people and things exist, then the probability of abuse is inherent in the construct — not only of women by men, and children by both women and men, but of the earth itself and of nation by nation.

AS A CHILD

What happens to a white, middle-class, North American girl child in a world in which power is seen and justified theologically as power over? — A world in which God is seen as the enforcer at the top of the power pyramid, and all other beings are subordinated to those above them in the pyramid? — A world in which the language speaks of the divine Power being humble and loving, merciful and mild, full of invitation and grace, while this same power is backed up with the ultimate hierarchical power of coercive enforcement?

Memories. Memories of hymns sung in church. "God the omnipotent king who ordaineth." (446)[1] "I would be true ... humble ... pure ... strong." (489) Memories of the elephant on the stairs, coming up with fear in his trunk, and loud feet. Coming after me. The unknown abuser, whose only trace is my dreams of elephants and night terrors and the certainty that bed is not a safe place.

Almost no memories of the first ten years. Gone, into the beat of the elephant's feet. And then remembering I must let the boys win, because they should win, because it was their place to win. Remembering eighth-grade despair, because though determined to let the boys win that summer, to be the lady my mother desired, I came home in tears after beating all but one of them at arm wrestling. Girls do not beat boys. It is not their place.

Memories. Memories of not running for the president of the state Pilgrim Fellowship or the senior class in high school, because that was for boys. They had, or should have, the power over. Memories of Mother's admonition, "Don't lift heavy weights, Susie, now that you are a lady in your teens. You might harm yourself." Memories of boys going on canoe trips for the weekend and girls not being allowed to do the same. Too dangerous. Someone might come upon us in the woods. We might drown.

Memories of my big brother following me from bed to bed, wanting something, something I knew not what, something wrong and frightening and insistent, but he was Older Brother, and if he asked, he should be given. He was the big brother. He knew better. It was his power, his right. I remember appealing to the same brother to stop my father from molesting me. "I can't, Susie. Pops is bigger than I am. He's stronger." He had the right, the right to define, not only who he was, but who we were.

"Be good, Susie. Don't rock the boat. Submit. God is in his heaven. The church is a safe place. You belong there. God the real father will take care of you. He has ultimate power over everything, and he will guide you and protect you. Submit. Be pure. Be brave, for there is much to dare."

Memories of Vati, Austrian "foster father" to sixteen-year-old Susie, the exchange student, insisting he simply had to have one more kiss, one more caress, because his need was so strong, and I (why did it take five revisions of this essay to say "I" here, rather than "the girl"?) was so attractive. "You might as well be twenty-one, a grown-up. You are who I say you are, Susie." Power to define who I was. Who I am.

Suicide. That's the answer. Drive into that abutment. No one would know. A recurrent dream of a family party. Everyone there. Someone brings a baby and places it on the hi fi speaker. A longing, yearning Susie picks it up and watches it turn to ashes and cinders in her arms. Every night. Same ashes. Vati in his black Mercedes 220, black homburgs. Night terrors. Power over. God will take care of you. He is in control. If you will submit. If you will be pure. "God the omnipotent king who ordaineth." "We come unto our fathers' God." (271) Father with the knee in the groin. Vati with the insistent hands and the wife at the bottom of the stairs, waiting, calling. "At the name of Jesus every knee shall bow... 'Tis the Father's pleasure we should call him Lord... in your hearts enthrone him; there let him subdue all that is not holy, all that is not true." (197)

Memories of church camp. Glimpses of another power — power at the center, in the midst, power from the strength and courage of commonality and mutuality. The extraordinary assertion that while power over could coerce bodies, it had no ultimate authority. Black women singing, marching, proclaiming that the present hierarchy is wrong, that black people too are human beings, whether or not those with power over them accept their claim. "Keep your eyes on the prize... hold on, hold on." "Jesus walked this lonesome valley..."

"That cause can neither be lost nor stayed, which takes the course of what God has made, and is not trusting in walls or towers, but slowly growing from seed to flowers."[2]

A kernel. A glimpse of another way, a power with, in the midst, affirming, strong. Sung from the center of Christ, who overturns pyramids and undermines hierarchy.

NOW A YOUNG WOMAN

My destiny is to be the wondrous second theme in Brahms's first symphony, the supportive, developing, swelling music, which helps build to the climactic finale, returning to the great, flowing sweep of the harmonious chords. Never those chords myself. I am lesser. I am supportive, not independent. Not interdependent. I have learned well.

Philosophy classes, theology classes. Women carry the image of God only derivatively, only when they are together with their husbands, but the man "is the image of God as fully and completely as when the woman too is joined with him in one."[3] A woman preaching is like a dog walking on its hind legs, says Dr. Samuel Johnson. Aristotle tells me that women are misbegotten males. Plato tells me that the Lydian mode must be banned from the Republic because it is too sensuous, too feminine. Aquinas declares that in our original state, women are by nature servile and under subjection. Medieval history, the Enlightenment, the nineteenth century, the twentieth century — they all tell me how imbecilic women are, how our nature is lesser, lower, derivative, incomplete. And the adviser for my master's thesis is relieved that I am doing an historical study, because women can do church history but are incapable of doing theology.

Memories. Memories of groups of men, castigating the emasculating young woman for participating in the group discussion as though she had a right to be there, for teaching the class, teaching men. They tell obscene jokes to drive her out because they reserved the power to define who she was, who they were. She had no right there. Not in the boys' club.

Memories of the church as a safe place, as the one place where I was accepted, had a purpose, was supported, not threatened. Where the youth minister made it clear how many delightful things he would like to do to me.

Another church, another country. Memories of a choir, men and boys, striding the echoing aisles, singing to God the king, praying to God the father in the name of all men. Even here, I do not fit. I do not belong. I am a yes, but. Yes, of course you are a person, but not fully, not wholly, not completely. Real people are men. They have the right, the responsibility to define, both themselves and the others who are lower than they in the pyramid. Of course. Power over gives that right, that responsibility.

This churchly reality, this embodiment of God, is not, they tell me, coercive love. This world, this theology grounded in an image of God who has power over all things, stems from a love that is not coercive, that is divine, that will not let me go. This is a love that surpasses all loves, that cannot be compared with human love; that intends that we do God's will, not our own. Our own will is evil and needs purging, needs cleansing. Let your holy flame "freely burn, till earthly passions turn to dust and ashes in its heat consuming." (239) This is a love that consumes all that is evil, all that makes me wrong and bad; it is a love that sets me free.

"Hold on...hold on...."

"Hearts open slowly, so slowly..."[4]

A PARADOX

Only when I have totally given up who I am, then and only then will I become who I truly am. But I am no one. I have no right to define who I am. Only as I attain the definition given me by the Other or the others higher on the pyramid do I become a person. But there is no one here. There never has been anyone here. Pride is not my failure. It is nothingness; it is powerlessness that is my despair. What then shall be consumed, if nothing is? How can there be a paradox of being and nothingness when there is only nothingness? I have no place to stand that is who I am, except as I am derived from the Other or from others.

A paradox. The extraordinary Christian symbol, dressed up with crowns and gold, diamonds and glitter, the symbol at the core of Christian faith — the cross. Why the cross? The symbol of powerlessness, of death, of torture and abandonment. Would it be our symbol were there no ascension after the empty grave, no rising to the right hand of God? Would it be our symbol if the powerlessness of the Friday called Good did not become the power over, the victory over that we sing at Easter?

The Sunday school awards are the cross and crown. Not the cross. Or if the cross is the center, if *kenōsis* ("emptying oneself") is the core, then the implied reward is always there. Do this, live this, and you will sing and dance with God, when you have become nothing and God has become all.

POWER OVER

Ultimately power over. Limitless, eternal, omnipotent, omniscient, omnipresent. There must be. If there isn't such a power, such a being, we would invent one, or become cynics, or head into the despair of Sartre, staring nothingness in the face with dignity, moving forward into the meaning that can only be created by ourselves.

"That cause can neither be lost not stayed . . ."

"Hold on . . . hold on . . ."

But there must be. There must be power over. I want there to be. It must exist. It cannot be that there is not in this universe such a power, such a being. How else will injustice be recompensed? How else will suffering make any sense? The suffering of the children, the broken, the disappeared — there must be an ultimate power, a coercive power, somewhere.

Holy Week. The powers of evil, human powers of evil, attack and destroy the good, the loving. And we can endure, because we know that triumph over death and enthronement with power over the universe are yet to come. If only I cling there. If only I participate fully and completely in that power, then I too will have power over, if nothing else, myself. Not power with. Not communion. But triumph over evil.

Memories. What power over permitted, encouraged that nightmare trek from bed to bed? What power over blamed a girl for being so attractive to a fifty-four-year-old that he could not resist? What power over forced that elephant up those stairs?

What would the world look like if we had responsibility for our own power? If we owned it? If we were right to do so, theologically right? Correct in affirming our own reality and its connections with the divine? If the divine were empowerment, not burning fire? If the God of all gods were not coercion but matrix?

O fear. O terror. No ultimate Enforcer. No final Judge. We would be set loose upon ourselves. No bombs to keep us in place. No belts to threaten the child. No secrets that cannot be named. No frying pans hurtling across the room. No hanks of hair yanked from a scalp. No babies burning in ovens.

What would keep order? We are evil. We are selfish. We cheat and lie and destroy one another. If there were no ultimate power, what model would the world have? If there is no order to the universe, no steps of creation, no rungs of authority, no obedience and submission and divine right of rulers, how would we get along? Someone must stop the wrongs. There must be courts and prisons and judges and armies. There must be immoral society. There must be God and ultimate Coercer.

Foolish women. Foolish people. The dream is only that, a dream. It cannot be. There is the cross — and the triumph. There is the right hand of God and the scepter. There is obedience. There is power over, ultimately. Isn't there?

"And is not trusting in walls or towers..."

"Spirit, spirit of gentleness, blow through the wilderness, calling and free..."[5]

VISIONS OF POWER

I have visions of power with, commonality. "Spirit, spirit of restlessness, stir me from placidness, wind, wind on the sea." Power that increases the strength of all, that does not force or lord it over. Power to which every knee shall not bow, but in which every head shall stand tall and strong and free.

But. The Other has the right to define me. God has the right to define who he is, to define who all the created beings are that are made by him. That is the very nature of the divine Being to whom we owe our allegiance and our worship.

Here lies the basis for all the abuse we heap upon one another and upon the world around us. I have the right to define who you are, who or what the earth is, what my cat and dog are, what the land shall do and be, what nations shall be or become. I have the intrinsic right to define what the other is, insofar as I participate in the life of God.

You say, but no, only God has the right to make those definitions. And I ask, who interprets those definitions? Who declares the reality of those definitions?

For the last three thousand years, the answer has been men, and in the reality of the Western world in which Christianity has grown to full flower, that has meant white Western men. They have had the right to define, as they participate most completely in the life and reality of God imaged as male.

I begin to think of what it would mean to me as a woman if the Other with which I am to identify is imaged as female, rather than male. What does that do to the "power-over" questions? To the definitions given of self by the Other?

What becomes clear is why many men feel they have a duty to define, define the natural and the spiritual, the human and the animal and the inanimate, the universe. It is part of their divinely given responsibility in their identity with the Other.

Further, if the divine is imaged as female, and I am female, then I see more clearly the ambiguity that exists for men when they speak of the divine as the wholly Other. I cannot conceive of a female image as being totally other than I. There are some points of similarity, however removed, or else there is no point to the female image. It would sooner be animal or vegetable.

I then can understand why many men apparently work comfortably with a male god named "Other." Because such a god is not truly other. There are many points of similarity, however removed.

And I can then understand the source of the tension between the two strands of Christian tradition mentioned at the beginning of this essay. It arises from the Other/not-Other image of the divine. Furthermore, the levels of fury and anguish so many men display when faced with the image of God as female are explained by the recognition that, for them, such an image of the divine is truly other. Such a truly other God makes the tension intolerable for those who have hitherto lived so easily with it, exposes its elemental contradiction.

THE POSSIBILITY OF NO GOD

Perhaps there is not and never has been a God who controls all things. How then can we live? How can we live in a universe without an ultimate God who controls all things? God the omnipotent, with whom I am called to identify as servant, so that I will ultimately receive power over, as Jesus, the emptied one, received power over all things. That every knee should bow, as I did at the altar rail, and every tongue confess, that Jesus Christ is Lord. "Soldiers of Christ, arise, and put your armor on. Strong in the Lord of hosts, and in his mighty power." (384)

Is it not terrifying to think that we might be in a post-Christian world, in which God as we have known him, is truly dead and, more frightening, was never alive? Was never real? That all the tradition with which we, I, have identified, if only to war against, was wrong? Was it a misreading of the reality that made us the gift of the incarnation and resurrection? What if the pyramid doesn't exist? Never has existed? What if the cross doesn't have a crown? What if "hearts open slowly, and sing the songs of the dove?" What if holding on will bring the seed to flower?

What would the world be, how can we live, if bringing the seed to flower depends not on a God who is conceived as the power at the top of the pyramid, whose will cannot be thwarted, but on ourselves and our participation in the purposes of a divine power that can only be power insofar as we participate? What if there is radical divine dependence upon human and animal and inanimate reality?

What if there is no divine plan, no great Puppeteer in the sky, who knows all things and controls all things, so that we can be assured that ultimately, the will of God will prevail, no matter how bleak it looks now? What if there is no alpha and omega, and we are not caught in the middle, beyond our birth and before our death, simply trusting because we cannot see? What if the responsibility has been in our hands all these generations? What if we, both men and women, have misunderstood? And only now, as the greater terror reigns, and the skeletons line the valleys, only now as the future may disappear in fallout, can we see clearly.

POWER WITH

"The king shall come when morning dawns...not as of old as a little child, to bear and fight and die, but crowned with glory like the sun that lights the morning sky." (201) Such a victorious faith. Such an exultant faith, in the face of despair on the Friday we call Good. What if they misunderstood? What if the resurrection truly happened, but the power that was released was not power over but power with? Not the ability to control, but the ability to be with, to suffer with, die with, and rejoice within new life?

We, both women and men, are so completely enmeshed in an image of God as the controlling, defining Power out there and over us that it is very difficult to pull out new images, to conceive of power and the divine in different terms. If, however, we return the focus to Jesus, if we look at the revelation of God in the event of the life, death, and resurrection of Jesus, we may find a new way of seeing, a new way as old as the empty tomb, as old as the startled, wondering women running with ointments falling from their hands as they spread the news.

It may be that the revelation is one of power not as force and coercion, but as matrix, symbiosis, partnership. It may be that everything is connected, and my power, our power, is a crucial part of the whole. If that is so, the responsibility lies with me, with us, not to submit but to act. Not to coerce but to move with, to shape, to form, to assist in freedom, out of passion, not self-denial.

It may be that we have a choice — whether to continue in a falsified version of the Christian faith, which has at its core an understanding of ultimate reality as power over, or to reclaim the vision of the incarnation, the vision of power that lives from the center. The first choice gives me, however derivatively, the possibility of my own sphere of power over others. Power over those I love. Power over the students, the parishioners, the animals, the ground I work in the growing months. Power over my recalcitrant car, over my body.

The second choice overturns hierarchies of power over. It sings ancient songs and new ones, which croon of freedom and mutuality and interdependence and circles and connections. It sings of breaking shackles, rejecting all that which breathes death and doom and pyramids. It sings the enfleshment of the breathing, rejoicing, laughing future.

INCARNATION

dawn wind stirs
the tree tops
where the smallest slice
of waning moon rises
snow cushions the flanks of the earth
I see the roundness of the moon
suggested by its arc
I see spring asleep
in the black twigs and branches
*   I see the dance*
*   I am the dancer . . .*

oh God you were born
a human baby.
After nine months of dreaming
in the watery dark
you were shoved by the rhythm of nature
out into this bright harsh world.
Your small head pushed
through the bands of your mother's muscle and flesh
you emerged pale blue, still for a second
eyes closed and then a gasp, a cry,
your lungs seared by oxygen, coloring your blood red.
Pink and softer than you would ever be again
you lay at your mother's breast,
pillowed, wondering;
found the nipple and began to suck.

oh God how more glorious
than your "triumph over death"
as a man upon a cross
is your journey from the womb
as a helpless baby.
We each have been cast out
of that slow, all-answering darkness
into this world of light and screaming surfaces.

You walk
all of it through, with us.
Hallowed be thy name![6]

The Price of the Ticket
Racism, Sexism, Heterosexism, and the Church in Light of the AIDS Crisis

Emilie M. Townes

> In the church I come from — which is not at all the same church
> to which white Americans belong — we are counselled, from time
> to time, to do our first works over.... To do your first works over
> means to reexamine everything. Go back to where you started, or as
> far back as you can, examine all of it, travel your road again and tell
> the truth about it. Sing or shout or testify or keep it to yourself: but
> *know whence you came.*
>
> — James Baldwin, *The Price of the Ticket*

James Baldwin fans will recognize that my theme is taken from a recent
collection of essays by Baldwin bearing the same name. The title piece is a
biting and honest autobiographical essay on the America Baldwin knows
and on how we as white folk and black folk pay an awful price for the
brokenness of our culture, our religion, our sexuality, and our humanity.

The challenge to do our first works over is a powerful one. To reexamine everything. To go back to where we started, or as far as we can,
and examine it all. To travel once again the roads we have already passed
and tell the truth about it. To shout or remain silent, but to know from
whence we come.

The AIDS crisis challenges us to do our first works over again. It challenges us to grapple once again with racism and sexism and heterosexism
in ourselves as well as in the dominant society in America. Unless we do,
we will continue to divide and destroy ourselves.

RACISM AND SEXISM

The price of the ticket is shattering the silence.

Black women's lives have been structured by both racism and sexism,
not just as parallel realities but as interacting ones. Black women have
been called matriarchs, Sapphires, and castrators, names arising from the

roles many of us have had to play in the support of children, husbands, and black society in a larger racist and sexist society. At the same time, we have met the responsibilities in those roles as far as possible, given the constraints imposed on us, and nearly everyone assumes that black women are capable.

In this respect, our legacy differs considerably from that of the majority of white women. White culture, by and large, does not assume that white women are capable. Black women's legacy — one of clearing the fields, caring for the children of others as well as our own, often being the bearers of values for the black community and functioning in marginal positions — is a deviation from the norm and an anomaly in United States society.

Black women's lives are thus both similar to and different from those of white women. Our relationship with black men is also structured differently. Many black males, for instance, have come to believe in the sexist ideal that they are to be the providers for their families and *their* women, and they have closely guarded the few leadership roles allowed them by the dominant white culture. But historically and still today, they have been largely excluded from the public male realm. Black women are caught also: the sexist norm, for white women, is sometimes seen as valuable; it is also often impossible to reach. It brings a loss of autonomy and status; and yet the black situation of being forced into positions of critical responsibilities with few resources to meet them is unjust and destructive. The combined pressures of racism and sexism just about tear us apart — as women and as men and as women and men in relationship to one another.

When we have not voiced that pain and damage, the price of the ticket has been conflict between us, lack of understanding and solidarity, and our own diminished humanity. When we have taken advantage of even a small and often illusory privilege offered us, we too participate in oppression.

We must go back and reexamine what we have done.

HETEROSEXISM

The price of the ticket is shattering the silence.

We separate our bodies from our spirits. We have inherited this separation from years of church doctrine and theological treatises. The history of the church is one that neglects, ignores, or devalues the body. The history is that the body is lower than the mind and that Christians should live in the spirit, which means ignoring or subduing the body. To be religious means living and acting as split beings. And we are to express our sexuality only within the bonds of marriage.

We say that only a heterosexual marital bond is legal and morally acceptable. We have inherited this heterosexism as well as the mind-body dualism. And heterosexism encourages the separation and objectification of our bodies. One of its underlying premises is that the emotion expressed in same-sex relationships is only that of pure sex; we are blinded to the care and nurture that lesbians and gay men can and do have for one another.

The result of this heritage is that sexual activity continues to take place but in a sexually repressive and homophobic culture. I say "sexually repressive" even though the media, the church, and even our own personal observations may indicate that we are promiscuous. We are sexually repressed in the sense that we have made all kinds of compromises regarding our sexuality in order to live on this planet and in this society and to survive in the church.

We are sexually active while being sexually repressed, and this is a dangerous combination. We do not understand how our bodies function or how the bodies of our sexual partners function. We fumble in the dark on subjects such as teenage pregnancy. Time and again children repeat the all-too-familiar litany, "I never thought it would happen to me," and when asked if they were using any form of birth control, the answer is a resounding no.

Even in the face of a life-defying disease such as AIDS, countless folk remain ignorant of how it is transmitted, how to protect themselves from spreading or catching the HIV virus, or even that everyone needs to take precautions. It is *not* transmitted by ministering to our kindred who have AIDS; it is *not* transmitted by being in the same room with, or breathing the same air as, a brother or sister who has AIDS. It *is* transmitted by the mixing of body fluids through intimate social contact or sharing needles or by coming in contact with body fluids through openings on the rest of the skin that may be lesions or sores. It *is* spread from an infected mother to her baby before, during, or after birth. *That* is how AIDS is transmitted, and the church must start educating its members so that *we* spread truth instead of rumor and innuendo.

I was stunned when a young woman told me that before this AIDS thing she had no animosity toward gays, but now she thinks *they* are a menace to society. When I asked if she was practicing safe sex, she did not know what that was. She was not aware of the need for condoms or avoiding oral contact with the penis, vagina, or rectum. She was not aware that the use of intravenous drugs by her sexual partner who shares needles or even her sharing needles put her in the risk group for AIDS. She was unaware of the risk she runs in being sexually active without proper precautions, even in the light of the growing number of heterosexuals contracting the virus.

But we cannot stop there. In educating ourselves we need to know such basic facts as that the test to detect the HIV antibodies in the blood does *not* tell us if a person has AIDS or will develop AIDS; it *does* show if a person has ever been infected by the virus. We need to be aware of the ways women can be infected with the HIV virus. When we educate ourselves, so that we can educate others, we become aware of the fact that if a woman has shared intravenous needles or had sex without a condom with someone infected with the HIV virus, that woman is in the risk group. A woman using donor insemination to become pregnant is at risk if the donor is infected. Women who have sex only with other women are at low risk. But blood and vaginal secretions can spread AIDS between women.

As we begin to recognize that we are fighting history and tradition, it is easier to see that much of the response we have to gay men and lesbians comes from a subtle and deadly unwillingness to reexamine everything.

Another manifestation of the heterosexism within us is that we are blinded to the pain of more than 1 million Africans, male and female, who now carry the AIDS virus. Fifty thousand of them have contracted what in Africa they call "the Horror," and over half have now died. The fear is that it is now too late for the populations of Zaire and Uganda. But the heterosexism in our culture prevents us from hearing that American brothers and sisters on a global level are dying, that AIDS is not just a "gay white male" disease, but is pandemic — is global.

Blacks and Hispanics in the United States are disproportionately affected by AIDS mainly from intravenous drug abuse. Blacks and Hispanics make up 20 percent of the population but are 37 percent of male AIDS victims and 73 percent of female victims. Black and Hispanic children, infected from the mother, account for 81 percent of children infected. The heterosexism in the black and Hispanic communities allows too many in those communities to believe that if they are not gay men, they do not have to worry. Meanwhile, there are no effective antidrug programs in communities of the dispossessed.

Heterosexism's continued presence means the devaluation of people. It permits the social, political, economic, and theological systems that encourage us to deny parts of our being, and this denial allows the continuing destruction of all of us.

Heterosexism feeds and reinforces the racism, sexism, and classism that we have not addressed. It sets the stage, for instance, for black women being beaten and raped on a New York State college campus in the late 1970s. When they tried to come together around women's issues with white women and other women of color, they received threatening phone calls accusing them of a lack of solidarity with black men and destroying the black community and family with lesbianism.

Heterosexism keeps us from drawing the connections between the multitude of injustices that we, as a people of faith, must find ways to eradicate. Fear of AIDS blinds us to the mind-boggling statistic that if a person of color and a white person are diagnosed with AIDS on the same day, the life expectancy of the person of color is nineteen weeks while the life expectancy of the white person is two years.

And this is the society we are called to minister to as the children of Abraham and Sarah.

MINISTRY: TASK OF THE CHURCH

The price of the ticket is shattering the silence.

We are called to be ministers — laity and clergy. The price of our ticket is to shatter the silence we maintain by allowing our own homophobia and our own heterosexism to choke our words and crush our passion for justice.

As people of faith, we must sit down and regroup and strategize, for tomorrow is coming. The death that comes from AIDS and the need to comfort not only those who are living with AIDS but also those who will be left behind is our responsibility. Tomorrow is coming; it is a lesson I learned well growing up black and female in North Carolina. As long as I have tomorrow, as long as you have tomorrow, as long as we have tomorrow, there is always the possibility that by shattering the silence and saying a clear, unambiguous word we will be faithful toward those who are suffering, who are being ostracized and threatened with concentration camps and quarantines, who are left to die alone.

The price of the ticket is truth. Truth requires integrity and stubbornness and fury. Two million people in the United States may have already been exposed to the HIV virus. Some in the religious community have declared AIDS to be God's righteous judgment upon persons they believe to be living in violation of God's will. Some people defend the rightness of the epidemic in order to defend the goodness of God. From where I stand, serving as a pastor to a predominantly white, gay, and lesbian church and working with black folk in my community, the AIDS crisis points to the reality that we have shattered the world to which God gave order and have created a fragmented society in which far too many folk are pushed aside and excluded — we have abandoned one another. It says little about the goodness of God; it says volumes about our inhumanity to others.

The price of the ticket, my sisters and brothers, the price of the ticket as people of faith, is justice. When fighting injustice, the greatest task is not to lose faith or courage or hope or humor. It means to keep pushing and shaking the foundations of bigotry and hatred and ignorance. It means that we are to be responsive to the ever evolving self-revelation of God in our lives and to change when we are no longer relevant or caring or loving. Laws are fine, but they can destroy us if followed without question or critique.

No matter how you feel about homosexual and bisexual men, drug abusers, hemophiliacs, or the increasing heterosexual population that does not fall into any of these categories, the call to do justice has intrinsic to it the command to reach out with compassion without reservation. Where you are now shapes the kind of ministry you can develop to those with AIDS, but that does not preclude *some* form of ministry. It can run the gamut from working directly with those who have AIDS and their families to working for legislation and rules that do not discriminate against the victims.

The price of the ticket is grace. Faith is ultimately a word of grace, not judgment. God's intention is to justify, save, and redeem humanity, not on the basis of discrimination between better or worse persons but on the basis of God's own gracious election. We are God's agents in this process, and when we try to subvert God's will, we, in effect, try to win our own salvation.

God is with us as we seek to make sense out of the nonsensical, proclaim justice and mercy in the midst of despair, and break down barriers and phobias in our yearning for wholeness. When we are open and honest with ourselves, we realize that all those things that foster the racism and sexism and classism within us also foster the fear we have of AIDS. The dynamic that allows a child to exist in poverty is the same one that allows us to fear our bodies and treat ourselves as pieces of a puzzle rather than a magnificent design. That dynamic is sin. It is sinful to allow any of our brothers or sisters to suffer or be discriminated against or to die without our reaching out or taking responsibility for our actions as sexual beings.

What should we be about? Insuring the protection of civil and human rights, making sure hospitals are giving treatment to people with AIDS (PWAs), supporting their right to work, ensuring that the HIV antibody test is used lawfully, monitoring the policies of insurance companies, stopping funeral homes from taking advantage of the families of PWAs or from refusing to handle the bodies of PWAs, supporting efforts to house people with AIDS — including single mothers who have children living with them.

What should we be about? Opposing any proposals to quarantine people who have AIDS, ARC, or HIV antibodies in their blood; stressing the need for hospice programs to address the unique needs of people with AIDS; writing and agitating for state and national funds for AIDS research; and pushing programs that address the whole area of social problems — poverty, racism, sexism.

What should we be about? Beginning with ourselves. We must take a long, hard, honest look at how we participate in the oppression of others and our own oppression by our own racist, sexist, heterosexist beliefs and practices. Institutions can undergo lasting change only if the people who are responsible for creating, maintaining, and eradicating them are willing to change as well.

> In the church I come from — which is not at all the same church to which white Americans belong — we are counselled, from time to time, to do our first works over. . . . To do your first works over means to reexamine everything. Go back to where you started, or as far back as you can, examine all of it, travel your road again and tell the truth about it. Sing or shout or testify or keep it to yourself: but *know whence you came.*[1]

Yours in Sisterhood
A Lesbian and Bisexual Perspective on Ministry

Deborah H. Carney
and Susan E. Davies

Women who are lesbian and bisexual in the North American churches have a unique theological perspective to offer. They live and work in a context that has warped, subverted, and denied their very existence because of their sexuality. And yet they continue to live in the church, serving as pastors, deacons, secretaries, presidents, trustees, Sunday worshipers, choir members, missionaries, executives, and committee and board members. What vision allows these women to survive and work in the very context that is also destructive of their lives?

In order to find out what sustains lesbian women, the authors surveyed fifty-five lesbians in the eastern United States and Canada. Questionnaires were distributed through seminary contacts and informal church channels, as there is no denominational or educational listing of women who are lesbian or bisexual and also working within the church. Distribution of the questionnaire was spotty, precisely because no one knows who many of the women are or where they are working. We were dependent on regional meetings and informal networking, and even then, we heard of many women who were unable to return the questionnaires because such a simple, anonymous action would be too dangerous to their continued work.

Some of the women were still in seminary; others were working in ordained ministries or other positions; but all were within the same structures that seek to expose and tear down the lives these women have chosen to lead.

The results of the survey were profoundly moving. We cried with some of our sisters, laughed with others, shook our heads and raged, and were touched by the honesty of all. This essay is a summary of the survey in narrative form. We offer it to the reader as a picture of what has happened and as a vision of what might be.

Respondents

The return rate was 18 percent — nine lesbians and one who considered herself bisexual. Seven respondents were ordained; one had finished seminary but was not ordained; and the others were still in seminary. Denominationally, the respondents were United Church of Christ (2), United Church of Canada (2), United Methodist (3), Episcopal (1), Roman Catholic (1), and Community Church (1). Ethnically, the respondents were Italian American, Reformed Jewish, and white Anglo-Saxon Protestant. We regret no women of color completed the survey. Their absence not only skews our results but reflects the racist nature of the avenues open to us for distribution.

Of the respondents, three were fully "out" at seminary, and five were out selectively. Two did not know their sexual identity until after graduation. Only one woman was completely out to her ordaining board; three were out selectively, and the rest either did not know themselves when they were in the ordination process or were convinced they would not be ordained because there was "too much homophobia." One woman responded, "My partner and I decided not to take the chance." Another said, "Maybe, maybe I could have been ordained, but I never would have been hired."

Oppression in the Church

In order to test the amount of oppression lesbian women experience in the church and during theological education, we asked if the women experienced discrimination while in seminary or afterward, and if so, from whom.

Throughout the process of education and ordination, the respondents said they found much discrimination. Straight students topped the list of discriminators at seminary, followed closely by the administration, other lesbian or bisexual women, financial aid officers, and professors. Those who had been ordained ranked discrimination by conference or diocesan staff first, followed closely by placement committees, other lesbian and bisexual women, and gay men.

Oppression Among Lesbians

We asked about the amount of internalized oppression the women found within the lesbian community. Both the closeted women and those who were out reported many incidents.

The women who were out found that closeted women discriminated against them because they were leery of "guilt by association." Others were terrified of being discovered. One woman claimed that closeted

women feared contamination, while yet another reported that her closeted sisters were angry at the out lesbians because they seemed so
happy.

The closeted women also related stories of discrimination from out
women. They were accused of "not being honest" and were told they
were afraid. Some out lesbians were reported as very vocal and hostile toward their closeted sisters. Feelings of resentment, accusations of failure,
and impatience flowed on both sides.

The women responded to such situations by various means. Many reported making a "constant check of one's own integrity," while trying to
maintain open dialogue. Another replied: "It was/is very painful. I try
to rationally discuss the issue and love them the best I can." Even though
some women "felt rejection," they kept going, proclaiming their right
to be who they are. They had "credible straight friends," who acted as
"advocates" for them and their lifestyles. Several answered that protecting themselves by denial or lying made them very uncomfortable, and
yet they were reluctant to throw their "pearls before the swine." One
reported always questioning every person's actions; another conversed
with people to understand the basis for their behavior toward her, her
partner, and others like her.

Effective Defense

We wanted to know what the women had found to be effective for
defusing the homophobia they faced. A small number reported that the
Bible was a good tool. One spoke particularly of how her understanding of Pauline theology had helped her cope with and try to defuse
the homophobia with which she was confronted. Several others said
the Bible simply was not effective as a tool. "Jesus said nothing about
homosexuality." "The Bible has no concept of sexual orientation."

The majority of responses, however, called for a change in social structures, along with discussion of the ethical imperatives based on Jesus'
ministry. They spoke of the importance of playing down the sexual
focus and developing images of lesbian women as part of the whole
of creation. One suggested the church deal more justly with homophobia. Several spoke of their own and others' need to receive acceptance
from God before the rest of the church will be able to accept them.
And most were convinced that sexual orientation was God's choice, not
one's own.

Almost all the women spoke of the need for telling their own personal
story, for experiencing with others the positive works and worth of lesbian women. They were also convinced of the need for confrontation.
"Bigots don't respond to education. They must be evangelized."

Church Support

We asked them next where they had found support within the structure of the church. How had they gathered the strength to live in the homophobic context and continue the fight?

Four women said they had not sought any support; they were afraid of one another. Some belonged to the United Church of Christ Caucus for Gay and Lesbian Concerns. One was a member of Affirmation, the Methodist group supportive of gay men and lesbian women. Another sought out the Metropolitan Community Church, which welcomes gay men and lesbian women. Dignity, the Roman Catholic organization, was "too male," while the Conference of Catholic Lesbians did not meet often enough.

One seminary group, Triangles, was mentioned as a source of support, where people were able to share their experiences. From another seminary came the report that an off-campus meeting had been proposed for both closeted and out lesbian women and gay men. The students refused to attend because they did not know one another and feared that the word might escape to denominational or seminary authorities. And so they remained hidden, not only from the church but from one another as well.

Difficulty in Ordination

In response to the question of whether it was now more or less difficult to be an ordained minister or seminary student, seven women responded it was more difficult. "AIDS and feminism have really made things very difficult," reported one woman. They also thought that now that lesbianism is more openly discussed, people are on the alert. And some denominations (the United Methodist Church was mentioned here) were experienced as even more homophobic now than in previous generations.

Church members were reported to be more suspicious now of single people, especially single women. One was asked directly by a search committee member if she was a lesbian. Although she denied it, she did not get the position she was seeking.

Inroads are being made, however. Three people felt being lesbian was easier now. One was supported by the conference and denomination, and another reported that "it is more openly discussed and more support groups arise." She felt that the more lesbians there are, the more it shakes the church, the more acceptance there is.

And still other respondents reported that lesbianism was neither more nor less of a problem now. "It is only a problem when things happen."

Attitude of the Church

The women were also asked whether they found the church as a whole more open or closed to gay men and lesbian women than it had been in the past. Overwhelmingly, the answer was more closed. The Methodists will not ordain "self-avowed" practicing homosexuals and will defrock those whom they have already ordained. "We are still second-class members of the Holy Family." "Falwell and the moral majority have continued to color and prejudice attempts of all churches." One woman was convinced that the church wants to do justice but is too worried about the short-term and long-term effect on finances.

Those few who found the church more open said that the increased awareness of "our existence" is causing a shift, "especially in Northern California." The church and society are more "tolerant," but she felt it will be some time before lesbian women and gay men reap the benefits.

Some women in institutional ministries also noticed improvements in attitude. Several found institutional chaplains more accepting of individual women, although most of the same chaplains were reported to be unable to justify lesbianism itself. Those who worked in government-operated institutions, such as prisons or state hospitals, found not only no improvement but some regression. One woman in a non-governmental institutional ministry found it easier to be out in her work than in other contexts she had known, but she still found it important to remain on the sidelines of her sisters' struggles.

Those who had sought ordination and been denied took a variety of alternative steps. One woman relied on those in power to assist her and found the whole experience made her feel cheap. Another woman stayed in the counseling profession, while stating she will always be a minister whether or not she is ordained. One woman appealed to every church court possible and is trying to decide what she will do, while another simply switched denominations, and a third found a way to support herself, remaining in the congregation and regularly reapplying. She attempts to keep the issue ever in the system and always on the agenda.

Advice to Seminarians

We asked them if they had any advice for women entering seminary. Their answers follow:

"Stay rooted in the local church despite the pain and frustration. Know the great distance between seminary and the local church."

"Know what you really want and why. Know where your integrity line falls and live by it."

"Take care of yourself. Don't sacrifice personal support for institutional gain."

"Check out the school and the support afforded there. It all depends on where you're going."

"Be faithful to Christ who called you. The road is not easy; let Christ be your guide."

"Seek counseling. Recognize that our struggle may not see fruits in our lifetime. Live with patience and grace and blessed unrest."

"Be prepared for battle and pain and heartache. Seek out helpful spaces and nurture them. Don't waste time on nonsupportive people. Find the women's community."

"Decide whether to be open or in the closet and then know what your options are from there."

"Maturity is essential. Don't start young."

"Be clear about the difficulties of the closet. Don't think you can have a relationship and a job too. And if the whole thing blows up, make use of the support systems available to you."

"Don't give up on the Spirit."

Theological Bases for Oppression

What, we asked, were the theological bases for the oppression of lesbian women? "None," said one woman, who went on to say, "True theology detests proof texting in favor of the context of the times. Theological laziness is the basis of oppression."

The other responses had two themes, sex and hierarchy. Those who thought that oppression stems from the construct of a hierarchy of creation spoke of the body-spirit dualism and pointed out that "There is no oppression of lesbians, but rather of all women, the poor and the disenfranchised. It stems from the fall and the understanding of sin." "Males are normative, and females derive their identity from being responsible to males." This divine ordering of the universe is threatened by lesbian women. Christian culture and tradition contain a hatred of women, especially of those not in the patriarchal mold.

The respondents who pointed to sex and sexuality as the problem said that the church as a whole needs to come to terms with the entire area of sexuality, for heterosexual people as well as for gay men and lesbian women. Because the church has not yet done so, it refuses "to see us as total beings" but only as "merely sexual." The refusal is linked to a denial of sexuality as a whole and to the projection of sexuality, especially "bad" sexuality on the "other," in this instance, lesbian women and gay men.

In developing this theme of the denial of, and rigidity about, sexuality, another woman cited the classic positions: "The Bible forbids homosexuality. Man and woman are meant for each other. Sex is to occur for procreation reasons only. Therefore same sex is unnatural and breaks down the family as God intended it to be. See the command in Leviticus 19, 'be fruitful and multiply.'" It is important, she felt, for lesbian women to know the arguments often used against them.

Yet another woman pointed to the "innate fear of the unknown." She thought that people see God in their own image and then decide what God's will on earth shall be. She was one of those who thought that more education and experience with lesbian and bisexual people would help the church lose its fear of the unknown quantity such people represent and enlarge its image of God.

Experience as a Resource for Reflection

We also asked the women how they interpreted their experiences as a resource for theological reflection. One reported that theology has become a "matter of relationship." Another stressed the importance of "more solidarity with other oppressed groups." A third said that the "Bible stories are my stories. The story of Lazarus can be used as a coming out story." And yet a fourth reflected on "God's pain at watching the institution which claims to be God's body on earth."

Conflict Between Lifestyle and Vows

Moving more closely to questions of personal integration, we asked the women about any potential conflicts between their lifestyle and their ordination vows. Their responses follow:

"I am sometimes overwhelmed with despair, anger, and pain about my own ordination. But I love my church and have seen it respond faithfully to other issues. Perhaps being on the inside can help."

"My vow to uphold the church is not in jeopardy as there is no denominational statement regarding lesbians. Yes, I am called, but I have no mystical power via ordination."

"If faithfulness depends on ordination, I should sell insurance."

"Sometimes I wonder if ordination was subordination."

"The church teaches many things I disagree with. But I feel committed to evangelize the church. It is up to them to kick me out. I am not going to let them get the best of me by leaving."

"I don't agree with all the teachings of the church, but I do agree with the theological task and with the church's overall propensity to pluralism, progressiveness, and the spirit of the gospel of Jesus Christ. That concern for community causes me to remain in the church."

Personal Relationships

Many women are or wish to be in a personal relationship. We asked how such relationships fared while the women were in seminary or in ordained vocation. We heard much pain and some joy.

Some relationships broke up in seminary because of the stress, the lack of communication, the personal changes commonly experienced by everyone in seminary, and the strain of one being closeted while the other was out. One woman asked, "Is it possible to have a relationship based on mutuality when the career of one means both must be closeted?" Another found her relationship enriched by her growth and seminary friends. "I tried to make her part of my process, and our therapist helped a lot too."

Those who have completed seminary found much the same situation. One was not in a relationship but would like to be. However, she was three hours from the nearest major city and found it "virtually impossible to meet people." Others had "terrific therapy bills," and phone bills that are "out of sight" and experienced other stresses by the fact that the "church doesn't acknowledge our covenant." As a result, those who were in relationships found that "relationships and church life cause much pain."

On the more positive side, one reported that the "community knows who we are and how we want to live. We act as family in public, and she's been active in the parish." Another reported that "Conversation with [my] partner helps [me] gain perspective." The first woman, however, acknowledged that "If it is necessary we will choose each other over the church."

Being Lesbian in the Church

Our last question asked how they felt about being a lesbian or bisexual woman in the church. Again, we found a combination of pain, strength, and affirmation. Responses ranged from "like a fence sitter" to "I feel good about myself; I'm mad as hell at the church." Most reported a struggle with their own sexual identity, before, during, or after seminary, which in one instance included the support of "Christian feminist women [who] lovingly encouraged me to deal with feminism and my sexuality." All found strength, healing, and joy in acknowledging their identity. "I have my own self-awareness. A lesbian is who I am. I belong in the church as a human being who is female, white, middle-aged, brunette, etc. Not in spite of or because of." None were happy about being closeted or about its effect on their relationship, but one spoke for many when she said, "Now I feel strong, my skills are strengthened.

I have more compassion and confidence, joy, humor. I can speak my mind and take risks."

Telling the Truth

At the end of the survey we asked the women what they wanted us to do with their materials.

They wanted us to tell the truth. We have shared their advice and reflected on the choices they made — to stay in, to come out, or to sit on the fence. We have shared their fears and their hopes. Some wanted us to be honest about the rage and find ways to share it. We have tried to do so.

The ten women who responded to our survey on lesbian and bisexual women in ministry have a vision that sustains them. It is a vision of a church and a world in which belonging and identity will not be dependent upon one's sexual orientation or cultural status but rather on the pluralistic, progressive spirit of Jesus Christ. They represent different ethnic and denominational backgrounds, as well as different means of addressing the problems of life as a lesbian or bisexual woman within the church. Each finds herself in the classic dilemma of having received a vision of wholeness and health, justice and shalom, from the very institution that denies both the embodiment of that vision and often her very right to exist. And yet they stay, at least for the time being, determined to evangelize the church they love, to "teach by example and precept," and to live with "patience and grace and blessed unrest."

We thank them for their courage.

Social Structures and Sexuality

Production, Reproduction, and Dominion over Nature

Carolyn Merchant

The new economic and scientific order emerging in sixteenth- and seventeenth-century Europe would be of lasting significance for both nature and women, for at its ideological core were the concepts of passivity and control in the spheres of production and reproduction. Disorderly female nature would soon submit to the controls of the experimental method and technological advance, and middle- and upper-class women would gradually lose their roles as active partners in economic life, becoming passive dependents in both production and reproduction.

EFFECTS OF CAPITALISM ON THE ROLE OF WOMEN*

In hierarchical society, women's economic and social roles were defined by the class to which they belonged through birth or marriage. In the lower orders of society, peasant and farm wives were integral parts of a productive family unit. Married women carried a heavy burden of labor — childbearing and childrearing, gardening, cooking, cheese and soap making, spinning and weaving, beer brewing, and healing. Unmarried women worked as servants in another household, as unskilled labor in mowing, reaping, and sheepshearing, or at spinning and weaving. Urban women worked in the crafts or trades, owned shops, were members of craft guilds, and even occasionally worked at construction and ditch digging. At the upper levels of society, noblewomen were busy supervising the economic activities of the estate, owning and managing property, and keeping accounts.

* Heads added.

"Production, Reproduction, and Dominion Over Nature" by Carolyn Merchant is adapted from two chapters in *The Death of Nature: Women, Ecology and the Scientific Revolution* by Carolyn Merchant (San Francisco: Harper & Row, 1980). Copyright © 1980 by Carolyn Merchant. Reprinted by permission of HarperCollins Publishers Inc.

Within preindustrial capitalism, women's economic roles became more restrictive and their domestic lives came to be more rigidly defined by their sex as women, rather than by their class. The ideal developing for the upper-class and well-to-do bourgeois wife was a life of leisure, symbolizing the success of her husband's economic ventures. In countries on the cutting edge of the capitalist advance (such as Italy in the fourteenth and fifteenth centuries and, as will be elaborated in this chapter, England in the sixteenth and seventeenth centuries), the contraction and redefinition of women's productive and domestic roles was consistent with changes in the ideology of sexuality.[1]

In Renaissance Italy (ca. 1350–1530), where a mercantile economy had developed much earlier than in northern Europe, men's public lives were expanding, while urban women's were contracting into domesticity. Many medieval Italian girls had been raised in the court of an educated noblewoman — which functioned as a cultural center in determining social values and mores — but in the Renaissance their education emphasized morality, chastity, and readings in the newly recovered classics of Greece and Rome. This shift presupposed male public and female domestic spheres....

In seventeenth-century England, significant changes were taking place in the productive work of women in domestic life, in the home, in family industries producing and selling foods for the local market, in early capitalist industries (such as agriculture, textile manufacture, and the retail trades), and in professional employment. The direction of the change was to limit and curtail the married women's role as a partner, so that she became more dependent on her husband. In the sphere of reproduction, women midwives were losing their monopoly over assisting at childbirth to male doctors. Simultaneously, the female's passive role in biological generation was being reasserted by physicians and natural philosophers. The witch and her counterpart, the midwife, were at the symbolic center of a struggle for control over matter and nature essential to new social relations in the spheres of production and reproduction.

Women and Production

Aristocratic women of the Elizabethan era managed the business affairs of their estates during their husband's absence and after his death; yet Restoration "ladies of quality" often had "nothing better to do, but to glorify God and to benefit their neighbors," the expectation that women should be trained in business affairs having by then markedly decreased.

Under subsistence agriculture, the wives of yeomen and husbanders had participated in the family farming operation, the profits of which benefited and were shared by the whole family. But as yeomen became wealthy agricultural improvers and market farmers, hiring more servants and day laborers, their wives withdrew from active participation in daily farm work, devoting more time to pleasure. These changes reduced the married woman's ability to support herself and her children on her husband's death.

Male day laborers in the new capitalist agricultural operations were completely dependent on the wages earned for their labor to support their families, having no land on which to grow family food. A wife's earnings, if she worked outside the home, were considerably less than her husband's, because her capacity for outside employment was reduced by the number of small children to be cared for at home, and the health and nutrition of the family suffered as a result. If her husband deserted her, a mother encumbered by children was unable to engage in sufficient productive work to support her family.

The English export market for woolen goods was one of the earliest and most important capitalist industries. Women played no role as cloth-iers or wool merchants, and little mention is made of them as assistants in the business ventures of their husbands, their employment being con-fined to wage work, primarily in the spinning branch of the industry. Women bought wool and, when not occupied in agricultural produc-tion, spun it at home and sold the yarn on the market. If, however, a wife was forced to work outside the home, the wages she earned were insufficient to provide both food and clothing for her and her children, although an unmarried spinster could support herself. By 1511, women had been forbidden to weave, because strength was needed to operate the looms. A widow, however, was allowed to continue the weaving in-dustry of her husband, directing the servants employed by him as long as she remained unmarried. In addition to spinning, women also partic-ipated in the bleaching and fulling operations. In periods of depression in the industry, fathers all too frequently deserted their families to seek work elsewhere or to become "masterless" vagabonds, leaving women with their children as the objects of charity.

In the retail trades, women fared well as long as the family operated as a productive unit, the wife helping in her husband's business and taking it over if widowed. But as the trades and crafts began to adopt the capi-talistic mode of employing wage workers, the wives of master craftsmen had less opportunity for participating, while the wives of journeymen, who had hitherto received guild privileges through marriage, were now excluded from the new journeymen's organizations, which sought to pro-tect the man's position vis à vis the master. These wives either became more dependent on their husbands, who were said to "keep them," or were forced to enter the marketplace on their own. They were able to become apprentices in women's trades such as hat making and cloak making, but as a group gradually lost ground in trades such as baking, butchering, fishmongering, and brewing, as rules and statutes began to limit the numbers of persons engaged. By the end of the seventeenth century, women had lost control of the brewing trade, an occupation that in earlier times they had monopolized.

Women and Reproduction

Until the seventeenth century, midwifery was the exclusive province of women: it was improper for men to be present at such a private and mysterious occurrence as the delivery of a child. Midwives were professionals, usually well trained through apprenticeship and well paid for their services to both rural and urban, rich and poor women. Yet no organization of midwives existed that could set standards to prevent untrained or poverty-stricken women from taking up the practice. Moreover, women were excluded from attending universities and medical schools where anatomy and medicine were being taught.[2]

Seventeenth-century London midwives, rightly or wrongly, considered themselves a responsible, well-trained group of women. But by 1634, the midwife profession was being threatened by the licensing of male surgeons who wished to practice midwifery with forceps, a technology that would be available only to licensed physicians. The midwives had complained to the bishop of London that such a practice was often marked by violence and that men had insufficient experience with deliveries. The Chamberlen family, which had invented the forceps, was attempting to establish educational and legal restrictions on their use. Earlier, in 1616, the Drs. Peter Chamberlen, elder and younger, had tried to form a corporation of midwives. The midwives doubted the Chamberlen's ostensible motives to educate and organize them because they feared that the latter would attempt to assume sole licensing authority. They favored the older delivery methods of which they had knowledge and called the new forceps method a violent practice. Their 1634 petition directed against Peter Chamberlen III stated,

> Dr. Chamberlane...hath no experience in [midwifery] but by reading....And further Dr. Chamberlane's work and the work belonging to midwives are contrary one to the other, for he delivers none without the use of instruments by extraordinary violence in desperate occasions, which women never practiced nor desired, for they have neither parts nor hands for that art."[3]

In addition to the Chamberlens, other doctors of the period were sharply critical of the practices of midwives. William Harvey, noted for his discovery of the circulation of the blood, and one of the four censors of the Royal College of Physicians responsible for enforcing the College's monopoly over licensing laws, took issue with some of their methods in his essay "On Parturition" at the end of his *Exercitationes de Generatione Animalium* (On Generation), 1651:

> Hence, it is that midwives are so much to blame, especially the younger and more meddlesome ones, who make a marvellous pother when they hear the woman cry out with her pains and implore assistance, daubing their hands with oil, and distending the passages, so as not to appear ignorant in their art — giving besides medicines to excite the expulsive powers, and when they would hurry the labor, retarding it and making it unnatural, by leaving behind portions of the membranes, or even of the placenta itself, besides exposing the wretched woman to the air, wearing her out on the labor stool, and making her, in fact, run great risks of life. In truth, it is far better with the poor, and those who become pregnant by mischance, and are secretly delivered without the aid of a midwife; for the longer birth is retarded the more safely and easily is the process completed.[4]

. . .

While women's productive roles were decreasing under early capitalism, the beginning of a process that would ultimately transform them from an economic resource for their families' subsistence to a psychic resource for their husbands, the cultural role played by female symbols and principles was also changing. The female world soul, with its lower component, *Natura,* and the nurturing female earth had begun to lose plausibility in a world increasingly influenced by mining technology essential to commercial capitalism. The older organic order of nature and society was breaking up as the new mercantile activities threatened the ideology of natural stratification in society.

Symbolic of these changes were the midwife and the witch. From the perspective of the male, the witch was a symbol of disorder in nature and society, both of which must be brought under control. The midwife symbolized female incompetence in her own natural sphere, reproduction, correctable through a technology invented and controlled by men — the forceps. But from a female perspective, witchcraft represented a form of power by which oppressed lower-class women could retaliate against social injustices, and a source of healing through the use of spirits and the regenerative powers of nature. For women, the midwife symbolized female control over the female reproductive function. But until medical training became available to women and licensing regulations were equalized for both women and men, women had no opportunity to compare the effectiveness of the older, shared traditions of midwifery as an art with the new medical science.

DOMINION OVER NATURE

Disorderly, active nature was soon forced to submit to the questions and experimental techniques of the new science. Francis Bacon (1561–1626), a celebrated "father of modern science," transformed tendencies already extant in his own society into a total program advocating the control of nature for human benefit. Melding together a new philosophy based on natural magic as a technique for manipulating nature, the technologies of mining and metallurgy, the emerging concept of progress and a patriarchal structure of family and state, Bacon fashioned a new ethic sanctioning the exploitation of nature.

Bacon has been eulogized as the originator of the concept of the modern research institute, a philosopher of industrial science, the inspiration behind the Royal Society (1660), and as the founder of the inductive method by which all people can verify for themselves the truths of science by the reading of nature's book.[5] But from the perspective of nature, women, and the lower orders of society emerges a less favorable image of Bacon and a critique of his program as ultimately benefiting the middle-class male entrepreneur. Bacon, of course, was not responsible for subsequent uses of his philosophy. But, because he was in an extremely influential social position and in touch with the important developments of his time, his language, style, nuance, and metaphor became a mirror reflecting his class perspective.

Nature as a Female to Be Tortured

Sensitive to the same social transformation that had already begun to reduce women to [being] psychic and reproductive resources, Bacon developed the power of language as political instrument in reducing female nature to a resource for economic production. Female imagery became a tool in adapting scientific knowledge and method to a new form of human power over nature. The "controversy over women" and the inquisition of witches — both present in Bacon's social milieu — permeated his description of nature and his metaphorical style and were instrumental in his transformation of the earth as a nurturing mother and womb of life into a source of secrets to be extracted for economic advance....

Bacon was also well aware of the witch trials taking place all over Europe and in particular in England during the early seventeenth century. His sovereign, while still James VI of Scotland, had written a book entitled *Daemonologie* (1597). In 1603, the first year of his English reign, James I replaced the milder witch laws of Elizabeth I, which evoked the death penalty only for killing by witchcraft, with a law that condemned to death all practitioners.[6]

It was in the 1612 trials of the Lancashire witches of the Pendle Forest that the sexual aspects of witch trials first appeared in England. The source of the women's confessions of fornication with the devil was a Roman Catholic priest who had emigrated from the Continent and planted the story in the mouths of accused women who had recently rejected Catholicism.

These social events influenced Bacon's philosophy and literary style. Much of the imagery he used in delineating his new scientific objectives and methods derives from the courtroom, and, because it treats nature as a female to be tortured through mechanical inventions, strongly suggests the interrogations of the witch trials and the mechanical devices used to torture witches. In a relevant passage, Bacon stated that the method by which nature's secrets might be discovered consisted in investigating the secrets of witchcraft by inquisition, referring to the example of James I:

> *For you have but to follow and as it were hound nature in her wanderings, and you will be able when you like to lead and drive her afterward to the same place again.* Neither am I of opinion in this history of marvels that superstitious narratives of *sorceries, witchcrafts, charms,* dreams, divinations, and the like, where there is an assurance and clear evidence of the fact, should be altogether excluded.... howsoever the use and practice of such arts is to be condemned, yet from the speculation and consideration of them ... a useful light may be gained, not only for a true judgment of the offenses of persons charged with such practices, *but likewise for the further disclosing of the secrets of nature. Neither ought a man to make scruple of entering and penetrating into these holes and corners, when the inquisition of truth is his whole object —* as your majesty has shown in your own example.[7] (Italics added.)

The strong sexual implications of the last sentence can be interpreted in the light of the investigation of the supposed sexual crimes and practices of witches. In another example, he compared the interrogation of courtroom witnesses to the inquisition of nature:

> I mean (according to the practice in civil cases) in this great plea or suit granted by the divine favor and providence (whereby the human race seeks to recover its right over nature) *to examine nature herself* and the arts upon interrogatories."[8]

Bacon pressed the idea further with an analogy to the torture chamber:

> For like as a man's disposition is never well known or proved till he be crossed, nor Proteus ever changed shapes till he was *straitened* and *held fast,* so nature exhibits herself more clearly under the *trials* and *vexations* of art [mechanical devices] than when left to herself.[9]

The new man of science must not think that the "inquisition of nature is in any part interdicted or forbidden." Nature must be "bound into service" and made a "slave," put "in constraint" and "molded" by the mechanical arts. The "searchers and spies of nature" are to discover her plots and secrets.[10]

Nature as a Woman to Be Exploited

This method, so readily applicable when nature is denoted by the female gender, degraded and made possible the exploitation of the natural environment. As women's womb had symbolically yielded to the forceps, so nature's womb harbored secrets that through technology could be wrested from her grasp for use in the improvement of the human condition:

> There is therefore much ground for hoping that there are still laid up in the womb of nature many secrets of excellent use having no affinity or parallelism with anything that is now known . . . only by the method which we are now treating can they be speedily and suddenly and simultaneously presented and anticipated.[11]

Bacon transformed the magical tradition by calling on the need to dominate nature not for the sole benefit of the individual magician, but for the good of the entire human race. Through vivid metaphor, he transformed the magus from nature's servant to its exploiter, and nature from a teacher to a slave. Bacon argued that it was the magician's error to consider art (technology) a mere "assistant to nature having the power to finish what nature has begun" and therefore to despair of ever "changing, transmuting, or fundamentally altering nature."[12]

The natural magician saw himself as operating within the organic order of nature — he was a manipulator of parts within that system, bringing down the heavenly powers to the earthly shrine. Agrippa, however, had begun to explore the possibility of ascending the hierarchy to the point of cohabiting with God. Bacon extended this idea to include the recovery of the power over nature lost when Adam and Eve were expelled from paradise.

Due to the Fall from the Garden of Eden (caused by the temptation of a woman), the human race lost its "dominion over creation." Before the Fall, there was no need for power or dominion, because Adam and Eve had been made sovereign over all other creatures. In this state of dominion, mankind was "like unto God." While some, accepting God's punishment, had obeyed the medieval strictures against searching too deeply into God's secrets, Bacon turned the constraints into sanctions. Only by "digging further and further into the mine of natural knowledge" could mankind recover that lost dominion. In this way, "the narrow limits of man's dominion over the universe" could be stretched "to their promised bounds."[13]

Although a female's inquisitiveness may have caused man's fall from his God-given dominion, the relentless interrogation of another female, nature, could be used to regain it. As he argued in *The Masculine Birth of Time*, "I am come in very truth leading to you nature with all her children to bind her to your service and make her your slave." "We have no right," he asserted, "to expect nature to come to us." Instead, "Nature must be taken by the forelock, being bald behind." Delay and subtle argument "permit one only to clutch at nature, never to lay hold of her and capture her."[14] ...

The new method of interrogation was not through abstract notions, but through the instruction of the understanding "that it may in very truth dissect nature." The instruments of the mind supply suggestions, those of the hand give motion and aid the work. "By art and the hand of man," nature can then be "forced out of her natural state and squeezed and molded." In this way, "human knowledge and human power meet as one."[15]

Here, in bold sexual imagery, is the key feature of the modern experimental method — constraint of nature in the laboratory, dissection by hand and mind, and the penetration of hidden secrets — language still used today in praising a scientist's "hard facts," "penetrating mind," or the "thrust of his argument." The constraints against penetration in Natura's lament over her torn garments of modesty have been turned into sanctions in language that legitimates the exploitation and "rape" of nature for human good. The seventeenth-century experimenters of the Accademia del Cimento of Florence (i.e., The Academy of Experiment, 1657–1667) and the Royal Society of London who placed mice and plants in the artificial vacuum of the barometer or bell jar were vexing nature and forcing her out of her natural state in true Baconian fashion.[16]

Scientific method, combined with mechanical technology, would create a "new organon," a new system of investigation, that unified knowledge with material power. The technological discoveries of printing, gunpowder, and the magnet in the fields of learning, warfare, and navigation "help us to think about the secrets still locked in nature's bosom." "They do not, like the old, merely exert a gentle guidance over nature's course; they have the power to conquer and subdue her, to shake her to her foundations." Under the mechanical arts, "nature betrays her secrets more fully...than when in enjoyment of her natural liberty."[17] ...

The New Atlantis: A Mechanistic Utopia

Bacon's utopia, the *New Atlantis,* was written in 1624, shortly before his death. In contrast to the organic egalitarian societies of Campanella and Andrea, in which women and men were to receive much the same education and honor, the social structure of Bacon's Bensalem was hierarchical and patriarchal, modeled on the early modern patriarchal family. . . .

[In the family] . . . the "Father" exercised authority over the kin and the role of the woman had been reduced to near invisibility. The shipwrecked visitors to Bensalem were invited to a "Feast of the Family" headed by the "Father of the Family, whom they call the Tirsan."[18] The Father was described entering the room where the feast was to be held followed by "all his generation or lineage, the males before him and the females following him." The mother, however, although present, was kept hidden behind a glass partition.

> If there be a mother from whose body the whole lineage is descended, there is a traverse [partition] placed in a loft above on the right hand of the chair, with a privy door and a carved window of glass, leaded with gold and blue, where she sitteth but is not seen.

After the opening ceremony, the Father began the dinner alone, "served only by his own children, such as are male, who perform unto him all service of the table upon the knee, and the women only stand about him, leaning against the wall." After the guests had been served in the room below, hymns were sung to the fathers: Adam, Noah, Abraham, the Father of the Faithful and the Savior. Then in order of age the Tirsan blessed his children in the name of the "everlasting Father, Prince of Peace." The son chosen to be in the house with him was named Son of the Vine and given the family's golden cluster of grapes to bear before his father in public places.

The Logic of Interstructured Oppression
A Black Womanist Perspective

Marcia Riggs

The term interstructured oppression is frequently used in feminist thought to describe the relationship between gender, race, and class oppression. On the one hand, the term means that sexism, racism, and classism are interrelated — that the three simultaneously create oppression. On the other hand, this assertion of interrelatedness is meant to signify an inclusive perspective and analysis (one that takes into account different groups of women) on the part of the writer. In this essay, I am contending that the present use of the term is misleading (perhaps even counterproductive) with respect to the ethical positions to engender liberation. My aim here is to explore the logic of what the assertion of interstructured oppression means for the way ethical decisions are made, particularly ethical decisions concerning the claims of women of different races and classes in relation to one another within a socioreligious, liberationist, ethical framework. The essay has three parts: (1) a brief explication of the black womanist experience and perspective, (2) a discussion of some understandings of interstructured oppression, and (3) a conclusion suggesting some socioreligious ethical implications of the discussion in the first two parts.

THE BLACK WOMANIST EXPERIENCE AND PERSPECTIVE

The term womanist was coined by Alice Walker to designate the experience and perspective of black women who advocate feminism.[1] Walker gives four definitions of "womanist"; part of the second definition, which follows, is pertinent to this discussion: "[A woman] committed to survival and wholeness of entire people, male *and* [her emphasis] female."[2] The term womanist has now been adopted by other black female writers, including black female religionists whose writing seeks to expose the "tri-dimensional phenomenon of race-class-gender oppression."[3]

Accordingly, I maintain that the following points outline features of the black womanist experience and perspective as well as tasks that the black womanist theologian or ethicist undertakes.

First, the womanist experience is inextricably bound up with the struggle of black people for liberation from race, gender, and class oppression in the United States.

Second, the womanist perspective has as a fundamental guiding premise a principle of collective solidarity. This means that black women understand their individual autonomy to be interdependent with the collective position of blacks in this country.

Third, womanists engage in at least these four tasks: (a) uncovering the roots of a womanist tradition through an examination and reintegration of black women's experience into black history in particular and American history in general; (b) debunking social myths about black womanhood so as to undermine the black woman's acceptance of sexist oppression against her, the black man's acceptance of patriarchal privilege, and the white woman's acceptance of white racist privilege; (c) constructing black womanist theology and religious ethics in light of the first two tasks so that these disciplines are broadened to include nontraditional bases and sources for theological and ethical reflection; and (d) envisioning *human liberation* (not solely racial/ethnic-group or gender-group liberation) under God, that is, black womanists are proposing a *decidedly inclusive* perspective, which is acutely aware of the need for simultaneous liberating work from all oppression.

Moreover, in terms of a socioreligious, liberationist, ethical framework, black womanist theologians and ethicists retrieve elements within the Judeo-Christian tradition that can have practical liberative force in the church and society. We black womanists reflect theologically and ethically from within both the prophetic tradition of the Bible and the tradition of our black foremothers, developing our liberative conscience by which we expose and assess values of domination wherever they are operative — in the black church and community and in the society and world at large.

A LOGIC OF INTERSTRUCTURED OPPRESSION

The discussion in this section analyzes understandings of interstructured oppression in the writings of white feminist theologians and ethicists in light of the weak and strong ethical stances that derive from them. Typically, white feminist theologians and ethicists assert relationality as a key concept when they write about interstructured oppression. Here relationality emphasizes the idea that there is an intrinsic connection of gender that binds women of various racial/ethnic groups and classes to one another.

The black womanist both disapproves of and affirms this concept of relationality. On the one hand, she disapproves because of relationality's proclivity toward a weak ethical stance. By weak, I mean that the basis for making ethical decisions is inadequate because morally relevant factors are ignored. That is, this idea of relationality produces a weak ethical stance because the intrinsic gender connection between women refers only to their biological bond, and the biological basis for bonding transcends and ignores specific sociohistoric roots of oppression.[4] For example, there are significantly different sociohistoric bases of gender oppression for black and white women. The debasement of black women (stemming from the sociohistoric experience of slavery in the nineteenth century) has been the means of denial of personhood, while idealization (deriving from the sociohistoric experience of the cult of true womanhood in the nineteenth century) has been the means of debasement for white women. Thus, while in both situations black and white women were and are oppressed because of their biological sex, sociohistoric realities produced (and continue to produce) different expressions of gender oppression for the two groups of women. This idea of "biological" relationality does not then encourage its supporters to consider and make hard ethical choices. There is an inability to accept the fact that different sociohistoric roots of gender oppression will require sacrifices on the part of some groups of women in relation to other groups of women. There is an ethical weakness because there is no acknowledgment of complicity, that is, that some women have privileged status (whether because of race or class) and participate in the oppression of other women who lack such privilege.

On the other hand, the black womanist affirms the concept of relationality because of its relevance for a strong ethical stance when it does not ignore sociohistoric realities.[5] By strong, I mean that the basis for making ethical decisions includes the morally relevant factors of sociohistoric particularity, which differentiate various groups of women and hold them accountable to one another. A strong ethical stance is feasible because moral responsibility is empirically grounded and moral obligations are experientially determined. Those who espouse sociohistoric relationality recognize that the intrinsic biological connection between women provides a necessary but insufficient condition for liberative interconnection. Sociohistoric relationality requires women engaged in liberative moral agency to make hard ethical choices, that is, to determine priorities among the competing claims of diverse groups of women because of our radically different bases of gender oppression and in light of the sociohistoric context in which we are interacting.

It is with this latter concept of sociohistoric relationality, which generates a strong ethical stance, that a black womanist logic of interstructured oppression begins. For such a logic has a contextual, interactive, sociohistorical, socioethical basis.[6] This means that the black womanist logic insists that sexism, racism, and classism are at the same time parallel processes (having independent effects) and contextually interactive processes (providing contexts for each other) in oppression. As black women, we experience sexism, racism, and classism simultaneously, as well as sharing racist and classist oppression with black men in the macrocontext of the patriarchal, white racist, capitalist United States. But we also experience these oppressive processes in micro-contexts (such as the black community and church or a predominantly white theological school) wherein one or the other of these processes (1) is the predominant cause of oppression, (2) evokes qualitatively different responses, or (3) has the same oppressive consequences for black women as for other women.

Furthermore, in recognizing a sociohistoric relationality, the black womanist calls for a logic of interstructured oppression that allows her to engage always in comprehensive liberative activity (activity that does not require that she place priority on either her femaleness or her blackness). She speaks out of her sociohistoric particularity to the interconnection of oppression. Bell Hooks sets forth a way to reconceptualize feminism that can serve as a cornerstone of the black womanist logic:

> Feminism as a movement to end sexist oppression directs our attention to systems of domination and the inter-relatedness of sex, race, and class oppression. Therefore, it compels us to centralize the experiences and the social predicaments of women who bear the brunt of sexist oppression as a way to understand the collective social status of women in the United States. Defining feminism as a movement to end sexist oppression is crucial for the development of theory because it is a starting point indicating the direction of exploration and analysis.[7]

SOCIORELIGIOUS ETHICAL IMPLICATION

At the beginning of this essay, I noted that the black womanist experience and perspective lead black womanist religionists to envision *human liberation* under God from a *decidedly inclusive* perspective, which is acutely aware of the need for simultaneous liberative work from all oppression. In the second part of the essay, I proposed that a womanist logic of interstructured oppression assumes sociohistoric relationality and has a contextual, interactive, sociohistorical, socioethical basis. Here I will outline briefly what this means for socioreligious, liberative, ethical reflection and action.

First, the black womanist vision of human liberation under God is based upon an understanding that we are human in sociohistoric particularity. This means that the vision of human liberation (rather than merely racial/ethnic-group or gender-group liberation) recognizes that we are all connected to one another by our creatureliness under God, yet we are estranged from one another by oppressive sociohistoric realities such as sexism, racism, and classism. Thus, the socioreligious ethical imperative is to overcome oppression through sociohistorical liberation for the sake of reunion with one another who, as creatures of God, are persons of equal worth entitled to socioeconomic, sociopolitical justice and equality.

Second, this socioreligious ethical imperative, the quest for reunion through sociohistoric liberation, is mandated from a theocentric perspective — by a God who is liberating the oppressed. Consequently, ethical reflection begins with the condition of the oppressed in a specific sociohistoric context and with the premise that we are coparticipants with God in God's liberating activity within society and the world. We are called by God to be responsible moral agents of liberative activity who make nonoppressive relationships the earmarks of God's presence and activity.

Third, as responsible moral agents of liberative activity, we must be guided in our actions by ethical principles determined in light of both our sociohistorical situation and the norm of nonoppressive relationships. For example, an ethical principle of the renunciation of privilege is experientially sound and may become operative for both morally responsible white feminists and black womanists, depending on the context in which they find themselves. In the macro-context of white racist, patriarchal, classist American society, the principle of renunciation should have some prima facie status for the way white women render liberative ethical decisions and action in relation to black women and other women of color. In a micro-context such as a historically all-white, male-dominated theological school, white women and black women are obviously not in a position of privilege and are not required to enact the principle of renunciation in relation to the men who have control in that context. Nevertheless, those same white women and black women have privileged status (socially as well as economically) with reference to other white and black working-class, lower-class, and poor women in society and must weigh whether or not the choices they make within the academy (even in matters such as what they teach and write) can have actual liberative consequences for the latter. In fact, white feminists and black womanists within the academy may have to choose whether or not to renounce the life of the scholar who is an advocate on behalf of her more oppressed sisters for some more directly participatory role in a feminist-womanist movement to restructure radically the society in which we live.[8]

Finally, as the black womanist finds that she must never lose sight of the fact that she is bound to all black people and that alleviating sexist oppression is a part of alleviating racist oppression, a logic of interstructured oppression from a black womanist perspective asserts these foundational premises: the eradication of gender oppression cannot occur fully apart from the eradication of race and class oppression. Hard ethical choices will need to be made in light of the sociohistorical, sociopolitical, and socioeconomic realities that constitute the complexity of interstructured oppression we seek to overcome.

Heterosexism
Enforcing Male Supremacy

Carter Heyward

In the dismembered world, we make love not to the living body of the Goddess but to her corpse. Power becomes sexualized. When all power is cast as domination, we can only feel our power through dominating another, and can give way only through our submission to another's control. The Master colonizes our orgasms.
— Starhawk, *Truth or Dare*

Growing up in an Irish Catholic family, sex was the ultimate forbidden subject. Ours was a family of silence and lies. Little was said out loud, only acted out and denied....As the youngest of eight children...I did my best to live out the Christian and family virtues of servanthood, purity, silence, and obedience....

In looking at my sexuality, I divide my lifeline into pre-Epiphany 1988 and post-Epiphany 1988. The word "epiphany" means sudden realization. The Epiphany is a Christian feast day celebrating the world's knowledge of the presence of Jesus Christ. It is also my birthday. I chose this significant day for my own personal epiphany. On January 6th of this year I walked into my therapist's office and announced that I wanted to discuss a previously taboo topic — my sexuality. I walked out with the knowledge that I was a victim of incest at my father's hands....

My mind has painted layers of forgetfulness over memories of my father's unpredictable acts of violence toward me. It has only been a month since I first consciously realized that my father raped me. My tears can be triggered by anything or nothing these days, but my sexual

"Heterosexism: Enforcing White Male Supremacy" by Carter Heyward is reprinted from *Touching Our Strength: The Erotic as Power and the Love of God* by Carter Heyward (San Francisco: Harper & Row, 1989). Copyright © by Carter Heyward.

responses are dead. I am protecting myself now as I was
unable to protect myself as a little girl. . . . I cannot look
at my sexuality without addressing how abuse has shaped
it. Today my reaction to abuse is to shut down sexually.
— Monica, theological student

Heterosexism is a foundational historical structure of our lives.
Heterosexism is the social and political force named by Adrienne Rich
as the "institution of compulsory heterosexuality."

Rich describes how the "lie" of compulsory heterosexuality distorts
women's lives in particular:

> The lie of compulsory female heterosexuality today afflicts not just
> feminist scholarship, but every profession, every reference work,
> every curriculum, every organizing attempt, every relationship or
> conversation over which it hovers. It creates, specifically, a profound
> falseness, hypocrisy, and hysteria in the heterosexual dialogue, for
> every heterosexual relationship is lived in the queasy strobe light of
> that lie. *However we choose to identify ourselves, however we find ourselves
> labeled, it flickers across and distorts our lives.* [My emphasis.]
>   The lie keeps numberless women psychologically trapped, trying
> to fit mind, spirit, and sexuality into a prescribed script because they
> cannot look beyond the parameters of the acceptable. It pulls on the
> energy of such women even as it drains the energy of "closeted" les-
> bians — the energy exhausted in the double-life. The lesbian trapped
> in the closet, the woman imprisoned in prescriptive ideas of the "nor-
> mal" share the pain of blocked options, broken connections, lost
> access to self-definition freely and powerfully assumed.[1]

Mario Mieli speaks in a similar fashion of "heterosexual ideology":

> The repressive society only considers one type of *monosexuality* as
> "normal," the heterosexual kind, and imposes *educastration* with a
> view to maintaining an exclusively heterosexual conditioning. The
> Norm, therefore, is heterosexual. [My emphasis.][2]

Heterosexism is the basic structure of gay/lesbian oppression in this
and other societies. Heterosexism is to homophobia what sexism is to
misogyny and what racism is to racial bigotry and hatred. Heterosexism
is the *structure* in which are generated and cemented the *feelings* of fear
and hatred toward queers and dykes, and toward ourselves if we are
lesbians or gaymen. Dialectically, such feelings serve also to secure the
structure. They thereby strengthen not only such traditional patriarchal
religious institutions as christianity, which have helped set the structure
of compulsory heterosexuality in place, but also more deeply personal
"institutions," such as the self-loathing of homosexual youths and the
hatred of such youths by others.

A "structure" is a pattern of relational transactions that gives a society its particular shape. Consider the analogy of a house. If there is a structural problem, we do not fix it by changing the wallpaper or rearranging the floor space. We cannot solve the structural problems of class elitism, racism, heterosexism, or any other "ism" by rearranging our institutions in such a way as simply to accommodate those who historically have been marginalized from the center of social, political, and economic power. To solve the structural problems we must dig deeply into the foundations of our common life in order to discover the rot. Only then can we begin to reconstruct the house in such a way as to provide adequate, trustworthy space for us all.[3]

"Structure" denotes the interconnections between what may appear to be unrelated phenomena — such as the taking of foster children away from gay parents in Massachusetts; the granting of child custody to a heterosexually abusive father in Mississippi; the acquittal in Michigan of a nineteen-year-old man who admitted to raping his eight-year-old neighbor because she was "seductive"; the drowning of a young gay man in Bangor, Maine, by teenagers who thought he was "effeminate"; and the statement by a woman who, hearing of this murder, said, "Well, he probably made a pass at one of the boys." Heterosexism is a configuration of relational power in which such events are held together not merely as related but as critical parts of the whole configuration. Each event secures and reinforces the public educational impact of the others. This is how we learn to fear and hate others and ourselves.

Charlie Howard was not thrown off the bridge in Bangor simply because he happened to be an "effeminate" individual who had the misfortune of running into some particularly homophobic boys.[4] Charlie Howard was killed because all-American kids are taught by church, synagogue, and state to fear and hate fags. The three young men who killed Charlie Howard stand, in a representative sense, for the prevailing sexual moral ethos of our mainstream religions and our society. We cannot make the connections — between ecclesial tradition, homophobia, misogyny, and, in this case, murder — unless we see that no incident can be understood apart from the social structures that have shaped it. As an ugly act of wrong relation, gaybashing forces us to examine the structure of heterosexism as a *foundational resource of alienated power*.

CAPITALISM AND THE DEVALUATION OF PERSONS*

In a profit-consumed economic order such as ours the value of persons is diminished. The accumulation of capital on the part of the wealthy and

* Heads added.

the hope for wealth on the part of the rest of us take precedence over the essentially nonmonetary value of human beings and other earthcreatures as valuable in our own right — because we are who we are. To claim we are valuable because "we are who we are" may, to our ears, sound "romantic" or "soft" or "simply a matter of faith." If so, we may have a clue of the depth of the cynicism that holds us collectively in its grip at this historical moment.

We humans, together with other earthcreatures, are diminished in the context of a late-twentieth-century capitalist global order. In this context, the capacity to love our bodies, enjoy a strong sense of self-esteem, take real pleasure in our work, and respect and enjoy either ourselves or others very much is a diminished capacity. In a very real sense, we have lost ourselves — that is, ourselves as a people, united with one another and other creatures.

This loss of ourselves and one another is what Marx meant by "alienation."[5] In an alienated situation, we do not relate as humanely as we might desire. It is not that we may not want to be caring people. It is rather that, unbeknownst to us (usually to the extent that we hold power-over others in the society), we are captive to social forces that are running our lives. Most of us do not see the extent to which we are playing roles in society as if we had no choice. As individuals, to the extent that we are among the powerless, we do not have much "choice" — not if we want to live decently or, for many of us, if we want to survive (I'm referring here especially to poor people and people of color, and most especially to poor women of color).

For most United States citizens with access to survival resources, a pre-occupation with "freedom" and its concomitant "privileges" of private ownership and private possession has its origins far beyond the realm of the individual's intention. All of us have received the message that the individual's freedom is our noblest possession, nobler than a quality of caring and dignity we might provide for one another. In the United States, among people of economic privilege, freedom is more important than justice. Whenever there must be a tradeoff, the freedom of the few will take precedence over justice for all.

Most of us learn that we should share what we have with others, especially the "less fortunate." But the dominant message in our civil and religious education is that the freedom of the individual must come first — especially for white propertied males. Men of color, all women, and the poor learn a similar lesson, but our capacities to achieve derive from our real or imagined relationships to white propertied males, whose right to set the agenda for the whole society has become a first principle of our civil religion.

POWER AND POWERLESSNESS

In our alienated society, power has come to mean *power-over* others' lives, well-being, senses of self-worth, and survival. Power has come to mean domination by a few over the lives and deaths of many. I am referring to the real and daily domination of all human and other natural resources. The food we eat, the air we breathe, the energy we burn, the love we make, even the dreams we nurture, are controlled to a significant degree by the structural configurations of power that have been shaped by the interests of affluent white males who usually fail to see any more clearly than the rest of us the exploitative character of their own lives.

We and those with power over us have learned to assume that this alienation is natural. The state of being lost to ourselves and others is just the way it is and, in fact, must be if we are to preserve any portion of the social order we white folk tend to characterize as "free." In an alienated social order, it is necessary to be out of touch with the sacred value of that which is most fully human — common — among us. To be common is not a worthy aim for human beings who, in this situation, must strive to be "exceptional."

It's important that we recognize the extent to which an acceptance of this state of affairs as "just the way it is" characterizes contemporary United States society. Such massive resignation generates a sense of powerlessness, a collective depression, in which we lose our capacities for hope. For, while alienated power is not shared, alienated powerlessness is. It moves us slowly toward our undoing as a people on this planet.

To combat this sense of powerlessness, many people have organized against nuclear war, against the Contras, against the so-called Right to Life movement, against racism. Yet it remains to this day unclear to many of us — at least those of us who are white middle-strata folk — what we are organizing *for*.

Alienated powerlessness is a social force that takes much of our most creative energy simply to withstand. It is easier to struggle *against* it than to generate fresh vision of a new and better social order. In an alienated situation, it's easier to be reactive than creative. The debilitating character of alienation creates reactionary progressives (such as the Democratic Party), a portent of pernicious things to come, as an entire society slips further away from the possibility of a common dream and a common good.

Audre Lorde's vision of the erotic as power is a creative social, emotional, spiritual, and political vision. Radically and simply, Lorde moves immediately into the heart of power as power-with, which for her is the erotic in our lives. In giving this deeply personal and political movement a voice, she speaks prophetically of who we can be together as we name and resist the structures of alienated power that keep us divided, separated, isolated, and depressed.

> [The erotic] — that deep and irreplaceable knowledge of my capacity for joy — comes to demand from all of my life that it be lived within the knowledge that such satisfaction is possible, and does not have to be called *marriage,* nor *god,* nor an *afterlife.*
>
> This is one reason why the erotic is so feared, and so often relegated to the bedroom alone, when it is recognized at all. For once we begin to feel deeply all the aspects of our lives, we begin to demand from ourselves and from our life-pursuits that they feel in accordance with that joy which we know ourselves to be capable of. Our erotic knowledge empowers us, becomes a lens through which we scrutinize all aspects of our existence, forcing us to evaluate those aspects honestly in terms of their relative meaning within our lives. And this is a grave responsibility, projected from within each of us, not to settle for the convenient, the shoddy, the conventionally expected, nor the merely safe.[6]

In sharp, violent opposition to this vision, alienated power is possessed, not shared. It is quantitative, not qualitative. Under advanced capitalism, alienated power is incarnated and symbolized by accumulation of wealth and property; manufacture, sale, and usage of guns and bombs; and the forcible thrusting of a penis into an unwanting vagina.

In this realm of greed and violence, more and bigger is best. We have it or we don't. It's natural to want it — for everyone to want wealth, for small countries to want bombs, and for women to want penises. In the moral ethos of the dominant social order, it is assumed that such power as capital, explosives, and rape can be used for either good or ill, depending on the purposes and judgment of those exercising it.

In this situation, no action is, in and of itself, evil — except that which challenges the established order of alienated power relations. So, for instance, while hunger may be a problem, communism, which threatens the individual white male's autonomy and his rights to private ownership, is evil. While wife-battering may be too bad, gay sex, which threatens the established order of male control of female sexuality, is evil. While incest may be a shame, lesbian mothers embody the forces of evil that threaten to bring down the entire sacred canopy of alienated power.

SEXUALITY AS OUR WAY OF BEING

In its fullest sense, theologian James Nelson writes, our sexuality is

> our way of being in the world as female or male persons. It involves our appropriation of characteristics socially defined as feminine or masculine. It includes our affectional-sexual orientation

toward those of the opposite and/or same sex. It is our capacity
for sensuousness."[7]

Or, as Beverly Harrison suggests, it "deepens and shapes our power of
personal being. Our sexuality represents our most intense interaction
with the world. Because this is so, it is also a key to the quality and
integrity of our overall spirituality."[8]

Our eroticism is the deepest stirring of our relationality, our experience of being connected to others. In the context of alienation, our
eroticism, the root of our relational capacity, is infused with the experience of alienation. We are electrified by alienated power dynamics, turned
on by currents of domination and submission that are structured into
the world we inhabit. As mirrors of the world, our bodyselves reflect the
violence intrinsic to the dynamics of alienated power. What we know,
what we feel, and what we believe is mediated by images, symbols, and
acts of domination and control.

We learn to associate survival — how we control our future, more
basically, that we have a future — with symbols and acts of domination
and violence. Whether at home, as is often the case, or elsewhere, children learn that whether or not might makes right, it shows who's in
charge: a whipping by daddy, a war movie on television, a rock video
about gang rape, a speech by the president about the so-called freedom
fighters in Nicaragua.... These are paradigmatic lessons, unforgettable
in the most embodied sense, by which we learn to experience our most
personal world as fraught with the tension of being either more or less
in control of our own daily lives.

We learn what it means to be child, parent, woman, man, dark, light,
poor, rich, jew, christian, bad guy, good guy, bottom or top, down or
up, less or more, powerless or power-more, vanquished or victorious.
The dynamics of alienated power relations shape our sexualities as surely
as they do the Pentagon budget.

Ours is a sadomasochistic society, quite literally, in that we have
learned to sit back and enjoy the fruits of domination and submission.
It is, for many of us, most of what we know to be relationally possible.

ALIENATED POWER

In the praxis of alienated power, the power of mutual relation is
in eclipse. We have difficulty believing and immersing ourselves in the
empowerment born of honest friendship. Relative to the overwhelming character of alienation, we are able to experience creative relational
power primarily in glimpses, intimations, art, and — if we are lucky —
the sustaining of good friendship.

We may believe that the mutuality we experience in relation to some others is *good,* but we have not learned to trust it as *powerful:* the fulcrum of our capacity to survive and to affect the world around us.

We have come to assume, affectively if not cognitively, that while mutuality is playful and recreational, staying in control is the stuff of real creation. In this situation, mutuality doesn't seem to be an empowering relational dynamic, because in this context it isn't: *Mutuality does not breed alienated power. It transforms it.*

We have mastered our lessons as students of alienation: If we want to be successful, worthy women and men in this society, we must accept the fact that our power is generated by dynamics of control. We cannot allow ourselves to believe that the primary intensity and energy that emerges among friends and comrades gives us any serious control over our own lives. We learn to disbelieve in our most creative and redemptive power and become architects of our own isolation.

The sexual effects of disbelief in our relational power are staggering. So deluged are we by the romance of domination that most girls and boys, while they are still quite young, are well under the captivating spell of an eroticism steeped in fantasies of conquest, seduction, and rape. Such eroticism is "normal" : that in which boy takes and girl is taken. Feminist theorists have demonstrated convincingly the extent to which "normal" human sexuality is synonymous with male gender domination. Any sexual desire or erotic stimulation that deviates from the normative status of male gender domination has been considered (until recently by the medical profession, and still by most mainline religions) to be "abnormal" or "wrong." While such abnormality includes homosexuality, it does not always include rape, especially "date rape," "marriage rape," or the forcible entry of a man's penis into the body of a woman or girl whom he knows (read: to whose body he has a "right").[9] As data mount on the sexual violence perpetrated by men against women and girls, it becomes evident that rape, father-daughter incest, and other forms of sexual violence against women and children are considered, if not exactly "right," at least understandable and even tolerable by a shocking number of judges, therapists, and clergymen, who not infrequently are among the perpetrators.[10]

But we must watch carefully, because many of us experience the daily dynamics of domination and control most frequently as benign, not brutal; natural, not perverse. Abusive power can be difficult to detect, name, challenge, and expunge. Abusive dynamics, for example, are basic, even sacred, to traditional modes of parenting, religious leadership, physical, emotional and spiritual healing, and teaching. In such relational transactions, movement in or toward mutuality is ruled out by those who, in the traditional arrangement, exercise power-over others.

The process of becoming more fully mutual cannot happen in any relationship in which control must be maintained forever primarily by one party. Mutuality is impossible wherever the configuration of power is unchanging. In the praxis of alienation, this is how all significant relationships between individuals and groups have been structured.

It is vital, morally and spiritually, that we realize that we all participate in these fundamentally flawed relational dynamics of domination and submission. We can't escape them entirely without leaving the world, but we can help create a better way. To do so we need one another's friendship and solidarity. We must be patient, persevering, and tender with one another and ourselves. It will take years, decades, a long time, to learn, with one another, that our power to love is stronger than the fear that festers in our alienation.

HETEROSEXISM AND ALIENATED POWER

Sexism is a structure of alienated power. It refers to the alienation between men and women, specifically to the historical complex of practices and attitudes that are essential to men's control of women's sexuality and thereby women's lives. *Heterosexism* is a logical and necessary extension of sexism. It is cemented in the false assumptions (1) that male gender superiority is good (natural, normal), and (2) that in order to assure sexism in the social order, men must be forced — if necessary — to control women's sexual activity.

Penetrating to the core of sexism, heterosexism heralds the recognition that, in order for women's sexual activity to be controlled, men's sexual activity must be imposed upon women. If women are to stay on the bottom of the male-female social relation, men must stay on top of women. In this way, men must be willing to do their part in preserving the structure of sexism. Otherwise, patriarchal, androcentric power relations will not prevail. Things will fall apart: romantic love between men and women, marriage and family as we know them, traditional values, the authority of traditional religious teachings, the stability of the social order, the security of the nation, everything predicated upon men's control of the world as we know it.

Heterosexist ideology is put in place to convince us that "normal" women are sexually submissive to men, and that "real" men sexually dominate women. Only when we understand heterosexism as the fundamental means of enforcing sexism and therefore as intrinsically bound up in the oppression of women, do we begin to understand why, historically, the gay/lesbian movement has come on the heels of the women's

liberation movement. We begin also to see why feminists are clear that
so-called women's issues and gay issues cannot be attended politically
with any long-term effectiveness as long as their proponents attempt to
keep them separate. The National Organization of Women in the early
1970s and the mainline protestant denominations have made this mistake. When we attempt not to confuse women's liberation with gay/
lesbian liberation, we disregard deep organic connections between gender and sexual politics. In so doing, we subvert the possibility of any
authentic gender or sexual transformation in our society and religious
institutions.

Understanding the links between sexism and heterosexism may help
illuminate also why so many openly self-affirming gaymen are feminists,
and why so many frightened and ashamed homosexual men are not.[11]
A gayman who understands the *sexist* character of his own oppression
knows that those who govern the structures of patriarchal capitalism are
determined to use his body to enforce the sexual control of women's
lives. He is able to comprehend his homosexuality not simply as a private orientation or preference, but rather as a form of resistance to
sexism, not necessarily chosen consciously, but a form of resistance
nonetheless.

Those men, on the other hand, who experience their homosexuality
as simply a private dimension of who they happen to be and what they
happen to like fail generally to understand the feminist liberation commitment to making the connection between women's liberation and that
of gaymen and others. Unable to make connections between their own
private lives and the oppression of women, such homosexual men (whom
the church always has gladly ordained) frequently are not merely indifferent to women's plight, but are hostile toward feminists and gaymen for
having made sexuality a matter of public interest, thereby threatening to
invade their privacy.[12]

Homosexual people, like everyone else in heterosexist society, are
homophobic. We are afraid of what our sexual involvement with members of the same sex may mean about us (that we are not "normal") or of
what its consequences may be for us (forfeit of job, marriage, children,
friends, ordination, and so on).

Our homophobia bears serious consequences for us. Many homosexual men and women are so terrorized by the meaning and potential
consequences of their sexual orientation or preference that they cannot
let themselves see the sexual politics of their own lives. Disempowered
by fear, they fail to imagine the creative power inherent in struggling for justice and solidarity on behalf of the oppressed — including
themselves.

Isolated, depressed, and cut off from the roots of their power in right relation, the wellspring of faith, these sisters and brothers do not yet believe that struggle is a name for hope.[13] But our lives are linked with theirs, and we should remember to make room for them at the table whenever they are able to come forth.

Marriage, Market Values, and Social Justice
Toward an Examination of Compulsory Monogamy

Mary E. Hobgood

You must therefore set no bounds to your love, just as
your heavenly Father sets none to his.
> — Matthew 5:48 (New Jerusalem Bible)

He knew exactly what she meant: to get to a place where
you could love anything you chose — not to need permission for desire — well now, *that* was freedom.
> — Toni Morisson, *Beloved*

We have an economic system...that's...not democratic.
If we believe in democracy, we have to believe in it in all
facets of our lives...our economy...our workplace...
our relationships. Now I don't have all the answers on
how to get there....But the solution is not the status
quo.
> — Michael Moore, *Lepoco Newsletter*

Sexuality too narrowly confined in marriage has been too
rigidly forbidden in friendship; both marriage and friendship have suffered from the separation of sexuality and the
more general energy of love and life itself. We have not
dared to say, "I love my friend."
> — Carolyn Heilbrun, *Writing a Woman's Life*

I have refused men who loved me...if they in turn were
loved by another woman but did not love her in return.
I am the kind of woman who could positively forbid a
married lover to leave his wife.
> — Alice Walker, *Living by the Word*

While we may sacrifice everything we have [in our commitment to another], we may not sacrifice everything we

115

are. We may not sacrifice in a final sense our autonomy.
We may not sacrifice our capability for union and com-
munion with God and human persons.
— Margaret Farley, *Personal Commitments*

To borrow a quip from ethicist Marvin Ellison, I am going to
write about "what we have always wanted — just sex!"[1] The issue
of justice and sex, however, is an enormous one. The way sexuality
is structured in Western society is both a result and a reinforce-
ment of all other social relations, including economic ones. Justice
in the area of sexuality is, therefore, related to justice in other
areas. In this essay I wish to examine some of these connections between sexuality and capitalism in the dominant culture of this United
States. My thesis is that sexual and capitalist ideologies work in
tandem to impoverish human relationships both within and outside
marriage.

THE MYTH OF ROMANTIC LOVE
AND MONOGAMOUS MARRIAGE

In American society mature, human sexuality is *married* sexuality. That
is, it is heterosexual, monogamous, and organized around child rearing.
Since the 1960s, a part of the traditional sexual ethic — celibacy in singleness — has given way to tolerance for sexual exploration and activity
for singles *only because* it is assumed that these relationships are a prelude
for marriage. Indeed that assumption explains how the phenomenon of
gay-bashing functions to restrain the sexual freedom recently afforded
heterosexuals. Hatred toward gay people — as homosexual and "promiscuous" — promotes the ideology that the only worthy relationships are
not only heterosexual but are also monogamous. Both heterosexuality
and monogamy are compulsory in a society that sees traditional marriage
as the norm.[2]

In middle-income white society traditional marriage is sustained by
the ideology of romantic love, which in turn supports a polarized and
hierarchical gender structure.[3] The ideology of romantic love tells us
that there is one person from a different sex, and one person only, who
will fulfill me by making up for the lack in my own gender. This person
alone is capable of meeting all of my emotional and sexual needs. The
ideology of romantic love encourages us to look outside ourselves to one
other person as the primary source of one's happiness and fulfillment.
We are thereby taught to abdicate responsibility for ourselves and our
own well-being. Instead we are expected to be dependent on our partner
for fulfillment.

Restrictions Based on Gender

We are familiar with the restrictions in gender roles that are reproduced in children to maintain this system of dependency. Gender role restrictions suppress natural similarities between males and females and exaggerate differences. They also perpetuate a hierarchy of values. The traits allowed in males — such as physical, sexual, and financial prowess — are considered the more important ones and are rewarded accordingly by society. The traits allowed in females — such as care and concern for the physical and emotional well-being of persons — are considered lesser values or are held in contempt in the public arenas of business and international politics.

In addition, males must deny their expression of tender and vulnerable emotions, as they maintain rigid boundaries between themselves and others. They are taught to seek dominant positions over all women and over other men whenever possible. For example, middle-income men are taught to fear mutuality with women and to feel safe only when they are helping them.

When men and women both work outside the home, the same pattern of gender restriction and hierarchy obtains. Women are thought to be naturally fit for work at home and for those lower-paying outside jobs related to housework, while men are thought naturally fit for leisure at home and better-paying outside jobs.

The ethic of compulsory monogamy undergirding dependent romantic love and a hierarchical gender system keeps the nuclear family in relative isolation because it prohibits married partners from engaging in other relationships of significant emotional depth. Both partners are taught that they are to forsake everyone else, that is, to deny their capacities for union and communion with any other persons. This ethic of restricted relationships encourages a dependency pattern of two differently sexed half-selves, who become fused to a greater or lesser degree. The autonomy required for true intimacy and mature interdependency is eroded. Intimacy involves both the ability to draw close *and* the ability to maintain autonomy. One pastoral counselor has remarked that "most marriages need both more closeness and more distance."[4] A sexual ethic that restricts relationships and the development of personal wholeness and autonomy also fosters dependency and inhibits the capacity for intimacy.

The myth of romantic love functions to keep this dependency pattern safely in place. Ironically, it does this by offering a limited exception to the norm of gender role complementarity. Through the myth of romantic love, or true love with "the one and only," one woman (and one only) can overcome her inferior status to a man and become a beloved. Similarly, in one instance only, a man can overcome the masculine taboo against vulnerability and tenderness and become a mutual lover to his beloved. In this one instance, a man is allowed to be vulnerable in a way that does not jeopardize his usual dominance as helper or exploiter in relationships with women. The "magic," or unreasonableness, of romantic love gives the woman status (as a mutual partner) and gives the man permission to be vulnerable and to exercise mutuality (as a giver of love) that each usually does not have. The institution of compulsory monogamy functions as the sole exception to the rule that keeps nonmutual gender roles safely intact in the other aspects of life.[5]

The Power of the Traditional Ethic

The ideology of romantic love and the system of traditional marriage that it supports continue to dominate Christian sexual ethics, even though most people are not now monogamous with a life-long partner. In cross cultural studies, scholars have shown for some time the extensiveness of societies that have not placed prohibitions on multiple mates.[6] Statistics tell us that in our own society, monogamy as a proper means to order a legitimate and faithful love is not working for many people. We are all familiar with the knowledge that in the past two decades, the divorce rate soared, peaking at one out of every two marriages ending in divorce.[7] Also on the rise are those who acknowledge extramarital intimate relationships while they are married. Possibly as many as 55 percent of wives and 60 percent of husbands become sexually involved with someone other than their spouse by the age of forty. Multiple relationships are now so common that social researchers no longer consider them deviant behavior. Surprising to some, these new extramarital relationships are experienced by many as enhancing their primary marital commitment, not competing with it.[8]

Today, in the late twentieth century, we are also faced with a new social context for marriage. Because of significantly longer lifespans and fewer incidences of death in childbirth than in previous history, it is possible that the typical marriage today could last for well over half a century. As one observer put it, "Forever is much longer now." Perhaps the present divorce rate is doing what higher mortality rates used to do for the durations of marriages in the past.[9] Perhaps the exclusivity demanded by traditional marriage is too heavy a burden for many relationships that hope for permanence today.

Yet, in spite of such limited historical practice and such obvious contemporary failure, the traditional ethic retains enormous power. Why does the assumption persist that monogamous, reproductive sexuality is the only way to order legitimate loving? Why have plural forms of sexual and marital relationships not gained a respected place in the political economy? One of the primary reasons a new sexual ethic will meet enormous resistance in American society is that traditional marriage is vital to capitalism.

Christian ethics must appreciate more fully the role of traditional heterosexual morality as a form of social control that serves the interests of capitalism. We need serious consideration of how this morality, which enjoys such ideological hegemony both in religion and society, fails to serve freedom, intimacy, community, or social justice.

CAPITALISM AND MONOGAMY

Although the ethics of compulsory, heterosexual monogamy has a history older than capitalism, traditional marriage is essential to capitalism in many ways.[10] Given the great resistance to an alternative sexual ethic in American society, I think it crucial that we begin to explore some of the ways that capitalist and marriage ideologies reinforce each other. We need better to appreciate the qualities of the relationship that Christian ethics affirms when it promotes the institution of marriage.

Supporting Inequality in the Labor Market

The gender system created by traditional marriage has served the interests of capitalism, first of all, by supporting inequality and alienation in the labor market. In order for firms to survive in a capitalist economy, they must make increasing amounts of profit, outdo competitors, and strive to achieve monopoly control over the market. Since escalating wages threaten profit, capitalists are interested in keeping wages down and in maintaining a secondary labor sector of lower-paying, low-benefit, dead-end jobs, chiefly populated by white women and minorities. Despite the civil-rights movement and the feminist movement, government statistics in the 1980s showed that more than 60 percent of employed minority men and women and more than 70 percent of employed women of all races held jobs in the lower-paying secondary labor sector.[11] Along with the social structure of racism, the gender system, which trains people in dominant or subordinate domestic roles, serves capitalism by making people assume that segmented public labor is natural. Wage differentials between whites and people of color and between men and women make a tremendous amount of profit for individual capitalists and are essential to their survival in the economic system.

Condoning Ownership and Control

In addition to supporting the two-tiered, capitalist labor market by reproducing an unequal division of labor in the traditional family, a second way in which marriage supports capitalism is by condoning domestic relationships that are similar in quality to those in the industrial sphere. Because capitalists own and control production, they have the social power to assume control of workers. Similarly, one who is married in white, middle-income culture is allowed to assume a kind of ownership and control, not only of the children, but also of the spouse. While ownership of the spouse is especially the prerogative of men, who enjoy dominance in the conventional family, it is also allowed to women insofar as the single sexual standard has become the ethic of white, middle-income society.

Possessiveness of persons and scarcity of resources are key components of the ideologies of capitalism and marriage. As incomplete halves of a possible whole, we are dependent on reciprocal, exclusive love for our fulfillment. This belief is so absolute that American culture has assumed that denial by one spouse of sexual access to the other is grounds for divorce or even for emotional, physical, or sexual abuse. The culture has also assumed, usually with great vengeance, that no husband — and among those who accept the single standard no wife either — should have to tolerate a spouse who is intimate with another.

Further, until monopoly control is reached, in either the sexual relationship or the business enterprise, the situation is one of fierce competition. Love, like capital, is limited. If one person gains some, another person always loses. Therefore, it is wrong to develop intimate relationships with persons other than one's legal partner. To protect access to one's supply of love, it is acceptable to read one's spouse's mail, listen in on phone calls, monitor appointments, or even, in the extreme of this way of thinking, abuse and kill her. If spouses belong to each other exclusively, then why not?

Ideologies that support possessiveness on the ground of assumptions of scarcity also support addictive controlling behaviors that are rampant in capitalist culture. Spouses seek to control the other by keeping the relationship patterned, predictable, exclusive, and isolated. Otherwise, as a half-self, their basic well-being may be threatened. Because their primary need is their own emotional survival, spouses are often not capable of seeing each other in his or her own terms.

We are socialized to think of this fused relationship, which condones intrusive and controlling behavior, as love. In capitalist culture there is great confusion between love and control, and there is tremendous pressure to define the purpose and function of others, whether economically or emotionally, in reference to ourselves. If we have been brought up to believe that our security depends on owning goods and having exclusive rights to our spouse, then sharing is a threat to our safety. Compulsory monogamy, the structure of traditional marriage, is particularly suited to capitalism because it requires ownership of and monopoly control over the spouse's sexual and emotional resources.

The Similar Roles of the Market and the Spouse

A third way that capitalist and marriage ideologies reinforce each other is in the similar roles played by the market and the spouse.[12] Capitalism fetishizes, or gives magical powers to, the market and gives unquestioned status to its function of setting prices. Capitalism makes the market the sole determinant of the economic value of the products we use. Capitalist ideology obscures the reality that products are valuable because human sweat and ingenuity have molded material reality into instruments that serve human needs, because in capitalism most people are alienated from their labor. It is the capitalist, not they, who decides how their labor is organized and what it is used to produce.

In a similar way, traditional marriage fetishizes, or gives unquestioned status to, the spouse as the sole source of emotional and sexual value. This ideology obscures the reality that the real determinant of sexual and personal value is within us. Our own rich human capacity for spontaneous feeling and mutual appreciation makes possible our union with others.

The ideology of marriage also substitutes duty to the spouse for attentiveness to one's own emotions and appreciating one's own capacities for rich interpersonal relationship with others. In this system, friendship between men and women is demeaned. Significant relationships with any other persons are degraded as "affairs" and held in contempt.[13] And it isn't just sex that people fear. Even more threatening is the prospect that strong friendship might develop. In this system, any relationship of emotional importance is supposed to lead to and be subsumed by marriage.[14]

Capitalist ideology justifies the economic suffering of those who are prohibited from having full access to their own human labor, that is, those who are prohibited from deciding what their labor produces, how their labor is organized, and how profits from that labor are invested. So also the ideology of romantic love and the system of heterosexual monogamy justify the suffering of those who are prohibited from having full access to their own affections and their rich potential to love in a variety of ways. They justify the suffering of those who are forbidden to make decisions about whom they are to love and in what ways they are to love. The authority of the market and the authority of the marriage contract block our responsibilities to expand our moral capacities in work and love. As capitalism impoverishes the laborer, so traditional marriage impoverishes the lover.

In addition, we must not forget the wider consequences of lending support to the notion that one person's body can belong to another. This idea of bodily possession, or ownership, which has been at the base of traditional marriage, fuels other beliefs extremely destructive in their consequences, ideas such as the following: citizens belong to the state, workers belong to capitalists, women and their reproductive capacities belong to men, children belong to parents. When bodily integrity is compromised in any way, we open the door to such atrocities as child abuse, sexual violence, denial of reproductive rights for women, state-sponsored torture of citizens, and the denial of our right to work, our right to love, and our right to die.

Lack of Freedom of Choice

A fourth way that capitalist and marriage ideologies reinforce each other is that neither capitalism nor marriage supports choice. Our cultural and ideological context assures us that both capitalism and heterosexual monogamy are the only legitimate ways to order economic activity and human loving. Both market ideology and the myth of romantic love rest on systematic illusions of voluntary selection and spontaneous response that exist in extremely restricted ways and are sustained by structural inequality between the sexes. As long as women are taught self-doubt, submissiveness, and the denial of our own desire and as long as we are not as economically powerful as men, marriage will remain a less-than-voluntary arrangement. As long as men are taught to repress tenderness and vulnerability, to fear mutuality, and to depend on women to do their emotional work, they will not develop the capacities necessary for rich human loving and mature partnership.

Further, both systems seek security and privilege in the form of monopoly control of the market or the spouse. Greater freedom in economic choice and a wider range of intimate relationships are viewed as threats that could destabilize the systems. And this, of course is correct: authentic choice in marriage would necessitate the economic equality of all women and men, as well as their freedom to engage in a variety of mutual relationships of significant emotional depth. Only under these conditions would men and women have the freedom *not* to choose or genuinely to choose and *rechoose* each other as primary partners.

Repression

A fifth way conventional sexual ethics aids capitalism is by repressing human feeling and our right to direct and control our lives, even our sexual lives. This restriction promotes our uncritical submission to external authorities, including our cooperation with the discipline of the capitalist work week. For example, historians of the witch hunts of the sixteenth and seventeenth centuries show how witch burning functioned to demonize female sexuality and socially independent women. Early capitalists, with the full force of religious teaching behind them, used rigorous discipline of sexual instincts as an efficient means to create an obedient work force. They restricted sex to marriage and helped keep women at home replenishing the labor force.[15] In addition, as the success of sexually explicit advertising on consumer demand shows, sexual repression serves capitalism because people turn to the market to satisfy repressed sexual needs.[16] There are also strong connections between sexual repression and the violence and militarism necessary to fuel capitalist expansion. Male distancing from the body and from emotions is essential to the project of warfare, whether it be killing on the battlefield or a killing in the market. Violence of all kinds, including the wife and child abuse rampant in American homes, feeds on the anger and resentment of those whose own sexual and emotional hungers go unmet.[17]

A capitalist sexuality, therefore, fears the erotic, fears that desire to form deep connections with others and with the cosmos. We are taught to associate this longing with evil and sin. The erotic drive impels us to transform physical, emotional, and spiritual energy into tangible sacred matter — a house, a meal, a song, a relationship. It impels us to form flesh-and-blood connections with persons, creatures, the earth.[18]

In an erotophobic culture, romantic sex exclusively directed toward a legally recognized one-and-only is sanctified. Other sexual activity is trivialized or demeaned and prohibited by religion. We learn instead to degrade our sexual capacities and hold our sexual longings in contempt. Men speak of "spewing sperm," "jerking off," "getting one's jollies." Women have traditionally been silent about sex, since naming it and enjoying it have supposedly been the prerogative of men. Today we can speak more openly about sex, but the legacy remains. Many of us believe that if sex isn't evil, it is at least a self-indulgent luxury that mature persons can well do without.

Tragically, a culture that supports dominant and subordinate relationships and the repression of sexual desire will suffer enormous amounts of violent sex, including addictive, promiscuous sex. This creates a situation in which it is easy to confuse sexual abuse with our physical need to be touched and held and our need for deep bonding with others. We must be clear that it is nonmutual relationships that should be censured and struggled against, not our physical and sexual needs themselves. Christian theologians and ethicists, such as James Nelson and Carter Heyward, argue that the incarnation of our longing to connect with others and our world — or the actualization of eros — is a participation in divine activity. As Heyward says, it is our very "godding" in this world.[19] Indeed, communities in which people see their bodies as divinely empowered instruments to touch, to hold, and to provide and receive physical comfort and pleasure could not tolerate the enormous abuse that most human bodies in our world suffer daily.

INJUSTICE AND SOCIAL CHANGE

As long as we are alienated from our erotic potential and forbidden to touch others in loving and tender ways, nonmutual relationships will seem normal and moral, and we will be numbed to injustice in the larger society. As long as our sexual ethic places such restricted limits on passion and we must forfeit the support of enriching relationships with others, we will be diminished in the energy we need for real social change. Romantic love and compulsory monogamy set up barriers between people and actively promote dishonest and fearful relationships between women and men.[20] Experience has taught many of us how gender-determined roles and a restricted sexual ethic have, at best, reduced our capacities for satisfying mutual relationships and deprived us of many dimensions of our sexuality. At worst, we bear in our bodies and spirits the wounds created by the violence of this sexual system. And it is indeed a violent system that forbids many forms of self-empowering mutual sex and creates a scarcity of options for love and nurture, thus inviting debilitating abusive sex. As we grow in awareness of the scars so many of us bear from being caught in such a violent social structure, we must not continue to grant this structure legitimacy.

In the meantime, a strategy of eliminating the double standard and making compulsory monogamy apply equally to men does not change the essential erotophobic and impoverishing nature of this institution. Rather we should struggle for economic equality between women and men and a multiplicity of new and more mature forms of marriage and of sexual and nonsexual friendships. We need new forms of marriage in which primary relationships of all kinds — heterosexual, homosexual, bisexual, monogamous, nonmonogamous — may be publicly celebrated. We need a society in which all persons, regardless of marital status, have legal protection and economic support.

Despite competitive capitalist ideology, our partners and our friends do not have to be in competition with one another. People are irreplaceable others. One relationship, no matter how central, cannot fully substitute for another. We do not have to choose between good relationships. Rather, we need all the friends with whom we may be blessed. Good relationships enhance other good relationships and are the building blocks for healthy communities. Whole, self-affirming people can understand and respect the common stages of all relationships and will not place in competition the early and more intense stage of a new relationship with the less intense but more richly textured stage of an older one.[21]

Monogamy may be a value to all of us some of the time and to some of us all of the time, but it is a value only if it is chosen, not assumed or demanded. We should see commitment as a process, not a once-and-for-all total surrender that abdicates our responsibility to ourselves, to others who might enrich our lives, and to our own process of growth and change. Love, including married love, thrives only as mutual recognition and passionate connection between two distinct selves fully capable of healthy self-love and personal satisfaction in their separate lives. Love has to do with cherishing the unique purpose of this other person and furthering that purpose, including respecting diversity in the other's need for intimacy and supporting the other's growth and change. The intensity of erotic union is determined not by gender difference (or sameness for that matter) but by the connection one makes to a core aspect of a truly distinct self. Since each relationship calls forth different parts of the core self, some of us may need to give and receive this kind of recognition from more than one other person in a lifetime. Multiple relationships may be liberating for some of us because each relationship enables us to experience a different part of ourselves. I agree with the ethicist Eleanor Haney, who says that we are in the process, perhaps only the earliest stages, of learning who we are as persons and as sexual beings.[22]

As long as children are reared in abusing homes that do not create an environment for self-acceptance, people will seek safety and status in erotic relationships that cannot provide them. It will no doubt take a long time to work through the jealousies, anxieties, and dependencies created in people who are exposed to authoritarian patterns of child rearing and the ethics of competitive romantic love that help to maintain capitalism. In the meantime we can remember that expectations are often self-fulfilling prophecies. If we believe that marriages cannot survive if spouses have vital, loving relationships with others, the chances are very high that marriages will indeed break up in these circumstances. But if we assume that vitality in a partnership is enhanced by spouses having rich affectional lives apart from as well as with each other, then we will not experience our attractions to others as threats to our primary commitments.

It is important to ask ourselves, What kind of communities might we create if we did not promote unequal and monopolistic relations between men and women; if most erotic longing were not trivialized, demeaned, and prohibited; if we supported many different scripts for the ways men and women choose to organize marriage and friendships; if we were free to love whomever we find mutuality with and were nurtured and energized by more than one other?

To the immediate outcry that we would sink into promiscuity and debauchery, I answer that I believe that our fear of chaos masks our fear of choice — for example, choices about the levels of responsibility in our commitments and the time and energy we have available to them.[23] We deny our vocation to be self-regulating moral agents when we fear that we cannot act ethically apart from prohibitive and restrictive laws.[24] Indeed, love and mutuality can never be forced or coerced. They only flourish when we are willing to share power and vulnerability. As Sharon Welch says, we must abandon the Western ethic of control and be courageous enough to replace it with an ethic of risk.[25]

Both sexual and economic ethics must take a hard look at what is actually being promoted by capitalist and marriage ideologies. A more self-defeating plan could scarcely be conceived for society than the alienation of human beings from our own feelings and from our own labor, from our own capacities to love and from our own work. Most of us do not experience the empowerment of authentic mutuality in our jobs and intimate relationships because work and marriage are "not constructed as if friends matter."[26] And we wonder why loneliness is high, energy is low, and prospects for genuine community among us often seem so bleak.

A viable sexual ethic for the twenty-first century must come to terms with the concrete realities of people's changing lives and needs. The theologian Bernard Haring, among many others, called us years ago to appreciate that moral knowledge has always been culturally conditioned. Historicity, he says, is an essential, not an accidental, structure of moral reason.[27] We must come to terms with our changing history, with the insights of social researchers about healthy relationships coexistent with marriage, and with new understandings about the impoverishing nature of romantic, capitalist marriage. To serve the needs of social justice, Christian ethics should play a role in demystifying traditional sexual morality as people struggle to create new, more mature, and more just forms of marriage, friendship, and human community.

No Rock Scorns Me as Whore

Chrystos

5:32 am — May

    The water doesn't breathe   No rowdy boats disturb her serenity
    I dream of days when she was this way each moment   Days
when no one went anywhere full of loud pompousness self-importance
    Days when dinosaurs were not being rudely dug up for their re-
mains   Days when order dignity & respect were possible   Days
when the proportions of things were sacred   O the moon in a dawn
sky is good enough
    Where are the people who cry "I am I am" as the gulls do? They rope
themselves off with labels   They stand inside a box called their job,
their clothes, their political & social opinions, the movies or books they
read   I've never believed those items which is why I was considered
crazy   I want to know the truth   I glimpse under that malarkey
called "civilization"   Maybe people have become so stupid as a result
of having too many machines   The company we keep
    It is clear to me that the use of nuclear power is dangerous — as
is almost every other aspect of the dominant culture   Including the
manufacture of the paper on which this is written   No produce from
Vashon Island can be sold because the earth there is poisonous from
the chemicals Tacoma's paper plant produces   My life is a part of
the poisoning & cars   Alternate energy sources cannot fuel what
"America" has become   I know this way of living will not last much
longer   I accept it I will be glad if we destroy ourselves   We have
made a much bigger mess than the dinosaurs   Other ways will follow
    Perhaps not   It is none of our business   I draw because I

"No Rock Scorns Me as Whore" by Chrystos is reprinted from *This Bridge Called My Back: Writings by Radical Women of Color,* ed. Cherie Moraga and Gloria Anzaldúa (Watertown, Mass.: Persephone Press, 1981). Copyright © by Chrystos.

can't think what else to do until the end   Maybe it will take longer
than I think   I'm not willing at the moment to give up the electric
blanket I am under & I do not notice too many radicals giving up their
stereos, hot showers, cars & blenders   Energy to run those machines
must come from somewhere   No protest march will alter the head-
on collision   *Nothing short of completely altering the whole culture will
stop it*   I don't think that all of the people here could be supported
on an alternative culture   Well if they manage to make a revolution
they'll kill lots of people   Most could not survive adjustment to
simpler life & so they will unknowingly fight it even the radicals
Another case of lecturing vegetarians in leather shoes

    Although it is heresy to admit it, many Indian people could not sur-
vive either   It takes a lot of power to manufacture a can of Budweiser
       We have become as poisoned as the eagle's eggshell   We have
fought   We still fight   Most of us have died fighting   Some
of us walk around dead inside a bottle   I am ashamed   I am
heartbroken   I still fight to survive   I mourn   I get up   I
live a middle class life. Sometimes

    We have lost touch with the sacred   To survive we must begin to
know sacredness   The pace which most of us live prevents this   I
begin only now to understand faint glimpses of the proper relationships
of time, of beings   I don't dig for clams because that is the main food
of many birds here   I have an abundance of other food available to
me   Too many humans clam this beach already   A stronger &
stronger sense that I want to grow food ourselves   Probably that
is not possible   I'm not thrilled about the idea of slaughter and I
am not a vegetarian   We'll see   Gradually, I am taught how to
behave by new teachers   By leaves, by flowers, by fruits & rhythms of
rain   My mother & father were not good teachers   They are too
deeply damaged by this culture which is one of obliteration   I don't
know why I see differently than they do   My blessing and burden

    The depth that I seek here only comes when I remove the ears in my
mind   Ears discourage my honesty & because I am so isolated here
honesty is absolutely essential to my survival   There is no way to
"be nice" to a tree or politely endure a thunderstorm   I am stripped
of pretensions as I was at nine by the wild gentle beauty of California before everybody came with stucco track houses & turquoise plastic
couches   I am a child again here   A child frightened by the idea
of progress, new housing, more strangers   I begin to love these lines
of dark trees as I loved the hills to which I belonged as a girl   Those
hills hold nothing now   Mostly leveled   Without deer, without puma, without pheasant, without blue-bellied lizards, without quail,

without ancient oaks   Lawns instead   Deeply disgusted by lawns
     Stupid flat green crew cuts   Nothing for anybody to eat
  I am still in love with the mystery of shadows, wind, bird song
The reason that I continue despite many clumsy mistakes, is love   My
love for humans, or rather my continuous attempts to love, have been
misdirected   I am not wise   However there is no shame when
one is foolish with a tree   No bird ever called me crazy   No rock
scorns me as a whore   The earth means exactly what it says   The
wind is without flattery or lust   Greed is balanced by the hunger of
all   So I embrace anew, as my childhood spirit did, the whispers of
a world without words
  I realized one day after another nuclear protest, another proposed bill
to make nuclear waste disposal here, that I had no power with those
My power rests with a greater being, a silence which goes on behind the
uproar   I decided that in a nuclear holocaust, for certainly they will
be stupid enough to cause one if their history is any example, I wanted to
be planting corn & squash   After there will be other beings of some
kind   They'll still need to eat   Aren't the people who come to
take clams like those who lobby at the airport for nuclear power? Who
is not guilty of being a thief?   Who among us gives back as much as
we take?   Who among us has enough respect? Does anyone know the
proper proportions?   My distant ancestors knew some things that are
lost to me & I would not have the insidious luxury of this electric heat,
this journal & pen without the concurrent problems of nuclear waste
storage   When we are gone, someone else will come   Dinosaur
eggs might hatch in the intense heat of nuclear explosions   I will
be sad to see the trees & birds on fire   Surely they are innocent as
none of us has been
  With their songs, they know the sacred   I am in a circle with that
soft, enduring word   In it is the wisdom of all peoples   Without
a deep, deep understanding of the sacredness of life, the fragility of each
breath, we are lost   The holocaust has already occurred   What
follows is only the burning brush   How my heart aches & cries to
write these words   I am not as calmly indifferent as I sound
I will be screaming no no no more destruction in that last blinding light

Sexuality and Economic Reality
A First World and
Third World Comparison

Elizabeth M. Bounds

I am a dancer.* I come from a poor family in the city
[Manila]. My father was a soldier in Korea, and I was
seven when he died. I would have liked to go to high
school, but we could not afford it.

When I left school, I was thirteen years old, and got
married. We had three children, but were not getting on
very well, so decided to separate. One child went to live
with my husband, I had two children to support. I learnt
to dance and took a job in a nightclub. I got good money
and could feed, clothe and educate my children....

I only do this work for the money, because of my two
sons. In 1968, I married a German and we had two children. He tried to take me to Germany, but I didn't want
to go because he treated me like a dog. When he returned
to Germany, he took our two children with him. It was
then that I left Manila and came to Olongapo† because
I could make better money here. The American sailors
have lots of money....

Sometimes I make more than US $400/month if there
is a ship in port. If there is no ship, then I make only about
$70. I have a bank account and have saved and educated
my two boys. I hate my job. If I am not drunk, I cannot
dance. I have been in this club for seven years and stay
here because it is the only place where I can make such
good money. Recently, a friend of mine died, and I have
adopted her two children....

I am a very independent person. I think men are weak
because they need a woman all the time. I feel sorry for
them. Also, I hate them because they are so brutal.
— Liza, a voice from the Philippines

* Dancing in a club in the Philippines usually includes periods of time selling drinks and one's body
to customers.
† Red light district around the United States Naval Base at Subic Bay.

Liza's story is the story of an oppressed and exploited woman.[1] It seems to call on those of us with privileged American lives to *do something*, to make it possible for Liza to live as she dreams to. It is this impulse, a combination of a feminist ethic of care and a commitment to alleviate suffering, that drew me into the study of Asian prostitution after meeting women like Liza in Thailand, Korea, the Philippines, and Japan.[2]

Yet as I have continued to listen to the voices of Third World women and to study the realities of prostitution, I have realized that my impulse to help and care is not enough. Truly to try, as a white woman, to stand in solidarity with these Asian sisters requires more than good will. It requires analyses and strategies that name differences and point to intertwined structures and accountabilities.[3]

No theory stands in isolated objectivity but simultaneously reflects and transforms its social context.[4] Consequently, theoretical adequacy is linked to the relation between the social location of the theorist and her subjects. Much available analysis of prostitution, both in the United States and overseas, is done by First World, white, middle-class women like myself who stand outside in a position of class and race privilege. Such work frequently portrays the women as victims of dehumanization who are unable to speak or act for themselves. Other analyses erase differences between the writer and audience on the one hand and the writer and the subject on the other to present a false commonality. Either way, the women become the objects of theory rather than the subjects of their lives.

Understanding differences *and* similarities is part of the accountability necessary for developing a concrete ethic of solidarity and empowerment. Only through dialogue between those without privilege and those of us with privilege can the dimensions of feminist ethics begin to appear. Inequalities of power make such dialogue very difficult, but if we begin by paying attention to the voices of those who suffer, a process of liberation can slowly emerge.

Starting with such a standpoint of solidarity leads to two methodological norms. One is the development of a sufficiently *complex and nuanced theoretical model*. Asian prostitutes stand in a social context where structures of sex, class, economy, race, and imperialism all intersect. As a Korean Christian once told me, when you look at the situation of the lowest of the low, you see exposed the totality of the forces at work in any society. The challenge for feminist religious ethics is to develop theories that embrace this social complexity. Most past and current work blocks off some dimension of class or sex or race. Yet the objective social reality is a global polity and economy that draw us together in a web of interconnected social forces.[5] Any analysis, whether religious or secular, that ignores any dimension of this complexity cannot be descriptively adequate and thus also cannot be strategically adequate.[6]

The second methodological norm is that of *agency*. My assumption is that Asian prostitutes are already active moral agents, making positive moral choices within oppressive and immoral structures. An analysis of prostitution that does not take into account the perspectives and the ongoing agency of the women themselves necessarily gives rise to strategies of disempowerment. The central question is, What will enable these women to struggle for a better life?

What I outline here presents sex *and* class *and* race *and* military imperialism as components of an adequate feminist social theory based on historical and structural analysis. I will first examine the presence of these different structures in the lives of Asian prostitutes. I will then assess a major explanatory model for prostitution offered by women: the sexual-slavery model of United States radical feminism. Then I will present the economic-and-social-agency model of Asian feminists. The ways in which these models illuminate questions of difference, agency, and empowerment will help clarify tensions within both United States and global feminist work.

THE LIVES OF ASIAN PROSTITUTES

Prostitution in Asia involves the influences of the military, the economy, sex, and race. At one level, the daily reality of Asian prostitutes is easy to describe. The women live lives characterized by overwork, poverty, and the lack of health care or any form of social security. Accounts by and about Asian prostitutes take on a painful similarity, whether the prostitution described is in Thailand, Japan, Korea, or the Philippines.

In the bars or dance clubs, the women have a variety of jobs. They dance, serve drinks, sell sex, and clean up. They may receive some minimal hourly wage, but their real income is dependent on the number of customers who buy drinks or sex. In Thailand, a customer might pay $5 for a drink, of which the woman may receive $2.50. She has to serve ten drinks in an evening, however, before she gets any portion of the income. In the Philippines, a woman might dance for a flat rate of $1.20 for the evening. She will make more money if a customer asks her to "go out" ($3 for the club and $3 for the woman).[7]

If the women work in a massage parlor or take customers to another room or a hotel for sex, they earn a different set of fees. Little of the money, however, comes to them. In a cheap hotel in Thailand, a customer may pay $6 for a woman, of which the woman herself will receive only $1.50. In the Philippines, a woman at an expensive Manila hotel could cost $70 for a night. Of this $34 will go to the travel agent,

$15 to the hotel, $10 to the woman's "regular" club, leaving $8 for the woman herself.[8]

As in everything else, there is a hierarchy in prostitution. Working in a massage parlor is higher class than working in a bar. Working in an expensive hotel is higher class than working in a cheap hotel. For Thai women and Filipinas, working in Japan, rather than at home, is better paid and thus more prestigious. As a woman becomes older, she is less desirable and can slip down into the poorer and more disreputable clubs. As her position changes, so do her customers. Top prostitutes in Korea or Thailand will be servicing Japanese and Western businessmen-tourists and United States soldiers. As their fortunes decline, they will be in contact with more and more of their own countrymen.

The working situation is a combination of stress, danger, and control. At the simplest level, wearing high heels and bikinis leads to twisted ankles and colds. Venereal diseases and drug and alcohol abuse are always present, with the added recent threat of AIDS. The women are under the constant direction of their manager-owner, who provides their housing and their clothing, and, if they are bonded women, owns their lives. Peasant girls in Thailand are sold by their struggling parents into "contracts," or bonds, which mean that the girl is at the mercy of the owner until she has earned the contract payment. Some of these bonded women are kept in their room in chains, as was tragically revealed in a club fire at a Thai resort, which killed several women imprisoned in a back room. Filipinas may enter into work contracts with clubs in Japan where the owners retain their passports and return tickets, making them virtual prisoners in a country where they cannot even understand the language.

How many women prostitutes in Asia are there? As with any supposedly illegal activity, it is difficult to obtain accurate statistics. In the late 1970s, the official count in Bangkok was 100,000 to 200,000, but unofficial estimates were 500,000 to 1,000,000, or 10 percent of all Thai women between the ages of fourteen and twenty-four. In 1978, in Manila there were 7,003 prostitutes registered but probably more than 100,000 in the streets, which does not include the thousands of women at the United States base towns of Olongapo and Angeles.[9]

The Military

Although forms of prostitution have existed in Asia for centuries, the growth of mass prostitution was linked to the entrance of Western powers and their armies. As the imperial empires grew, the problem of providing women for the growing national armies of the European world was transferred to Asia. "The Road to Mandalay," a popular British soldier's song in the nineteenth century, spoke of the soldier's "neater, sweeter maiden in a cleaner, greener land!"[10]

By the early twentieth century, Japan had begun to replace Europe as the major power dominating Asia. At first the Japanese armies brought their own women, who were bonded servants purchased from Japanese peasant families. By the 1920s, when the empire was prospering, laws were passed banning Japanese women from prostitution, which meant the substitution of women from Japanese-occupied Asian territories. During World War II, an estimated 50,000 to 70,000 Korean women were sent as comfort troops to the Japanese front. Most of these women were killed during the war or by the Japanese at the time of their surrender to the Allied forces.[11]

After 1945, the United States replaced Japan as the major military presence in Asia and the Pacific. The Korean and Vietnam wars brought thousands of soldiers not just to Korea and Vietnam but also to the rest and recreation (R and R) centers in Japan, Okinawa, the Philippines, and Thailand. The support bases spawned a parasite culture of bars, clubs, and hotels. At the height of the Vietnam War, there were estimated to be half a million prostitutes in Saigon. At the same time, R and R outside Vietnam had to be offered. The United States developed alternatives in Thailand, where 50,000 to 70,000 soldiers visited annually, and around its bases in the Philippines, where 100 troop ships (each carrying hundreds of soldiers) docked each year at Subic Bay.[12] For both areas, the United States presence and expenditures (probably $5 billion on the Thai bases alone) meant the creation of a new industry: drinks, dancing, and sex.

The end of the Vietnam War and the beginning of the Nixon policy of containment brought changes to these parasite cultures. In Okinawa, Korea, and the Philippines, the continued presence of the United States military allowed the bar culture to continue more or less without pause. Yet the decrease in steady United States clientele required a search for new customers among tourists and businessmen. In Thailand, communities whose economies had developed around military bases at the expense of any other kind of development had no alternative sources of income.[13] As it turned out, they continued to serve United States and, increasingly, Japanese and European men in a different, but related, economic sector.

The Economy and Tourism

For most Asian countries, the United States, Europe, and Japan are the key economic partners, necessary for trade relations, development aid, and currency exchange. The entrance of Japanese and Western capital into Asia has meant a restructuring of Asian economies and the development of particular economic sectors. Western-dominated institutions, such as the World Bank and the International Monetary Fund, "sell" aid packages that tie Asian economies into a global system of dependency through industrialization-dominated exports. In order to receive aid, a country must open itself to the maximum possible foreign investment aimed at the sectors where a "comparative advantage" (the presence of natural or other resources) is considered to be found. Tax barriers are abolished, wages are kept low, and labor unrest is eliminated (through measures such as banning all labor unions) in order to attract foreign investment and keep export products competitively priced. Countries are completely dependent on foreign markets, foreign funds, and foreign technologies. Since they produce goods for export rather than goods to meet the needs of their people, they soon also become dependent on imported food and other supplies.

Until the early seventies, Asian countries were considered to have an advantage in agricultural production. A poor market and low prices however, depressed agricultural export prospects. As the development of agribusiness artificially expanded the production of certain products for export, and farmers struggled to live off the sales of one or two crops rather than growing what they ate, the self-sufficiency of small-family production was destroyed. When a rural family could not maintain itself, the children migrated to the city to seek jobs. They provided a cheap labor pool for the new forms of low-skilled, multinational, technological production that were entering Asia, as the "comparative advantage" shifted from agriculture to manufacture of textiles, clothing, and electronic goods.

By the late seventies, tourism was also appearing as a new source of Asian economic development, promoted in development aid packages. Asian countries were seen to have the "comparative advantage" of beautiful beaches and low-wage service workers. Tourism is a capital-intensive industry, requiring funds for roads, modern multistoried buildings, and sewage and electrical systems.[14] In spite of the size of capital investment, tourism is not necessarily a high-productivity business, especially for the host countries. Part of any income generated flows out to pay off the foreign loan financing the development. Much of the tourist infrastructure — hotels, planes, tour packages — is foreign-owned and foreign-operated so that between 40 percent and 75 percent of the profits eventually also leave the country.[15] Management jobs often go to foreign workers, leaving domestic workers to serve the needs of foreigners in the lowest-paid and lowest-skilled jobs.

Prostitution is, of course, a "vital" foreign need. Sexuality is sold as one of a country's natural resources, whether through the implied sexuality of airline advertisements or the explicit inclusion of sexual services within package tours for Western and Japanese men. As a Norwegian travel brochure says, "Prostitution is part of Thai culture. They wish to give you care and sex."[16] Although the Philippines, Thailand, and Korea all have legal bans on prostitution, they have supported it as a large tourist industry and use the law only against the prostitutes, not against the owners of bars and brothels. A former minister of tourism in Thailand told local governors not to avoid offering "some forms of entertainment...you might consider disgusting and shameful" because they created jobs.[17] Prostitution is a key sector of the economies of these countries, turning the state into a pimp.

The Gender System

Historically, Asian women have played many different roles from chief agricultural producer to subservient domestic. The economic changes of the past decades have simultaneously reproduced and altered different facets of the sexual division of labor and the sociocultural position of women. In the Philippines and Thailand, for example, women had been the chief farmers and producers of food. When the domestic agricultural sector was transformed into export-oriented production, development aid and technology were aimed at men rather than women. Consequently, females became the more expendable labor force, required to migrate for work in cities and export-processing zones.[18] Simultaneously, the jobs available in tourist and military entertainment and in factories were categorized as women's jobs, requiring docility and dexterity. Male definitions of sexuality described women's role as providing sexual service or doing demeaning, low-paid work on a "temporary" basis, since all women were assumed to be working temporarily until they married.

Malaysian economist Noeleen Heyzer suggests three factors leading to Asian women's involvement in prostitution.[19] The first is the psychological factor of a sense of low self-worth, which must be seen in relation to the conflicting interaction of traditional sexual moralities with Western cultural influences. As was true in Western industrialization, women's initial entrance into the work force is accompanied by an ideology of working women as sexually "loose"[20] (which is one reason why Asian women can cross easily between factory work and prostitution). Women in the factories and especially women in the bars are generally considered unmarriageable. Thus the idea that these women will drop out of the labor force is false. Rather, they will continue to move within a marginal sector of factories, shops, bars, and clubs. Women who have traditionally been socialized to consider themselves as worth less than men now also blame themselves for their "sinful" condition.

The second and third factors are the pull of excitement and pay in the sex industry combined with the push of no alternatives such as education, work, or marriage. A typical assembly-line job in the Philippines pays a woman no more than $100 a month for ten-hour-to-twelve-hour days in six-day weeks, carried out under poorly ventilated, debilitating conditions.[21] By contrast, Liza can make as much as $400 a month as a dancer in the military bars in Olongapo. Even more money is promised if she contracts as a dancer-hostess in Japan. Although this salary may be precarious, depending on the number of ships in port or the number of drinks or sex acts a woman can sell, club life seems to offer more personal freedoms and financial rewards.

From my own experience of speaking with Asian women prostitutes, I would add another dimension to Heyzer's third factor. The women feel tremendous responsibility for the welfare of their families, which include parents, siblings, extended family, and children. Many women in Manila, Bangkok, or Japan have left their children (often the illegitimate offspring of soldiers or tourists) in the home villages, cared for by their mother, sister, or aunt. For almost all Asian prostitutes, the major reason for working is to send money home. Given the higher income available in the bars and the deep responsibilities and commitments they have to their families, Asian women make a reasonable economic choice when they go into prostitution.

The participation of Asian women in the modern work force as prostitutes simultaneously transforms and reproduces the traditional sexual division of labor. Prostitution reproduces a traditional sexual role for women as servants of men, part of the "culture-bound sexual morality,"[22] within a new Westernized context.[23] Although women are freed from the constraints of the traditional roles of family life, they live under a new form of male sexual dominance, practiced by men who are not their kin. For many, a traditional marriage is a sign of success as they hope to leave behind the image of being a "bad woman" and find some security in their lives.

The Factor of Race

Hidden in the discussion so far has been the question of race. The relation of foreign military powers to Asian countries has always embodied imperial power and racism. Western nations not only aimed to acquire territory in Asia, but they also justified these acquisitions in light of the "backwardness" of the conquered. Asians appeared to the West as alternately mysterious and barbaric, examples of a frightening "otherness" that had to be conquered. Racism lies behind the images of exotic and alluring Asian women (evident in the British soldier's song and the

Norwegian tour brochure) and of docile and dexterous Asian women workers. Racism lies behind the United States soldiers' view of Filipinas as "little brown fucking machines."[24] And racism lies behind the historical substitution of other Asian women as Japanese army prostitutes and the present-day substitution of other Asian women for Japanese women as prostitutes for Japan's new business army in the downtown clubs in Tokyo and Osaka.[25] Perhaps the best summation of the mixture of race, nationalism, and sexuality found in Third World prostitution was stated by Rudo Gaidzanwa, a Zimbabwean professor: "[these white men] feel their currency entitles them to exercise on a micro scale what their countries do on a macro scale."[26]

AN ANALYTIC MODEL OF PROSTITUTION IN THE WEST

Until the Enlightenment, prostitution was generally tolerated in Western European society as a necessary outlet for dangerous sexual forces. Augustine wrote, in *De Ordine*, "Prostitutes in a city are like a sewer in a palace: if you get rid of the sewer, the whole palace becomes filthy and foul." Such tolerance was rooted in a Neoplatonic Christian cosmology that divided the universe into spirit and flesh, light and dark, male and female. The prostitute embodied the lower, dark, female sexuality, which men had simultaneously to control and use.[27]

By the beginning of the early modern period, society, rather than individual criminals or prostitutes, came to be seen as a body that needed to be purified and regulated.[28] The growth of urban centers in Europe meant that prostitution was no longer a few women at a local inn but many women in a crowded and visible district. The problem of prostitution came to be addressed both through coercive laws and ideological domination. The state developed its coercive power through a police force and government regulatory bodies. They spawned laws covering all aspects of prostitutes' lives — medical exams, pass laws, and prohibition of approach and "unseemly" behavior.[29]

On the ideological level, an intense moral debate was carried on by middle-class voluntary reform organizations in the Victorian era. Women were no longer seen as dangerous and lustful but as weak and victimized. The popular image of a prostitute was of a "demoralized creature treading the downward path ending in drunkenness, destitution and disease."[30] The emphasis was on the immorality created by the new factory conditions and on the individual victims, rather than on the lack of economic alternatives. Strategies for reform aimed at providing rehabilitation centers where women would be strictly regulated and be taught "useful" skills that would never lead to anything but subsistence work.

The reform organizations, which were central to the development of European and United States white feminism, used an analysis based upon "sentimental moralism, prurient details, and a focus on passive, innocent female victims and individual evil men." Thus the prostitutes were "objects of concern, rather than active participants in the struggle."[31] They were described and contained as helpless individuals requiring moral reform.

Present-day radical feminist analysis continues this middle-class emphasis on purity and passivity in the context of a structural, rather than an individualistic, analysis. Kathleen Barry, Andrea Dworkin, and, until recently, Charlotte Bunch have described prostitution as female sexual slavery explained by "ONE universal patriarchal oppression of women which takes different forms in different cultures and different regions." Female sexuality is the product of "male dominance, of sexual violence, and enslavement."[32]

The emphasis on male violence and sexual domination excludes consideration of race and class. Dworkin has said that attention to economic factors inevitably leads to anti-women analyses. Diana Russell's analysis of rape as a factor driving women into prostitution blames rape solely on male socialization without considering the economic deprivation experienced by many male batterers, not to mention the complex construction of masculinity in the history of United States black men.[33] In this view, all prostitutes are "victims of many forms of domination by men which are exercised through structures of sex, racism, and class."[34]

The classification of prostitutes as victims of patriarchy excludes the notion that prostitutes may be exhibiting agency and self-determination in her work. *Any* acceptance of their status, even if qualified, means endorsing the "assumption that sex is a male right" and reducing "all women to the lowest and most contemptible status." Barry admits that claims of choice are made by prostitutes themselves, but says that these "represent the ideology of male domination."[35]

The exclusionary emphasis on patriarchy leads radical feminists to classify every woman as equally a victim of patriarchy. Catherine MacKinnon writes that prostitution is "the fundamental condition of women."[36] Such a universal claim conceals difference, including the difference of class and skin privilege possessed by many radical feminists. And such a universalist model leads to elitist and racially blind strategies. An example of the consequences of this analytic model occurred at a 1988 conference on prostitution sponsored by the Coalition on Trafficking in Women (linked to Women Against Pornography). In spite of the large numbers of racial or ethnic women engaged in prostitution, there were only a few Third World women speakers and no United States racial or ethnic women speakers. Further, although each Third World speaker emphasized the critical role of the economy and the presence of the United States military as factors in creating and maintaining prostitution in her country, the First World women leaders simply ignored their analysis. As Lisa Go, a Filipina present, said, the First World women had a "narcissistic preoccupation" with their own psychology while maintaining silence over their complicity in racial and military oppression.[37]

STRATEGIES OF DEALING WITH PROSTITUTION IN THE EAST

The tension at the 1988 conference on prostitution focuses the difference between the perspectives of white women in the First World and racial or ethnic women in the Third World. Present in all Asian analyses of prostitution is a clear recognition of the importance of foreign military and economic power. For Third World women, says Go, the issues are gender *and* class *and* imperialism.[38] We will encourage, says GABRIELA, the Philippine women's organization, "the struggle for [women's] equality and empowerment as an integral part of the overall struggle for true freedom, democracy and justice for our people."[39] Sexuality is seen within a framework of exploitation shaped by economic and international power.

The broadened analysis leads to strategies that simultaneously affirm the women's worth *as they are now* and recognize the long-term need for social transformation. The ultimate goal for Asian women activists is the creation of nations without crippling economic dependency on the First World and without the monopoly of land and resources by a tiny elite. Short-term strategies aim to empower prostitutes to recognize their own worth and through that awareness enter into the broader struggle.

In the Philippines, the Buklod Center in Olongapo offers daily support to the women while linking them through GABRIELA to the national movement for social change. In Thailand, EMPOWER offers English classes because knowledge of English helps the women bargain better with their customers and gain more control over their conditions of employment, with the possibility of the eventual creation of a prostitutes' union. EMPOWER believes that the first step must be a recognition of the important role prostitutes already play as economic agents, as "they are the major productive force of the state entertainment industry . . . the largest [source of] income of the country."[40] Given the working conditions and pay scales of other forms of employment, the group affirms Asian women's choice of prostitution as a sensible economic decision.

A further difference between First and Third World discussions of prostitution appears in the question of legal strategies. In the First World, debates range over whether prostitution should be banned more

effectively (the radical feminist view) or decriminalized (the view of prostitutes' organizations such as COYOTE and the International Prostitutes'
Collective). Although Asian women would support legal bans on coercion into prostitution, the decriminalization issue is not a major concern.
In a discussion of international legal strategies at the Trafficking on
Women conference, Aurora Javate de Dios of GABRIELA and Mi Kung
Lee of the Korea Women's Association United had one strategy — removal of the United States military presence. The struggle for national
self-determination is the context for their feminist strategizing.

ANALYSIS AND ACCOUNTABILITY

The brief review of prostitution offered here suggests some requirements for those of us who wish to do feminist ethics in solidarity within
a global, multiracial context. First, we must do a full social analysis
that includes the many dimensions of oppression and power. Without
complete analysis, we cannot reveal the complexity of social violence underlying prostitution. Nor will we have an adequate basis for developing
the variety of comprehensive strategies needed to actualize what Beverly
Harrison terms the norm of "full personhood and agency of women"
in our differing situations.[41] To omit a dimension means omitting the
pain of particular women — rendering this suffering incapable of being
named and transformed.

Second, we must formulate an ethic in dialogue with other voices,
some of which are just now coming to speech and to writing. For example, white radical feminists condemn prostitution as a manifestation of
patriarchal sexuality, while Asian feminists broaden the social context of
sexual experience but for reasons of culture and strategic priority speak
little of sexuality itself. In both situations, women's actual experiences
are hidden behind dominant Western sexualized culture. In the United
States poor white and racial and ethnic women, both heterosexual and
lesbian, are beginning to describe their own sexualities, a process less evident in Asia, which may provide sources for more adequate theorizing
about different forms of patriarchy and sexuality.[42]

Third, we must be self-conscious in our theory and strategy about
our own social location. Without such consciousness, we risk silenc-
ing oppressed women by making them objects rather than subjects and
agents of analysis. The blindness of United States radical feminism described here is the blindness of class and race privilege that has been
detrimental to coalition and solidarity work among women within this
country and among women from different countries. As the black American womanist Bell Hooks writes, "White women both promote a false
image of themselves as powerless, passive victims, and deflect attention

away from their aggressiveness, their power (however limited in a white supremacist, male-dominated state), their willingness to dominate and control others."[43] Feminist ethics must work to make visible the invisibility and bring to speech the silence of *all* women. This is work we must do together, but we can only begin to become united after power is named, reclaimed, and shared.

How Men Have (a) Sex
An Address to College Students

John Stoltenberg

In the human species, how many sexes are there?
Answer A: *There are two sexes.*
Answer B: *There are three sexes.*
Answer C *There are four sexes.*
Answer D: *There are seven sexes.*
Answer E: *There are as many sexes as there are people.*

I'd like to take you, in an imaginary way, to look at a different world, somewhere else in the universe, a place inhabited by a life form that very much resembles us. But these creatures grow up with a peculiar knowledge. They know that they have been born in an infinite variety. They know, for instance, that in their genetic material they are born with hundreds of different chromosome formations at the point in each cell that we would say determines their "sex." These creatures don't just come in XX or XY; they also come in XXY and XYY and XXX plus a long list of "mosaic" variations in which some cells in a creature's body have one combination and other cells have another. Some of these creatures are born with chromosomes that aren't even quite X or Y because a little bit of one chromosome goes and gets joined to another. There are hundreds of different combinations, and though all are not fertile, quite a number of them are. The creatures in this world enjoy their individuality; they delight in the fact that they are not divisible into distinct categories. So when another new-born arrives with an esoterically rare chromosomal formation, there is a little celebration: "Aha," they say, "another sign that we are each unique."

"How Men Have (a) Sex: Address to College Students," by John Stoltenberg reprinted from *Refusing to Be a Man: Essays on Sex and Justice* by John Stoltenberg (New York: Meridian Books, Penguin Group, 1990). Used by permission.

These creatures also live with the knowledge that they are born with a vast range of genital formations. Between their legs are tissue structures that vary along a continuum, from clitorises with a vulva through all possible combinations and gradations to penises with a scrotal sac. These creatures live with an understanding that their genitals all developed prenatally from exactly the same little nub of embryonic tissue called a genital tubercle, which grew and developed under the influence of varying amounts of the hormone androgen. These creatures honor and respect everyone's natural-born genitalia — including what we would describe as a microphallus or a clitoris several inches long. What these creatures find amazing and precious is that because everyone's genitals stem from the same embryonic tissue, the nerves inside all their genitals got wired very much alike, so these nerves of touch just go crazy upon contact in a way that resonates completely between them. "My gosh," they think, "you must feel something in your genital tubercle that intensely resembles what I'm feeling in my genital tubercle." Well, they don't exactly *think* that in so many words; they're actually quite heavy into their feelings at that point; but they do feel very connected — throughout all their wondrous variety.

I could go on. I could tell you about the variety of hormones that course through their bodies in countless different patterns and proportions, both before birth and throughout their lives — the hormones that we call "sex hormones" but that they call "individuality inducers." I could tell you how these creatures think about reproduction: For part of their lives, some of them are quite capable of gestation, delivery, and lactation; and for part of their lives, some of them are quite capable of insemination; and for part or all of their lives, some of them are not capable of any of those things so these creatures conclude that it would be silly to lock anyone into a lifelong category based on a capability variable that may or may not be utilized and that in any case changes over each lifetime in a fairly uncertain and idiosyncratic way. These creatures are not oblivious to reproduction; but nor do they spend their lives constructing a self-definition around their variable reproductive capacities. They don't have to, because what is truly unique about these creatures is that they are capable of having a sense of personal identity without struggling to fit into a group identity based on how they were born. These creatures are quite happy, actually. They don't worry about sorting *other* creatures into categories, so they don't have to worry about whether they are measuring up to some category they themselves are supposed to belong to.

These creatures, of course, have sex. Rolling and rollicking and robust sex, and sweaty and slippery and sticky sex, and trembling and quaking and tumultuous sex, and tender and tingling and transcendent sex. They have sex fingers to fingers. They have sex belly to belly. They have sex genital tubercle to genital tubercle. They *have* sex. They do not have *a* sex. In their erotic lives, they are not required to act out their status in a category system — because there *is* no category system. There are no sexes to belong to, so sex between creatures is free to be between genuine individuals — not representatives of a category. They have sex. They do not have a sex. Imagine life like that.

Perhaps you have guessed the point of this science fiction: Anatomically, each creature in the imaginary world I have been describing could be an identical twin of every human being on earth. These creatures, in fact, *are us* — in every way except socially and politically. The way they are born is the way we are born. And we are not born belonging to one or the other of two sexes. We are born into a physiological continuum on which there is no discrete and definite point that you can call "male" and no discrete and definite point that you can call "female." If you look at all the variables in nature that are said to determine human "sex," you can't possibly find one that will unequivocally split the species into two. Each of the so-called criteria of sexedness is itself a continuum — including chromosomal variables, genital and gonadal variations, reproductive capacities, endocrinological proportions, and any other criterion you could think of. Any or all of these different variables may line up in any number of ways, and all of the variables may vary independently of one another.[1]

What does all this mean? It means, first of all, a logical dilemma: Either human "male" and human "female" actually exist in nature as fixed and discrete entities and you can credibly base an entire social and political system on those absolute natural categories, or else the variety of human sexedness is infinite. As Andrea Dworkin wrote in 1974:

> The discovery is, of course, that "man" and "woman" are fictions, caricatures, cultural constructs. As models they are reductive, totalitarian, inappropriate to human becoming. As roles they are static, demeaning to the female, dead-ended for male and female both.[2]

The conclusion is inescapable:

> *We are clearly a multisexed species which has its sexuality spread along a vast continuum where the elements called male and female are not discrete.*[3]

"We are... a multisexed species." I first read those words a little over ten years ago — and that liberating recognition saved my life.

All the time I was growing up, I knew that there was something really problematical in my relationship to manhood. Inside, deep inside, I never believed I was fully male — I never believed I was growing up enough of a man. I believed that someplace out there, in other men, there was something that was genuine authentic all-American manhood — the real stuff — but I didn't have it: not enough of it to convince me anyway, even if I managed to be fairly convincing to those around me. I felt like an impostor, like a fake. I agonized a lot about not feeling male enough, and I had no idea then how much I was not alone.

Then I read those words — those words that suggested to me for the first time that the notion of manhood is a cultural delusion, a baseless belief, a false front, a house of cards. It's not true. The category I was trying so desperately to belong to, to be a member of in good standing — it doesn't exist. Poof. Now you see it, now you don't. Now you're terrified you're not really part of it; now you're free, you don't have to worry anymore. However removed you feel inside from "authentic manhood," it doesn't matter. What matters is the center inside yourself — and how you live, and how you treat people, and what you can contribute as you pass through life on this earth, and how honestly you love, and how carefully you make choices. Those are the things that really matter. Not whether you're a real man. There's no such thing.

The idea of the male sex is like the idea of an Aryan race. The Nazis believed in the idea of an Aryan race — they believed that the Aryan race really exists, physically, in nature — and they put a great deal of effort into making it real. The Nazis believed that from the blond hair and blue eyes occurring naturally in the human species, they could construe the existence of a separate *race* — a distinct category of human beings that was unambiguously rooted in the natural order of things. But traits do not a race make; traits only make traits. For the idea to be real that these physical traits comprised a race, the race had to be socially constructed. The Nazis inferiorized and exterminated those they defined as "non-Aryan." With that, the notion of an Aryan race began to seem to come true. That's how there could be a political entity known as an Aryan race, and that's how there could be for some people a personal, subjective sense that they belonged to it. This happened through hate and force, through violence and victimization, through treating millions of people as things, then exterminating them. The belief system shared by people who believed they were all Aryan could not exist apart from that force and violence. The force and violence created a racial class system, *and* it created those people's membership in the race considered "superior." The force and violence served their class interests in large part because it created and maintained the class itself. But the idea of an Aryan race could never become metaphysically true, despite all the violence unleashed to create it, because there simply is no Aryan race. There is only the idea of it — and the consequences of trying to make it seem real. The male sex is very like that.

Penises and ejaculate and prostate glands occur in nature, but the notion that these anatomical traits comprise a sex — a discrete class, separate and distinct, metaphysically divisible from some other sex, the "other sex" — is simply that: a notion, an idea. The penises exist; the male sex does not. The male sex is socially constructed. It is a political entity that flourishes only through acts of force and sexual terrorism. Apart from the global inferiorization and subordination of those who are defined as "nonmale," the idea of personal membership in the male sex class would have no recognizable meaning. It would make no sense. No one could be a member of it and no one would think they *should* be a member of it. There would be no male sex to belong to. That doesn't mean there wouldn't still be penises and ejaculate and prostate glands and such. It simply means that the center of our selfhood would not be required to reside inside an utterly fictitious category — a category that only seems real to the extent that those outside it are put down.

We live in a world divided absolutely into two sexes, even though nothing about human nature warrants that division. We are sorted into one category or another at birth based solely on a visual inspection of our groins, and the only question that's asked is whether there's enough elongated tissue around your urethra so you can pee standing up. The presence or absence of a long-enough penis is the primary criterion for separating who's to grow up male from who's to grow up female. And among all the ironies in that utterly whimsical and arbitrary selection process is the fact that anyone can pee both sitting down and standing up.

Male sexual identity is the conviction or belief, held by most people born with penises, that they are male and not female, that they belong to the male sex. In a society predicated on the notion that there are two "opposite" and "complementary" sexes, this idea not only makes sense, it becomes sense; the very idea of a male sexual identity produces sensation, produces the meaning of sensation, becomes the meaning of how one's body feels. The sense and the sensing of a male sexual identity is at once mental and physical, at once public and personal. Most people born with a penis between their legs grow up aspiring to feel and act unambiguously male, longing to belong to the sex that is male and daring not to belong to the sex that is not, and feeling this urgency for a visceral and constant verification of their male sexual identity — for a fleshy connection to manhood — as the driving force of their life. The drive does not originate in the anatomy. The sensations derive from the idea. The idea gives the feelings social meaning; the idea determines which sensations shall be sought.

People born with penises must strive to make the idea of male sexual identity personally real by doing certain deeds, actions that are valued and chosen because they produce the desired feeling of belonging to a sex that is male and not female. Male sexual identity is experienced only in sensation and action, in feeling and doing, in eroticism and ethics. The feeling of belonging to a male sex encompasses both sensations that are explicitly "sexual" and those that are not ordinarily regarded as such. And there is a tacit social value system according to which certain acts are chosen because they make an individual's sexedness feel real and certain; other acts are eschewed because they numb it. That value system is the ethics of male sexual identity — and it may well be the social origin of all injustice.

Each person experiences the idea of sexual identity as more or less real, more or less certain, more or less true, depending on two very personal phenomena: one's feelings and one's acts. For many people, for instance, the act of fucking makes their sexual identity feel more real than it does at other times, and they can predict from experience that this feeling of greater certainty will last for at least a while after each time they fuck. Fucking is not the only such act, and not only so-called sex acts can result in feelings of certainty about sexual identity; but the act of fucking happens to be a very good example of the correlation between *doing* a specific act in a specific way and *sensing* the specificity of the sexual identity to which one aspires. A person can decide to do certain acts and not others just because some acts will have the payoff of a feeling of greater certainty about sexual identity and others will give the feedback of a feeling of less. The transient reality of one's sexual identity, a person can know, is always a function of what one does and how one's acts make one feel. The feeling and the act must conjoin for the idea of the sexual identity to come true. We all keep longing for surety of our sexedness that we can feel; we all keep striving through our actions to make the idea real.

In human nature, eroticism is not differentiated between "male" and "female" in any clear-cut way. There is too much of a continuum, too great a resemblance. From all that we know, the penis and the clitoris are identically "wired" to receive and retransmit sensations from throughout the body, and the congestion of blood within the lower torso during sexual excitation makes all bodies sensate in a remarkably similar manner. Simply put, we all share all the nerve and blood-vessel layouts that are associated with sexual arousal. Who can say, for instance, that the penis would not experience sensations the way that a clitoris does if this were not a world in which the penis is supposed to be hell-bent on penetration? By the time most men make it through puberty, they believe that erotic sensation is supposed to *begin* in their penis; that if engorgement has not begun there, then nothing else in their body will heat up either. There is a massive interior dissociation from sensations that do not explicitly remind a man that his penis is still there. And not only there as sensate, but *functional* and *operational.*

So much of most men's sexuality is tied up with gender-actualizing — with feeling like a real man — that they can scarcely recall an erotic sensation that had no gender-specific cultural meaning. As most men age, they learn to cancel out and deny erotic sensations that are not specifically linked to what they think a real man is supposed to feel. An erotic sensation unintentionally experienced in a receptive, communing mode — instead of in an aggressive and controlling and violative mode, for instance — can shut down sensory systems in an instant. An erotic sensation unintentionally linked to the "wrong" sex of another person can similarly mean sudden numbness. Acculturated male sexuality has a built-in fail-safe: Either its political context reifies manhood or the experience cannot be felt as sensual. Either the act creates his sexedness or it does not compute as a sex act. So he tenses up, pumps up, steels himself against the dread that he be found not male enough. And his dread is not stupid; for he sees what happens to people when they are treated as nonmales.

My point is that sexuality does not *have* a gender; it *creates* a gender. It creates for those who adapt to it in narrow and specified ways the confirmation for the individual of belonging to the idea of one sex or the other. So-called male sexuality is a learned connection between specific physical sensations and the idea of a male sexual identity. To achieve this male sexual identity requires that an individual *identify with* the class of males — that is, accept as one's own the values and interests of the class. A fully realized male sexual identity also requires *nonidentification with* that which is perceived to be nonmale, or female. A male must not identify with females; he must not associate with females in feeling, interest, or action. His identity as a member of the sex class "men" absolutely depends on the extent to which he repudiates the values and interests of the sex class "women."

I think somewhere inside us all, we have always known something about the relativity of gender. Somewhere inside us all, we know that our bodies harbor deep resemblances, that we are wired inside to respond in a profound harmony to the resonance of eroticism inside the body of someone near us. Physiologically, we are far more alike than different. The tissue structures that have become labial and clitoral or scrotal and penile have not forgotten their common ancestry. Their sensations are of the same source. The nerve networks and interlock of capillaries throughout our pelvises electrify and engorge as if plugged in together and pumping as one. That's what we feel when we feel one another's feelings. That's what can happen during sex that is mutual, equal, reciprocal, profoundly communing.

So why is it that some of us with penises think it's sexy to pressure someone into having sex against their will? Some of us actually get harder the harder the person resists. Some of us with penises actually believe that some of us without penises want to be raped. And why is it that some of us with penises think it's sexy to treat other people as objects, as things to be bought and sold, impersonal bodies to be possessed and consumed for our sexual pleasure? Why is it that some of us with penises are aroused by sex tinged with rape, and sex commoditized by pornography? Why do so many of us with penises want such antisexual sex?

There's a reason, of course. We have to make a lie seem real. It's a very big lie. We each have to do our part Otherwise the lie will look like the lie that it is. Imagine the enormity of what we each must do to keep the lie alive in each of us. Imagine the awesome challenge we face to make the lie a social fact. It's a lifetime mission for each of us born with a penis: to have sex in such a way that the male sex will seem real — and so that we'll feel like a real part of it.

We all grow up knowing exactly what kind of sex that is. It's the kind of sex you can have when you pressure or bully someone else into it. So it's a kind of sex that makes your will more important than theirs. That kind of sex helps the lie a lot. That kind of sex makes you feel like someone important and it turns the other person into someone unimportant. That kind of sex makes you feel real, not like a fake. It's a kind of sex men have in order to feel like a real man.

There's also the kind of sex you can have when you force someone and hurt someone and cause someone suffering and humiliation. Violence and hostility in sex help the lie a lot too. Real men are aggressive in sex. Real men get cruel in sex. Real men use their penises like weapons in sex. Real men leave bruises. Real men think it's a turn-on to threaten harm. A brutish push can make an erection feel really hard. That kind of sex helps the lie a lot. That kind of sex makes you feel like someone who is powerful and it turns the other person into someone powerless. That kind of sex makes you feel dangerous and in control — like you're fighting a war with an enemy and if you're mean enough you'll win but if you let up you'll lose your manhood. It's a kind of sex men have *in order to have* a manhood.

There's also the kind of sex you can have when you pay your money into a profit system that grows rich displaying and exploiting the bodies and body parts of people without penises for the sexual entertainment of people with. Pay your money and watch. Pay your money and imagine. Pay your money and get real turned on. Pay your money and jerk off. That kind of sex helps the lie a lot. It helps support an industry committed to making people with penises believe that people without are sluts who just want to be ravished and reviled — an industry dedicated to maintaining a sex-class system in which men believe themselves sex machines and men believe women are mindless fuck tubes. That kind of sex helps the lie a lot. It's like buying Krugerrands as a vote of confidence for white supremacy in South Africa.

And there's one more thing: That kind of sex makes the lie indelible — burns it onto your retinas right adjacent to your brain — makes you remember it and makes your body respond to it and so it makes you believe that the lie is in fact true: You really are a real man. That slavish and submissive creature there spreading her legs is really not. You and that creature have nothing in common. That creature is an alien inanimate thing, but your penis is completely real and alive. Now you can come. Thank god almighty — you have a sex at last.

Now, I believe there are many who are sick at heart over what I have been describing. There are many who were born with penises who want to stop collaborating in the sex-class system that needs us to need these kinds of sex. I believe some of you want to stop living out the big lie, and you want to know how. Some of you long to touch truthfully. Some of you want sexual relationships in your life that are about intimacy and joy, ecstasy and equality — not antagonism and alienation. So what I have to say next I have to say to you.

When you use sex to have a sex, the sex you have is likely to make you feel crummy about yourself. But when you have sex in which you are not struggling with your partner in order to act out "real manhood," the sex you have is more likely to bring you close.

This means several specific things:

1. Consent is absolutely essential. If both you and your partner have not freely given your informed consent to the sex you are about to have, you can be quite certain that the sex you go ahead and have will make you strangers to each other. How do you know if there's consent? You ask. You ask again if you're sensing any doubt. Consent to do one thing isn't consent to do another. So you keep communicating, in clear words. And you don't take anything for granted.

2. Mutuality is absolutely essential. Sex is not something you do to someone. Sex is not a one-way transitive verb, with a subject, you, and an object, the body you're with. Sex that is mutual is not about doing and being done to; it's about being-with and feeling-with. You have to really be there to experience what is happening between and within the two of you — between every part of you and within both your whole bodies. It's a matter of paying attention — as if you are paying attention to someone who matters.

3. *Respect is absolutely essential.* In the sex that you have, treat your partner like a real person who, like you, has real feelings — feelings that matter as much as your own. You may or may not love — but you must always respect. You must respect the integrity of your partner's body. It is not yours for the taking. It belongs to someone real. And you do not get ownership of your partner's body just because you are having sex — or just because you have had sex.

For those who are closer to the beginning of your sex lives than to the middle or the end, many things are still changing for you about how you have sex, with whom, why or why not, what you like or dislike, what kind of sex you want to have more of. In the next few years, you are going to discover and decide a lot. I say "discover" because no one can tell you what you're going to find out about yourself in relation to sex — and I say "decide" because virtually without knowing it you are going to be laying down habits and patterns that will probably stay with you for the rest of your life. You're at a point in your sexual history that you will never be at again. You don't know what you don't know yet. And yet you are making choices whose consequences for your particular sexuality will be sealed years from now.

I speak to you as someone who is closer to the middle of my sexual history. As I look back, I see that I made many choices that I didn't know I was making. And as I look at men who are near my age, I see that what has happened to many of them is that their sex lives are stuck in deep ruts that began as tiny fissures when they were young. So I want to conclude by identifying what I believe are three of the most important decisions about your sexuality that you can make when you are at the beginning of your sexual history. However difficult these choices may seem to you now, I promise you they will only get more difficult as you grow older. I realize that what I'm about to give is some quite unsolicited nuts-and-bolts advice. But perhaps it will spare you, later on in your lives, some of the obsessions and emptiness that have claimed the sexual histories of many men just a generation before you. Perhaps it will not help, I don't know; but I hope very much that it will.

First, you can start choosing now not to let your sexuality be manipulated by the pornography industry. I've heard many unhappy men talk about how they are so hooked on pornography and obsessed with it that they are virtually incapable of a human erotic contact. And I have heard even more men talk about how, when they do have sex with someone, the pornography gets in the way, like a mental obstacle, like a barrier preventing a full experience of what's really happening between them and their partner. The sexuality that the pornography industry needs you to have is not about communicating and caring; it's about "pornographizing" people — objectifying and conquering them, not being with them as a person. You do not have to buy into it.

Second, you can start choosing now not to let drugs and alcohol numb you through your sex life. Too many men, as they age, become incapable of having sex with a clear head. But you need your head clear — to make clear choices, to send clear messages, to read clearly what's coming in on a clear channel between you and your partner. Sex is no time for your awareness to sign off. And another thing: Beware of relying on drugs or alcohol to give you "permission" to have sex, or to trick your body into feeling something that it's not, or so you won't have to take responsibility for what you're feeling or for the sex that you're about to have. If you can't take sober responsibility for your part in a sexual encounter, you probably shouldn't be having it — and you certainly shouldn't be zonked out of your mind in order to have it.

Third, you can start choosing now not to fixate on fucking — especially if you'd really rather have sex in other, noncoital ways. Sometimes men have coital sex — penetration and thrusting then ejaculating inside some-one — not because they particularly feel like it but because they feel they *should* feel like it: It's expected that if you're the man, you fuck. And if you don't fuck, you're not a man. The corollary of this cultural im-perative is that if two people don't have intercourse, they have not had real sex. That's baloney, of course, but the message comes down hard, especially inside men's heads: Fucking is *the* sex act, the act in which you act out what sex is supposed to be — and what sex you're supposed to be.

Like others born with a penis, I was born into a sex-class system that requires my collaboration every day, even in how I have sex. Nobody told me, when I was younger, that I could have noncoital sex and that it would be fine. Actually, much better than fine. Nobody told me about an incredible range of other erotic possibilities for mutual lovemaking — including rubbing body to body, then coming body to body; including multiple, nonejaculatory orgasms; including the feeling you get when even the tiniest place where you and your partner touch becomes like a window through which great tidal storms of passion ebb and flow, back and forth. Nobody told me about the sex you can have when you stop working at having a sex. My body told me, finally. And I began to trust what my body was telling me more than the lie I was supposed to make real.

I invite you too to resist the lie. I invite you too to become an erotic traitor to male supremacy.

Domestic Violence
Among Pacific Asians

Nilda Rimonte

This essay presents an overview of the phenomenon of domestic violence in the Pacific Asian community of Los Angeles.[1] Who are the women involved? Why do they get battered? Why do they stay? When do they leave? And how, if at all, do they differ from battered women of other races, other groups?

The typical Pacific Asian battered woman exhibits a wide range of characteristics. She may be a first-generation immigrant or a refugee. She may speak fluent English or any of the forty different Pacific Asian languages and dialects that are represented in Los Angeles County.[2] She may be highly educated or preliterate, have an income of $22,050 or make less than the legal minimum hourly wage. She may have arrived here legally or "creatively"; lived in the United States for years or be an imported bride of barely three months. Such a woman will in time also exhibit the characteristics of someone so badly abused that she feels helpless; so diminished in self-esteem that she feels she deserves nothing more; and so lacking in a sense of self that she is almost invisible to herself as well as to her family and community.[3]

Of the approximately three thousand Pacific Asian clients served by the Center for the Pacific Asian Family in Los Angeles between 1978 and 1985, one-third were Korean, one-third Southeast Asians (mostly Vietnamese), and the last third distributed among Chinese, Filipinos, Japanese, South Asians, Thais, Samoans, and others.[4] It should be noted that this breakdown reflects to some degree the presence of staff

"Domestic Violence Among Pacific Asians" by Nilda Rimonte is reprinted from *Making Waves: An Anthology of Writings By and About Asian American Women*, ed. Asian Women United of California (Boston: Beacon Press, 1989). Used by permission.

from, and their outreach to, specific ethnic groups. For instance, having Korean-speaking workers at the center from the start has resulted in more response from that community.[5]

During one recent two-year period, the residential caseload averaged about four hundred women and children annually. Of this number, about 120 are Korean, with approximately one-half being adult Korean women. This means that among Koreans more than one woman each week is so severely abused by her husband that she seeks the safety of shelter outside of her home. Only the severely abused seek shelter. Some women just call the hotline for help. Therefore the actual number of women who suffer from varying levels of abuse is probably much greater than these figures indicate.

WHY DOMESTIC VIOLENCE OCCURS

Domestic violence, or wife abuse, occurs among Pacific Asians as often as it does in the dominant community, in approximately one out of every two marital relationships. Factors contributing to this fact include the Pacific Asian family's traditionally patriarchal system and the attendant belief in the supremacy of the male; the socialization goals and processes which favor the family and community over the individual; the cultural emphasis on silent suffering versus open communication of needs and feelings; and the enormous adjustment pressures which test the limits of immigrants' and refugees' survival skills. Cultural norms and values directly or indirectly sanction abuse against women and tend to minimize it as a problem in the community.

Traditionally Pacific Asians conceal and deny problems that threaten group pride and may bring on shame. Because of the strong emphasis on obligations to the family, a Pacific Asian woman will often remain silent rather than admit to a problem that might disgrace her family. If domestic violence is made public, the topic is given short shrift. Community leaders prefer to view it chiefly — if not entirely — as the result of economic and social adjustment pressures. In short, if the cause of stress was removed from the environment, abuse of women would cease.

This is an over-simplified explanation of domestic violence. Pacific Asian women are truly at great risk because their families are unusually vulnerable. Despite their financially successful image, many Pacific Asian families can survive only on the combined incomes of husband and wife, who are often overworked by an average of six hours per week.[6] This need for both spouses to work creates changes in the family and sex role system. These changes are perceived as liberating by the woman, but extremely threatening by the man. Often he will describe these changes as the Americanization of his Asian wife.

To be American, from the Pacific Asian perspective, is to enjoy individual freedom, be self-determined, and be self-defined. Pushed by economic needs, and then exposed to the Western ideals of independence and self-reliance, the Pacific Asian woman does change. She begins by demanding changes in the home itself, particularly in areas that by culture and habit have been exclusively hers — housework and childcare, for instance.

Already humbled by his lack of control in the new and alien world, and perhaps also feeling a sense of failure, the Pacific Asian man resists the change. He insists on his accustomed privileges and esteemed place: she mustn't change; she mustn't turn her back on her ethnic culture; she mustn't become Americanized. She mustn't, that is, abandon him.

Such dependency is made clear in the desperate efforts of abusive husbands to retrieve women whom they have abused and who have fled for their lives. This dependent relationship is more than just the anxious attachment of the insecure and the psychologically impaired. It is the "relentless reciprocity" — Sartre's phrase — that exists between the oppressor and the oppressed. Because one's identity and status is derived from the other, if one person ceases to exist, so does the other.

The community's earlier explanation of domestic violence, blaming the circumstances, is only denying the problem. It also denies the victims the right to look for alternatives and ignores their need to seek help. It also does not question the man's assumed right to beat women during times of stress, or the woman's assumed obligation to respect that right.

Thus a woman is first brutalized, and then pressured to conceal her victimization. Fear, guilt, and shame are the means by which pressure is applied. Hence the community shelters the inequality between women and men and nurtures the ancient patriarchal family structure.

A healthy family by Western standards has an open structure. Members are allowed to be individuals and to communicate their feelings freely.[7] This ideal contrasts starkly with the controlled, conforming style of Pacific Asians, in which a high value is placed on one's strict accountability to the family. The Pacific Asian family has a closed structure. Communication is restricted and decision making is vertical. Power in the marriage is hierarchical. Even in extended families power belongs to the most senior male, often the woman's father-in-law.[8]

Studies have shown that the more closed the system is, the more disordered and dysfunctional the family becomes.[9] They also show that men's limited ability to express their feelings results in a continual state of explosiveness and possible violence.[10]

This does not mean that the Pacific Asian family is by nature dysfunctional; it is merely more responsive to the needs of men than to those of women. The Pacific Asian family has been the traditional source of support and nurturance to its members. The emotional and economic security that the individual finds within the bosom of her family are seen to compensate for the harsh restrictions and de-emphasis on individuality. Even the achievements of individual Asians are generally laid at the doorstop of a highly supportive family which throws the full weight of all its resources behind the aspiring individual — albeit for the glory and future economic well-being of the family itself.

Nevertheless, this system, which is propped up by traditional sex roles, that is, male dominance, results in a power imbalance. Wherever that imbalance exists — especially without the mediating presence of elders — there is always at least the potential for violence.

SEEKING SHELTER

It is still true, for the most part, that the family remains the major source of support for Pacific Asian individuals. Tradition requires the individual to turn first to her immediate family and then beyond in widening concentric circles: to the extended family, to the community, and last to an agency that is perceived as culturally hospitable and linguistically accessible.

However, even if this support system remains intact outside the homeland — which is questionable because of changes in the structure due to immigration — the Pacific Asian woman faces betrayal. First, her attacker comes from the very group to which she has been taught to turn. Second, when relatives are available, they often discourage her from taking steps toward safety and rescue because they too believe in the traditional role of women. Even when they recognize her need to risk family disapproval for the sake of survival, they often are in no position economically to provide significant assistance. Third, community gatekeepers are interested in maintaining the status quo in order to preserve the culture. Church leaders, for example, preach the acceptance of private suffering for the sake of peace. In any case, the Pacific Asian woman is often ineluctably alone.

A shelter away from relatives and the community becomes for the woman her first, if not only, alternative for both support and refuge. This is particularly true if she is fleeing physical as well as emotional abuse.

Studies in the dominant culture indicate that women stay in abusive relationships for both economic and psychological reasons.[11] Women know that escape may mean greater poverty for themselves and their children. This has been called in various studies the "feminization of poverty."

The process is particularly prevalent with battered Pacific Asian women. This is true because they often have few marketable skills, limited English, and neither the knowledge of how to get around the city nor the means to do so. So for them the prospect of suddenly becoming the single head of an impoverished household can be extremely daunting. Given the threat of the unfamiliar and having been socialized to function well only within the home, they often lack the self-confidence to leave. They may prefer the security of the predictable — even if the predictable includes the certainty of abuse.

If a woman does leave, she must face the possible loss of control over her children. If she is a first-generation immigrant, she may be bewildered by her children, who grow up in America embracing Western values and behaviors and who are in turn bewildered by her values. She often says the children's need for a father as a source of control is one of her major reasons for staying in the abusive relationship.

There is also the matter of coping with loneliness and the often unspecified need for sexual companionship. Because discussion of this subject is taboo for many Pacific Asians, it is frequently glossed over if not actually ignored. Only when a counselor encourages an open discussion of sexual needs do women freely acknowledge this as another reason for either staying with or returning to an abusive partner.[12]

CHOOSING TO LEAVE, RETURN, OR BE INDEPENDENT

Some women do manage to leave the abusive relationship, even if only temporarily. And given the Pacific Asian culture and the psycho-dynamics of abuse, this act is an extraordinary gesture of self-assertion.

The most frequently cited reason for seeking shelter is a woman's fear for her own life and for that of her children. This is especially true when one or more of the children have already been physically or sexually abused, or inadvertently injured during a domestic fight. The reason cited second is a woman's desire to leave while she is still young enough to rebuild her life, preferably with another partner. Thus, her flight from home represents a paradox of hopelessness about her ability to manage an abusive relationship and hopefulness about the possibility of life without violence.

The woman who chooses to leave suffers from intense conflicts. She comes from a culture where the ideals of personal independence and individual freedom are alien. Instead the ideals of mutual obligation and family interdependence are valued. So, first of all, she feels guilt about having chosen herself and her goals over those of her family; she feels she has betrayed her ethnic values. She also experiences shame about her failure to live up to community-prescribed roles and behaviors; she is deeply concerned about what the community might think of her. Finally, her children — depending on their ages and on the relationship with their father — bring pressures to bear on her decision to stay away or return.

Sometimes the pressures are too great and the woman returns to the abusive relationship, often for very much the same reasons that originally compelled her to leave. She is the woman whose conflicts remain unresolved despite a stay at a shelter. She is not uncommon. Since her respite at the shelter is brief compared to the years of exposure she has had to traditional Pacific Asian values, she is inclined to return to her husband.[13]

Let us emphasize again that given her background and limited resources, the woman who chooses to leave an abusive situation, however temporarily, has taken extraordinary action. The woman who chooses to be independent after her stay at the shelter is even more unusual. Choosing not to be a victim a woman strikes out for herself and goes against the tradition in which she was raised and by which she defines herself. For a woman raised in a conformist and other-directed culture, this choice requires immense courage. It also requires mobilization of resources and support from others to maintain that independence.

STRATEGIES FOR INTERVENTION

The strategies that can help battered Pacific Asian women before, during, and after their stay at a shelter are many. Intervention must be well coordinated and sufficiently comprehensive in response to their multifarious and complex needs. The words "mobilization of resources" are most apt, for not only does the woman have to gather up her internal and personal resources, but the shelter and community must also orchestrate their resources.

Though the woman who returns to an abusive relationship, the woman who chooses independence, and the woman who stays but reaches out for help all have their own particular needs, they all share some common ones as well. They need practical assistance, such as housing, food, work, financial help, legal aid, childcare, transportation, police protection. More than those things, however, they need to be taught to see for themselves, and then to make decisions based on their own perceptions and priorities.

The first steps for the battered woman are to see herself as a victim, how she became one, and that she has a choice not to be one any longer. Understanding how victimization takes place and how to avoid it not only helps in her immediate situation, but also in the larger contexts of culture and society.

Next, she must learn to speak. It is alarming how so many Pacific Asian women still rely on silence as a way of communicating their feelings — particularly hurt and anger. They rely on silence to keep the family intact.

Finally, she must learn to act. But on what will she act? She will decide among the various alternatives she is assisted to explore, once armed with accurate information about property and child custody laws, immigration laws, and domestic violence laws. In short, she will act when she knows her rights and obligations. This is particularly urgent for the battered woman who was brought to the United States by a green card holder (a permanent resident), or who came hoping to become one herself via marriage.[14] What happens next depends on which course the woman selects.

If she chooses independence and becomes a single parent, single parenting education will be tremendously important. She will also need practical help, that is, respite care, childcare, and emotional support for the difficult task of managing a separated family.

If she returns to her husband, the challenge could be even greater. For if she is to avoid abuse, or better yet, eliminate it altogether, her family environment must change. Counseling for the abused and the abuser alike is needed because the woman who leaves and then returns is not the same person she was before. Now at the very least she knows there are other women in much the same position as she; that she has a right not to be abused; that there are people with resources willing to help; and that life without violence is possible.

BATTERED WOMEN IMMIGRANTS: A SPECIAL CLASS

Immigrants and refugees all confront loss. What is lost is the security which comes with the familiar; in its place is a whole set of new and unfamiliar demands and expectations. This unfamiliarity coupled with rejection in the new community creates enormous feelings of social incompetence, confusion, isolation, and cultural alienation.[15]

In order to cope in the new country, immigrants are forced to accept change, but the change involves still another kind of loss. This time the loss is of traditional beliefs, attitudes, roles, and lifestyles.[16] For instance, to ask an unemployed Pacific Asian man to modify his expectation of his working wife is to ask him to accept diminution of his status, to risk losing face before his own family and community. To suggest to a battered Pacific Asian woman that she can choose not to be a victim is to challenge the view by which she has always lived, to wit, that as an individual she does not count for very much and that only her roles and functions within the family have any value.

Both of these examples are extreme, involving the uprooting of individuals from the cultural values on which their identity is based. Tension between the demands of the new environment and an individual's ability to conform can breed illness and sometimes violence.[17]

Asian Pacific cultures allow a certain amount of violence as a behavior-shaping tool and a way of venting frustrations. Nonetheless such violence seems acceptable only when directed at women and children and other social inferiors.

Acknowledging that the use of violence as a form of power and control is rooted in and sanctioned by a culture does not mean, however, that the culture is itself the problem. The problem is still the battering. Shifting responsibility for battering from the abuser to the cultural system means that the individual is not held responsible. If this is true, then there is no victimizer and consequently no victim. Without a victim, no law has been broken, and therefore there is no crime. An additional problem results from blaming the culture: Because the system of beliefs, values, and norms is difficult to alter, those working for the abolition of violence against women and children could feel paralyzed by the enormity of their task.

CHILDREN OF VIOLENT HOMES

Throughout most of this essay domestic violence has been discussed as if it meant only abuse against women. This is because women have always been perceived as the primary victims. The reality, of course, is much broader. Children who accompany abused mothers to shelters have sometimes been abused themselves. At the Center for the Pacific Asian Family, for example, two-thirds of the population in the shelter are children. One-fourth of them have been abused; the remaining three-fourths are at risk of abuse by both the father and the mother.[18]

All the children who have witnessed abuse and violence in their homes have been traumatized. Children of violent homes are "terrified, at a loss of what to do, feeling responsible and guilty for the violence and for their mother's having to leave the home. . . . Moreover, these children are passive and withdrawn, use aggressive behavior to handle situations, and have impaired peer relations."[19] They also suffer from "pseudo-maturity, resulting from their having been made to play an adult role, encouraged by parents who are themselves emotionally immature."[20]

The children at the Pacific Asian shelter exhibit all these symptoms. But because they are the offspring of immigrant mothers, they have the added burden of playing mediator between the home and the outside world. They are equipped to do so because as children they acquire facility with English more quickly than their elders. All this causes a role reversal of monumental proportions.

Aside from the emotional difficulties, children who witness or suffer abuse learn to use violence as a way of coping and a means of communicating. Because they see violence as a normal way of living, they become predisposed to marrying abusers or becoming abusers themselves. Thus, "children suffer simply because they live in a battering household."[21] Without doing anything else, before even stepping out of their homes, their futures are already compromised.

Any intervention strategy must necessarily include the treatment of all children of violent homes. Preferably, such treatment is done in conjunction with the treatment of mothers at the shelter, with a follow-up program when they leave to return home or become independent. The object of such treatment must be to change the mothers' and children's behavior to one without verbal abuse or physical violence.

CONCLUSION

The use of violence as a means of coping and of getting what one wants is a learned behavior; it is a choice that the abuser makes. Fortunately, it can be unlearned. An abuser needs to choose again, this time deciding to acquire nonviolent interpersonal skills. Indispensable to this first step is taking responsibility for one's actions.

For the abused woman, a willingness to commit to change and the courage to confront all the difficulties is required. This commitment is also required of the community.

Pacific Asians have always been proud of the role of the family in their cultural and economic survival. It is time for Pacific Asians to reevaluate this role. Does it have meaning for Pacific Asians living in a Western culture? If not, what does, and what can?

It would be ironic if the cultural concept of a strong family should be the very force that would cause the family to disintegrate. Perhaps an approach to changing culture and institutions is to change individuals. In articulating the mission and philosophy of the Center for the Pacific Asian Family I wrote in 1979 that "adaptability is the hallmark of the survivor species." I believe this to be true of the Pacific Asian.

Disability, Sexism, and the Social Order

Debra Connors

Soon after I began losing my vision, a friend asked if I would join her in a newly-forming support group of disabled women. My response was, "What do you mean *disabled*? *I'm* not disabled. I just can't *see,* that's all!" She agreed — the label was degrading and not at all how we felt about ourselves. Certainly it was better than *handicapped*. Residents of the state institution where I once worked and children on telethons were handicapped. Yet *disabled* was no consolation. It resounded with an all-encompassing, somehow too final thud in my ear.

A few years later, a classmate asked that I not refer to her as *disabled*. It offended her. She considered herself a person with a disability, she said, and would not be reduced to her deafness. A disability, she explained, is a physical or mental impairment. A handicap is a set of social conditions which impede our independence. Disabilities become handicaps only when we allow them to become insurmountable. We then become disabled; we become our disabilities.

DISABLED BY SOCIETY*

Disabled, handicapped, differently-abled, physically or mentally different, physically challenged, women with disabilities — this is more than a mere discourse in semantics and a matter of personal preference. *Disabled women* is the term which most accurately characterizes our position in American society. Sexism and able-ism work in concert to disqualify us from vast areas of social life. Our unique set of barriers is further compounded by discrimination based on our race, age and sexual preference.

* Heads added.

"Disability, Sexism and the Social Order" by Debra Connors is reprinted from *With the Power of Each Breath: A Disabled Women's Anthology,* ed. Susan E. Browne, Debra Connors, Nanci Stern (San Francisco: Cleis Press, 1985). Copyright © 1985 by Debra Connors, Susan Browne, and Nanci Stern. Reprinted with permission of Cleis Press Inc., P.O. Box 8933, Pittsburgh, PA 15221.

Objectified as women and as medical, social work and charity cases, disabled women have been deeply invalidated as human beings. We have been disabled by our society. No euphemism will change this.

Disability is not a medical problem: nor is able-ism just a set of prejudicial ideas about disabled people. Disability is a societal institution which has developed alongside capitalism. Our societal position has been shaped by history and is inextricably woven into the fabric of American culture. There is no reason to assume that medical conditions are disabilities or that they should necessarily be stigmatizing. History reveals that policies, practices and ideas regarding disabled women have been socially constructed.

Disability first became institutionalized with the enactment of England's Elizabethan Poor Laws (1598–1601).[1] As the old feudal order gave way to mercantile capitalism, unemployment emerged as a new social phenomenon. Serfs who had lost their birthright to land as a result of the enclosure movement and old and sick people who had been ejected from their hospital and monastery shelters under the Protestant Acts of Dissolution flocked to market towns and cities which were unable to absorb them and ill prepared to cope with the problems they posed. With neither work nor relief available, life for most urban dwellers was characterized by suffering and protest. The Poor Laws were designed to squelch social unrest and control the vagabonds.

Prior to the Poor Laws, the Catholic Church had been the primary social service institution in medieval England. It provided a steady but slim trickle of alms to the poor. Travelers and old and sick people found shelter in the many hospitals (hospitality houses) under the governance of the monasteries. Pilgrims were charged a fee. Permanent residents of the hospitals were required to take vows of poverty and turn their few possessions over to the Church. Hospital life was severe and avoided by all who could manage to do so.[2] More generally, needy families received alms from the parish priests, if and when funds were available and depending on the political climate. Serfs expected charity and the Church sought to absolve itself as the major land and serf holder by redistributing to the poor a meager portion of the produce it had expropriated from them.

ELIZABETHAN POOR LAWS AND LATER LEGISLATION

The Elizabethan Poor Laws differed from feudal custom in several important ways. They drew a distinction between those who were "deserving" and "not deserving" of charity. Poverty and unemployment came to be viewed as personal problems and defects of character. Receipt of charity became cause for humiliation. Newly defined as those who "could but would not work," able-bodied paupers were put to labor in workhouses. Children of poor families (orphans) were placed out as apprentices. Blind, old and lame people and others with "diverse maladies" were given licenses to beg. Those who were discovered begging without a license were publicly whipped. Overseers of the poor were appointed in each municipality to collect and establish poor taxes, remove vagabonds to their places of birth and charge their families responsible for the care of those deemed incapable of self-care.[3] Almshouses were established for the care and incarceration of "invalids" and were administered by the overseers of poor people.

Persons who were ill or had physical impairments were legally defined as unemployable social dependents, incapable of self-care and in need of governance. Feudal paternalism had taken on a municipal guise. Those who were able to find employment or employ themselves were more directly taxed for the care of those who were destitute and were threatened with debtors' prison for failure to remit taxes to the overseer. This contributed to the opprobrium with which all "charity cases" were met. Poor relief was intended to restore social order, but it was never able to accomplish this. The social causes of poverty and unemployment were obscured in the Protestant work ethic and the working class began to be divided against itself.

The English Poor Laws were exported to the North American colonies and changed very little until 1935, when responsibility for and administration of poor people shifted from local, county, and state to federal jurisdiction.[4] Like their historical antecedents, the Social Security Act and other New Deal measures were introduced in a period of high unemployment and social unrest. The federal government created some employment opportunities for able-bodied men and women. Disability continued to be defined as an inability to pursue an occupation because of physical impairment. Unemployment and disability have yet to be addressed as political and economic conditions endemic to capitalism.

DISABILITY AND THE NEED TO WORK

The point to be made is, it hasn't always been the case that persons with medical or psychiatric disorders were categorically disabled — unemployed and unemployable. Indeed, the only persons free from labor in feudal Europe were the aristocrats. Some critically ill, contagious and dying persons were exempted from work in the hospitals, but most performed services in them.[5] Bands of wandering minstrels who were blind, deaf and lame traveled from manor to manor, carrying messages and providing entertainment in exchange for food and shelter.[6] There is little record of the daily lives of serfs, as literacy was reserved for the ecclesiastical class, but it seems reasonable to conclude that everyone contributed to the manorial and family economies in whatever means they were able. Blind women, for example, spun yarn and wove cloth. There is no evidence to indicate that those who could not walk were not allowed to use their hands. Life was hard, scarcity tended to be the rule, and labor was short during periods of plague. Survival depended on maximizing everyone's abilities.

Disabled people were denied passage to the American colonies, either as free persons or as indentured servants. But, many who began their journeys in good health arrived quite ill and famished, as did enslaved Africans. Farm-centered family economies, plantation slavery, and tenant farming predominated in America until the end of the nineteenth century. Women, men, children and elders, whether firm or infirm, contributed to family survival. Accidents and disease were common, but none could afford to be idle. Slaves harmed by brutality were not permitted respite. Disabled people have always existed and have always worked. Many no doubt labored beyond their capacities because there was no choice. They might have welcomed reprieve. But, in the urban-industrial cities, others found themselves in enforced idleness, unable to secure employment and with no means of support.

DISABILITY AND CAPITALISM

Disability became more fully institutionalized during the emergence of industrial capitalism. Industrialization had the potential to eliminate a substantial degree of disability, since machine power came to replace human power in many sectors of the economy. (The present computer revolution holds a similar promise.) Instead, more stamina was required of workers, industrial accidents caused more unemployability, and efforts were made to eliminate disabled people. The industrial revolution, hailed as the epitome of human potential, often worked against the realization of that possibility.

Once time became money, workers who could not keep pace with the assembly line were systematically disabled from productive activity. Profit, after all, is created by paying workers less than the value of the work they have done.[7] It is less profitable to hire employees who work more slowly than young able-bodied candidates. Since profit is the motive force of capitalism, workers with impaired profit generating abilities are regarded as useless — like broken machines.

Yet, less physical strength and dexterity are required to perform more tasks in today's work place than ever before.[8] Apparently disabled workers are no longer less profitable to employ. We, too, can be exploited at the maximal rate, at least until cost is considered. Workers who require adaptive equipment, a reader, sign language interpretation, a flexible work schedule, architectural reconstruction of the work place, or a non-standard mode of work performance are unlikely to find work. Facilitation, accommodation, adaptive equipment and architectural redesign are expensive and avoidable, simply by hiring workers who do not need them.

One corporation, at least, would seem to disagree.[9] A recent study concluded that it is no more costly to hire disabled than non-disabled workers. Disabled workers were said to be as efficient [as] and missed less work time than their co-workers. This superficially cheery picture soft-pedals the harsh truth that only those who can be fit into the corporate machine, as it exists, are ever hired. No report is given about the various physical attributes of these employees, which is obviously an important question. People with chronic progressive illnesses do miss more time from work, either due to fluctuating health or the fact that medical appointments are usually only available during business hours. Employers need not be aware of the added expenses involved in hiring a disabled person because either government subsidies or the employees pay the cost of our employability. We do not raise the cost of insurance plans because health insurance usually excludes pre-existing conditions. We should hardly be surprised to learn that these workers are satisfactory. They were no doubt carefully selected for their race, class, age, religion, appearance, gender — and of course — health.

What is tucked away, out of sight, by image-oriented approaches is that unemployment — and, thus, disability — is a necessary feature of a capitalist political economy. Business and industrial expansion *require* that a sector of the population be held in reserve — ready and willing to work for minimum wages. The conditions of unemployed and disabled workers serve as a constant reminder to even the most dissatisfied active worker that *any* job may be preferable to no job at all. The presence of readily available replacements effectively holds down wages and threatens unions. Fear and blame associated with unemployment mystifies its social origins and keeps workers in their place.[10]

Idealized notions of full employment do not include disabled people and old persons. Our unemployability is a given. We are not personally blamed for a dependence which is perceived to be beyond our control. We are pitied instead. Able-bodied people may lose their jobs, their lives may be falling apart, perhaps they've lost their partners or children, still a consoling friend will assure them, "at least you've got your health." Health offers hope for beginning anew, for taking personal control of a twist of fate. Illness and injury spell doom.

DEPENDENCY AND INDIVIDUALISM

This pity — this doom writ large — has been called the common denominator of disabled people's oppression. We are said, by social scientists,[11] to suffer from the *opinions* others hold of us. We are viewed as "abnormal," "defectives," "deviants," partial persons who are not quite human. Our needs are a sign of our disgrace. Given our unemployable status and our reliance on family, friends and social services to cope with an inaccessible environment, it is not irrational that we are categorically defined as dependents in need of care. Able-ism is not only an oppressive idea; though, had anyone conspired against us, they couldn't have created a more effective institution.

It is unpardonable in an individualist society to fail to be "self-sufficient." Our society values a false sense of independence which results in pain and a sense of worthlessness for women and men whose capabilities have been ignored and whose potential has been uniformly underdeveloped. Yet, independence does not truly reflect anyone's reality. As a species, we are emphatically *interdependent*.[12] Disabled people cannot be independent, not because we are pitiable or helpless, but because we are human.

Americans are particularly unmindful of the many persons on whom we daily depend for survival. A market economy — a cash nexus — obscures this fact. Moreover, class relations are hidden by the ideology of individualism. We firmly believe that if we are able to purchase the goods and services we are not able to produce for ourselves, we are free of dependence. Conversely, if we are not able to buy them, we suspect we do not deserve "charity." Those who are able to purchase a false sense of independence are revered and are a measure by which the working class evaluates its members. The fact that some grow rich at the expense of their employees is conveniently ignored, while people who are systematically disadvantaged are criticized for their dependence.

The stigma of dependence may be all but inescapable for disabled people. Society's resources are unavailable to us because we have been structurally defined as unemployable. It is considered a "special" privilege for us to be able to obtain an education, have a job or job skills, use public facilities, or have access to medical care, sub-minimal social support and freedom of mobility. Without the financial resources to pay an attendant to enable us to negotiate an environment that was not designed for our participation, we are often isolated and may be led to prioritize our own needs — some as absolute and life-sustaining and others as "luxuries." Disability has become so institutionalized against a back-drop of Protestant individualism that we may question our own abilities and worthiness to live self-managed, interdependent lives.

Unequal distribution of wealth in feudal society was explained as divine will. Disease, famine and ill-fortune were a sign of having fallen from spiritual favor. Science has displaced religious authority since then and the oracular task of explanation has fallen to biological determinists. Religious appeals to a "calling" could not account for the immense fortunes of a few and the severe poverty of many. Social and medical scientists put forth theories of natural selection to legitimize the increasingly polarized class relations which evolved with the industrial revolution. Evolution, they argued, was in progress. The fit were thriving; the poor, who were by definition "unfit," had simply met the final outcome of their biological destinies. Policy makers were warned not to tamper with nature by providing for the welfare of destitute families.[13]

BIOLOGICAL DETERMINISM

The myth of independence and theories of social evolution essentially disguised and have continued to disguise the structural causes of virtually all social problems.[14] Biological determinism is the well-established idea that the personalities, capabilities and social positions of individuals are fundamentally and inevitably determined by their biological appearance or genetic characteristics. Science has justified and apologized for discrimination against women, third-world people, religious and ethnic groups, old people, lesbians and gay men and disabled people. While much of what was determined to be natural about social inequalities has been exposed as a conscious effort to manufacture myth, the legacy of these experiments retains a powerful strong-hold upon our imaginations and finds expression in our social policies and in our prejudiced attitudes.

Scientific able-ism is a specific instance of biological determinism. Based on our biological characteristics, medical science and legislatures have worked in harmony to determine our membership. At various times throughout our history, attics, freak shows and circuses, hospitals, residential asylums, segregated schools and sheltered workshops have been established as our natural and proper environments. Myths concerning our feebleness, unnaturalness, beastlike sexuality or asexuality, ill-fittedness to parent, violent hostility and inherent evil prospered through time and have helped to keep us in our proper places.

Able-ist movements of the late nineteenth and early twentieth centuries regarded disability as problematic for society, but not — once again — as a socially constructed problem. As with the earlier Poor Laws, solutions tended to be directed toward individuals. Past and current reform movements — whether liberal or conservative — try to fix the symptoms of what are structural problems, leaving the sources quite untouched. The eugenics and rehabilitation movements, for example, treated disability as a condition to be eliminated or corrected at an individual level. They were generally praised as humanitarian efforts.

EFFECTS OF THE EUGENICS MOVEMENT

The early eugenicists were medical scientists who essentially conducted an experiment in genocide. They sought to improve the quality of the human gene pool by preventing the births of disabled infants. Numerous studies were conducted in an attempt to document the hereditary nature of such diseases as diabetes, blindness and epilepsy, as well as [such] deviant social behaviors as poverty, prostitution and criminality. Birth control literature, previously held in high disregard, suddenly found its way into the hands of poor women. Heredity counseling was advised for those with questionable genes in order to dissuade them from having children. State legislatures provided for the forced sterilization of mentally retarded women.

Despite the fact that evolution does not operate on an individual level and that most physical and emotional conditions are not inheritable, the search continues to this day for scientific documentation of genetically transmitted deviance. Recreational, automobile and industrial accidents, environmental pollution, iatrogenic disease, job-related stress and the impending threat of nuclear holocaust can safely be said to be among the major causes of physiological and psychological distress. Reproductive control of women's bodies continues, whether our genes or the genes of our partners are fallaciously considered problematic for society and our species. Twenty-seven states still provide for the sterilization of mentally retarded women. "Misdiagnosis" and coercion have led blind, deaf, deaf-blind, third-world and poor women to be sterilized against their will. Birth control chemicals are still routinely dispensed to women in some institutions. Genetic counseling, available at most major medical centers, has found its way into popular opinion. (This is not to imply that information available through genetic counseling should not be made available to prospective parents but rather to point out the historical and frequent current misuse of genetic counseling.) Prenatal diagnosis, which the early eugenicists sought to discover, has been praised as a miracle of modern medicine, one which has made all too clear that only children who might some day be permitted to be "productive" are welcomed into the world.

Common notions of disability continue to objectify us as patients. We are the failures of modern medicine, the "cases" whose births could not be foreseen and for whom there are no known cures. We testify against the omnipotence of medical science and represent a frightening truth. We are feared and hated and viewed as hopeless patients in all of our daily environments.

The consequences of viewing disabilities as irreparable impairments have been severe and far reaching. The investigatory nature and narrow conceptual scope of medical science — isolate the "defect," measure it, correct it, mask it, and/or eliminate its recurrence — have often culminated in the abuse of disabled people. Somehow, physicians often forget that we are whole people. Humanitarianism, the supposed good of the patient, and the advancement of medical science are too often put forth as rationale for treating us as human rats, on the operating table and in the laboratories. The situation is rife with potential for personal violation and injustice.

MEDICINE FOR PROFIT

Monopolized by the American Medical Association, medicine is produced and practiced for profit. Illness is a private problem for which individuals assume private responsibility. Because local, state, and national health care programs are insufficient, because private insurance generally excludes pre-existing conditions and because disabled people are economically disadvantaged, we are generally unable to pursue needed health care — whether real or doctrinal — "independently." Our only choice may be to submit to experimentation. Personal, professional and societal messages about the virtue of health and the disgrace of disease render us a captive audience. If we are not willing to try every new experiment, no matter how slim the chance of cure or survival, we are blamed for wishing to remain impaired, either for opportunistic or masochistic reasons. Grateful for services we suspect we do not fully deserve and cannot justifiably refuse, we are unwittingly led to participate in our own abuse.

Women patients are more likely than men to be medically abused. Our physical and psychological concerns have been ignored, misdiagnosed and invalidated. Our physical symptoms have been treated as products of our imaginations. Psychotropic drugs are commonly prescribed as an all-purpose remedy to discount psychological distress. Vital information has been withheld and reserved for professionals. Disabled women have been medically controlled. Health, like disability, is politically defined by medical, insurance and governmental bureaucracies.

Our identities as patients have developed alongside the eugenics movement and the professionalization of medical science. In addition, education was becoming more specialized and more scientific during the late-nineteenth and early-twentieth centuries. Both medical and educational reforms presumed what the English Poor Laws had decreed — that disabled people are unemployable and, therefore, in need of paternalistic care and governance. Rather than rehabilitating an able-ist society, medical science attempted to cure disabled people and educational reformers sought to correct them. Both of these individual solutions failed miserably, and not without harsh consequences.

CORRECTING THE DISABLED

The obvious solution is a fundamental restructuring of society. Instead, efforts remain focused on correcting *us*. Once medicine has failed, social workers, special educators and rehabilitators are called in to fix what are perceived to be our disabilities. Individual solutions merely mask fundamental causes, if they work at all. Structural impediments to our employability cannot be eradicated by teaching us to type, make brooms, or run a computer. Rehabilitated workers remain largely disabled — underemployed or unemployed.

It would be absurd to deny the importance of literacy and the value of having marketable skills. For disabled people, quality education has long been non-existent, primarily because it was assumed we had no use for it. Educational resources and the efforts of teachers were thought to be wasted on us. The early efforts of doctors, teachers, and philanthropists to solve disability by teaching disabled people to be "productive" demonstrated the futility of education as a solution.

Graduates of late-nineteenth century schools for blind, deaf and mentally retarded students found themselves without jobs and with no way to support themselves. Discouraged by this situation, the residential schools responded by establishing sheltered workshops, generally as an annex to the schools themselves. Broom factories, which employed blind workers, are a classic example. Sheltered workshops paid their employees less than subsistence wages, from which the cost of their room and board was then deducted. Frequently, these charges exceeded earnings and families were required to contribute to the support of workshop employees. When laws were enacted to ban prison workshops, only because of their unfair market competition, sheltered workshops for disabled people were exempted on the grounds that they were charitable institutions.[15] There is nothing charitable about exploiting workers and draining their resources such that many were never able to leave the institutions which profited from their labor. They were effectively enslaved. Those who controlled and incarcerated them argued that they were providing disabled workers with self-esteem and a sense of purpose.

State and private schools discovered teaching and communication methods for those who had previously been presumed uneducable. If some good came out of these schools, however, their results cannot possibly justify their inhumane means. Philanthropists became disillusioned when it was discovered that education did not necessarily facilitate employment or employability. Education was all but abandoned in most of the schools; they became warehouses for society's misfits.

Rehabilitation has recently been given new momentum and, again, has been hailed as the solution to our problems. Laws which seek to protect disabled people from educational and employment discrimination based on our physical or mental differences continue to presuppose our unemployability. Section 504 of the Rehabilitation Act, for example, applies principally to persons who are unable to work *because of a disability*.[16] This is a clear-cut case of biological determinism being used to reform institutionalized disability.

DILEMMA OF DISABLED WOMEN

The dilemma of disabled women is especially poignant. Categorically, women have been significantly "disabled" from participating in skilled industrial, policy making and business spheres of society. Medical and/or psychiatric theories of biological inferiority, sexual dimorphism and hormonally induced "hysteria" have been sought to justify discrimination based on our sex. Domestic work and child rearing, whether [or not] we have worked outside of the home, have been determined to be our natural — instinctual — occupations. Disabled women have been disqualified from domestic and wage work, in a double bind of biological predestination.

We experience institutionalized sexism in special education and rehabilitation programs. Vocational counselors, who have the authority to determine "appropriate" placements *for* us, often channel women into traditional "women's work." If we can type, sew and cook, we are considered rehabilitated. Inadequate education is likely to influence our scores on vocational aptitude tests, disqualifying us from training in non-traditional occupations. A lack of positive role models may influence our awareness of career possibilities for disabled women. Moreover, counselors often deny our own aspirations as impractical or inappropriate because we are women and disabled. Programs which may actually benefit some individual women more often control us.

On the other hand, the eugenics movement continues to shape the domestic life of disabled women. Victorian-era beliefs associating sex for women strictly with procreation have led to our being viewed as asexual. When we are sexual, our sexuality has been viewed as beast-like and in need of paternalistic control. Sex education is popularly thought to be misguided for disabled girls and women. Chastity belts seem to be in more appropriate order, especially since disabled women are regarded as unmarriageable and unfit to be mothers.

Popular notions of feminine beauty manufactured by cosmetic and fashion industries, myths of heredity and the private structure of the nuclear family have limited disabled women's potential for fulfilling traditional role prescriptions. Women who cannot perform an endless array of household and parenting responsibilities "independently" are considered unmarriageable and unfit mothers. Family wages are typically inadequate to hire someone to shop, transport children, cook, launder, clean or provide other consumer services. This privilege is reserved for the elite. If wages were enough to cover the cost of domestic accessibility, wage workers would have to be paid better. This arrangement would certainly be objectionable to employers, who refuse to be concerned with the "private" lives of employees. Disabled women are effectively disqualified to be housewives and mothers.

SUPERFLUOUS PEOPLE

Current social welfare policies continue to place disabled women in a category of superfluous people. If we decide to marry, we may lose a substantial portion of our income. We are discriminated against in employment opportunities, even when it is no more costly and as profitable to employ us. When we are unable to find employment, we are forced to demonstrate to the bureaucracy that we are, in fact, unemployable. "Disincentives" to employment are built into the Social Security Act. Once our earned income has reached the poverty level, we are likely to be ineligible for any services at all.[17] This means that chronically ill women are asked, for example, to choose between having access to food or [to] medical care. Our survival is thus threatened by employment. Able-ism has been built into the system; our poverty has been institutionalized. We cannot escape the clutches of bureaucratic control.

Our survival is also threatened when we do not comply with the demands of law and our administrators. Welfare benefits are intentionally below the minimum wage in order to provide "incentive" to employment. We are relegated to dire poverty but are not expected to be able to subsist on such little income. Social workers know that we "cheat" the system by failing to report "under the table" employment and gifts of money from relatives, both of which would automatically be deducted from our welfare checks. They expect us to find additional means of support; yet, our very survival raises suspicions. Our survival is an act of resistance in a society which would just as soon eliminate us and is also a testament to our resourcefulness. Instead of encouraging our resourcefulness, we are interrogated no less than once a year. For this we are expected to be grateful.

In the wake of the women's liberation and independent living movements, disabled women have been thrown into a myriad of contradictions. Many of us have found satisfying employment, live in accessible communities and homes and participate in reciprocal and rewarding relationships. Our resistance to sexism and able-ism has created better lives for many and increased opportunities for some individuals. Still, far too many of us remain in institutions. Poverty and isolation are far too prevalent in most of our lives. Our different abilities are not appreciated or acknowledged. Reforms in public services are in jeopardy. Funding has been cut and "special" programs have been eliminated. Able-ist oppression has been internalized and has divided us hierarchically against ourselves. We are experiencing a backlash against our collective protest and stand to lose much of what we've gained because we have not fully challenged the institutionalized nature of able-ism.

INCREASED VISIBILITY

As we forge our way into new territories, disabled women have become more visible. Attitudes towards us are changing. Sensationalist television, for example, now features disabled women, but only disabled women who have "overcome their disabilities." We are praised for our "independence" and our refusal to be reduced to our disabilities. With little regard for the fact that we are legally defined as unemployable and that unemployment characterizes most of our lives, women who remain on social welfare programs are now criticized for continued dependence which is beginning to be perceived as a choice. Our collective resistance to systematically generated disability has been undermined. We must refuse to be co-opted by the idea that disabilities are personal shortcomings.

Disabled women have always resisted our no-win societal position. Indeed, the English Poor Laws, educational and medical reforms and recent welfare legislation have come about only because we have demanded them. We have refused to be incarcerated in "schools" and asylums. Able-ist notions that we are pitiable patients and charity cases have been exposed as efforts to keep us isolated, dependent and discounted. Our history is rich with demonstrations, lobbying and petitions. But these have been answered with reforms that disguise and continue the paternalistic suppression against which we have struggled. Our disabled status remains intact, as does the system which gave rise to it.

In essence, disabled women have demanded participation in a political economy which oppresses all workers. A small percent of the population owns most of the wealth and grows wealthier by exploiting employed and unemployed workers. Individualism mystifies the fact that our society is class structured. Ideals of equality and democracy mean that individuals are free to compete against disabled people, women against women and political movements against one another as we compete for too few jobs, for piecemeal gains and for validation of our cause. If we are to actualize our ideals of a true democracy and personal freedom, we must come together as disabled women and form alliances with other systematically disadvantaged groups in order to effect fundamental changes. Finding our own place within the system simply will not be enough.

sus plumas el viento
for my mother, Amalia

Gloria Anzaldúa

Swollen feet
tripping on vines in the heat,
palms thick and green-knuckled,
sweat drying on top of old sweat.
She flicks her tongue over upper lip
where the salt stings her cracked mouth.
Stupid Pepita and her jokes and the men licking
her heels,
but only the field boss,
un bolillo, of course, having any.

    Ayer entre las matas de maíz
    She had stumbled upon them:
    Pepita on her back
    grimacing to the sky,
    the anglo buzzing around her like a mosquito,
    landing on her, digging in, sucking.
    When Pepita came out of the irrigation ditch
    some of the men spit on the ground.

    She listens to Chula singing *corridos*
    making up *los versos* as she
    plants down the rows
    hoes down the rows
    picks down the rows

"sus plumas el viento" by Gloria Anzaldúa is reprinted from *Borderlands/La Frontera: The New Mestiza* by Gloria Anzaldúa (San Francisco: Spinsters/Aunt Lute Books, 1987). Copyright © 1987. Reprinted by permission of Aunt Lute Books (415) 558-8116.

the chorus resounding for acres and acres
Everyone adding a line
the day crawls a little faster.

She pulls ahead
kicking *terremotes;*
el viento sur secándole el sudor
un ruido de alas humming songs in her head.
Que le de sus plumas el viento.
The sound of hummingbird wings
in her ears, *pico de chuparrosas.*

She looks up into the sun's glare,
las chuparrosas de los jardines
¿en dónde están de su mamagrande?
but all she sees is the obsidian wind
cut tassels of blood
from the hummingbird's throat.

She husks corn, hefts watermelons.
Bends all the way, digs out strawberries
half buried in the dirt.
Twelve hours later
roped knots cord her back.

Sudor de sobacos chorriando,
limpia de hierba la siembra
Claws clutching hoe, she tells the
two lead spatulas stirring the sand,
jump into it, *patas,* wallow *en el charco de mierda,*
breathe it in through the soles of your feet.
There was nothing else but surrender.
If she hadn't read all those books
she'd be singing up and down the rows
like the rest.

She stares at her hands
Manos hinchadas, quebradas,
thick and calloused like a man's,
the tracks on her left palm
different from those on the right.
Saca la lima y raspa el azadón

se va a mochar sus manos,
she wants to chop off her hands
cut off her feet
only Indians and *mayates*
have flat feet.

Burlap sack wet around her waist,
stained green from leaves and the smears of worms.
White heat no water no place to pee
the men staring at her ass.

Como una mula,
she shifts 150 pounds of cotton onto her back.
It's either *las labores*
or feet soaking in cold puddles *en bodegas*

cutting   washing   weighing   packaging
broccoli spears carrots cabbages in 12 hours   15
double shift the roar of machines inside her head.
She can always clean shit
out of white folks toilets — the Mexican maid.
You're respected if you can use your head
instead of your back, the women said.
Ay m'ijos, ojalá que hallen trabajo
in air-conditioned offices.

The hoe, she wants to cut off...
She folds wounded birds, her hands
into the nest, her armpits
looks up at the Texas sky.
Si el viento le diera sus plumas.

She vows to get out
of the numbing chill, the 110 degree heat.
If the wind would give her feathers for fingers
she would string words and images together.
Pero el viento sur le tiró su saliva
pa' 'trás en la cara.

She sees the obsidian wind
cut tassels of blood
from the hummingbird's throat.

As it falls
the hummingbird shadow
becomes the navel of the Earth.

bolillo — a derogatory term for Anglos meaning hard crust of loaf of white bread
entre las matas de maíz — between the corn stalks
terremotes — sods
El viento sur secándole el sudor — The south wind drying her sweat
un ruido de alas — a sound of wings
¿En dónde estaban las chuparrosas de los jardines de su mamagrande? — Where were the hummingbirds
   from her grandmother's gardens?
Sudor de sobacos chorriando limpia de hierba la siembra — The sweat dripping from her armpits, she
   weeds the plants.
manos hinchadas, quebradas — swollen, broken hands
mayates — a derogatory term for Blacks
como una mula — like a mule
Ay m'ijos, ojalá que hallen trabajo — Oh my children, I hope you find work
Si el viento le diera sus plumas — If the wind would give her its feathers
Pero el viento le tiró su saliva pa' 'trás en la cara — But the wind threw her spit back in her face.

The Salt of the Earth[*]

Paula Lorraine Roper

I

There has been an abomination of the land and the old folks
creak in "just ain't na'tral" tones
    rocking forth and back
    refusing to sit or stand
    upon the ground
afraid to walk in huddled stance across this season that creeps
with infertile speed over camomile and red sage

mumblin' 'bout "spirits hovering low"
Yea even in the desecrated bowels   of the earth
that refuses
to heave   relieve   conceive
    Bare sounds moan of tools unworthy
    to penetrate
    the neglected garden
    weed infested gash

and
the old folks creak in "just ain't na'tral" tones
suspiciously reluctant to alternate steps
across the silence that will not yield
without the proper rain

[*] Thanks to Beverly Van Patterson for the title and for Glenda Masingale Dalcourt, Gloria Johnson, Gail Whitlow, and women everywhere.

the old men spit in earnest effort
spinning effigies of spittle
easing the dryness of their memories

the old women squat upon
the old corpse
chanting for the blood of their youth
shrouded bridal beds long gone   long ago

the old men's tools are withered
and the young   men with heedless indignation
inch their plows from furrow to furrow
to sowed impotency

knowing only now   that
without the blessing of the moon shower

their hoes are hopeless in opening
the hurt   hard   earth

    Blessed Terra, pray for us
    Blessed Terra, bleed our sins away

bored and burdened
the womb cries and denies

the young men hear   and
hold limp heads in sticky hands
chanting shame-filled ejaculations
for the advent   of   scattered seeds

sanguinary rain ceased
in screech-owled silence
from door to door from house to house
stopped
when

II

She   in arthritic   repulsion
ceased
weaving his dreams
at
Her loom

came down from the cross
recoiled outstretched legs and arms
held head up from chest-pressed
suffocation
        gave up the ghost
        like a cheap bottle of wine
turned Her back
        flexed   arched   removed
Sat up   Stood up
        moving like hinges on
a door unaccustomed to pleasant entry

deceiving the parchedness
with   arrogant   discharge
She thumbs her nose at the   moon

The young men plead
for   the come
        of repentance

The old folks pray   for
the coming of
        a Spring

making Rag sacrifices
to the unforgiving womb...

Refusing to Be "Good Soldiers"
An Agenda for Men

Marvin M. Ellison

In the past two decades, male violence has been the focus of intense debate within the feminist movement. Men have rarely participated in that movement, but their absence is not entirely due to antifeminism. As Bell Hooks observes, some women, especially those who have identified all men as the enemy, have perpetuated a traditional (that is, sexist) sex-role division by assigning to women exclusively the task of "cleaning up the mess" and creating a feminist revolution. At the same time, Hooks rightly acknowledges that all men do support — and benefit from — sexist oppression in one way or another, but even so,

> it is crucial that feminist activists not get bogged down in intensifying our awareness of this fact to the extent that we do not stress the more unemphasized point which is that men can lead life-affirming, meaningful lives without exploiting and oppressing women.[1]

Men, as well as women, are socialized passively to accept sexism as the "natural" order of things and to internalize its ideology and norms as fixed and unalterable. While none of us men in Western culture is more "blameworthy" than another for the sexism we have internalized, each of us must assume responsibility for eliminating sexism and ending our complicity in the oppression of ourselves and others.

Becoming responsible as men does not mean leaning on women to do our political and emotional work for us, nor does it mean taking charge of the feminist movement. Rather, we men have our own work to do in order to reclaim the power to change our lives in more humanizing directions, as we become strong advocates for the well-being of women and children and for their increased empowerment to become the "subjects of their lives."

I suggest three areas for us men to explore together in order to strengthen ourselves for constructive participation in the movement to eliminate violence from our lives: (1) studying our lives as men, especially our sexualities, and reclaiming the centrality of bodily connectedness; (2) breaking our silence about the abuse of male power and supporting *and* confronting one another as we do so; and (3) accounting for the "faith within us" to sustain the struggle for a far different world, one without patriarchal privilege and devoid of the violence that sustains male gender superiority.

What follows is exploratory and suggestive of only a partial agenda, that men will need to delineate and refine together. I address these remarks directly to men because it is our work of which I am speaking, but I trust women will participate in the process as well, if only to continue to hold us accountable for our words and our deeds.

One preliminary observation: patriarchy, the social structure built on male gender privilege and the power of men to control women and less powerful, socially marginalized men, is perpetuated by the acceptance and internalization of its ideology of masculinity. Insofar as men identify and comply with patriarchal ideology, we will seek but also most often exaggerate the power that this system grants to us as men. Although men as a group do have more power than women, the majority of men do not exercise significant personal power in Western society or experience secure control over our own lives. Moreover, no matter how much power the system has given to any one of us, this power is useful only in keeping things going according to present rules and dynamics, not in changing things in any fundamental way. When men deviate from, or actively resist, the status quo, power is taken away from us. Often that resistance is met with punishments, including the loss of job, status, social respectability, and life itself. Gay men, as nonconformists to patriarchy, are the prime illustration of those considered traitors to the "male cause."

The power to change comes not from the patriarchal system but from another source — our ability to connect with ourselves and others and then passionately to forge an alternative possibility. The good news, as Tony Eardley identifies it, is that while "the ideology of masculinity is generalized and pervasive, and molds us all," none of us is simply a passive recipient of it, "any more than all women have accepted their own ideological designation."[2] To own up to the discrepancy between the ideological standard for men and our own lived experience makes possible a way to reinforce our need and our responsibility to make choices that are life-enhancing both for ourselves and for others.

STUDYING OUR LIVES, OUR SEXUALITIES

For us men to study our lives, we need to look carefully at our own experiences and struggles. At the same time, we need to understand how others perceive us and how we and the world we have created are experienced by others, especially by those least powerful and well placed in Western society. Examining our role in that preeminently masculine occupation, war making, is a good place to start.

Training to be a "good soldier" is a process of instilling macho-masculinity, an intensification of the typical male socialization process in which men are trained to be violent, aggressive, controlling, and emotionally detached. Men are socialized to "toughen up" in order to be able to dominate and coerce other people without self-reflection or guilt. Such toughening is necessary so that men will willingly use violence and inflict suffering upon others, as well as tolerate their own pain and risk their own deaths.

Military training involves distancing the self from one's own body, from other people's bodies, and from the emotions. During basic training, a young recruit's insecurity about his own sexuality and manhood is systematically manipulated in order to link sexuality with aggression and domination. Because manhood is a quality to be achieved and, therefore, something that can either be lost or never firmly established, men are threatened with basic insecurity about their own worth in a male system that generates fear, uncertainty, and self-doubt about one's adequacy and ability to "make the grade." To avoid becoming an "unreal man," that is, like a woman or like less powerful men in this culture, men strive desperately to establish their superiority. They prove their fitness to do their duty by assuming control, by violence if necessary, over their own bodies and bodily senses, but also by controlling others and nature itself. As one Vietnam veteran describes his experience in basic training,

> The primary lesson of boot camp, towards which all behavior was shaped, was to seek dominance.... All else was non-masculine.... Recruits were often stunned by the depths of violence erupting within themselves. Only on these occasions of violent outbursts did the drill instructor cease his endless litany of "you dirty faggots" and "Can't hack it little girls?" After a continuous day of harassment, I bit a man on the face during hand-to-hand combat, gashing his eyebrow and cheek. I had lost control. For the first time the drill instructor didn't physically strike me or call me a faggot. He put his arm around me and said that I was a lot more of a man than he had previously imagined. In front of the assembled platoon [he] gleefully reaffirmed my masculinity.[3]

The ideology of war and the ideology of masculinity are intertwined. Both are based on contempt for women and on a corollary fear of homosexuality. Homosexuality is especially fearful because it represents a deviation from and break with the strongest and most familiar social control on sexuality in Western culture, the patriarchal social pattern of compulsory heterosexuality. Heterosexism insists that both men and women conform to stereotypic gender roles and to dominant-subordinate power dynamics. This elaborate social construction of human sexuality is ideologically built on two assumptions: on gender dualism, that there are fundamental differences and an unalterable inequality between men and women, and on gender hierarchy, that male superiority and control over women is natural and good.

According to this heterosexist code, which the military strenuously reinforces, moral legitimacy is granted only to certain configurations of power and only to certain sexual and social relationships. When men are on top, all is well with the patriarchal world. Men remain members of the club especially by avoiding the realm, the tasks, and the concerns of women. Men who do not play their dominant role, either by choice or by accident, are viewed as failed men. They are perceived as homosexuals, whether accurately or not, and like women, that is, without power and status. Winner or loser, on top or on bottom, are the only outcomes available to the patriarchal imagination.

The modern soldier as a "killing machine" bears a striking resemblance to modern patriarchy's other cultural hero, *homo economicus,* the corporate executive who makes a killing in the market or arranges for plant closings without serious regard for the human and social costs involved. Both roles reflect the abstractionism, or remoteness from reality, that is so characteristic of the masculinist ethos. Taught to fear and repress their feelings, especially feelings of pain and vulnerability, men literally lose connection with themselves and others, so that "the man who kills from a distance and without consciousness of the consequences of his deeds feels no need to answer to anyone or to himself."[4]

Disassociation from the body and from the emotions is at the root of this absence of moral sensitivity to the suffering men inflect on ourselves and on others. Since we are connected to ourselves and to the world only in and through our bodies, when we no longer feel and experience our bodily connectedness, we literally lose touch with reality. As men who batter others give ample testimony, those not able to feel their own pain are more likely to inflict pain on others. In the process, they may in fact not know what they are doing or what is being done in their name, a situation also true in war.

How might we deal with this emotional illiteracy and engage in a process to, literally, "come to our senses"? Glenn Gray offers a provocative suggestion that the appeals of war will dissipate only as men experience a radical inner change and emotional reorientation, a process of gaining genuine closeness and intimacy with ourselves, other people, and the natural order. Physical proximity by itself does not guarantee such intimacy, as battered women can certainly attest. Genuine relationship, or deep connectedness, is possible only as we recover intimacy, the embodied capacity to let go of control and experience mutual delight in one another's company.

Deepening awareness of our need and capacity for intimacy in relation to women is critical but not more so than in relation to other men, both those more powerful and those less powerful than ourselves. As Joseph Pleck has rightly observed, "Ultimately, men cannot go any further in relating to women as equals than they have been able to go in relating to other men as equals."[5] Examining issues of intimacy with other men is especially needed, for homophobia and heterosexism teach us that "real men" must exercise power over other men as well as over women and that closeness to other men signals effeminacy and loss of manhood.

For me, the gift of the profeminist men's movement has been the invitation together with other men to explore friendship and take mutual delight in sharing physical touch and gestures of care and nurture. Because patriarchy assigns women to deal with matters of intimacy and emotional nurture, we men have depended almost exclusively on women friends and female lovers to find the personal support and comfort that now we are slowly discovering we can both give to and receive from other men. In honoring our love for other men, we also come to celebrate our love for our own selves. Only in self-acceptance do we find the source of our personal power to live securely in touch with our own value and the value of others.

Regaining intimacy also requires reclaiming the centrality of erotic power in our lives. Embracing the erotic and the sensuous as a source of our knowledge and empowerment goes against the dominant culture's wisdom that men are associated only with the "higher" things of the mind, of the spirit (not body), and of the will's control over the body and over nonrational spontaneity. It also challenges the patriarchal assumption that the passions are tainted and intrinsically corrupt and corrupting. As Audre Lorde argues,

> We have been raised to fear the yes within ourselves, our deepest cravings. . . . When we live outside ourselves, and by that I mean on external directives only, rather than from our internal knowledge and needs, then . . . we conform to the needs of a structure that is not

based on human need, let alone an individual's. But when we begin
to live from within ourselves...then we begin to be responsible to
ourselves in the deepest sense.[6]

Women, first of all, but also gay men are the designated "carriers"
of the erotic in Western culture. The best test of men's willingness to
take the body seriously is how well gay men are respected and listened
to as unique male resources for living passionately and gaining strength,
through bodily intimacy, in the struggle to resist the dynamics of masculinist oppression. Because gay men celebrate love for men's bodies and
refuse to "disincarnate" their own lives by insisting upon the integrity
of body *and* spirit, they embody a wisdom empowering for all men to
honor the erotic as creative life-source as well as the well-spring of desire
to value our own unique identities in relation to others. As we gain trust
in our ability to name ourselves and our needs and to discern what is
genuinely life-giving for us, we also learn to respect and appreciate that
process in others.

In patriarchy, as in capitalism, all self-directed human needs and desires are denied or strenuously frustrated, except those that have been
cultivated to maintain the smooth functioning of the present social order.
Enormous pressure is applied to discount one's own feelings and sen-
sibilities as "merely" subjective and idiosyncratic and to accept external
guides for what is "truly" desirable and worthy of our respect. That so
many men put up with unsatisfying jobs, for example, in exchange for
the dubious reward of being considered a "real man" who earns his own
keep and can rule the roost when he goes home is but one illustration
of how our manly acceptance of "doing our duty" thwarts us from living on the basis of our own deepest desires and needs. When we fear
and ignore the erotic, we also give over our trust and power to external
authorities to know better than ourselves what is life-giving for us.

Whenever we are cut off from the sensuous wisdom of the body and
from the knowledge that our feelings communicate, we lose the much
needed capacity to experience our own pain and joy, as well as losing
a deeply felt sense of connectedness to all that is around us. When we
are deeply in touch with our own desires, vulnerabilities, and passion
for life, we will be less inclined to inflict pain on others, but equally
important, we will also become less willing to tolerate abuse of ourselves. Recovery of body connectedness and of our capacity to give and
receive pleasure, therefore, has direct bearing on the problem of violence
in our culture. As James Nelson comments, there is now considerable
research that shows "close connections between peacefulness and the experience of body pleasure, and between violence and suppression of body

pleasure."[7] Studying our lives and our sexualities in order to increase our ability to experience body pleasure is thus our first work in eliminating violence from our lives.

BREAKING OUR SILENCE ABOUT MALE VIOLENCE

As men we rarely gather to talk about our lives and discuss how we are implicated in violence. When the subject is addressed, my experience has been similar to Tony Eardley's that we men "are often confused, defensive, self-doubting or self-hating and resentful. A challenge to sexual violence may itself produce a violent reaction."[8]

That silence might be explicable if all men were, indeed, rapists or batterers. The fact that only some are does not explain our general reluctance to address the problem of male violence. Another explanation might be that all men feel the guilt and shame of male violence, but as studies regularly indicate, men who are violent against women and children rarely, if ever, experience remorse or contrition. The fact that women, not men, have traditionally been the service providers, relegated to "bind up the wounds" of those who have been violated and abused by others, may account for some of our distancing from these issues, but I have another hunch about our silence and confusion.

As part of a patriarchal society, we men fear isolation and rejection from the company of men. To acknowledge candidly the reality and depth of the problem of male violence requires courage for any man who dares to risk speaking the truth and to hold himself — *and other men* — accountable. Because any departure from the dominant male role, as well as all direct confrontations about the "limits of masculinity," incurs costs for the individual man, speaking out about male violence is likely to generate fear in us of being repudiated by other men as disloyal and "unmanly." Precisely for this reason, I think Sally Gearhart is right to argue that the danger for most women is not the individual man, who may in fact be deeply sympathetic to feminism and engaged in personal resistance to dominant male gender roles. Rather, the danger is "in the phenomenon of male bonding."[9]

Glenn Gray is helpful on the reality of men closing ranks with one another. He notes that in war, "the most potent quieters of conscience are evidently the presence of others who are doing the same things," as well as the awareness that the soldier is acting under orders from those "superior" to himself who will answer for his own conduct.[10] I would add that a more telling possibility is that individual men who abhor violence keep silence for fear of alienating other men or of being themselves subjected to their ridicule and other men's violence.

Two social psychologists, John Sabini and Maury Silver, have examined various research projects about the formation of moral conscience and the capacity of persons to challenge institutional dynamics of injustice and oppression. They argue that "moral drift" occurs when individuals are afraid to speak publicly about their objections to violation and abuse. In one experiment they reviewed, a model prison was set up and staffed by volunteers, each assigned to a role as prisoner or guard. Although many of the "guards" soon displayed acts of brutality toward their "prisoners," some men showed moral sensitivity and refrained from any violence or abuse. These "good guards," however, never spoke out to reproach any of their comrades for their misconduct, and the brutality rapidly escalated unchecked. As Sabini and Silver conclude, "The failure to establish publicly the wrongness of a particular action gives it an implicit legitimacy." Although the public establishment of a moral consensus among men about the limits of acceptable male behavior may not, by itself, restrain or inhibit certain actions, "at the very least, the *failure to condemn* allows those who ignore simple moral requirements to do so more easily."[11]

We men do violence by our silence, as well as with our fists. Men who batter their partners, for example, believe that most men support them. Therefore, it is particularly important for us to communicate, in visible, outspoken ways, that abuse by men is unacceptable behavior and will not receive our endorsement. Moreover, we must model publicly as well as privately our enthusiastic support for the empowerment of women as agents of their own lives and well-being and accept our responsibility to educate and work with other men to change our own masculinist behavior patterns and attitudes. Only when we men passionately and energetically join in a broad-based social-protest movement to critique and challenge male violence will a strong enough shift occur in the prevailing moral climate, which, at present, too easily minimizes or denies these abuses of male power.

One lesson for us is a warning "not to go it alone" but to connect with other men for mutual support and empowerment. Power for change is found in collective, shared power. The lone warrior, even the most courageous moral crusader, is too easily intimidated and isolated or burns out.

A second lesson is this: men who personally reject the use of violence but do not engage in confronting other men remain untrustworthy allies in the struggle. A concern for one's own personal purity and for maintaining one's status as a "good guard" in the midst of brutality does little to alter the conditions which perpetuate the violence. Gay men often experience this phenomenon from "liberal" straight men who are tolerant themselves but who fail to speak out against homophobic acts and speech from their male associates. In fact, even the presence of a few "good guards" helps to legitimate the prison system as good, decent, and reasonable.

Each of us is implicated in the violences that permeate our world. Where systemic injustices prevail, no one has clean hands. Just as in a racist society it is a delusion to regard oneself as nonracist, so in a violent society it is impossible to be totally nonviolent, for the institutions we help to maintain by our silence and conformity do the violence for us. Our struggle as men is to become passionately antiracist, antiviolent, antipatriarchal. Fortunately, as Barbara Smith reminds us, "it is neither possible nor necessary to be morally exempt in order to stand in opposition to oppression."[12] What is necessary is to take a stance of resistance, join with others in that struggle, and hold oneself accountable as to how one's own power affects the lives of others for good or ill.

When men become as vocal and organized as women now are in the movement to end violence, among nation states as well as in the family, a major step will be made toward delegitimating and removing the violences from our own lives.

ACCOUNTING FOR THE FAITH WITHIN US

The struggle to transform ourselves and our world is simultaneously a political and a spiritual process. To believe that a just and nonviolent world is possible requires me to "hope against hope" that my brothers and I may contribute to that transformation, even though violence is deeply entrenched and we face incredible odds. Reclaiming our power to change our lives — and to be changed — is essential to any liberating spirituality. How we name, nurture, and share that power is never a morally neutral or inconsequential matter. The particularities of how we as men experience and articulate our faith will vary, but *what* power we hold as sacred and life-giving needs exploration.

Patriarchal spirituality fosters a quest for transcendence as the highest good, a life beyond vulnerability and dependence on others and an acquisition of absolute control. Allegiance to the male warrior-god sends us scurrying after power-as-domination and in futile search for mastery, for that alienated and alienating power to affect others without being affected ourselves. Small wonder that the "god-*phantasie*" of male supremacy, to use Dorothée Soelle's phrase, is a cold, aloof, and indifferent spectator, who is, literally, "above it all," untouched and untouchable and neither interested in nor affected by human struggles.

To place what is most sacred, valued, and worthy of our loyalty outside the realm of what we see and touch and sense often leads to the abuse and disregard of the integrity of our own bodies, those of others, and of the physical world. By locating what is sacred above and beyond us, we maintain a patriarchal split-consciousness, which allows us to inflict and to suffer pain and violation in pursuit of a transcendent, otherworldly, and unmanifest good beyond ourselves. Violence is often justified in the name of defending such abstractions, including the honor of patriarchy's "Lord God almighty," "Western civilization," and "man's home as his castle." Such abstractions lure us away from the embodied goodness that sustains our lives and only encourage us to distance ourselves from others, as well as from the consequences of our own actions. Those of us who came of age during the Vietnam era experienced the pull of patriarchy toward violence as we struggled against it in order to honor and act upon our deep desire and commitment for peaceful connection with distant people quite different from ourselves. War resistance was as much a spiritual as a political struggle to refuse to become "good soldiers" and to become more powerful lovers of peace and justice.

To honor the flesh-and-blood connections between persons as sacred and inviolate, as well as the web of interrelatedness linking all of life, is to grasp a different experience of transcendence and of the holy. In liberation perspective, transcendence is not a quest for control and mastery but rather the capacity to turn toward the "familiar and evident" and deeply enjoy the pleasure of mutual well-being and at-homeness. That experience, however partial and fragmentary in our lives, affirms that gentleness and power coexist in ways that alone make life worth living. Liberation faith finds its truth in the discovery and enrichment of the "blessed ties" that bind us together with all that is and in the strengthening of genuine solidarity among all peoples. The only spirituality worthy of our devotion is one that cultivates the mutual well-being of bodies and spirits together, ours and all others.

For us men, what faith actually grounds and moves us will be most evident in the actions we are inspired to undertake for our own sake and for the renewal of our world. Not all actions will generate a future for this planet in which life worth living and worth sharing may flourish. Our taking due care to nurture the faith within us and among us will have unavoidable spiritual and, therefore, humanly significant import. With Denise Levertov, may we men be well advised on this score: "Let our different dream, and more than dream, our acts of constructive refusal generate struggle. And love. We must dare to win not wars, but a future in which to live."[13]

PART TWO

THE LAND WE SEEK

Personal Statements

Perpetual Settlement

Cihuatlyotl, Woman Alone

Gloria Anzaldúa

Many years   I have fought off your hands, *Raza*
father mother   church   your rage at my desire to be
with myself,   alone.   I have learned
to erect barricades   arch my back against
you   thrust back fingers, sticks   to
shriek no   to kick and claw   my way out of
your heart   And as I grew   you hacked away
at the pieces   of me   that   were different
attached your tentacles   to my face and breasts
put a lock between my legs.   I had to do it,
Raza,   turn my back on your crookening finger
beckoning   beckoning   your   soft brown
landscape, tender *nopalitos*.   Oh,   it was hard,
Raza   to cleave flesh from flesh   I risked
us both   bleeding to death.   It took   a long
time   but   I learned   to let
your values   roll off   my body   like water
those I swallow to stay alive   become tumors
in my belly.   I refuse   to be taken over   by
things   people   who fear that hollow
aloneness   beckoning   beckoning.   No self,
only race *vecindad familia*.   My soul   has always
been yours   one spark   in the roar of your fire.
We Mexicans are   collective animals.   This I
accept   but my life's work   requires autonomy

"*Cihuatlyotl*, Woman Alone" by Gloria Anzaldúa is reprinted from *Borderlands/La Frontera: The New Mestiza* by Gloria Anzaldúa (San Francisco: Spinsters/Aunt Lute Books, 1987). Copyright © 1987. Reprinted by permission of Aunt Lute Books. (415) 558-8116.

like oxygen.   This lifelong battle has ended,
Raza.   I don't need to flail against   you.
Raza india mexicana norteamericana,   there's nothing more you can chop off   or graft on me that
will change my soul.   I remain who I am, multiple
and one   of the herd, yet not of it.   I walk
on the ground of my own being   browned and
hardened by the ages.   I am fully formed   carved
by the hands of the ancients,   drenched with
the stench of today's headlines.   But my own
hands whittle   the final work   me.

Out of the Depths, O God, We Call to You

WORDS: Ruth C. Duck
MUSIC: Ann MacKenzie

Out of the depths, O God, we call to You.
Wounds of the past remain, affecting all we do.
Grant us the healing light we need so much.
Here in this community, heal us by your touch.

Out of the depths of fear, O God, we speak.
Breaking the silences, your truth and light we seek.
Grant us acceptance, friends who hear, who bear.
Here in this community, hold us in your care.

God of the loving heart, we praise your name.
Dance through our lives and loves; anoint with Spirit flame.
Grant us your presence in flesh'd, familiar face.
Here in this community, heal us by your grace.

"Out of the Depths." Text copyright © by Ruth C. Duck. Music copyright © by Ann MacKenzie.

Out of the Depths, O God, We Call to You

WORDS: Ruth C. Duck
MUSIC: Ann MacKenzie

Out of the depths, O God, we call to You. Wounds of the
Out of the depths of fear, O God, we speak. Break - ing the
God of the lov - ing heart, we praise your name. Dance through our

past re - main, af - fect - ing all we do. Grant us the heal - ing
si - lenc - es, your truth and light we seek. Grant us ac - cept - ance,
lives and loves; a - noint with Spir - it flame. Grant us your pres - ence in

light we need so much. Here in this com - mu - ni - ty, heal us by your touch.
friends who hear, who bear. Here in this com - mu - ni - ty, hold us in your care.
flesh'd, fa - mi - liar face. Here in this com - mu - ni - ty, heal us by your grace.

"Out of the Depths." Text copyright © by Ruth C. Duck. Music copyright © by Ann MacKenzie

La Conciencia de la Mestiza
Toward a New Consciousness

Gloria Anzaldúa

Por la mujer de mi raza
hablará el espíritu.[1]

José Vasconcelos, Mexican philosopher, envisaged *una raza mestiza,*
una mezcla de razas afines, una raza de color — la primera raza síntesis del
globo. He called it a cosmic race, *la raza cósmica,* a fifth race embracing
the four major races of the world.[2] Opposite to the theory of the pure
Aryan, and to the policy of racial purity that white America practices,
his theory is one of inclusivity. At the confluence of two or more genetic
streams, with chromosomes constantly "crossing over," this mixture of
races, rather than resulting in an inferior being, provides hybrid progeny,
a mutable, more malleable species with a rich gene pool. From this racial,
ideological, cultural and biological cross-pollinization, an "alien" consciousness is presently in the making — a new *mestiza* consciousness,
una conciencia de mujer. It is a consciousness of the Borderlands.

UNA LUCHA DE FRONTERAS / A STRUGGLE OF BORDERS

Because I, a *mestiza,*
continually walk out of one culture
and into another,
because I am in all cultures at the same time,
alma entre dos mundos, tres, cuatro,
me zumba la cabeza con lo contradictorio.
Estoy norteada por todas las voces que me hablan
simultáneamente.

"La conciencia de la mestiza: Toward a New Consciousness" by Gloria Anzaldúa is reprinted from
Borderlands/La Frontera: The New Mestiza by Gloria Anzaldúa (San Francisco: Spinsters/Aunt Lute
Books, 1987). Copyright © 1987. Reprinted by permission of Aunt Lute Books. (415) 558-8116.

The ambivalence from the clash of voices results in mental and emotional states of perplexity. Internal strife results in insecurity and indecisiveness. The *mestiza*'s dual or multiple personality is plagued by psychic restlessness.

In a constant state of mental nepantilism, an Aztec word meaning torn between ways, *la mestiza* is a product of the transfer of the cultural and spiritual values of one group to another. Being tricultural, mono-lingual, bilingual, or multilingual, speaking a patois, and in a state of perpetual transition, the *mestiza* faces the dilemma of the mixed breed: which collectivity does the daughter of a darkskinned mother listen to?

El choque de un alma atrapado entre el mundo del espíritu y el mundo de la técnica a veces la deja entullada. Cradled in one culture, sandwiched between two cultures, straddling all three cultures and their value sys-tems, *la mestiza* undergoes a struggle of flesh, a struggle of borders, an inner war. Like all people, we perceive the version of reality that our culture communicates. Like others having or living in more than one culture, we get multiple, often opposing messages. The coming together of two self-consistent but habitually incompatible frames of reference[3] causes *un choque,* a cultural collision.

Within us and within *la cultura chicana,* commonly held beliefs of the white culture attack commonly held beliefs of the Mexican culture, and both attack commonly held beliefs of the indigenous culture. Subcon-sciously, we see an attack on ourselves and our beliefs as a threat and we attempt to block with a counterstance.

But it is not enough to stand on the opposite river bank, shouting questions, challenging patriarchal, white conventions. A counterstance locks one into a duel of oppressor and oppressed; locked in mortal combat, like the cop and the criminal, both are reduced to a com-mon denominator of violence. The counterstance refutes the dominant culture's views and beliefs, and, for this, it is proudly defiant. All re-action is limited by, and dependent on, what it is reacting against. Because the counterstance stems from a problem with authority — outer as well as inner — it's a step toward liberation from cultural domination. But it is not a way of life. At some point, on our way to a new consciousness, we will have to leave the opposite bank, the split between the two mortal combatants somehow healed so that we are on both shores at once and, at once, see through serpent and eagle eyes. Or perhaps we will decide to disengage from the dom-inant culture, write it off altogether as a lost cause, and cross the border into a wholly new and separate territory. Or we might go an-other route. The possibilities are numerous once we decide to act and not react.

A TOLERANCE FOR AMBIGUITY

These numerous possibilities leave *la mestiza* floundering in uncharted seas. In perceiving conflicting information and points of view, she is subjected to a swamping of her psychological borders. She has discovered that she can't hold concepts or ideas in rigid boundaries. The borders and walls that are supposed to keep the undesirable ideas out are entrenched habits and patterns of behavior; these habits and patterns are the enemy within. Rigidity means death. Only by remaining flexible is she able to stretch the psyche horizontally and vertically. *La mestiza* constantly has to shift out of habitual formations; from convergent thinking, analytical reasoning that tends to use rationality to move toward a single goal (a Western mode), to divergent thinking,[4] characterized by movement away from set patterns and goals and toward a more whole perspective, one that includes rather than excludes.

The new *mestiza* copes by developing a tolerance for contradictions, a tolerance for ambiguity. She learns to be an Indian in Mexican culture, to be Mexican from an Anglo point of view. She learns to juggle cultures. She has a plural personality, she operates in a pluralistic mode — nothing is thrust out, the good the bad and the ugly, nothing rejected, nothing abandoned. Not only does she sustain contradictions, she turns the ambivalence into something else.

She can be jarred out of ambivalence by an intense, and often painful, emotional event which inverts or resolves the ambivalence. I'm not sure exactly how. The work takes place underground — subconsciously. It is work that the soul performs. That focal point or fulcrum, that juncture where the *mestiza* stands, is where phenomena tend to collide. It is where the possibility of uniting all that is separate occurs. This assembly is not one where severed or separated pieces merely come together. Nor is it a balancing of opposing powers. In attempting to work out a synthesis, the self has added a third element which is greater than the sum of its severed parts. That third element is a new consciousness — a *mestiza* consciousness — and though it is a source of intense pain, its energy comes from continual creative motion that keeps breaking down the unitary aspect of each new paradigm.

En unas pocas centurias, the future will belong to the *mestiza.* Because the future depends on the breaking down of paradigms, it depends on the straddling of two or more cultures. By creating a new mythos — that is, a change in the way we perceive reality, the way we see ourselves, and the ways we behave — *la mestiza* creates a new consciousness.

The work of *mestiza* consciousness is to break down the subject-object duality that keeps her a prisoner and to show in the flesh and through the images in her work how duality is transcended. The answer to the problem between the white race and the colored, between males and females, lies in healing the split that originates in the very foundation of our lives, our culture, our languages, our thoughts. A massive uprooting of dualistic thinking in the individual and collective consciousness is the beginning of a long struggle, but one that could, in our best hopes, bring us to the end of rape, of violence, of war.

LA ENCRUCIJADA/ THE CROSSROADS

A chicken is being sacrificed
    at a crossroads, a simple mound of earth
    a mud shrine for *Eshu,*
    Yoruba god of indeterminacy,
who blesses her choice of path.
She begins her journey.

Su cuerpo es una bocacalle. La mestiza has gone from being the sacrificial goat to becoming the officiating priestess at the crossroads.

As a *mestiza* I have no country, my homeland cast me out; yet all countries are mine because I am every women's sister or potential lover. (As a lesbian I have no race, my own people disclaim me; but I am all races because there is the queer of me in all races.) I am cultureless because, as a feminist, I challenge the collective cultural/religious male-derived beliefs of Indo-Hispanics and Anglos; yet I am cultured because I am participating in the creation of yet another culture, a new story to explain the world and our participation in it, a new value system with images and symbols that connect us to each other and to the planet. *Soy un amasamiento,* I am an act of kneading, of uniting and joining that not only has produced both a creature of darkness and a creature of light, but also a creature that questions the definitions of light and dark and gives them new meanings.

We are the people who leap in the dark, we are the people on the knees of the gods. In our very flesh, (r)evolution works out the clash of cultures. It makes us crazy constantly, but if the center holds, we've made some kind of evolutionary step forward. *Nuestra alma el trabajo,* the opus, the great alchemical work; spiritual *mestizaje,* a "morphogenesis,"[5] an inevitable unfolding. We have become the quickening serpent movement.

Indigenous like corn, like corn, the *mestiza* is a product of crossbreeding, designed for preservation under a variety of conditions. Like an ear of corn — a female seed-bearing organ — the *mestiza* is tenacious, tightly wrapped in the husks of her culture. Like kernels she clings to the cob; with thick stalks and strong brace roots, she holds tight to the earth — she will survive the crossroads.

Lavando y remojando el maíz en agua de cal, despojando el pellejo. Moliendo, mixteando, amasando, haciendo tortillas de masa.[6] She steeps the corn in lime, it swells, softens. With stone roller on *metate,* she grinds the corn, then grinds again. She kneads and molds the dough, pats the round balls into tortillas.

> We are the porous rock in the stone *metate*
> squatting on the ground.
> We are the rolling pin, *el maíz y agua,*
> *la masa harina. Somos el amasijo.*
> *Somos lo molido en el metate*
> We are the *comal* sizzling hot,
> the hot *tortilla,* the hungry mouth.
> We are the coarse rock.
> We are the grinding motion,
> the mixed potion, *somos el molcajete.*
> We are the pestle, the *comino, ajo, pimienta,*
> We are the *chile colorado,*
> the green shoot that cracks the rock.
> We will abide.

EL CAMINO DE LA MESTIZA / THE MESTIZA WAY

Caught between the sudden contraction, the breath sucked in and the endless space, the brown woman stands still, looks at the sky. She decides to go down, digging her way along the roots of trees. Sifting through the bones, she shakes them to see if there is any marrow in them. Then, touching the dirt to her forehead, to her tongue, she takes a few bones, leaves the rest in their burial place.

She goes through her backpack, keeps her journal and address book, throws away the muni-bart metromaps. The coins are heavy and they go next, then the greenbacks flutter through the air. She keeps her knife, can opener and eyebrow pencil. She puts bones, pieces of bark, *hierbas,* eagle feather, snakeskin, tape recorder, the rattle and drum in her pack and she sets out to become the complete *tolteca.*

Her first step is to take inventory. *Despojando, desgranando, quitando paja.* Just what did she inherit from her ancestors? This weight on her back — which is the baggage from the Indian mother, which the baggage from the Spanish father, which the baggage from the Anglo?

Pero es difícil differentiating between *lo heredado, lo adquirido, lo impuesto*. She puts history through a sieve, winnows out the lies, looks at the forces that we as a race, as women, have been a part of. *Luego bota lo que no vale, los desmientos, los desencuentos, el embrutecimiento. Aguarda el juicio, hondo y enraízado, de la gente antigua*. This step is a conscious rupture with all oppressive traditions of all cultures and religions. She communicates that rupture, documents the struggle. She reinterprets history and, using new symbols, she shapes new myths. She adopts new perspectives toward the darkskinned, women and queers. She strengthens her tolerance (and intolerance) for ambiguity. She is willing to share, to make herself vulnerable to foreign ways of seeing and thinking. She surrenders all notions of safety, of the familiar. Deconstruct, construct. She becomes a *nahual,* able to transform herself into a tree, a coyote, into another person. She learns to transform the small "I" into the total Self. *Se hace moldeadora de su alma. Según la concepción que tiene de sí misma, así será.*

QUE NO SE NOS OLVIDE LOS HOMBRES

"Tú no sirves pa' nada —
you're good for nothing.
Eres pura vieja."

"You're nothing but a woman" means you are defective. Its opposite is to be *un macho*. The modern meaning of the word "machismo," as well as the concept, is actually an Anglo invention. For men like my father, being "macho" meant being strong enough to protect and support my mother and us, yet being able to show love. Today's macho has doubts about his ability to feed and protect his family. His "machismo" is an adaptation to oppression and poverty and low self-esteem. It is the result of hierarchical male dominance. The Anglo, feeling inadequate and inferior and powerless, displaces or transfers these feelings to the Chicano by shaming him. In the Gringo world, the Chicano suffers from excessive humility and self-effacement, shame of self and self-deprecation. Around Latinos he suffers from a sense of language inadequacy and its accompanying discomfort; with Native Americans he suffers from a racial amnesia which ignores our common blood, and from guilt because the Spanish part of him took their land and oppressed them. He has an excessive compensatory hubris when around Mexicans from the other side. It overlays a deep sense of racial shame.

The loss of a sense of dignity and respect in the macho breeds a false machismo which leads him to put down women and even to brutalize them. Coexisting with his sexist behavior is a love for the mother which takes precedence over that of all others. Devoted son, macho pig. To wash down the shame of his acts, of his very being, and to handle the brute in the mirror, he takes to the bottle, the snort, the needle, and the fist.

Though we "understand" the root causes of male hatred and fear, and the subsequent wounding of women, we do not excuse, we do not condone, and we will no longer put up with it. From the men of our race, we demand the admission/acknowledgment/disclosure/testimony that they wound us, violate us, are afraid of us and of our power. We need them to say they will begin to eliminate their hurtful put-down ways. But more than the words, we demand acts. We say to them: We will develop equal power with you and those who have shamed us.

It is imperative that *mestizas* support each other in changing the sexist elements in the Mexican-Indian culture. As long as woman is put down, the Indian and the Black in all of us is put down. The struggle of the *mestiza* is above all a feminist one. As long as *los hombres* think they have to *chingar mujeres* and each other to be men, as long as men are taught that they are superior and therefore culturally favored over *la mujer*, as long as to be a *vieja* is a thing of derision, there can be no real healing of our psyches. We're halfway there — we have such love of the Mother, the good mother. The first step is to unlearn the *puta/virgen* dichotomy and to see *Coatlapopeuh-Coatlicue* in the Mother, *Guadalupe*.

Tenderness, a sign of vulnerability, is so feared that it is showered on women with verbal abuse and blows. Men, even more than women, are fettered to gender roles. Women at least have had the guts to break out of bondage. Only gay men have had the courage to expose themselves to the woman inside them and to challenge the current masculinity. I've encountered a few scattered and isolated gentle straight men, the beginnings of a new breed, but they are confused, and entangled with sexist behaviors that they have not been able to eradicate. We need a new masculinity and the new man needs a movement.

Lumping the males who deviate from the general norm with man, the oppressor, is a gross injustice. *Asombra pensar que nos hemos quedado en ese pozo oscuro donde el mundo encierra a las lesbianas. Asombra pensar que hemos, como feministas y lesbianas, cerrado nuestros corazones a los hombres, a nuestros hermanos los jotos, desheredados y marginales como nosotros.* Being the supreme crossers of cultures, homosexuals have strong bonds with the queer white, Black, Asian, Native American, Latino, and with the queer in Italy, Australia and the rest of the planet. We come from all colors, all classes, all races, all time periods. Our role is to link people with each other — the Blacks with Jews with Indians with Asians with whites with extraterrestrials. It is to transfer ideas and information from

one culture to another. Colored homosexuals have more knowledge of
other cultures; have always been at the forefront (although sometimes
in the closet) of all liberation struggles in this country; have suffered
more injustices and have survived them despite all odds. Chicanos need
to acknowledge the political and artistic contributions of their queer.
People, listen to what your *jotería* is saying.

The *mestizo* and the queer exist at this time and point on the evolutionary continuum for a purpose. We are a blending that proves that
all blood is intricately woven together, and that we are spawned out of
similar souls.

SOMOS UNA GENTE

Hay tantísimas fronteras
que dividen a la gente,
pero por cada frontera
existe también un puente.

— Gina Valdés[7]

...Many women and men of color do not want to have any dealings
with white people. It takes too much time and energy to explain to the
downwardly mobile, white middle-class women that it's okay for us to
want to own "possessions," never having had any nice furniture on our
dirt floors or "luxuries" like washing machines. Many feel that whites
should help their own people rid themselves of race hatred and fear first.
I, for one, choose to use some of my energy to serve as mediator. I
think we need to allow whites to be our allies. Through our literature,
art, *corridos,* and folktales we must share our history with them so when
they set up committees to help Big Mountain Navajos or the Chicano
farmworkers or *los Nicaragüenses* they won't turn people away because
of their racial fears and ignorances. They will come to see that they are
not helping us but following our lead.

Individually, but also as a racial entity, we need to voice our needs. We
need to say to white society: We need you to accept the fact that Chicanos
are different, to acknowledge your rejection and negation of us. We need
you to own the fact that you looked upon us as less than human, that
you stole our lands, our personhood, our self-respect. We need you to
make public restitution: to say that, to compensate for your own sense
of defectiveness, you strive for power over us, you erase our history and
our experience because it makes you feel guilty — you'd rather forget
your brutish acts. To say you've split yourself from minority groups, that
you disown us, that your dual consciousness splits off parts of yourself,
transferring the "negative" parts onto us. (Where there is persecution
of minorities, there is shadow projection. Where there is violence and

war, there is repression of shadow.) To say that you are afraid of us, that to put distance between us, you wear the mask of contempt. Admit that Mexico is your double, that she exists in the shadow of this country, that we are irrevocably tied to her. Gringo, accept the doppleganger in your psyche. By taking back your collective shadow the intracultural split will heal. And finally, tell us what you need from us.

BY YOUR TRUE FACES WE WILL KNOW YOU

I am visible — see this Indian face — and yet I am invisible. I both blind them with my beak nose and am their blind spot. But I exist, we exist. They'd like to think I have melted in the pot. But I haven't, we haven't.

The dominant white culture is killing us slowly with its ignorance. By taking away our self-determination, it has made us weak and empty. As a people we have resisted and we have taken expedient positions, but we have never been allowed to develop unencumbered — we have never been allowed to be fully ourselves. The whites in power want us people of color to barricade ourselves behind our separate tribal walls so they can pick us off one at a time with their hidden weapons; so they can whitewash and distort history. Ignorance splits people, creates prejudices. A misinformed people is a subjugated people.

Before the Chicano and the undocumented worker and the Mexican from the other side can come together, before the Chicano can have unity with Native Americans and other groups, we need to know the history of their struggle and they need to know ours. Our mothers, our sisters and brothers, the guys who hang out on street corners, the children in the playgrounds, each of us must know our Indian lineage, our afro-*mestizaje,* our history of resistance.

To the immigrant *mexicano* and the recent arrivals we must teach our history. The 80 million *mexicanos* and the Latinos from Central and South America must know of our struggles. Each one of us must know basic facts about Nicaragua, Chile and the rest of Latin America. The Latinoist movement (Chicanos, Puerto Ricans, Cubans and other Spanish-speaking people working together to combat racial discrimination in the market place) is good but it is not enough. Other than a common culture we will have nothing to hold us together. We need to meet on a broader communal ground.

The struggle is inner: Chicano, *indio,* American Indian, *mojado, mexicano,* immigrant Latino, Anglo in power, working class Anglo, Black, Asian — our psyches resemble the bordertowns and are populated by the same people. The struggle has always been inner, and is played

out in the outer terrains. Awareness of our situation must come before
inner changes, which in turn come before changes in society. Nothing
happens in the "real" world unless it first happens in the images in
our heads.

EL DÍA DE LA CHICANA

I will not be shamed again
Nor will I shame myself.

I am possessed by a vision: that we Chicanas and Chicanos have taken
back or uncovered our true faces, our dignity and self-respect. It's a
validation vision.

Seeing the Chicana anew in light of her history, I seek an exoneration,
a seeing through the fictions of white supremacy, a seeing of ourselves
in our true guises and not as the false racial personality that has been
given to us and that we have given to ourselves. I seek our woman's
face, our true features, the positive and the negative seen clearly, free of
the tainted biases of male dominance. I seek new images of identity, new
beliefs about ourselves, our humanity and worth no longer in question.

*Estamos viviendo en la noche de la Raza, un tiempo cuando el trabajo se
hace a lo quieto, en el oscuro. El día cuando aceptamos tal y como somos y
para en donde vamos y porque — ese día será el día de la Raza. Yo tengo
el compromiso de expresar mi visión, mi sensibilidad, mi percepción de la
revalidación de la gente mexicana, su mérito, estimación, honra, aprecio,
y validez.*

On December 2nd when my sun goes into my first house, I celebrate
el día de la Chicana y el Chicano. On that day I clean my altars, light
my *Coatlapopeuh* candle, burn sage and copal, take *el baño para espan-
tar basura,* sweep my house. On that day I bare my soul, make myself
vulnerable to friends and family by expressing my feelings. On that day
I affirm who we are.

On that day I look inside our conflicts and our basic introverted racial
temperament. I identify our needs, voice them. I acknowledge that the
self and the race have been wounded. I recognize the need to take care
of our personhood, of our racial self. On that day I gather the splintered
and disowned parts of *la gente mexicana* and hold them in my arms.
Todas las partes de nosotros valen.

On that day I say, "Yes, all you people wound us when you reject us.
Rejection strips us of self-worth; our vulnerability exposes us to shame.
It is our innate identity you find wanting. We are ashamed that we need

your good opinion, that we need your acceptance. We can no longer cam-
ouflage our needs, can no longer let defenses and fences sprout around
us. We can no longer withdraw. To rage and look upon you with contempt is to rage and be contemptuous of ourselves. We can no longer
blame you, nor disown the white parts, the male parts, the pathological
parts, the queer parts, the vulnerable parts. Here we are weaponless with
open arms, with only our magic. Let's try it our way, the *mestiza* way,
the Chicana way, the woman way."

On that day, I search for our essential dignity as a people, a people
with a sense of purpose — to belong and contribute to something greater
than our *pueblo*. On that day I seek to recover and reshape my spiritual
identity. *¡Animate! Raza, a celebrar el día de la Chicana.*

EL RETORNO

All movements are accomplished in six stages,
And the seventh brings return.
— *I Ching*[8]

Tanto tiempo sin verte casa mía,
mi cuna, mi hondo nido de la huerta.
— "Soledad"[9]

I stand at the river, watch the curving twisting serpent, a serpent nailed
to the fence where the mouth of the Rio Grande empties into the Gulf.

I have come back. *Tanto dolor me costó el alejamiento.* I shade my eyes
and look up. The bone beak of a hawk slowly circling over me, checking
me out as potential carrion. In its wake a little bird flickering its wings,
swimming sporadically like a fish. In the distance the expressway and
the slough of traffic like an irritated sow. The sudden pull in my gut, *la
tierra, los aguaceros.* My land, *el viento soplando la arena, el lagartijo debajo
de un nopalito. Me acuerdo como era antes. Una región desértica de vasta
llanuras, costeras de baja altura, de escasa lluvia, de chaparrales formados
por mesquites y huizaches.* If I look real hard I can almost see the Spanish
fathers who were called "the cavalry of Christ" enter this valley riding
their burros, see the clash of cultures commence.

Tierra natal. This is home, the small towns in the Valley, *los pueblitos*
with chicken pens and goats picketed to mesquite shrubs. *En las colonias*
on the other side of the tracks, junk cars line the front yards of hot
pink and lavender-trimmed houses — Chicano architecture we call it,
self-consciously. I have missed the TV shows where hosts speak in half
and half, and where awards are given in the category of Tex-Mex music. I
have missed the Mexican cemeteries blooming with artificial flowers, the
fields of aloe vera and red pepper, rows of sugar cane, of corn hanging

on the stalks, the cloud of *polvareda* in the dirt roads behind a speeding
pickup truck, *el sabor de tamales de rez y venado*. I have missed *la yegua
colorada* gnawing the wooden gate of her stall, the smell of horse flesh
from Carito's corrals. *He hecho menos las noches calientes sin aire, noches
de linternas y lechuzas* making holes in the night.

I still feel the old despair when I look at the unpainted, dilapidated,
scrap lumber houses consisting mostly of corrugated aluminum. Some
of the poorest people in the U.S. live in the Lower Rio Grande Valley, an
arid and semi-arid land of irrigated farming, intense sunlight and heat,
citrus groves next to chaparral and cactus. I walk through the elementary
school I attended so long ago, that remained segregated until recently. I
remember how the white teachers used to punish us for being Mexican.
How I love this tragic valley of South Texas, as Ricardo Sánchez calls
it; this borderland between the Nueces and the Rio Grande. This land
has survived possession and ill-use by five countries: Spain, Mexico, the
Republic of Texas, the U.S., the Confederacy, and the U.S. again. It has
survived Anglo-Mexican blood feuds, lynchings, burnings, rapes, pillage.
Today I see the Valley still struggling to survive. Whether it does
or not, it will never be as I remember it. The borderlands depression
that was set off by the 1982 peso devaluation in Mexico resulted in
the closure of hundreds of Valley businesses. Many people lost their
homes, cars, land. Prior to 1982, U.S. store owners thrived on retail
sales to Mexicans who came across the border for groceries and clothes
and appliances. While goods on the U.S. side have become 10, 100,
1000 times more expensive for Mexican buyers, goods on the Mexican
side have become 10, 100, 1000 times cheaper for Americans. Because
the Valley is heavily dependent on agriculture and Mexican retail trade,
it has the highest unemployment rates along the entire border region; it
is the Valley that has been hardest hit.[10]

"It's been a bad year for corn," my brother, Nune, says. As he talks,
I remember my father scanning the sky for a rain that would end the
drought, looking up into the sky, day after day, while the corn withered
on its stalk. My father has been dead for 29 years, having worked himself
to death. The life span of a Mexican farm laborer is 56 — he lived to be
38. It shocks me that I am older than he. I, too, search the sky for rain.
Like the ancients, I worship the rain god and the maize goddess, but
unlike my father I have recovered their names. Now for rain (irrigation)
one offers not a sacrifice of blood, but of money.
"Farming is in a bad way," my brother says. "Two to three thousand
small and big farmers went bankrupt in this country last year. Six years

ago the price of corn was $8.00 per hundred pounds," he goes on. "This year it is $3.90 per hundred pounds." And, I think to myself, after taking inflation into account, not planting anything puts you ahead.

I walk out to the back yard, stare at *los rosales de mamá*. She wants me to help her prune the rose bushes, dig out the carpet grass that is choking them. *Mamagrande Ramona también tenía rosales*. Here every Mexican grows flowers. If they don't have a piece of dirt, they use car tires, jars, cans, shoe boxes. Roses are the Mexican's favorite flower. I think, how symbolic — thorns and all.

Yes, the Chicano and Chicana have always taken care of growing things and the land. Again I see the four of us kids getting off the school bus, changing into our work clothes, walking into the field with Papí and Mamí, all six of us bending to the ground. Below our feet, under the earth lie the watermelon seeds. We cover them with paper plates, putting *terremotes* on top of the plates to keep them from being blown away by the wind. The paper plates keep the freeze away. Next day or the next, we remove the plates, bare the tiny green shoots to the elements. They survive and grow, give fruit hundreds of times the size of the seed. We water them and hoe them. We harvest them. The vines dry, rot, are plowed under. Growth, death, decay, birth. The soil prepared again and again, impregnated, worked on. A constant changing of forms, *renacimientos de la tierra madre*.

> This land was Mexican once
>   was Indian always
>   and is.
>   And will be again.

Stealing the Thunder
Future Visions for American Indian Women, Tribes, and Literary Studies

Paula Gunn Allen

Strange things begin to happen when the focus in American Indian literary studies is shifted from a male to a female axis. One of the major results of the shift is that the materials become centered on continuance rather than on extinction. This is true for both traditional tribal literatures and contemporary poetry, fiction, and other writings such as autobiography, journals, "as-told-to" narratives, and mixed-genre works. The shift from pessimism to optimism, from despair to hope, is so dramatic that one wonders if the focus on male traditions and history that has characterized the whole field of American Indian literature and lore was not part of the plot to exterminate Native American tribal peoples and cultures and to extinguish their aboriginal title to land, resources, and moral primacy of the Americas.

Of course, plots or conspiracies do not characterize American politics or scholarship, as we all know. But popular ideas about American Indians — warriors, chiefs, colorful befeathered veterans of the wars of progress, colonialism, imperialism, or whatever one wants to call it, brave noble, dying but brave braves — hauntingly pervade the American mind, and behind them lurks the image of the hostile, bloodthirsty savage, the redskin who howls out of the wilderness intent on the total destruction of innocent Christian families trying to build a nation founded in liberty, justice, and moral truth.

"Stealing the Thunder: Future Visions for American Indian Women, Tribes and Literary Studies" by Paula Gunn Allen is reprinted from *The Sacred Hoop: Recovering the Feminine in American Indian Traditions* by Paula Gunn Allen (Boston: Beacon Press, 1986). Copyright © 1986 by Paula Gunn Allen. Reprinted by permission of Beacon Press.

THE SHIFT FROM HE TO SHE*

However he is viewed — sympathetically or with suspicion and terror — the Indian is always *he*. Certainly *she* never rides tall and noble in the saddle, face framed in savage splendor with plundered feathers of great fighting birds. *She* never parlays in powwow council with the white man, offering the peace pipe/calumet to the gods, asking that the proceedings be blessed by heathen powers. *She* never dies at Sand Creek or Wounded Knee. *She* is not the old shaman who gives advice to the young and sends them to the mountains to find their vision; *she* does not have the visions that tell of a nation's destruction. *She* does not stand on the top of a bluff weeping for the broken hoop of the nation. *She* is not revered in the memory of Americans as shaman, warrior-chief, peacemaker.

In the annals of American Indian literary lore there has been no female Red Cloud, Sealth, Logan, Black Elk, Lame Deer, or Rolling Thunder to bear literary witness to the shamanistic traditions of American Indians; there has been no female Sitting Bull, no Crazy Horse, no Handsome Lake, no Wovoka, no Sweet Medicine. And because there have been no great and noble women in that essentially literary cultural memory called tradition, there is no sense of the part that women have played in tribal life either in the past or today.

But let us suppose that among the true heroes were and are many women. Suppose the names of Molly Brant, Magnus, Pocahontas, Sacagawea, Malinalli, Nancy Ward, Sara Winnemucca, and scores of others were the names that came to mind when we thought of the noble and sacred past of the tribes. Suppose that when we heard the tribal deities referred to we thought of Thought Woman, Sky Woman, Cihuacoatl, Selu — that theirs was the name of god, the Great Spirit. Let us for a moment imagine that all the great deeds and noble philosophies, all the earth-centeredness, egalitarianism, medicine systems of sacred power, all the life ways and values of the Native Americans from the northern barrens to Tierra del Fuego, are woman-inspired and woman-maintained. Let us imagine this truth and see how it affects our understanding of American Indian literature. Enabling Americans to imagine, to recognize, and to acknowledge that truth is what my scholarly and creative work has been about for almost fifteen years, and the implications of that shift in perception are at least as exciting as the second coming would be.

---

* Heads added.

A GYNOCRATIC CONTEXT

What I have done, am doing — putting women at the center of the tribal universe — is not particularly revolutionary, though it has entailed groping around in a false dark created by the massive revisionism of tribal life and thought that characterizes American literary scholarship in the field, a revisionism that has trickled down into tribal attitudes and thought and therefore into what the tribes have preserved in their oral traditions. But I am from a gynocratic tribal society, and so I have been aided by my background in locating material that points to the truth about the nature of the tribes prior to Anglo-European invasion and conquest.

My tribe, the Keres Pueblo Indians of the Southwest, put women at the center of their society long ago. Of course, they don't say *they* did it, they say *She* did it. That She is Thought, Memory, Instinct, Tradition, and Medicine or Sacred Power; that She is ritual, ceremony, food, and shelter; that She is the ways by which these are developed — the bringer of them and the teacher of them and the creator of them. Where I come from, the people believe traditionally that nothing can happen that She does not think into being, and because they believe this they say that the Woman is the Supreme Being, the Great Spirit, the Great Mystery, the All-Being. This WomanGod, Thought/Thinking Woman they call Spider Grandmother, acknowledging her potency as creator, as Dream/Vision being, as She Who Weaves existence on all material and supermaterial planes into being.

This is not extraliterary material I am discussing; it is the heart of the literary impulse. For literature comes out of tradition, and traditionally in the gynocratic tribal world, woman is at the center of existence. That means that for writers such as Leslie Marmon Silko, Carol Lee Sanchez, Paula Gunn Allen, Simon J. Ortiz, N. Scott Momaday, Janet Campbell Hale, D'Arcy McNickle, James Welch, Beth Brant, Joy Harjo, Linda Hogan, Wendy Rose, Maurice Kenny, Elizabeth Cook-Lynn, Diane Burns, Gerald Vizenor, Geary Hobsen, nila northSun, Mary TallMountain, Ray Young Bear, and many more, the centrality of the feminine power of universal being is crucial to their work and to the study and teaching of it.

THE EFFECTS OF GYNOCRACY ON THE STUDY OF AMERICAN INDIANS

These writers are not all Keres, though the first four named are, but they are all Indians. Many of them come from clearly woman-centered, or gynocratic, tribal societies, and others, those who hail from northern or southern Plains tribes or northern Algonkian tribes, have powerful female deities and female-centered social and spiritual structures. As we move into the 1990s and my lone voice is joined by the growing multitude of women's voices across the country and within the profession of writing and of literary scholarship, the facts of tribal gynocracy, or powerful woman-focused traditions, will [have] impact more and more decisively on the study and teaching of American Indian literature as well as on other areas of American Indian life.

The impact will develop along the following lines:

- Women writers will have more and more accessibility to female traditions from which to write and think and will be more greatly empowered to use these resources. In turn this increase in woman-focused literature will generate growing understanding of the real nature of pre-Columbian tribal life. The idea of Indian in the contemporary public mind will shift from warrior/brave/hunter/chief to grandmother/mother/Peacemaker/farmer. It also means that central "Indian" symbols such as feathers, wampum, war bonnets, war paint, bows and arrows, and tomahawks will be replaced by corn meal and corn pollen, corn mothers, metates, grinding stones, hoes, plows, pottery and basket designs, and the like, and the understanding of the tribal traditions as warrior-oriented will shift to an understanding of them as peace-oriented. For the tribes were largely peaceful, and peace was upheld by the presence of powerful women shamans and women's councils. That all housing, most food production and preparation, most medicine, and ritual was and is done by or through the empowering agency of women and that the tribes as a whole never viewed women as objects of scorn or contempt, fit only to bear burdens and do all the work, will become common knowledge. The emphasis on "special" beings like sachems, "priests," and chiefs will shift to an emphasis on the whole of the tribe, the whole of the tribal cosmos — for such was and is the focus of traditional American Indian life and such was the basis of gynocracy and tribal belief in the prowess of women.

- Male writers will not be able to simply "plug into" existing popular notions about Indians but will be forced to write and think more creatively, more accurately, and more honestly about their tribes, their lives, and their histories.

- Critics who are interested in either traditional or contemporary American Indian literature will have to dig more deeply into existing materials on Indian women to be able to illuminate the works they hope to explicate or teach. In the process, they will locate "lost," buried, and hidden materials about women in tribal traditions, providing an ever-widening pool of lore and symbols for writers to draw upon.

- At the very least, critical understanding of the cultural traditions of American Indians will shift rather smartly as a result of the shift from a male to female focus in tribal America. This by itself will result in a net gain for the Indian people because as long as they are seen as braves and warriors the fiction that they were conquered in a fair and just war will be upheld. It is in the interest of the United States — along with the other political entities in the western hemisphere — to maintain that foolish and tragic deception, and thus the focus has long been on Indian as noble or savage warrior who, as it happens, lost the war to superior military competence. The truth is more compelling: the tribes did not fight off the invaders to any great extent. Generally they gave way to them; generally they fed and clothed and doctored them; generally they shared their knowledge about everything from how to plant corn and tobacco to how to treat polio victims to how to cross the continent with them. Generally Chief Joseph, Sitting Bull, Crazy Horse, and the rest are historical anomalies. Generally, according to D'Arcy McNickle, the Indian historian, anthropologist, and novelist, at least 70 percent of the tribes were pacifist, and the tribes that lived in peacefulness as a way of life were always woman-centered, always gynecentric, always agricultural, always "sedentary," and always the children of egalitarian, peace-minded, ritual, and dream/vision-centered female gods. The people conquered in the invasion of the Americas by Europe were woman-focused people.

- All the interpretations and conclusions [of] scholars in the fields of folklore, ethnology, and contemporary literary studies will have to be altered, all the evidence reexamined, and all the materials chosen for exemplification of tribal life — which at present reveal more about academic male bias than about the traditions and peoples they purport to depict — will have to be redone. This is because the shift in focus from a male to a female axis recontextualizes the entire field.

For clarity here I must note that literary studies in the field of American Indian studies [are] not purely literary in the sense that the discipline is pursued in the west. We critics of Indian literature must be cultural, historical, and political as well as literary scholars because neither traditional peoples (and their literatures) nor contemporary poets and writers can write outside a cultural, historical, and political context. Factual contextualization of the tribal and contemporary literary materials of Indian people is central to the pursuit of literary studies in the field, and when a critic such as myself — or a poet and writer such as myself and scores of others — moves the focus from male to female traditions, recontextualizing the materials on and about American Indian life and thought, the huge changes I have described necessarily must occur in the whole field.

- Finally, the most important implication of the shift in focus is the one with which I began these essays: the traditions of the women have, since time immemorial, been centered on continuance, just as those of the men have been centered on transitoriness. The most frequently occurring male themes and symbols from the oral tradition have been feathers, smoke, lightning bolts (sheet lightning is female), risk, and wandering. These symbols are all related in some way to the idea of the transitoriness of life and its wonders. The Kiowa death song (a male tradition that was widespread among Plains tribes) says, "I die, but you live forever; beautiful Earth, you alone remain; wonderful Earth, you remain forever," telling the difference in the two traditions, male and female.

FROM THE TRANSITORY TO THE ENDURING

The male principle is transitory; it dies and is reconstituted. The female principle, which is immanent in hard substances (like the earth, minerals, crystals, and stones), wood, and water, is permanent; it remains. Male is breath, air, wind, and projectile point; female controls, creates, and "owns" breath, air and wind, bird and feather, and the hard substance from which the projectile point is shaped. Female is earth, sun, moon, sky, water in its multitudinous forms and its ever-generating cycle, corn, mother of the deer, mother of the gods, bringer of fire and light, and fire itself (which is why the women are its keepers among many if not most groups). He is what comes and goes, she is what continues, what stays.

When we shift our attention from the male, the transitory, to the female, the enduring, we realize that the Indians are not doomed to extinction but rather are fated to endure. What a redemptive, empowering realization that is! As the Cheyenne long have insisted, no people is broken until the heart of its women is on the ground. Then they are broken. Then will they die.

The plot that we all know doesn't exist has been contrived to convince Indians and everyone else that Indians are doomed to extinction, to throw to the ground every woman's heart. It has been carried out by the simple process of subjecting our cultures, lives, traditions, rituals, philosophies, and customs to Christian patriarchal scrutiny, seeing only the male in them, putting male bias into systems that never had it, interpreting rituals, customs, philosophies, and attitudes in male-biased terms and generally creating out of whole cloth the present male-dominating view about the tribes and their significance.

Women's rituals, ceremonies, traditions, customs, attitudes, values, activities, philosophies, ceremonial and social positions, histories, medicine societies, and shamanistic identities — that is, all the oral tradition that is in every sense and on every level the literature of the tribes — have been largely ignored by folklorists, ethnographers, and literary critics in the field of American Indian studies. These traditions have *never* been described or examined in terms of their proper, that is, woman-focused context. Actually, it is primarily the context that has been ignored — vanished, disappeared, buried under tons of scholarly materials selected and erected to hide the centrality of women in tribal society, tribal literature, and tribal hearts and minds. The data [have] been studiously recorded, then filed. Sometimes it surfaces in print, distorted almost out of recognition by the wholesale revision of the context in which it occurs. In the Keres way, context is female and it is God, because it is the source and generator of meaning. A vanished context is the same as a meaningless pile of data, and it is the same as a vanished source of meaning, a vanished God. Destroying the context parallels the destruction of women; in this case it also parallels the destruction of a race. It amounts to Deicide.

In this way the hearts of the women have been forced to the ground because the power of imagination, of image, which is the fundamental power of literature, is the power to determine a people's fate. By the simple expedient of shifting the view back to its original and rightful position, the whole picture changes, and it becomes clear that our heart is in the sky. We understand that woman is the sun and the earth: she is grandmother; she is mother; she is Thought, Wisdom, Dream, Reason, Tradition, Memory, Deity, and Life itself. *Nos Vemos*.

Sexual Being:
Burden and Possibility
A Feminist Reflection on Sexual Ethics

Eleanor H. Haney

In this essay, I wish to outline a normative, feminist* sexual ethic. The essay proceeds in four steps — an introduction to what I mean by "feminist," a summary of the dominant sexual ethic and the way it has been shaped by Christian themes, a feminist vision of sexuality, and a normative feminist approach to issues of sexuality.

A FEMINIST FRAMEWORK

I write as a white professional woman deeply committed to feminism. That commitment means for me being pro-woman. This is the heart of feminism, its core — loving and celebrating women, grieving over our pain and terror, raging against the violence done to us, naming clearly the "structures of enemyhood" that divide us, tracing the webs that connect us to one another and to all other being, and living toward a vision of friendship and sufficiency. It means being pro-me, — valuing my experiences and wisdom, celebrating and caring for myself, drawing on the resources of my life in shaping an ethic, and taking responsibility for naming myself as an authority in matters of theology and ethics.

That commitment includes accepting the limits of my experiences and of the scars and distortions and inaccurate biases I bring to my action and reflection. It demands naming and struggling to overcome the ways I am privileged by, and profit from, the oppressions I seek to transform and the ways I internalize them.

---

* *Feminist* is the word that has meaning for me. Many women of color prefer *womanist,* a word that emerges out of experiences and a heritage somewhat different from mine. Some men use *pro-feminist* or some other term. Each way of naming ourselves will shade somewhat differently the material that follows.

"Sexual Being: Burden and Possibility" by Eleanor H. Haney is reprinted in a different form in *Vision and Struggle: Meditations on Feminist Spirituality and Politics* (Portland: Astarte Shell Press, 1990).

Commitment to feminism includes understanding women's lives in the context of a range of oppressions. We are pressed down and the life squeezed out of us. We are cheap labor; on our backs others have made fortunes. Working two and three jobs, caring for everyone else, living in worry and fear, we are beaten down and crushed. Our talents and strengths have been ignored; we have been channeled into subordinate, controlled, routine areas of society or made into instruments to sell cars, liquor, furs, perfumes, and sex.

We have been beaten and raped and killed. We have seen our children, family, and friends fed into cannons, gas chambers, slavery, and drugs. Genocide and the possibility of our own death through violence drum through our lives and are momentarily transcended in our ceremonies and ecstasies.

We have been trivialized and scorned — expected to hold the human fabric of society together through homemaking and volunteer work and then mocked and satirized and discounted for our efforts.

Commitment to feminism means understanding and challenging patriarchy as only one expression of oppression yet integrally related to all others. It means challenging racism in ourselves and in dominant institutions with the same commitment with which we challenge patriarchy. More: it means challenging particular webs of racism, classism, ableism, ageism, heterosexism, and humanism (putting people, actually restricted groups of people, at the center, at the expense of the earth). I must address this interstructuredness, not simply its multiplicity.

Commitment to feminism, finally, means living toward a vision, not in conformity with oppression and not simply in noncooperation but also in light of an alternative. I try to live in fidelity toward the twin vision of friendship and justice — of a time when the structures of enemyhood will be broken, when people and the earth can move toward patterns of healing and health, when life can be sustained with dignity and security, and when the artistry of each life will be valued above rubies — not to mention national security and corporate profit.

What then is a feminist framework? It is a multi-textured perspective that weaves together the diversities of oppression in their commonality and particularity, that roots me at the intersection of women's oppression with other forms of oppression and privilege, and that offers me an alternative vision of how our lives could be and *ought* to be.

THE SOCIAL CONSTRUCTION OF SEXUALITY

There is a dominant social construct of sexuality in the United States. It is the result of a pattern of ideas, expectations, and institutions that arose in the course of Western, European history and has become part of the dominant structures of our lives. Its intellectual roots are a blend of Greek and Christian concepts available to the church during the Middle Ages. In the two major articulations of a Christian understanding of sexuality, Augustine appropriated Neoplatonic concepts, and Thomas Aquinas Aristotelian ones. Both men worked within religious and social institutions that were hierarchical and patriarchal. Although the ideas of the two men are not identical by any means, they developed several themes that still help to shape the dominant ways of thinking about sexuality today.

Themes That Shape Thinking About Sexuality

With Augustine's writings as a resource, I wish briefly to summarize three of those themes.

BODY AND SOUL. The first of these is philosophical — the relation of body and soul. The question of that relationship was a major one for the Neoplatonic philosophers, the dominant philosophical school of his day, and Augustine simply inherited the problem.

Neoplatonic thought held that reality is a series of emanations outward from the One that is beyond all things, beyond all concepts, beyond all values, in whom or which there is no multiplicity or division. Through emanations from the One come, in order, Mind, Soul, individual soul, and the material world. Each level is organically related to the preceding one, yet distinct from it, like rays of light emanating from a sun but without any lessening of the sun. An individual person consists of body and soul, both ultimately from the One. Nevertheless, the body is further removed — and inevitably has less value than the soul.

Augustine inherited the problem and the philosophy as well as other theological concepts, including those of the fundamental goodness of creation and of the incarnation. Influenced by his theology, Augustine held that the body as well as the soul constitutes the human being, but he was ambivalent about the relationship. In some of his early work, he wrote that the body is a "snare."[1] Later he said it is the "spouse" of the soul. Influenced equally by the hierarchical context of his society, he wrote that the right relation of the body to the soul is obedience. As a result of the fall, however, the body now disobeys the soul. The human condition is now (after the fall) one of loss of control over the body and specifically over sexual impulses.

> Disobedience, inevitably, and most justly, drew upon itself a loss of control shown both in the failure of the fallen man [sic] to control his body and to resist sexual passion, and...by a subjection to the lust to dominate others.[2]

Existence after the fall, in other words, is one of lust and subjection —
politically as well as sexually. The lust for gold, the lust for power and
fame, and the lust for sexual activity are all consequences of the loss of
control over the materiality of our lives.

PROCREATION. A second theme is the emphasis on procreation. Augustine and Thomas differed in their reasons, but they agreed on the
conclusion: the only appropriate purpose for intercourse is procreation.
In speculating about intercourse as it might occur without lust, Augustine wrote:

> those parts, like all the rest, would be set in motion . . . without the
> seductive stimulus of passion, with calmness of mind . . . [and with]
> a spontaneous power . . . the male semen could have been introduced
> into the womb of the wife with the integrity of the female genital
> organ being preserved.[3]

SEXISM, MISOGYNY, AND HOMOPHOBIA. The third theme is the interrelated pattern of the sexism, misogyny, and homophobia of the society
within which Augustine wrote, a pattern that he also appropriated. It includes assumptions about the essential superiority of men, for instance.
Men may have lost control over their sexuality, but they are expected
to remain chaste through "manly discipline," while women can remain
chaste only through subjection to a "strict watch" on them.[4] Further,
he drew a parallel between the man-woman relation and the soul-body
relation. As the body is to obey the soul, so the wife is to obey the husband. Augustine wrote that the ideal relationship is one in which there
is "a certain friendly and true union of the one ruling, and the other
obeying."[5] And since men are superior to women, even the body of a
man is superior to the body of a woman — and should not be treated as
if it were a woman's body. Augustine wrote, "The body of a man is as
superior to that of a woman as the soul is to the body."[6] His point was
to condemn male homosexual behavior; men should not have sex with
other men because, in effect, it makes the body of one of the men like
that of a woman. An assumption that may also have been behind that
assertion was that male homosexual behavior meant that one person was
active and one was passive; one played the role of a man and the other
the role of a woman. Those assumptions reflected two further assumptions — that "woman" was "passive" and that one's male personhood
was devalued if one behaved like a woman.[7]

These themes form part of the intellectual legacy that has shaped the
way we today understand our sexuality and its institutions. This legacy
views sexuality as a problem, specifically a problem of control. It narrowly
restricts the sphere of appropriate sexual activity. It assumes that sexuality
in men and women is different. It devalues women as well as sexuality,

and it perpetuates a hatred of homosexuality, rooting that hatred in a hatred of women.

Institutionalizing the Legacy

Today the intellectual legacy described in the previous section is institutionalized in the dominant ethos, in law, and in the dominant institution of the nuclear marital family. It helps to maintain oppression, notably patriarchy, racism, capitalism, and heterosexism. A major consequence of this institutionalization is our profound alienation from ourselves and from one another.

ETHOS. Three beliefs in particular are central to the dominant sexual ethos.[8] The first is the belief that there is an essential human sexual nature that includes two sexes, male and female, and two genders, masculine and feminine, which both correspond to and are opposite to each other. The belief includes the assumption that the two sexes or genders are mutually attracted to each other, although a few people have deviated from this norm. The second belief is that sex is a powerful force and one that in general drives men more than it does women. Scholars have created a language of drive and need to reflect this assumption.

The third belief is that at the same time sexual activity needs to be controlled. On the basis of this belief, a variety of expectations, laws, and behaviors have developed to control it. Sexual activity has been severely restricted, although in such a way as also to allow the powerful force its outlet. It has been restricted largely by restraining certain groups of women, women of the same social and economic class as the men whose sexual needs are so powerful. At the same time, therefore, prostitution has been allowed and encouraged. "Lower-class" women, slave women, and others outside the circle of women who are potential partners for men of the dominant class are expected (by the dominant class) to be promiscuous and/or available for the taking. A thriving pornographic industry has also been encouraged.

This ethos has also permeated interpersonal relationships. From my experience, at least, people bring to relationships assumptions about the irrational and powerful force of sex. We also tend to believe that that force is going to produce problems: our sexuality is not and probably cannot be integrated into the rest of our being. Like an addiction, it remains a potentially explosive drive that holds us captive.

SEXUALIZING OPPRESSION. This philosophical legacy is a major underpinning of many of the social oppressions we live with. Its primary tool has been the socially normative pattern of family organization. Today that is still the nuclear family.

The family has been a major means of controlling who is part of the dominant society and who is not and on what grounds. The double standard of restriction and promiscuity mentioned above drew the circle around the women who were "in." Those restricted "belonged" to dominant men. The others did not count.

The law also played a role in determining who was in and who was outside. Often in the past, slaves could not legally marry; today gay and lesbian people cannot marry.

Those who cannot be or are not married (particularly if they are women) are devalued, discriminated against, and often punished. Single-parent families are not considered to have the same value that two-parent families have. Households in which family members live among relatives and move from one residence to another as described in *All Our Kin,* a gay or lesbian couple, a teenage heterosexual couple, a single adult, four elderly women living in separate apartments in the same building — all of these patterns may be tolerated, the individuals dearly loved, and the reasons for their patterns of existence understood and accepted, but they are not considered equal alternatives to heterosexual marriage. They are not considered equally good. When they are, we will celebrate them in our religious communities as we now celebrate marriage. And we will use them as resources for the ways we picture the divine.

Not only are such relationships less valued; the people in them are socially much less powerful than married people. They are denied many financial and social benefits, they are often discriminated against, and they may even be punished.

The expectation that women belong in the family as wives and mothers — an expectation that, as we know it, arose much later than Augustine but was consistent with such earlier views of women as subordinate and not mentally equipped for leadership roles in society — is a still further instance of the way in which the family is utilized as a key means of maintaining many forms of oppression. This particular expectation was meant only for women who "belonged" to socially dominant men. It was never expected of working-class women, for instance. Nevertheless, it was also the norm for the entire society, just as marriage was the norm for all yet was never expected of all. This two-fold understanding of women's role meant that on the one hand most women in a society were in fact part of the labor force and on the other hand that they were a "secondary" or "extra" supply of labor. Since women's "real" role was homemaking, they did not have to be paid as much as men did. Women's labor was "supplementary" to what the household needed. Further, they were restricted to those jobs that were most like the jobs women did at home — service jobs, jobs for which special training was not needed and which were most dispensable either through automation or the contracting or expanding market. Expectations about the normative structure of the family, in other words, serve to perpetuate structural characteristics of capitalism — low wages and a reserve pool of labor.

Expectations about the dominant family pattern also perpetuate abuse. In sixteenth-century Europe, families of the rising capitalist class became increasingly patriarchal, bringing together the earlier idea of rule with that of ownership. This legacy remains in the dominant ethos surrounding expectations about family, specifically in the assumption that the family is a private sphere, that the husband "owns" the other members, and that how they act toward one another is no one else's business. Wives "belong" to their husbands; children "belong" to their parents as if they were possessions. Further, what happens in middle-class and upper-class families has been held to be no one else's business. Such views encourage and often sanction attitudes and actions in elite families that manipulate family members as objects of emotional or physical abuse. They are a significant part of the reasons why incest, battering, rape, and emotional abuse continue to be widespread in these families. In non-elite families, abuse exists also. The reasons are extremely complex — diverse combinations of cultural, personal, and economic — but, again, the expectations of the dominant class help significantly to shape and sanction such behavior.

Today, the norm of the marital nuclear family is still so powerful that it shadows even those who have rejected the idea and institution of legal marriage. This shadowing is a further way of perpetuating the dominant status quo. The shadow of the modern marital family is a nonmarital monogamy, a term that has come to mean a qualitatively distinct relationship and not simply one kind of relationship among others. Among most of my friends, for instance, "monogamy" is typically used to refer to a relationship that is serious, that involves commitment, that means settling down. Monogamy is an alternative or counter-cultural imitation of the "real thing," and it has most of the trappings of the legal institution of marriage. More value is placed on it than on other forms of relationships, and it involves a kind of permanence not expected of them.

ALIENATION. A major result of the foregoing influences is, for many women, a profound sense of alienation from our bodies and from one another. This alienation is not only an intellectual belief that the body — and specifically sexuality — is some "thing" separate from me. I experience this separation somatically and experience it as alienation. I have not been, and most of the people I know have not been or are

not, at home in or as our bodies. Whether we have accepted traditional understandings of sexuality or sought for alternative ones, we
remain to some extent alienated from our own bodies — our own
selves.

I find that this alienation remains even in two major nonfeminist challenges to the dominant approach to sexual ethics — the challenges of
"sexual liberation" and of the elevation of the norm of love as shaping
sexual identity and activity. The challenge of sexual liberation, popu-
larized in the '60s, did confront the legalism and the double standard
of the tradition. But it tended to accept the masculinist legacy of the
tradition as still normative and in that respect perpetuated many of its
assumptions and much of its dualism. Tremendous pressure remained,
now on women as well as men, to perform, and women still had to
handle unwanted and unintended pregnancies. Masculinist values of performance and uninvolved sexual behavior, of conquest and possession,
of an emphasis on technique, and of making pornography widely acceptable still made it difficult for us as women to recover our self-body and
its integrity.

The sexual-liberation challenge came largely from outside the church.
Inside, a number of Protestant and Catholic theologians began moving
away from addressing issues of control and toward identifying love as
the overarching concept and norm for the area of sexuality. Love became
central to understanding our createdness as sexual beings; love became
the norm to guide sexual activity. And the emphasis on love led to an
emphasis on the quality of a sexual relationship:

> Love...involves commitment to the other, the willingness to risk
> and entrust oneself to the other....Love is expectant. It recognizes
> the inexhaustible possibilities in the beloved....Love is the respect
> of individual identity. As such, it is communion.[9]

By and large, however, such love was still most fully expressed in a
traditional marriage, although there was a real recognition that a love
relationship could be homosexual as well as heterosexual.

At the same time, the emphasis on love tended to make a sexual
relationship very serious and romantically ideal. We could be much
more casual with one another in every other area of our lives except
in our sexuality (a stance that ignores the fact that sexuality actually permeates every area of our lives). Further, we were supposed to
live happily ever after or at an intense pitch of romantic love and
Christian care that only the mystics glimpsed in an earlier age. That
expectation was so ideal that we could hardly live up to it in an
ideal world, much less in this world where the experience of sex,

at least for women, is so often fraught with pain and even terror. Such a norm could too often further the alienation we experience, not heal it.

The two challenges, therefore — the celebration of sexuality and the norm of love — also perpetuate significant negative dimensions of the heritage. Further, locating the ethical challenge at the personal and interpersonal level of sexual experience renders it difficult to analyze thoroughly the extent to which sexuality is a social construct, created by and handed down to us through this legacy.

Much of the legacy I have just summarized is a dreary and destructive one. It is time to try to start anew, to think as freshly as we can about our being as sexual and about desirable patterns for our lives. It is time to do some imagining.

A FEMINIST VISION OF SEXUALITY

I see a society in which everyone has enough to eat and to wear and is able to do what is individually fulfilling and what furthers the good of all. In that society the values of authenticity, intimacy, respect, and shared power and nurture govern individual development and interpersonal relationships. All institutions are structured nonhierarchically and reflect those values. Thus, for instance, economic institutions are as careful of human and ecological well-being as individuals are.

It is a society shaped by a new paradigm for social organization and interpersonal life. It is a paradigm of friendship; it is not that everyone is expected to be friends with everyone else but that the principles and values inherent in the concept of friendship are the norms.

This paradigm exists as an alternative to what we have now. Within this paradigm, I see individuals, not institutionalized group identities. With power, production, and distribution of resources equally shared and people thereby secure, gender and other group categories are not institutionalized.

I see colored people, a rainbow of tones and hues, reflecting ethnic or racial roots but not penalized by them.

I see a society in which criteria of health, comfort, and one's frame and metabolism determine the shape of one's body; and interests, personality, and temperament determine one's attire.

In this society, everyone can be competent, and there are real expectations of excellence without the illusion that my competence is more (or less) valuable than the competence of others.

In this society, sexuality is not a drive, a need, a force; it is not a *thing;* it is our selves; it is the way humans respond to the world — physical impulses and changes, emotions, intentions, values. What we now call sexual relationships are dimensions of many relationships, dimensions that are themselves complex.

As people relate to one another in varying degrees of openness and focus, we no longer use the word *sex* to specify certain activities or relationships. Neither do we use such phrases as lovers, just friends, and a Platonic relationship. Those categories no longer make sense. Again, when I respond to someone, *I* respond. I may choose to focus on some particular dimension of a relationship, for example, a story someone is telling me, but at the same time there are all kinds of communication streaming between us.

The same dynamics occur between me and what has been called the natural world. My response to a dolphin, to my cat, to the ocean as I swim, is complex and rich, containing emotional, erotic, aesthetic, and cognitive dimensions.

Where such possibilities exist, we will acknowledge a range of feelings, needs, and intentions. They may include a longing to hold and to be held, caressed, comforted, and reassured. They may include a joy and need to give ourselves in passion and compassion, in play and healing, in sharing and renewing.

In this dream society, we experience and give to others and to ourselves pleasure, ecstasy, care, communion, and union. We can experience those in many different activities — talking, singing, meditating, praying, kissing, caressing any or all areas of a self, holding or receiving parts of a self, swimming, reading, dreaming. We are generous with ourselves, clear about our feelings and intentions, and powerful, that is, we take what action we choose.

We live within and enter into different kinds of relationships, each with its own expectations, commitments, joys, and reason for being. There are many different possibilities. No one is morally normative, and none requires or includes a license. Some people may choose to live together; others may live alone. The variations are many.

The commitments within each relationship will also vary. Two people may choose to live together for the rest of their lives and to reserve for themselves some of the ways of sharing their love and joy and pleasure and commitment. A person may live alone and commit herself or himself to be in weekly contact with three other people scattered over the globe. Another person may have several close, full relationships; each has its own distinctive way of expressing the meaning of the love that is shared. And so on and so on.

When children are born in this visionary society, they are wanted and cherished. Between those times, relationships and lives are not shaped by the fear and actuality of unwanted pregnancies. Men and women are expected to take and do take equal responsibility for ensuring that conception and birth are planned and welcomed events.

Each person is encouraged in every way possible — in interpersonal relations, educational contexts, the political life of the community, his or her work — to accept and celebrate one's own power to be and to act. Thus each person is encouraged and expected to enter into friendships and other relationships from a center of power that is not isolated and self-sufficient. Each person is encouraged to have as few or as many friendships and acquaintanceships and as much solitariness as fits her or his own being.

In this vision, the beauty and power of bodily shapes, sizes, and contours are appreciated and celebrated. The lines of a hand, the tones of skin, the planes of a torso, will be found in photographs and drawings in magazines and books and on public murals. The texture of a bear's fur, the curve of a wave, the outline of a tree, will also please and arouse. The images do not conform to any one expectation of what is beautiful and erotic in the human form or in nature. The vision I cherish, is, therefore, of a society in which integration replaces control and integrity replaces gender. It is a radical vision, in that the totality of our lives and relationships will be and must be transformed. It is a joyful vision because I can see our being well. And I think it is an inclusive vision because it celebrates pluralism without making one possibility normative.

TOWARD A FEMINIST ETHIC OF SEXUALITY

But we live today between the times. My vision is utopian, ideal; clearly I cannot expect or even hope for its fruition in my lifetime, if ever. As feminists, womanists, and others committed to social justice and peace, we live neither in utopia nor simply in the status quo. We live toward a vision *and* within the status quo; we challenge the structures that oppress women and other beings; we seek alternatives to and within the present structures. We live, therefore, in a three-fold reality, which sets the framework for my understanding of feminist ethics and its bearing on our sexual being.

Dimensions of Feminist Ethics

Feminist ethics is concerned with three different but related activities — vision, analysis, and action. The values and principles that I name *feminist* are the criteria for shaping a good, or desirable vision; for identifying and analyzing structures of privilege and oppression; and for shaping specific actions in this time between the times.

The critical values for me, in this ongoing spiral of naming, interpreting, critiquing, and valuing, are *justice, healing, power, survival,* and *life abundant.* They translate the vision of friendship into criteria that can shape our lives and actions today.

I picture these criteria as four interlocking circles. The circles have a partially independent existence, but their interlocking core makes the fifth, central value.

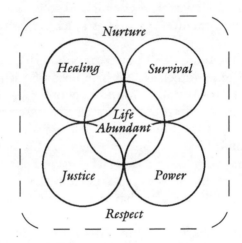

At the core, the four values are all the same thing — *life abundant,* fullness of life, well-being, individual and common good. Life abundant is a consequence of the other four values. The four, however, are not simply means to the end of life abundant. Justice, healing, power, and survival all have their own intrinsic value and the force of independent imperatives on us. We may not, for instance, always see the connections between doing justice and creating abundant life, but we are nevertheless obliged to do justice.

Further, suffusing all those values are two more values, *respect* and *nurture,* indicated by the broken line embracing all the circles. The broken line suggests these values inhere in all the circles. They do not form another separate circle. Respect and nurture refer both to structures and to attitudes, and they must be held together. Respect is honoring the being-becoming of each organism. But without nurture, respect can become indifferent, minimalistic. Nurture is actively tending to the well-being of each and all. But without respect, nurture can become manipulative and condescending.

The distinct, but organically related sections of the diagram are the four values of justice, healing, power, and survival.

JUSTICE. Justice is rooted in the affirmation that all beings have intrinsic worth. It calls us to work for economic sufficiency for all. It calls us to work for moral and legal equality among human beings and for the integration of human beings into sustainable ecosystems.

Justice should be normative for every area of life — social, political, economic, interpersonal, and interspecies. Justice toward nature, as among human beings, therefore, includes having available the conditions to sustain life with peace and security. It includes sharing those conditions in such a way that all can live with peace and security and sufficiency. It includes learning to live in cooperation and mutual caring with other human beings and the natural world.

HEALING. Healing calls for overcoming the scars of living in structures of oppression, scars that may be physical, emotional, or spiritual. Healing is not reconciliation, but it makes reconciliation possible. Healing means taking care of ourselves — taking the time to nurture ourselves, to enjoy one another and the incredible beauty of the world we live in. It means reducing stress, taking a vacation, meditating, praying, loving, writing poetry, singing, playing. It also often includes letting go of the tyranny of the past. Thus, for instance, healing may mean letting go of the tyranny of the scars of incest, not forgetting them but letting go of their ability to stunt or constrain one's life. As one is able to become free of those bonds, one can then act creatively on the memories.

Healing also means taking care of others — both human beings and nature. Establishing shelters, helping people work through pain and terror, and creating safe space for people to relax and begin to put their lives together in a meaningful way are examples of healing activities. Seeking to restore a lake that has been polluted is similar to trying to heal a body or soul that has been damaged.

POWER. Power calls us to take individual action, initiative, and to work toward the transformation of structures and personal attitudes to make possible further individual and shared initiative, responsibility, and authority. Power is the capacity to act; it is concrete, historical ability, not simply a theoretical possibility. Power is having the autonomy and resources to make decisions and carry through on them.

Power does not exist in a vacuum; one acts in the context of, and in relation to, many other people and the natural world. One's power, therefore, may be decreased or increased by the actions of others and by natural structures. In the long run, one's power to act is increased by negotiation and agreements with others and by working in harmony with nature. Further, if everyone is to be powerful, that is, able to exercise power, such power must be negotiated, mutually limited, and mutually exercised. Such a way of understanding how power works is consistent with the other principles of justice and healing and is, therefore, a desirable, or normative, way of understanding and using power.

This understanding is similar to what many feminists call *power with* in contrast to *power over*. The latter reflects and reinforces hierarchies of power and authority and is characteristic of structures of violence and injustice. There may be specific occasions in which the exercise of power over is appropriate, that is, occasions in which a pattern of command and obedience should exist, but those occasions should always be the exception rather than the rule and should themselves be grounded in consent. Where real consent may not exist, as in a child's consenting to an adult's wishes or commands, there is tremendous room for exploitation and abuse. Under such conditions, other measures must be instituted that respect a child and nurture its power.

SURVIVAL. Finally, survival both allows us and demands of us to take seriously our embeddedness in this historical moment, to accept where we are, to do what we need to do in order to live with some measure of dignity, security, and integrity, and to take the *next* step toward transformation. Survival has a bad name in much of traditional ethical reflection; it is seen as selfish or cowardly, for instance. But survival can be good. Oppressed people throughout the world have had to learn how to survive, and in surviving they have challenged systems of oppression. The tools of survival include deceiving and outwitting the oppressor, developing alternative ways of securing and sharing scarce resources, and finding ways to live under conditions of violence and deprivation. What psychologists call sexual frigidity, for instance, has often been a means of some women's survival in a context of powerlessness. Being "closeted' has been a standard means of survival for many gay and lesbian people.

Means of survival can also be very creative and rich. Mention has already been made of the alternative patterns developed by a poor urban black community as described in *All Our Kin*. The values in those patterns are actually much closer to how we ought to live than the values guiding the dominant and privileged members of society. In that respect, they offer us all new models of living. Alice Walker describes another way that helped her mother, and the mothers of many of us, to survive — tending a garden. Growing flowers, writing, creating some bit of beauty, are important means of surviving.

CRITERIA FOR RESPONSIBLE EXISTENCE. These four criteria exist as a normative context, a set of imperatives, a voice calling us to responsible existence. Our use of them will often be intuitive rather than consciously deliberate and reflective. Also, although some may be more relevant at certain times than others, it is their totality that reflects radical change and life abundant. Similarly, it is over our lifetime and that of the next generations that we effect desired change, not in isolated, abstracted "situations" of decisions, as so much of traditional Western ethics pictures the moral life. The criteria do not tell us what to do; they do not relieve us of the joys and burdens of responsible existence; they circle us; they keep us focused on the vision; they remind us of the plurality of changes necessary for moving toward that vision.

FINITUDE AND PLURALISM. A feminist ethic operates in the awareness that we live in the struggle; and in the struggle, our options are always finite. Seldom, if ever, do we have the option of making our vision purely real. Our only option at a given time may be to survive; but however few or many options we have, they are limited. What is *good,* therefore, is a good related to concrete possibilities, which are related in turn to the structures and circumstances of our particular lives.

Further, a feminist ethic is not only limited and concrete; it is also pluralistic. Our choices will and must be different.

Pluralism is one consequence of the fact that we do not all have the same options. It is also a consequence of the meanings of different options, meanings that are both personal and social. Social meaning refers to the understanding, value, and history around a given institution or practice or policy or event shared by a culture or subculture. White feminists' tendency to value friendship at the expense of family, for instance, may not be shared by those whose cultural experience is quite different.

In addition to differences of social meaning are differences of personal meaning. The understanding I have of my experience of sexual intercourse, for example, will inform my understanding of sexual ethics in a way that may be quite different from another person's.

This does not mean that a feminist ethic is simply relativistic. Although we stand at somewhat different places, we are or should be all engaged in a common struggle to transform structures of oppression toward visions of communal, individual, and ecological well-being. We will disagree about some of the specifics of the vision and of the analysis of the oppression, but there is and ought to be a large degree of shared understanding of what oppresses, what values ought to shape our vision of the "good" life, individually and communally, and what a truly abundant life would look like.

A REFLECTION OF OUR HISTORY. Finally, the options and choices we make as feminists will to some extent reflect oppression as well as move toward transformation. None of our choices will fully enable us to transcend our history and this time. We are embedded in structures, heritages, meanings, and personal experiences of domination, control, violence, denial, stereotyping, discrimination, privilege, power, and powerlessness. Our reflection and our actions will to some extent reflect those even as they may also try to transform them.

The good and the right, therefore, are not static, nor are they pure in some ideal sense. They are profoundly relational and the best we can do now.

Nevertheless, in this feminist ethic we are called to account, and demands are made on us. We are called to act by other people, and our actions are and ought to be challenged by others. We are called to act by dolphins and wild irises and are challenged by them. We are called to act by dimensions of ourselves that see the injustice and the violence or hear and are lured by the siren song of vision. We are called by restless, powerful, loving forces some call God or Goddess. The universe ceaselessly calls us to caring, to commitment, to struggle, to action. Hearing and heeding the call, however, is a stumbling, often painful, sometimes joyful process. Ethicists have variously described the moral life as similar to that of an artist, as a journey toward an end, as living in consistency with the orderliness of the universe or with the help of some other image. I sometimes think the moral life is like a baby's learning to walk. We do an awful lot of stumbling and falling on our faces!

Accepting Our Sexuality

Within the preceding framework, how might we now think about specific areas, dilemmas, and issues of sexual being and action? The first ethical consideration is positive. We can and do accept our sexual selfhood. Whether our own personal sexual reality is problematic, painful, joyful, ambiguous, or anything else, we begin with affirming and accepting it. Whether we are celibate, in a loving, heterosexual marriage, involved in sadomasochism, or move from one casual encounter to another, the first feminist ethical consideration is affirmation. We need not measure or label ourselves by some ideal, abstract yardstick. To do so would be to obscure and confuse the realities of our lives, the ways in which we participate in structures of oppression, must survive in them, and seek to transform ourselves and them.

Notice, our first ethical response to our sexuality is not wild, joyful celebration. Although celebration may be the appropriate affirmation for some, for many others, sexual life and experience are painful, confused, and even filled with terror. So the first response is affirmation, which may include, but is not synonymous with, ecstasy.

Affirmation does not occur in a vacuum. Affirmation in the struggle, in this time-between-the-times, is to understand our own situation in light of structures of privilege and oppression and to connect our situation to that of others. It is to understand and accept our sexual reality socially as well as personally and interpersonally.

If I affirm my life as a married woman as one that is fulfilling, I also affirm that marriage has been terribly destructive for many and that the normativeness of marriage has been even more destructive for whole groups of people. I must act to dethrone the moral power and authority of marriage, to make marriage available to gay and lesbian couples, or to address ways in which those who are single parents or live in some other familial pattern are not penalized economically and socially.

If I affirm my sexual reality as one of abuse, for instance, I can begin to gain insight into the reasons for the experience, reasons that do not blame me, and I can begin to determine what I want to do about that situation. I gain power. As I look at it in light of the criterion of healing, for instance, I may join an incest survivor's group. I may work at a battered women's shelter. As I look at it in light of justice, I may choose to work toward effective ways of restraining those who abuse.

Naming Our Sexuality

A second ethical consideration is to rethink, or rename, how we understand ourselves as sexual beings. This renaming is difficult. Not only our concepts and language but also our experiences are shaped by the social structures within which we have lived. So, although it is necessary, we cannot only "listen to our experience." What follows, therefore, is a preliminary reconceptualization of sexuality that has emerged for me as a result of years of trying to get in touch with my own sexual reality, listening to stories of others' experiences (primarily but not totally women's experiences), and sharing with other scholars analytical and constructive work.

GENDER AND SEXUALITY. I am both woman (gender) and female (sexuality). "Woman" is very much a historical, cultural designation. "Female" is a physical, emotional, intentional designation that to some extent transcends culture. Even "female," in other words, is cultural in part. It is a cultural phenomenon, for instance, to divide human beings into female and male and to make those distinctions either/or ones. If we were to take biology more seriously, what we call male and female exist on a continuum more than they do as categories.

Nonetheless, the fact that I am embodied in a certain way does shape my sense of myself. Size, body type, kind of genitalia, hormones, and musculoskeletal structure bear on my experience of myself. Just how they shape my reality is still largely an uncharted part of the pilgrimage.

LOVE. I grew up learning that people fall in love once and then get married, that they must not (cannot?) be in love with more than one person at a time, that they experience different kinds of love in different relationships, that there is a clear difference between love and lust, and that there are discrete and distinct categories of sexual partners.

I believe today that all those pronouncements are artificial, invalid, and valueless. The experience of a mother's love for her child, a mystic's love for the heart of the universe, a friend's delight in a friend, a person's love for a dolphin, are not so much different types as containing similar components of a complex phenomenon.

Love is a phenomenon that includes emotions, physiological responses, attitudes, values, intentions, and memories. A fearful memory—one of abuse, for instance—shades a person's love of God or the Goddess, of a partner, of a brother. Similarly, delight, affection, and care can all be present in romantic, religious, and parental love. Delight, affection, care, physiological changes, heightened awareness, commitments, fears, hopes, memories, anxieties, longings, attention, a sense of pleasure, anticipation, are all probably involved in most relationships we have called love or friendship. Mother love, spiritual love, and romantic love are not different kinds of love but motifs or dimensions of many relationships.

What then is love? I find myself using the word love very sparingly. When I do, and to the extent that I am consistent about it, I mean a combination of delight, affection, and loyalty in the most significant relationships with other beings — family and friends, the Goddess, and dolphins. Love includes a large element of what has traditionally been called *eros* ("being powerfully drawn to another"), but it also includes *philia* ("friendship") and *agape* ("disinterested care"); and it includes a commitment of loyalty to another's well-being and a secure sense of being at home in his or her presence.

I reserve other terms for other experiences. Falling in love, for instance, is a good description of that heady, also erotic, highly charged, lustful experience that often occurs at the beginning of a possible relationship. My own experience is that falling in love happens from time to time. When I am relatively powerful and competent, falling in love doesn't throw me into confusion. I enjoy it, and I am willing to wait and see if it matures into love. How I act on the experience of falling in love depends on many considerations of time, energy, other commitments, and an assessment of the consequences.

LUST. Similarly, it is necessary to rethink and revalue lust. Traditionally the term has both negative and positive connotations. Lust for money, lust for power, lust for a person's body, have negative connotations and suggest people — primarily men — out of balance and dangerous. Lust for life has a more positive connotation, as does the adjective lusty. What is consistent in both the negative and positive connotations are intensity, or passion, pleasure, and perhaps need. I wish to identify and affirm those dimensions of our human sexuality with the name lust. So lust is pleasure, highly charged pleasure. It is also intense desire, and it connotes the anticipation of pleasure, of savoring, enjoying the object of desire. When I lust, there is an excitement, energy, and electricity I experience in anticipation and in enjoyment. Lust may also on occasion reflect deprivation, deep neediness, insecurity.

Lust can exist by itself as the major feeling in a relationship. I am, for instance, not only an adult woman; I am also still a child and need to be mothered. A part of my lust for someone may well be this yearning to be mothered. Tremendous healing can occur when those needs are acknowledged, accepted, and ministered to. Similarly, I am not only a role — a mother — when I hold my son. I am a sexual self, and I may, therefore, experience sexual arousal. And I am not only a soul when I love the Goddess. Appropriately, Jim Nelson writes of having an erection during communion.[10] Finally, I have all of those feelings in relationships with close friends and acquaintances of either sex or gender. I may or may not act on any of those feelings, but they exist.

SEXUAL ORIENTATION. As a part of this process of renaming, therefore, I suggest we seriously experiment with language that moves us beyond the traditional categories. For instance, I suggest we eliminate hetero-, homo-, and bi-sexual terms as sexual categories, reserving them now for use as political-structural terms. As major categories of social control and oppression, they have helped to socialize us into stereotyped beings. Removing their dominance can enable largely hidden dimensions of our sexual nature to appear. Thus, we are all sexual beings, although we live in a heterosexist and homophobic society.

It is also important to maintain the terms gay and lesbian as political adjectives. Thus, I am a gay or lesbian person, not a gay, not a lesbian. Neither term is a category that constitutes me, but rather either may be descriptive of connections between my life and the history of a people whose sufferings and courage are now mine.

We also then need to create a term for those of us whose life and history are different but who are committed to justice for gay and lesbian people. The term straight is inadequate and disparaging. Perhaps *pro-lesbian* and *pro-gay* would work.

FAMILY. One traditional category that I have retained in the process of renaming is that of family, although to some extent I have redefined it. "Family" refers to the people to whom I have certain commitments. It includes people I love, some of whom are friends and some of whom

are biologically related. I do not, however, consider family all of those
to whom I am biologically related. Family commitments involve sharing
finances, sometimes sharing living space, significantly investing time and
energy to establish a deeply rooted relationship, making enduring commitments, and enjoying the secure sense of being at home with specific
others.

I have commitments to individuals among my nonfamily friends as
well as my family-friends. For me, those commitments include loyalty,
reliability, and sharing much of our lives. The commitments that I have
made to both groups include locating genital expressions of affection
only in the context of family or becoming family and only to one person within that context. The reasons for such commitments are related
to the particular configurations of my story and those of the people I
am close to.

It may be that, for me, the category of family is a transitional one.
In the future, it may disappear altogether. It may not seem healthy, empowering, or contributing to an abundance of life to distinguish between
family-friends and other friends. I am not clear about that. In this time-
between-the-times, however, the distinction helps to enable me both to
survive and to struggle toward transformation.

A DILEMMA OF SEXUALITY. In light of the foregoing discussion about criteria and reconceptualization, I wish to conclude with a brief exploration
of one continuing dilemma of sexuality — marriage and monogamy.
Marriage, as the traditional norm for sexual relationships, is deeply
embedded in our psyches and shapes our thinking and expectations
about alternatives. Many, many people who are committed to ending oppression nevertheless marry. Many substitute for marriage a long-term,
monogamous relationship, or, as it has come to be called, simply monogamy. Many enter into a covenant of commitment, which is the very
essence of marriage.

Many of us, therefore, who are opposed to the oppression that marriage reflects and reinforces yet marry or enter into an imitation of it.
Should we not simply refuse to live in such a pattern?

For some of us, that question will and should be answered affir-
matively. We may choose to live alone, without partners, but rich
in friendships and family relationships that contain many different
kinds of commitments and genital sexual expressions. We may live in
communities, again with many different kinds of interpersonal relationships.

In this time-between-the-times, however, those options may not seem
appropriate or possible. The reality of life for many of us is profound
alienation. Friendship and community structures barely exist; yet we

desperately need refuge, support, a place to be safe and healed with at least one close, loving friend. Realistically, both survival and healing may suggest a partnered, monogamous relationship.

Further, marriage may have different social meaning for different groups of people. For those who have traditionally been denied that option, for instance, it may be a critical expression of dignity and self-respect. Similarly, a wedding or other a ritual of commitment is one of the few widely recognized ways of symbolizing our intention to live in a permanent, caring relationship.

Those of us, therefore, who choose the legally valid option of marriage should be honest about the complexity and ambiguity of our actions. We are, in effect, perpetuating an oppressive structure even as we may also challenge it. Gay and lesbian weddings, for instance, do challenge the heterosexual norm. Similarly, marriages among black people in this country, who as slaves were denied it, may help to overcome some of the traumas of racist oppression.

Those of us who choose nonlegal monogamous relationships should also recognize the complexity and ambiguity of our actions. Insofar as those relationships imitate the hierarchical pattern and reflect the status and value accorded marriage in this culture, they also perpetuate oppression. The structure to a significant extent still stands. At the same time, they do also challenge the norm of a legal marriage.

In short, the most surviving, healing, empowering, and just response may be ambiguous with respect to moving us toward a vision of a society that reflects and nurtures the well-being of all creatures. Whether in the long run such necessary but relatively incremental changes will facilitate structural change is difficult, perhaps impossible, to say.

To continue to challenge structures, therefore, it is necessary to find still other ways to restrain the power and authority of the normative pattern. In doing this, it is important to remember that there is nothing innately wrong about two people choosing to live together for the rest of their lives in a relationship of commitment, love, and genital exclusivity. One possible challenge, therefore, is to begin to sever the social-political connections between an interpersonal choice and an oppressive pattern. This can be effected by taking actions that will at once honor more diverse patterns of relationships and, through legal action, extend to all familial groupings rights and privileges currently enjoyed only by traditional families.

Institutionalizing rituals to celebrate diverse patterns is one way to begin to sever the above connections. Honoring a range of commitments and relationships imbues many options with value, underscores the importance of taking care of one another, and makes relative the significance of a monogamous relationship. I know, for instance, of four elderly women who live in separate apartments in the same building, who consider themselves family. Those commitments could be recognized, honored, and celebrated. Other patterns can also be celebrated, among friends and in religious gatherings. Each such public occasion helps to build up a richly textured tapestry of values and valuable, pluralistic patterns of relationships.

Another way to challenge the social-political connections is to seek legislative changes that grant people in nonmarital and nonmonogamous family patterns the same legal rights and protections that traditional families have. These might include access to health-care coverage and to social security and pension benefits, for instance.

Finally, we must relate this work of justice to broader economic and social action. Only limited change will come from focusing primarily on sexuality. The freedom to explore and establish alternative, more just, interpersonal and family relationships is related to living in a society that offers economic security and sufficiency. It is related to living in daily patterns that support and enhance our senses of being and power and do not fragment and exhaust us. It is related to living in a society in which traditional gender expectations have disappeared. Family and friendship patterns are part of a larger whole and fit into and help to maintain other institutions. Only as they are also changed will we be able to move significantly toward justice and fulfillment in this area of our lives.

In conclusion, then, a feminist approach to concerns of our sexual existence is just as much political as it is personal, as much social as it is individual. It should be concerned as much with changing structures as with personal pleasure or fulfillment.

Second, it should start with the recognition of the historical character of sexuality — the way it has been constructed and the way that construction has become "natural." A primary feminist ethical task is the reconstruction of sexuality. I have sought to begin this task by envisioning sexuality in an ideal and just society, by analyzing the impact of the construction on our lives, and by identifying central normative ethical principles.

Third, this approach suggests that there is not a separate "sexual ethic." The principles delineated above are normative for our whole lives, not simply a certain aspect of our lives.

Fourth, a feminist approach to sexuality is pluralistic. The decisions we make will vary from one time to another and from one person to another. The differences of meanings, of heritage, of options, of the way one's life is shaped by privilege as well as oppression, will lead to different decisions, even if the criteria are shared.

Finally, a feminist approach illumines somewhat different dilemmas from traditional approaches. In the dominant traditional ethic, marriage is not problematical in the way that it is for some feminists. And I am arguing that for feminists, what we call monogamy ought to be more problematical than it seems to be but for reasons quite different from traditional ones.

You Do, I Don't

Mary E. Hunt

The most satisfying wedding I ever attended was in a Quaker meeting house followed by a swish reception with two lavender brides on the top of a chocolate wedding cake. The service was tasteful, with Quaker silence and well-chosen words. One participant remarked that Annie was "the reason for a smile of uncommon radiance on Lynnae's face." I quite agreed. They have lived happily ever after, at least for five years, with every sign of more to come.

Other such celebrations have been moving as well. Two friends exchanged rings and promises at an annual meeting of lesbian and gay Christians; their anniversary is always a weekend party. Two more took to the hills for an outdoor affirmation of their love surrounded by family, children, and friends. Still another couple chose to do it privately with a priest to witness their vows at home. I say, do whatever chimes your bells.

There is another side to all of this that deserves exploration lest we romanticize ourselves into a corner. Some celebrations have been videotaped with the tape lasting longer than the relationship. Others have been painful affairs with hurt over parental rejection exacerbated by family members unwilling to attend the ceremony. Still others have never gone beyond the discussion stage with intimacy issues surfacing and old tapes rolling about what marriage means. These folk have bailed out of the whole relationship. Love is like that sometimes.

The ups and downs of wedded bliss accrue to lesbian and gay people in equal measure to our heterosexual and bisexual counterparts, albeit with that extra added hassle that we are not supposed to marry. This extra measure is not incidental, but overcoming it should not be the only goal

This essay has been printed in a slightly different version in *Open Hands* 6, no. 2 (Fall 1990): 10–11.

as we reshape the world to make space for ourselves. The goal, mine at least, is to make love abound in a world where there is precious little of it.

The debate over to wed or not to wed is a sign of how far we have come as lesbian and gay people. That churches are seriously entertaining the notion of marriage for us makes me alternately delighted and skeptical. As long as certain rights and responsibilities accrue to heterosexuals who marry, I believe that they should also accrue to lesbian and gay people. But as long as lesbian and gay people have a choice, I urge us to take leadership in breaking the two-by-two pattern that is alleged to have begun with Noah and his nameless wife.

CELEBRATIONS OF FRIENDSHIP*

I think that friendship, not coupledness, ought to be the relational norm, especially within the Christian tradition. As I have argued in *Fierce Tenderness: A Feminist Theology of Friendship,* the heterosexual marriage norm is inadequate to the needs of most people and should be replaced by friendship. Everyone has been or at least tried to be friends. Children can learn the fine art of friendship. Friends can be of any age, race, or gender, albeit with systemic difficulties built in. Even pets can be our friends. It is with this in mind that I look carefully if critically at the move toward lesbian and gay covenants, commitments, yes, marriages, weddings, and happily ever after.

I do think the right of gays and lesbians to marry is essential to our liberation in church and society. Further, if children are to be brought into our homes with some semblance of security, perhaps marriage is a good start. Even more convincing to church people is the sacramental grace of marriage. At best it is the prayerful support of a loving community that is brought to bear on a given twosome.

Further, I have seen real good come out of ceremonies, like the healing of family bonds when siblings have come to witness their sister's covenant. I am even persuaded by John Boswell's research that same-sex marriage ceremonies have been part of early church history.

Still, I have strong reservations about same-sex marriages. Since most churches will not be offering Saturday slots on their wedding calendars to lesbian and gay people any time soon, we might as well discuss the issues before the industry closes in around us.

THE PROS AND CONS OF SAME-SEX MARRIAGES

First, two people need support to maintain and deepen a relationship. Lesbian women especially (perhaps less so for gay men) need to build

* Heads added.

strong networks of friends, an extensive and intensive support system within which to live and a safety net within which to fall. Why not celebrate that network instead of or in addition to a coupled relationship? For example, a friend who was moving invited all of her women friends to send her forth. It was a time to say what she meant to us, to wish her well, and to promise a permanent presence in her life even though she would be far away.

Second, coupled relationships are as much an economic covenant as an emotional one. Whether through joint checking accounts, life insurance beneficiaries, or other niceties of advanced capitalism, coupled relationships reinforce the notion of "just the two of us against the world," which keeps the wheels of the system running. I suspect that advanced patriarchal capitalism can stand a few stray same-gender couples here and there, especially in the top economic brackets.

Most people, however, would be better off if we socialized our resources, shared appliances and fancy cooking tools that we use rarely instead of having them in each home. What if we bought essentials cooperatively, instead of household by household, to lower costs? Granted the price of toilet paper is not the first thing one thinks of when deeply in love, but why reinforce the economic and social mode that has kept so many people down?

Third, same-gender coupling services reinforce the notion that relationships are forever and ever amen. Heterosexual marriages are styled this way, and as politically correct as the wording may be, the covenants I have witnessed have had that "forever" quality of which I am increasingly suspicious. It is not that I encourage promiscuity or reject stability. It is simply that I wonder if quantity (i.e., forever) and not quality (i.e., while it is healthy, life-giving, and community-enhancing for both persons) is really the issue when it comes to love.

Will commitment services tempt people (women especially, who sometimes stay together long after it is healthy to split) to persevere in a relationship that has been pronounced publicly? Will the partners feel constrained by their commitment to share their struggles with people who could help because the wedding created an illusion about the perfect couple?

Finally, if covenants were to become the norm within our communities, what does this mean about those of us who live, albeit some of us are in monogamous committed relationships, without benefit of such celebrations? Will we become the new "unwed mothers" and couples "living in sin" of heterosexual fame? Far-fetched as this may sound, I reject any move toward neo-puritanism that will gain lesbian and gay love respectability by mimicking the heterosexual model. I also wonder whether some of the urge toward same-sex commitment services isn't part of an unconscious move to make us "OK"; to sanitize our love, which needs no such soap and water; to mainstream us, when in fact the mainstream needs a good push in the direction of honesty.

This is precisely the point: the heterosexual and bi-sexual community has much to learn from us. We have much to teach: our strong reliance on one another for survival, not simply on our partner, if we have one, but on our community; life with dignity and fun even if we are not partnered; endless variety in how we make our lives work in the face of oppression. These are valuable contributions that, when taken seriously, will reshape the ethical norms of our [Western] society.

The two major contributions of every lesbian and gay person who is out are love and honesty. We are willing to say that we love whom we love. Our honesty gets us in as much trouble as our love. To survive, indeed to thrive, as many of us do, we have learned "that's what friends are for." Hence, I reiterate my intuition, nascent but increasingly compelling, that what we ought to celebrate is friendship, lots of it and often.

CELEBRATION OF FRIENDSHIP

What would such celebrations look like? Some of them would look like the commitment services I seem to be rejecting. That is, it might be two friends who wish to say something to each other and their friends about the meaning of the relationship and their commitments to it and to the individuals that form it.

But don't stop with that model. Let your imagination soar. Think of your dearest friends, the ones whom we call "family of choice," the ones without whom life would be meaningless. Think of far-flung friends, old friends, work and work-out colleagues who have become close over the years, a neighbor who has become a real mainstay, your sister or brother who has surprised you over the years by her or his love. The list is endless and so are the celebrations — parties, liturgies, an annual picnic, Thanksgiving at home, your birthday with presents for them, a letter in which you say it all to all. The form is not as important as the content, and the content is honest love, not just for one other, but for several, many, perhaps in the next life, for all.

The advent of same-sex ceremonies is not far off. They are a regular part of some churches, such as the Metropolitan Community Church, and other reasonable religious groups that take love seriously. Far from wanting to put an end to them, I urge that we expand their scope, widen their parameters, and begin to see how communal and personal life can be enhanced when such options are made available to everyone whether coupled or not. This initial exploration of options is meant to complement that movement so that we can turn the oppression of heterosexist patriarchy into the liberation of friends in all nations.

The New Improved Jewish Divorce
Hers/His

Vicki Hollander

When the phone rang with the news that my *get* (Jewish divorce) ceremony could take place the following day, I was ready. My civil divorce
had come through several days earlier, but it hadn't made me feel divorced. I was the one, not David,* who had insisted that we have a
traditional *get* as part of the divorce negotiations. We had been married
ten years, separated one year. We had a beautiful four-year-old daughter. The ending of the marriage was, for me, painful and completely
unexpected.

I know that many women feel hurt by the implicit sexism of the *get*
ceremony, but I didn't feel that way. I wanted to stand before the entire
Jewish community — including the most traditional — and have my
new status declared and validated. I believed that a Jewish ceremony,
unlike the civil event, might emotionally support me through a difficult
transition: from being married to being single, from parenting as a couple
to parenting alone.

I also knew that I had to construct a parallel ceremony. Five males
(one rabbi, two witnesses, David, and the scribe) would be present (along
with myself) at the traditional *get* ritual. I decided to assemble my own
cadre of supportive women friends. I worked out a schedule of guard-
duty shifts (a *shomeret*) in which different friends would accompany me
through the day. I also decided to write my own *get* document, to create
my own customs for the day, and to construct my own sort of support-
network *minyan* (quorum).

---

* David is not his real name.

"The New Improved Jewish Divorce: Hers/His" by Vicki Hollander from *Lilith*, Summer, 1990.
Copyright © by Vicki Hollander. Lilith, 250 West 57th Street, New York, NY 10107. Used by
permission.

On the one hand, I felt unspeakably sad and afraid; on the other, I felt strong and dignified, ready to claim this ancient ritual as my own, to recognize that the Jewish divorce ceremony was a route that was available to me for my own use in healing.

At dusk on the evening before the ceremony, I began a twenty-four-hour fast: I lit a white candle and started to compose my own divorce document (what I call a "document of transition" [see below]) using special textured paper that I had bought for the occasion and a real ink pen. I was all alone, and I sat on the living room couch watching the candle flicker in the December dark, thinking, crying, preparing myself for the fact that tomorrow my marriage would be officially over. Going to bed that night, I felt quiet but not alone, in the grip of a large unfolding thing, but also feeling in control of what was about to happen.

The next morning, wrapped in my *tallis* (prayer shawl), I said the *viddui,* a prayer of confession generally recited before one's marriage, on Yom Kippur, and on one's death bed. I wanted to acknowledge my part in the death of my marriage — the patterns I had perpetuated that were not healthy, the skills I lacked, the times I had not listened to my intuitive voice.

Paralleling Yom Kippur, I wore no jewelry and no makeup. I dressed in white, the color of the *kittel*. (The *kittel,* a burial shroud, is also traditionally worn by Jewish men on their wedding day and on various Jewish holidays.) In a white skirt, white blouse, and cloth shoes I felt bleached, cleansed, pure, and present. White felt right to me, a symbol both of death and of rebirth.

I stayed alone until mid-morning, needing time to feel sad, to reflect, to be with God. I would have liked to have had my family with me during parts of the day, but as my parents live in San Diego and my sister and brother-in-law in Cleveland that wasn't possible. My daughter had slept over at David's house and was now at school. I started to feel nervous and frightened, with a painful ache. So many relationships were now dying, and dreams, and parts of myself.

Joanne, my oldest friend in Seattle, picked me up at 10:30. We drove to the *shul.* Joanne sat by my side for about half an hour, through the first part of the ceremony. Around the large wooden table sat the two male witnesses, plus the officiating rabbi, the scribe, and David. Except for the scribe, I knew everyone else in the room. I could feel their sympathy. There was small talk and joking around. I think they were afraid I would cry if there was much silence. Although as a woman I was legally powerless at this ceremony, I felt I had a great deal of authority. I had the power to get to the emotional core of the situation.

The ceremony began with the rabbi explaining the proceedings to us. He asked, formulaically, "Are you ready to go through with this?"

I answered, "Yes."

David answered, "Yes."

There was a terribly mournful feeling in the room.

After some more formalities, the officiating rabbi said we could leave for two hours while the scribe hand-wrote the *get.* Joanne drove me to my friend Bria's apartment. I had not yet shown anyone my "document of transition," and I wanted both to hear it read by someone else and to read it aloud myself. I hoped it would cut through the numbness. Hearing it and then reading it, I felt both grief and the beginnings of resolution.

Bria drove me back to the *shul,* where a third friend, Joanna (not Joanne), met me. We entered the room for the last part of the ceremony, watching the completion of the writing of the *get,* the artful, calligraphic document inscribed with infinite precision. The officiating rabbi read it aloud in Aramaic; then he cut the parchment with a small blade, symbolically cutting our union, giving concrete form to the ending of our marriage.

He gave the parchment to David who dropped it into my open hands. I tucked it in between my left arm and my heart, as I was instructed to do. Holding the ripped document near my heart felt like a real enactment of what was happening: this most close and intimate part of my life was over. One small gesture captured a year and a half of what I had been feeling.

I then gave this beautiful, disfigured parchment back to the officiating rabbi, relinquishing it. I walked the traditional three steps backwards and three steps forward, signifying my acceptance of the document. I didn't feel at all shamed by my allegedly "passive," distaff role in this proceeding. As I took the steps, I could physically feel myself standing tall and walking straight. It felt like the ceremony was mine.

I waited until the very end to hand David (my now ex-partner) my "document of transition." Though I had not gotten to hear my own document read aloud in this room, I had heard it read aloud with Bria, and I felt satisfied. I was glad to be performing the final, closing rite.

The ceremony was over. It had felt foreign, yet greatly comforting. I was participating in an ancient ritual of unbinding, following the path of many people who had passed before me who also had been hurting and torn.

Joanna drove me back to my apartment. Slowly I bathed, adapting the customs of mourning rituals in which water is the symbol of purification and renewal. I changed from my white clothes into comfortable, colored, happier clothes. I had bought myself a new pair of colored earrings for the occasion — a present to myself.

At around 5 P.M., eight additional women friends joined us, making a *minyan*. Each woman brought a dish for dinner. We had salads, casseroles, wine, bread, and almond tarts for dessert. The meal was a combination mourner's meal of consolation and of transition.

Lighting colored candles, we spoke of endings and of new beginnings, each of us spontaneously sharing some ending and beginning from her own life. We sang the blessing over wine and talked about the meaning of this blessing — vines, rootedness, being connected with the earth, growth. It was a metaphor for our processes.

When we said the blessing over bread, we talked about how many co-ordinated actions are necessary to produce a loaf of bread — the finished product — no less the mystery of the initial grain. The talk was simple, which felt right. "I am not all alone," I said. "All of you have accompanied me through this difficult, coordinated process. Today marks not only the closure of my marriage, but formally recognizes how my friends have been with me through all of this." I thanked everyone, acknowledging that in my neediness through this crisis, I had made demands on my friends.

When we sang the *shehechiyanu* blessing (to mark my new beginning), we each reflected on what we wanted for ourselves now and in the future, what dreams we had. What new possibilities existed for me now? There had been so many changes. I was so aware of being a woman with women.

As the evening neared an end, we all went outside. Arm in arm, in small groups in the moonlight, reminiscent of the mourning ritual, we walked around the block. (At the end of sitting *shiva,* it is traditional to walk around the block, symbolizing the end of the mourning week.) My life's path would now be different.

When we came back to my apartment building, we formed a circle on the lawn. I talked briefly and quietly about my feelings throughout the day. Then we hugged and parted.

The ritual had begun at dusk and it ended at dusk. I felt very full, very satisfied. The day had, after all, been mine.

DOCUMENT OF TRANSITION*

On the _____ day of the week the _____ day of _____

574 __ since the creation of the world, the _____ day of

_____ 199 __ as we reckon time here in _____,

_____ I, _____ daughter of _____

& _____ (Hebrew names) _____

do depart from the bindings and vows of my marriage (kedushin)

that took place _____ years ago on _____ in

_____ to _____ son of _____ &

_____ (Hebrew names).

This day I am no longer bound to the task and to the commitment to cherish and honor you in faithfulness and in integrity as my husband.

This day I am no longer bound by honor or by law to affirm and maintain kedusha within our relationship.

This day I am no longer set aside, special to only you.

This day the kedushin vows become null and void. I am no longer bound by the vows of kedushin. Hereby, I am no longer kedusha to you, no longer your wife, and you are no longer kadosh to me, no longer my husband.

On this day according to our tradition I depart as a free woman.

I stand as a free agent in the Jewish community, in the world, and before myself.

I stand having completed our people's traditional way of unbinding a marital relationship.

I stand as a Jewish woman with dignity and with strength.

I stand restored to a single unit as a whole and complete person.

This shall stand as a document of release and a letter of freedom in accordance with the values of our people, Israel.

_____(woman's Hebrew name)

_____(woman's English name)

_____Witness

_____Witness

* This document draws upon the *ketubah,* the *get,* and my own writings.

Sexuality and the Eucharist

Deborah H. Carney

> In the Beginning there was no thing
> but the Goddess. She was all and
> EveryThing. She was the void. She
> amused HerSelf for what were days
> to her, eons in our reckoning. She
> played and loved HerSelf. She
> realized that She had never seen
> the course of Her pleasure. She
> felt the joy, the wetness, the
> ecstasy of the throbbing deep
> within her, but She had never seen
> the glistening fold Her fingers
> pleasured. She had never seen what
> felt like a pearl at the center of
> HerSelf.
>
> One day She surprised HerSelf as She once again took
> pleasure with HerSelf. She brought forth the pearl. It
> rolled out from beneath her legs. It was round, blue and
> green, shrouded in beautiful, floating wisps of clouds. She
> saw in the blue of the pearl Her reflection. She could, at
> last, on the still ocean waters, see what had never been
> seen before. Her joy overwhelmed Her, and She knew it
> was not enough to know this pleasure by HerSelf alone.
> She womyned the earth with beings like HerSelf and in
> each She planted a pearl of pleasure so that each womyn
> could know herSelf.
>
> — Felice Rhiannon

If Felice Rhiannon's words had been contained in the book of Genesis, this essay would not need to be written, for the connections between
one's sexuality and the spirituality of the eucharist would be clear and

basic.[1] Our sexuality, that is, the totality of our being, and our spirituality, that is, the entirety of the style and meaning of our relationship with that which we perceive as having ultimate worth and power, would be thoroughly interwoven and interconnected.[2]

The quotation above is obviously not Christian scripture. It is not even traditional Christian theological thought. Yet the womyning of beings on Earth so they might pleasure themselves in HerSelf has strong parallels with the incarnational theology of the church, and this story reflects my own experience of the interweaving of sexuality and spirituality as experienced in the eucharist.

The story presses me to explore the connection between the merging of two people in a mutual and intimate union and the union of a person with God in the Lord's Supper. Why do I experience the divine in two very different venues yet with the same intense awareness of holy presence?

SELF-GIVING

God's self-giving and self-communication are the foundation upon which the Christian sacraments are built.[3] Human self-giving and self-communication are the foundation upon which the sexual union between two people is built. That has been my experience. Human self-giving in mutuality and intimacy is celebrated in sexual union; human and divine self-giving in mutuality and intimacy is celebrated in the eucharist.

Self-giving is both simple and deeply complex. Western cultural history is full of complex heroic episodes of self-giving, Christian and pagan alike. Self-giving, however, is also a daily experience, unspectacular for the vast majority of people. Human self-giving is a common means of expression, which comes in diverse forms.

Self-giving is the means by which God is revealed to Christians, also in diverse ways. The supreme act of God's self-giving is the Christ event: "God so loved the world that God gave God's only begotten Child [John 3:16]." The supreme act of self-giving that Christians experience with each other is, for me, the sexual union with a loved one.

I experience self-giving in two fundamental ways: in the encounter with the divine in the eucharist and in the human encounter of mutual sexual union. The words and physical elements of the sacrament are the visible and tangible sign of God's self-giving. I know my self-giving, as well as my partner's, through our self-giving during the union of our sexualities. Our physical and spiritual presence to each other, our communication and sharing, occur at a level that is basic to my existence.

The eucharist and the sexual union, the spirituality and the sexuality, demonstrate my relationship to my partner and to God.

NOT OPPOSITES BUT PARALLELS

Traditional Christian theology would have one believe that sexuality and spirituality are at opposite ends of the spectrum. Sexuality, the carnal, has been considered the source and sign of human depravity, while spirituality, specifically the eucharist, has been called the medicine of immortality. The person who is spiritual, truly spiritual, is regarded by the tradition as having no need for sexual union, except, of course, to make more spiritual people.

I am convinced, however, that sexuality and spirituality must not and cannot be separated. The similarities, the parallels, between the two are immense. And, as we shall see, the experiences are not only parallel, they share common dimensions.

Mystic literature of all religious traditions uses sexual language to articulate the spiritual experience:[4]

> With this, our good Lord said most blissfully, "See how I loved you!" It was as if he had said, "My darling, behold and see your Lord, your God, who is your maker and your endless joy! See what delight and endless bliss I have in your salvation. For my love, enjoy it now with me."
>
> Thus I saw him and sought him, I had him and I wanted him — and this is, and should be, the way we commonly work in this, as I see it.[5]

What mystics gave us we still use. Human passion for the divine is often expressed in passionate language of the flesh. Eroticism is the closest and clearest symbol of complete longing available to most of us, and it is the language closest to the surface of awareness for most people.[6] Erotic love can sometimes constitute a primary education in loving preparation for a fuller recognition of agape.

The parallels may also be seen in the physical involvement in both experiences. The eucharist is celebrated using the whole body. In high liturgical churches, kneeling, standing, and sitting are all part of the experience, as well as touching and receiving. If we observe facial expressions before and after the taking of the elements, we note a marked difference. Prior to receiving the elements, individuals seem to have a look of serious concentration. After the feast the faces change. The look becomes one of joy and a delightful sense of fulfillment. Our sense of touch is used to feel the body. Our sense of taste is incorporated in drinking the blood. Hearing and seeing are two more ways the experience is heightened. If incense is used, even our sense of smell is put into action.

So it is with our sexual unions. We use our whole bodies. We touch, listen, smell, and taste. Each sense complements the others and serves to make us more fully aware. Here too the facial expression changes from the time we commence to make love until we savor what has just happened to our whole being.

Further, both the eucharist and the sexual act, if they are activities of mutuality and joy, promise unity while not erasing the individuality of each person. Both are the union or communion that bonds deeply unique individuals.

The mood appropriate to each is also telling. The mood for participating in the eucharist is a joyful sense of gratitude to God. So it is also in erotic union.

Our spirituality and sexuality also have eschatalogical dimensions. Both are earthly experiences of the ultimate unity promised to all in God's realm.

To take the bread and wine of the eucharist is to speak of a great covenant of love, agape. To take the joy and intimacy of the sexual union is also to speak of a great covenant of love, eros.

But sexuality and the eucharist not only have similar components. They merge into the same act. My experience is that my erotic life and my sexual self bring me into a realized agapic relation with God.

A SACRED MYSTERY

The act of sexual union has been considered a sacred mystery throughout history. Many early cultures regarded sex as a magical expression, designed to replicate the fertile powers of the gods. In ancient Greece and Rome sexual intimacy was the vehicle for communion with the deity. The term "temple prostitute," used by Christian scholars to describe this religious activity, is more accurately translated as "sacred virgin," words that more completely convey the intentions of its practitioners. As G. Rattay Taylor states, this form of sexual activity "was nothing less than an act of communion with God."[7]

I am not arguing for the physical merging of sexuality and spirituality on the communion table. I am, rather, arguing that sexuality and spirituality have been seen as a celebration of a very similar human desire. The desire is anchored in our need to be in relationship, in communion with other humans as well as with God.

Even Paul asserted that the act of marital sexual intercourse could have divine meaning and could celebrate the divine mystery.[8] The idea was submerged for centuries until it was picked up again, but not by the church. It was established again in literature by such writers as Shakespeare, John Donne, and D. H. Lawrence.

The sacredness of the sexual union allows me more deeply to appreciate the sense of the sacred in the eucharist. The church, as a community conscious of life's pervasive sexuality, should also recognize and respond appropriately to the often overlooked sexual dimensions of the eucharist. To deny that both sexuality and spirituality are at the core of a person's being and creativity only hinders the possibilities of human fulfillment.

EXPERIENCE OF THE DIVINE

If we begin to accept the interweaving of both, we must begin to express our deepest thoughts and concerns regarding the experience of the divine during the eucharist and during sexual intimacy. We need to release ourselves from the bondage of Christian dualism. We can no longer separate sexuality and spirituality. Life for the Christian is meant to involve the total self, including the sexual self. Relationship for Christians is with God and one another. They are mutual and intimate. God is with us at the altar rail in the passion of the spirit. God is also with us in the place of sexual union and in the passion of the flesh.

Many Christians sense, I think, that sexuality reaches far beyond those areas to which it has been confined by the church, far beyond the personal and private life of individuals. "We know that the whole creation has been groaning in travail together until now; and not only creation but we ourselves...groan inwardly as we wait for...the redemption of our bodies [Rom. 8:22–23]."

But where and when will this happen? The paradox of the incarnation is that it occurs in strange and unexpected places. We meet and we touch. Personal presence is always with us. And again we know the meaning of the Word become flesh. We understand anew the resurrection of the body. And we are ever surprised by the joy.

It is this sense of joy found in the elements of the eucharist, the body and blood of Christ, and in the elements of my sexuality, the mutuality and intimacy, that I want to convey. That does not mean I plan to announce to the world how much satisfaction I receive in being sexually active as well as in partaking of the eucharist.

It does mean I am stronger and more able to go forth and minister among people who may or may not share my experience and sense of the divine. It makes me acutely aware of the differences in theologies and in interpretations of Scripture and the Christian tradition. For just as my understanding is grounded in my sexuality, so is that of other people. No two sexualities are alike, and therefore no two people can experience spirituality in exactly the same manner.

I find this truth very liberating. It gives me hope for a world that is reconciled to God through the embodiment in Jesus Christ and through our own embodiment. I feel as if I were standing on a horizon of new-found reality for many people. I fantasize that sexual theology will, in the near future, become a means of understanding the nature of God and therefore of God's love for us. For me it is a means of grace as valid as the eucharist. As the eucharist is the pinnacle of my spiritual life, so the sexual union is the pinnacle of my sexuality. In both I find love, agape and eros. In both I find mutuality and intimacy. In fact, they have merged and become one tapestry, which clothes me in the love of God and in the love of other human beings.

For this I give thanks, both at the communion table and in the arms of my beloved.

Women, Men, and Black Theology

James H. Evans Jr.

Black feminism is one of the most serious challenges that black male theologians have faced. The anguished, passionate, and often angry hue and cry from the lips of black women cannot be ignored. Black women are speaking for themselves, and they are not only addressing the issue of their participation as full partners in the black liberation movement, they are also addressing the political implications of black male-black female relations.

In her book *Black Macho and the Myth of the Superwoman*, Michele Wallace levels an often scathing attack on what she describes as a recent history of chauvinism among black males in the United States. It has driven a wedge between black men and black women.

> I am saying, among other things, that for perhaps the last fifty years there has been a growing distrust, even hatred, between black men and black women. It has been nursed along not only by racism on the part of whites but also by an almost deliberate ignorance on the part of blacks about the sexual politics of their experience in this country.[1]

It is this distrust, argues Wallace, that has accounted for the inability of the black community to mobilize as it once did.

In her book *Beautiful, Also, Are the Souls of My Black Sisters,* Jeanne Noble locates the battle lines, not between black men and black women but between the black woman and anyone who is not totally committed to her liberation.

> It is not that black women don't want equal rights. It is more the case that we are "hanging loose" from total immersion in any other libera-tion movement unless and until the "new" liberators prove the depth of concern for the liberation of all people — black, poor, "other," as well as women.[2]

Noble believes, like Wallace, that black male chauvinism is a real problem in the black community. Noble argues, however, that the history of black women's strength will permit them to assert themselves as full partners in the black liberation movement and in the process lead black men to a fuller understanding of their own humanity.

In her article "The New Black Feminism: A Minority Report," Julia Mayo takes yet another approach. For her, the new black feminism is part and parcel of the black liberation movement.

> Black women today recognize that without liberation for the black male there can be no real freedom for anyone. There is no place in the present day scheme of things for black Delilahs. And Black women are determined to give birth to no more "raisins in the sun." The liberation the woman seeks is from the oppression which results from the color black, for it is the image of blackness to which she responds and which ties her to the black male.[3]

These three voices, though in some ways different, all point to the fact that the black community is being called upon to clarify its own identity. As the black community is challenged, so is the black church and its male theologians. Black male theologians are being asked whether or not black theology is sexist.

The importance of this challenge cannot be dismissed by saying that the feminist issue is a white one and not related to the struggle for black liberation. This challenge is coming from black women, not white women. And it is coming from black women who historically have been involved in the struggle for black liberation. Therefore, it is an issue that must be dealt with by black theologians on more than a superficial or cursory level.

Black theologians must look at the ways in which the question Is black theology sexist? affects the theological task at its heart — its norm and sources, scripture, tradition, and experience. James Cone has stated that "the sources and norm of Black Theology must be consistent with the perspective of the black community."[4] Therefore, black theologians must always be aware of any change in the perspective of the black community as well as diligent in their assessment of the consistency between that perspective and the norms and sources of black theology. In addition, black theologians must examine the meaning of "blackness" as an ontological symbol. In this way, black male theologians can begin to respond constructively to this question from within.

THE POINT OF DEPARTURE

The point of departure for black theology is to be found in the black community. The starting point of the black theological task must be located within the social and historical context of the black community because "one's social and historical context decides not only the questions we address to God, but also the mode or form of the answers given to the questions."[5] Only in the community where black people are terrorized, brutalized, emasculated, and killed can the reality of God's liberating activity be known. The purpose of God's salvation is to restore the integrity and humanity of black people.

The questions raised by black feminists, however, are, Have black theologians been oversimplistic and monolithic in their analysis of their point of departure? Is there uniformity of oppression in the black community or is the black woman, to use Marx's phrase, "the slave of a slave"? These questions are crucial to black theologians because they concern the social and historical context of their theological questions and answers. If the starting point for the theological task is to be found in the black community, then responsible questions concerning the social and historical context of that community must be taken seriously by black theologians. Black women are saying that the point of departure for black theology is to be found not only in that community where black people are terrorized, brutalized, emasculated, and killed but also in that community where black women are raped, exploited, and forcibly sterilized.

Frances Beale argues that black women and poor women are subjected to oppression that differs in kind, if not degree, from that experienced by black males.[6] As a surplus labor supply, they are the necessary victims of a capitalistic system. Thus, they are economically exploited. They are human "guinea pigs" on whom new birth control methods are tested to determine their safety for mass consumption. Thus, they are the first victims of a massive genocidal conspiracy. Finally, they are restricted by black males in their attempts to assert their full humanity. Thus, they are the intimate victims of the black man's quest for his long-delayed patriarchal rights. If the point of departure for black theology is to be found in the black community, then black theologians cannot ignore the overall experience of oppression within that community.

More important, however, is the fact that the test of the validity of the starting point of black theology is not found in the particularity of the oppressed community alone. Its validity is ultimately found in its faithfulness to the norm of all theological discourse, that is, to Jesus Christ as the oppressed One who has proclaimed release to the captives and liberty to the oppressed. It is in the light of this norm that our point of departure must be evaluated. If that is done, black male theologians will come to realize that the sexist oppression experienced by their sisters will not divert their attention from racist oppression, but will alert them to all the manifestations of evil suffered by African-Americans.

SCRIPTURE

Black theology is a theology in which scripture is important. "Black Theology," states James Cone, is "kerygmatic theology. That is, it is theology which takes seriously the importance of Scripture in theological discourse."[7] Thus, what black theologians say about God, humanity, and the world must be informed, in some fashion, by the biblical witness. "The Bible can serve as a guide for checking the contemporary interpretation of God's revelation, making certain that our interpretation is consistent with the biblical witness."[8] This checking is done within the context of the black community, whose perception of the Bible determines, in large part, its character as guide.

The black community's analysis of scripture is always done within the context of that community's idea of God and salvation. Thus, the Bible, while occupying a fundamental place in the life of the African-American Christian, is not subject to fundamentalist interpretation. It is not a book of rules for living, nor is it a set of inerrant proof texts.

> We should not conclude that the bible is an infallible witness. God is neither the author of the Bible, nor are the writers [God's] secretaries. Efforts to prove verbal inspiration of the Scripture are the result of [people] failing to see the real meaning of the biblical message: the liberation of [humanity]!"[9]

Thus, in reading the Apostle Paul's dictum "Slaves, obey your masters," for instance, black people were not placed into the either/or situation experienced by those who subscribe to the doctrine of the plenary verbal inspiration of Scripture. Black people were not compelled either to give up the quest for freedom or give up the Bible. Rather, they accepted Paul's statement in its own context.

This acceptance involved three crucial observations. First, Paul's statement does not exemplify the whole gospel and does not manifest its central thrust. Second, Paul was not addressing the slavery issue at that time. The relation of the gospel and human bondage was not the focus of the discussion. Third, Paul was not Christ but a dedicated, fully human servant of the Lord. Therefore, the apostle cannot be presumed to have possessed the "fullness" of the gospel, though he strove to attain it. The fullness of the gospel is evident in the missiological declaration of Jesus Christ to "set at liberty those who are oppressed." Thus, the meaning and authority of scripture are not found in its transliteration and simplistic application but in the fact that it points beyond itself to the reality of God's revelation. That revelation is the divine will to liberate the poor and oppressed, and in America it is God's promise to the black community.

The question about scripture that black feminist theologians such as Jacquelyn Grant raise is, "How can a Black preacher (or theologian) preach (or do theology) in a way which advocates St. Paul's dictum concerning slaves?"[10] That is, how can black male theologians justify the use of a liberated hermeneutic in reference to slavery, while retaining a fundamentalist interpretation in reference to women?

This question is crucial because it is aimed at the very seedbed of black biblical interpretation in two ways. First, if black biblical interpretation takes place within the context of the black community, then certainly the voices of more than 50 percent of that community ought to be heard. Second, this question calls upon black male theologians to "check" again their contemporary interpretation of God's revelation for consistency with the biblical witness. Black theologians must not make the mistake of assuming that the "fullness" of the gospel consists of "maleness." If black theology is based on a reading of scripture that reveals its message of liberation, black male theologians cannot be selective in their reading. If the hermeneutical circle of the Bible's message and meaning is not to become solipsistic, it must be an open circle, one that allows God to breathe into it continuously the breath of life.

TRADITION

Church tradition has always been an important theological source for African-American Christians. This tradition, however, has not been perceived by black theologians as a unified whole. That is, in looking at church history in the West, black people have observed two traditions, one that is their own and one that is not. "When Black Theology speaks of the importance of tradition, it focuses primarily on the history of the black church in America and secondarily on white western Christianity."[11] Thus, the appeal to tradition as a source of insight is primarily an appeal to the history of black religious experience in this country. Black church tradition, while not functioning in the manner that church tradition functions in Catholicism, is nevertheless one of the avenues through which God's truth is made known to us.

The appeal to black tradition takes the form of a question: What does it say to us, from the particularity of its own context, about the activity of God in the world? In answer, the black church simply presents its witness and testimony to the faithfulness of God. The tradition of the black church has exemplified protest, prophetic proclamation, and involvement in the struggle for liberation. One need only recall the ministries of

Andrew Bryan, George Liele, Nat Turner, Richard Allen, Absalom Jones, and others to see that the tradition of the black church is a tradition of struggle against oppression and bondage.

At the same time, there are moments in that tradition that manifest an unwillingness to engage in that struggle and a docile acceptance and even support of the structures of racism, bondage, and oppression. In these moments the black theologians must exercise their interrogative imperative and ask, When does the church cease to be the avenue of God's revelation? The appeal, then, that black theology makes to black church tradition is an appeal to that aspect which most visibly and faithfully witnesses God's activity in the world.

The question that black women ask is, What do we do about the blatant sexism in the tradition? The black feminist theologian Jacquelyn Grant relates an account in which Richard Allen, founder of the American Methodist Episcopal Church, refused to recognize the legitimacy of the ministry of a black woman, Mrs. Jarena Lee. Though he was impressed with her considerable talents and sincerity, he would not ordain her, because the A.M.E. "discipline...did not call for women preachers."[12] In questioning this tradition, one is immediately confronted with the fact that any answer must be informed by something in addition to black church tradition. Even Allen's appeal to the A.M.E. "discipline" to justify his position is informed by the particularity of the context in which he lived.

Black people, however, are not willing to scrap their church tradition. Black Christians insist on retaining their tradition with all its contextual limitations. Even though some aspects of that tradition may run counter to their perception of its central thrust, black people will not simply jettison them or ignore them. I believe the reason for this is that it is their tradition, made and sustained by black people alone. Their pride and personal investment in it have made fierce their grasp upon every jot and tittle. The persistence of this grasp is illustrated through a more recent, if not more personal, experience, which Grant relates. At the 1971 Annual Convocation of the National Committee of Black Churchmen held at the Liberty Baptist Church in Chicago, she approached the pulpit to place thereupon a tape recorder. She was told in no uncertain terms that women were not allowed in the pulpit area.[13]

Black feminist Christians are challenging black church tradition because it is their tradition also. Black male theologians must remember, in light of all this, that while tradition is a source of the truth, it is not the truth itself. Our tradition is not perfect but is an imperfect witness and instrument of a perfect and liberating God. As God has revealed to us a hint of freedom through tradition, that tradition cannot hold the fullness of God's revelation of freedom for black women and black men.

EXPERIENCE

Black experience is the context out of which black theologizing takes place. "This means that there can be no Black Theology which does not take the black experience as a source."[14] Only in our experience can we grasp the questions to which God is the answer. The experience of the black community in their struggle for liberation sharpens and clarifies the ultimate and divine meaning of that struggle. In the 1950s and early 1960s the civil-rights movement led by Martin Luther King Jr. gave new life to the then dormant quest for freedom. In the late 1960s and early 1970s the Black Power movement, led by Malcolm X, Stokely Carmichael, and others, gave an even greater exigency to that quest. It is this kind of experience that formed the context of black theology.

Black women, however, have questions about their role or lack thereof in these pivotal experiences. They also question the lack of weight given to their specific experiences as normative. Jeanne Noble relates the following incident.

> During the summer of 1972 a major black women's organization had enough cases to bring up affirmative appeals on behalf of well-trained black women seeking employment in two of the largest black organizations in the nation. At the last minute they decided that it was not sisterly to complain.[15]

Clearly, the question for black women is whether or not the peculiarities of their experience of racism and sexism are reducible to a general experience of racism. They note that the civil-rights movement was launched from the experience of a black woman, Rosa Parks, and that women were a clear majority of the rank and file. Yet, it was a male-dominated movement. Michele Wallace argues that part of the reason that the Black Power movement evolved from the civil-rights effort was to accommodate the growing militancy of black women.

> It was the restless throng of ambitious black female civil rights workers — as much as any failure of the Civil Rights Movement — that provoked Stokely Carmichael to cry "Black Power!"[16]

But the Black Power movement itself was epitomized by the grand, black, patriarchal image of Malcolm X. This often ambiguous experience is the contextual arena of black theology. Despite the ambiguity, however, black theologians must continue to take black experience seriously — the experience of the total community, both male and female. At the same time, while the black theologian must always affirm the particularity and significance, the importance and finiteness of our experience, he or she must always recognize that though black experience is a source of truth it is not the truth itself. Black experience itself is always open to the redemptive and liberating activity of God.

BLACKNESS AS AN ONTOLOGICAL SYMBOL

For black theology, "blackness" connotes something more, but not other than, skin color. To be black, then, has at least two levels of meaning. It means experiencing the oppression of being black in America. This experience is lived by all who are born into oppression and by all who enter into solidarity with the oppressed. It also means experiencing one's God-given freedom through the struggle for the liberation of the oppressed.

> First, blackness is a physiological trait. It refers to a particular black-skinned people in America who have been victims of white racist brutality.... Secondly, blackness is an ontological symbol for all people who participate in the liberation of [humanity] from oppression. This is the universal note in Black Theology.[17]

Thus, blackness connotes not only a skin color but also a state of being in the world. Blackness points to the dialectical and ontological experience of true humanity by moving out of oppression and into freedom. Blackness is ontological because the essential character of God, Israel, and Jesus, confirms it as such. "To say God is creator means that my being finds its source in God. I am black because God is black! ...To be a disciple of the Black Christ is to become black with him."[18]

Blackness, then, points to the imago Dei in humanity. Its concrete manifestation in Jesus Christ relates the will, being, and activity of God with the situation, condition, and aspirations of the chosen people.

The most radical challenge that black women present to black theology centers around the ontological meaning of blackness. Black theologians have faced this kind of question before from Latin American liberation theologies. Their question has been, Has the theological concept of blackness fallen prey to the limitations inherent in the cultural [capitalistic] concept of blackness? The Latin Americans wanted to know whether or not the concept of blackness had become limited or could it include those whose oppression was more than or other than racial in origin? Black theologians have boldly faced this question, coming as it did from allies and not foes. Indeed, James Cone's work *God of the Oppressed* seems directed, at least partially, toward responding to this question.

The black feminist challenge, coming as it does from within the black experience, is even more crucial. The black feminist question is this. Has the ontology of blackness become limited to the ontic status of maleness? While black theologians are claiming ontological status for blackness, have they unconsciously elevated the ontic status of maleness, thereby, in actuality giving blackness only a penultimate significance? This is exactly what Michele Wallace claims happened to the black male in the black liberation movement.

> The contemporary black man no longer exists for his people or even for himself. He has made himself a living testament to the white man's failures. . . . As long as he was able to hold onto his own black-centered definition of manhood his sense of himself was not endangered. But it was inevitable . . . that he would get the black and white perspectives confused. He is unaware that he has accepted a definition of manhood that is destructive to himself and that negates the best efforts of his past.[19]

If blackness is an ontological symbol, then it means more than physical blackness and also more than maleness. Blackness must not come to refer only to the deficiency of whiteness. It must mean the condition of an oppressed people who are throwing off the chains of their oppression and seeking to claim the freedom they already possess. Blackness must mean the racism and liberation from it experienced by black men. And it must also mean the racism and sexism and the liberation from that experienced by black women and men. If blackness as an ontological symbol refers to authentic humanity, then it cannot become simply a "living testament" to failure in white male-white female relations but must point to new relations. According to Jeanne Noble, "Black women are saying the opposite. They want to share freedom together. They want new relationships, not carbon copies."[20] Before this can occur, however, black men must take seriously the black women's search for authentic selfhood.

> Black women want to be involved. They demand to be involved. Black women want to be partners, allies, sisters! Before there is partnering and sharing with someone, however, there is the becoming of oneself. And the search and discovery of authentic selfhood on the part of black women has begun.[21]

The search for, and discovery of, authentic selfhood on the part of black women is part of the ontology of the black community. Though black men do not experience sexism directly, by entering into solidarity with our sisters, their problems become our problems. By accepting the divine demand to struggle against both sexism and racism in the black community, black men can experience blackness in both its male and female manifestations. It is only out of this kind of experience that black theologians can accompany all black people toward that eschatological community in which "there is neither slave nor free, male nor female."

WOMANIST RESOURCES FOR BLACK THEOLOGY

The experience of black women is not only a critique to which black male theologians must respond. It is also an indispensable resource for the doing of black theology. It is becoming clear through the study of the arts and the literature, philosophy, and theology being provided by black women that their particular way of seeing the world, construing the faith, and confronting oppression is an untapped resource for black theology. Delores Williams has demonstrated some of the theological insights that black imaginative literature holds.[22] She argues that literary works by black women writers provide valuable resources for the constructive task of theology because they do not conform to the traditional separation of reason and the imagination in human experience. To make use of these sources the arena of conversations among black theologians must be opened to women. The partnership of black women and men, along with the solidarity of black women, must be supported. The resources of black women's experience will inevitably expose the weaknesses of the original vision of liberation in black theology. The extent to which black male theologians simply accepted the absence of black women in their ranks and adopted the attitudes of white men toward black women may reflect the power of racist and sexist oppression to circumscribe the liberating vision of the oppressed. The vigor and determination with which black male theologians commit themselves to overcoming this failure will reflect the genuineness of their vision of freedom.

One of the ways in which black women have begun to change the shape of black theological discourse is to draw on their own cultural roots. One alternative is to undertake the theological task as working groups rather than as solitary thinkers. This alternative emulates the pattern of traditional African societies where the collective is the basic social unit rather than the individual. Another alternative is doing theology from the standpoint of ethics rather than systematics, so that one begins the theological task by asking how the group lives and witnesses in the world rather than with the systematic articulation of basic Christian doctrines. Still another alternative is the suggestion that theological discourse take the form of storytelling rather than philosophical discourse. In this way, black theology would contribute to the sustenance of black culture by embodying cultural values that can be transmitted even to children.

A second — and perhaps even more important — womanist contribution to black theology are the hidden sources for black theological reflection employed by black women. One of these sources is the reading of the Bible from the perspective of black women. Black women are rereading the Bible and deciding for themselves whether it is the solution to, or part of, the problems that they face. Katie Cannon has argued that black women have interpreted the Bible in distinctive ways made necessary by the particularity of their experience.[23] She concludes that the Bible has supported the historic quest of black women for freedom and dignity. Women's history is also being rewritten from the perspective of black women. The unheard testimonies of black mothers and daughters are being recovered and celebrated. Black women's spirituality is becoming appreciated as a means of both survival and liberation. Toinette Eugene has explored the ethical and theological dimensions of black spirituality in relation to sexism and racism.[24] She argues that the unifying power of "black love" is capable of healing the domestic wounds between black men and black women and, ultimately, restoring mutuality to their relations. These sources and the emerging methodologies of black women theologians point to the development of a distinctive theological perspective for black women; that is, a distinctive "womanist theology."

The black women's movement faces both overt and covert sexism. Therefore, black male theologians cannot expect black women simply to accept a verbal disclaimer that sexism on the part of black men is either nonexistent or has been overcome. Ultimately, only black women can make that determination. Black male theologians can, however, state what they believe to be the norm of all theological discourse and relate that norm to their encounter with black feminism. The norm of theological discourse is Jesus Christ, whose character and being are defined by his mission to liberate those who are oppressed. This norm indicates that wherever people are struggling to free themselves from oppression, Christ is there among them. This means that Christ is at work in the African-American community, siding with the oppressed. He is siding with black men and black women in their struggles for freedom. Thus, it is not the desire to be relevant, avant garde, or chic that determines the difference between true God-talk and mere verbal posturing. Rather, it is fidelity to the revelation of God in Christ Jesus that transforms our motives and words into praxis and praise.

Embracing Masculinity

James B. Nelson

Is there not something good, important, *and distinctive* about the experience of maleness itself? Something that can produce an energy which is not oppressive but rather creative and life-giving — and recognizably male? A "deep masculine" that men can find in themselves and justly celebrate? ...And, what is the place, if any, of that age-old emblem of manhood, the male genitals? Let us look at masculinity through this particular lens.

— Eugene Monick

PHALLUS

In his suggestive book *Phallos: Sacred Image of the Masculine,* Eugene Monick explores the psychic and religious dimensions of the male experience of his phallus, his erect penis.[1] Every male, he asserts, directly knows the meanings of erection: strength, hardness, determination, sinew, straightforwardness, penetration. Because erection is not fully under a man's conscious control, because the penis seems to decide on its own when, where, and with whom it wants erection and action, the phallus seems to be an appropriate metaphor for the masculine unconscious.

From time immemorial it has fascinated men. Numerous ancient expressions of phallic art and worship are well known, from the common representations on ancient Greek pottery, to the huge erection of the Cerne giant (carved in the first century B.C. by the Celts into a chalk hill in Dorset, England), to the modern-day Hindu cult of Shiva, where the phallus is an image of divinity.[2] Beyond such outward evidences of religious veneration, men of every time and place have known a religious

"Embracing Masculinity" by James B. Nelson is reprinted from *The Intimate Connection: Male Sexuality, Masculine Spirituality* by James B. Nelson (Philadelphia: Westminster/John Knox Press, 1988). Copyright © 1988 James B. Nelson. Reprinted by permission of Westminster/John Knox Press.

quality to their phallic experience. To adapt Rudolf Otto's words, it is the *mysterium tremendum*. Such encounters with the numinous produce responses of fascination, awe, energy, and a sense of the "wholly other."[3] Through the phallus, men sense a resurrection, the capacity of the male member to return to life again and again after depletion. An erection makes a boy feel like a man and makes a man feel alive. It brings the assurance and substantiation of masculine strength.

Yet, as with other experiences of the holy, males feel ambivalent about the phallus. Erections must be hidden from general view. They are an embarrassment when they occur publicly. Men joke about erections with each other but cannot speak seriously. The secret is exposed only with another person in intimacy or when a male permits himself to experience his potency alone. If the mystery is exposed publicly, somehow the sacred has been profaned.

Furthermore, there is a double-sidedness to the phallic experience. One dimension is the *earthy* phallus.[4] This is the erection perceived as sweaty, hairy, throbbing, wet, animal sexuality. In some measure it is Bly's Iron John maleness. Men who have rejected this may be nice and gentle, but they seem to lack life-giving energy. Their keys remain hidden under the queen's pillow — indeed, with the cooperation of the king, for the powers of social order always distrust the earthy phallus. And there is reason for distrust, because there can be an ugly, brutal side to the earthy phallus that uses others for gratification when this part of a man's sexuality does not find balance with other sides. Yet without the positive presence of earthy energy a man is bland. There is gentleness without strength, peacefulness without vitality, tranquility without vibrancy.

Men also experience the *solar* phallus.[5] Solar (from the sun) means enlightenment. A man's erect penis represents to him all that stands tall. It is proud. The solar experience of erection puts a man in touch with the excitement of strenuous achievement. It is the Jacob's ladder and the mountain climb, which rise above the earthy and the earthly. It is the satisfaction of straining to go farther intellectually, physically, and socially. Solar phallus is transcendence. It is the church steeples and skyscrapers that men are inclined to build. Solar phallus represents what most men would like to have noted in their obituaries. In Carl Jung's thinking, solar phallus is the very substance of masculinity. It is, he believed, *logos,* which transforms thought into word, just as eros (which he called feminine) transforms feeling into relatedness. I believe Jung misled us with his bifurcations of masculine and feminine principles, unfortunately grounding them in common gender stereotypes. Nevertheless, logos is an important part of the male experience both represented and invited by the solar phallus.

As with the earthy phallus, there is a shadow side to the experience of the solar phallus, too. It is the patriarchal oppression of those who do not "measure up." It is proving one's worth through institutional accomplishments. It is the illusion of strength and power that comes from position. It is the use of technical knowledge to dominate. It is political power which defends its ideological purity at virtually any price and then prides itself on standing tall in the saddle. It is addiction to the notion that bigger is better. The distortions of solar phallus are legion. Yet without its integrated positive energy, a man lacks direction and movement. Without the urge to extend himself, he is content with the mediocre. Without the experience of the wholly other, life loses its self-transcendence.

Thus far I have agreed in broad outline with Monick's significant analysis: the importance of both the earthy and the solar phallus, their integration, and the dangers of their shadow sides. Here, however, Monick stops. He believes that phallus, the erect penis, is *the* sacred image of the masculine. That seems to be enough. But it is not. Left there, I fear we are left with priapism.

In Roman mythology Priapus, son of Dionysus and Aphrodite, was the god of fertility. His usual representations were marked both by grotesque ugliness and an enormous erection. In human sexual disorders, priapism is the painful clinical condition of an erection that will not go down. Priapus and priapism are symbolic of the idolatry of the half-truth. Phallus, the erection, indeed is a vital part of the male's experience of his sexual organs. Hence, it is usually a vital part of his spirituality. But it is only part. Were it the whole thing, his sexuality and his spirituality would be painful and bizarre, both to himself and to others. That this in fact is too frequently the case is difficult to deny. Our phallic experience gives vital energy, both earthy and solar. But we also need the affirmative experience of the *penis*.

PENIS

In our daily lives, almost all men are genitally soft by far the greater share of the time. Genitally speaking, penis rather than phallus is our awareness, insofar as we are aware at all. (For economy in words, I will use "penis" for the organ in its flaccid, unaroused state.) We are genitally limp most of our waking moments, and while erections come frequently during sleep we are seldom aware of them.

Psychically, the experiences of phallus and of penis seem very different. An erection during waking hours claims my attention. Frequently I choose not to act upon its aroused urgency, and sometimes in embarrassment I hide its evidence. But its claims on my psychic awareness have an undeniable phallic imperiousness. The penis is different. Most of the time I am unaware of it. It is just there, part of me, functioning in my occasional need to urinate, but most often invisible from my conscious awareness, much as an internal organ. But when I am conscious of it in dressing or undressing, I am aware of its difference from phallus. Penis is considerably smaller. It is wrinkled. There is even something comical about the contrast (as a man's wife or lover occasionally might tell him). It has a relaxed humility. In its external existence it seems vulnerable, and with the testicles it needs jockstrap protection during the body's vigorous athletics.

In spite of the quantitative dominance of penis time, men tend to undervalue penis and overvalue phallus. Part of that, indeed, simply stems from conscious awareness. When the phallus is present, it demands our attention. The penis does not. Part of the difference, however, is a matter of intentional valuation. We have been taught and have learned to value phallic meanings in patriarchy: bigger is better (in bodily height, in paychecks, in the size of one's corporation or farm); hardness is superior to softness (in one's muscles, in one's facts, in one's foreign policy positions); upness is better than downness (in one's career path, in one's computer, in one's approach to life's problems). In "a man's world," small, soft, and down pale beside big, hard, and up.

Penis is undervalued, also, because we so commonly identify male energy and true masculinity with the vitality of young manhood. Infant males and little boys have frequent erections, but true phallus — the heroic sword raised on high — is the property of young manhood. As age comes upon a man, hardness changes and modifies. It is less apparent, less urgent, less the signature of his body. Phallus bears intimations of life and vigor, while penis bears intimations of mortality. Fearing mortality, men tend to reject the qualities of penis and project them upon women, who are then seen to be small, soft, and vulnerable, qualities inferior to the phallic standard. Wrinkles, so typical of penis, are not permitted in women if they are to retain their womanly attraction.[6]

But the undervaluing of penis and the overvaluing of phallus take their toll. The price is paid by all who suffer because of patriarchy, for this spiritual body dynamic, while hardly the sole cause of such oppression, surely contributes to it. But oppressors themselves are also oppressed in the process. So what is the price paid by men? One cost we must look at is the deprivation of a significant kind of masculine spiritual energy and power.

The history of Western spirituality reveals two traditional paths to the presence of God: the Via Positiva and the Via Negativa, the positive way and the negative way.[7] The former is a way of affirmation, of thanksgiving, of ecstasy. It is the way of light, the way of being filled by the sacred fullness and rising to the divine height. The Via Negativa is a way of emptying and being emptied. It is the way of darkness. It is sinking into nothingness and into the sacred depths. In spirituality, each way needs the other for balance and completion. The overdevelopment of one to the detriment of the other brings distortion. I believe that in the male experience the Via Positiva has profound associations with the phallus, while the Via Negativa correspondingly is connected to the penis. And in most men it is the latter which remains underrecognized, underclaimed, underaffirmed.

Consider some aspects of the Via Negativa as expressed by a great Christian mystic who knew this way, Meister Eckhart (1260–1327). It is quiet, not active: "Nothing in all creation is so like God as stillness." It is the darkness more than the light: "The ground of the soul is dark." It appears to be less rather than more: "God is not found in the soul by adding anything but by a process of subtraction." It is a deep sinking and a letting go: "We are to sink eternally from letting go to letting go into God." It is the abandoning of focus and attention: "One should love God mindlessly, without mind or mental activities or images or representations." It is the paradox of nothingness embracing something: "God is a being beyond being and a nothingness beyond being.... God is nothingness. And yet God is something."[8]

All such modes of the Via Negativa are a man's experiences of his penis, not his phallus. Think of sinking and emptying. The penis is empty of the engorging blood that brings hard excitement to the phallus. Its flaccidity is a letting go of all urgency. It has nowhere to go. It just is. It just hangs and sinks between the legs.

Sinking, emptying, is a way of spirituality.[9] It means trusting God that we do not need to *do,* that our *being* is enough. It means yielding to our tears that keep coming and coming once they begin. It means trusting ourselves to the darkness of sleep, so like the darkness of death. It means abandoning our own achievements and resting in the depths of meaning we do not create. Men often resist these things. But sinking and emptying are as necessary to the spirit's rhythms as they are to the genitals'. Without periods of genital rest, a man lacks phallic capacity. Without times of retreat to the desert, there is no energy for greening.

Or consider darkness, another theme of the Via Negativa. It seems related to the cosmic womb of our origins, and it has its own energy. Rainer Maria Rilke writes, "You darkness, that I come from/I love you more than all the fires that fence in the world...and it is possible a great energy is moving near me/I have faith in nights."[10] But most men are less at home in the darkness than in the light. We are heirs of the

Enlightenment, a male-oriented rational movement that sought to shed
light on everything. Our psyches seem to link darkness with death, and
fear of death is characteristic of the patriarchal society. Starhawk, speaking
of the holiness of darkness, maintains that the dark is "all that we are
afraid of, all that we don't want to see — fear, anger, sex, grief, death,
the unknown."[11]

The penis, in contrast to the phallus, is a creature of the dark. It
is resting. Asleep. Usually we are unaware of its presence, but we are
conscious of the presence of the phallus, just as we are aware of the
presence of light. Taught to prize light and fear the dark, we have also
been taught to prize the phallic virtues and to fear the meanings of penis.
Its quiescence seems symbolic of death, its limpness the reminder of
male-dreaded impotence, and fears of death and impotence are the cause
of much destruction. But without the darkness there is no growth, no
mystery, no receptivity, no deep creativity. Without the gentle dark, light
becomes harsh.

MASCULINE ENERGY: BEYOND ANDROGYNY

For a variety of reasons, men have come to believe that phallus is
the emblem of masculinity, the signature of true maleness. But this is
only partly true, and partial truths taken as the whole truth become both
demonic and self-destructive. A man's penis is as genuinely his reality as
is his phallus, and just as important to his male humanity. Spiritually, the
Via Negativa is as vital to him as the Via Positiva. It may also be the case
that men's overvaluation of phallus, and the undervaluation of penis,
is one important reason for our confusions about gender identities and
the notion of androgyny.

The concept of androgyny has been commonplace for some years.[12]
Most simply put, it denotes the integration within a single person of
traits traditionally identified by gender stereotypes as masculine and
as feminine. Thus, androgynous people characterize themselves both as
strongly self-reliant, assertive, and independent, and as strongly understanding, affectionate, and compassionate. Androgyny is an appealing
alternative to the oppressiveness of gender role stereotypes. It goes
beyond the false dualism of the belief that there are certain inherent
personality traits of the male and of the female. It moves us beyond
oppressive gender expectations into the possibility of a more genuinely
human liberation for each and for all.

The concept seems appealing theologically. Nicolas Berdyaev, the Rus-
sian philosopher-theologian, pressed the idea in 1919, long before its
currency in social psychology. There is, he declared, a fundamental androgyny of the human being created in the image of God, an androgyny

that the gender roles of the world have not destroyed. "In fact, 'in the beginning' it is neither man nor woman who bears the divine similitude. In the beginning it is only the androgyne ... who bears it. The differentiation of the sexes is a consequence of the fall of Adam." Now, estranged from our essence, we have a compelling desire to recover our lost unity through recovery of the lost principle. "It is by means of this femininity that the male-human can once again be integrated to the androgynous source of his nature, just as it is in God that the lover meets with the beloved, because it is in God that personality is rooted. And personality in God, in its original state, is androgynous."[13]

Berdyaev was ahead of his time. Most later male theologians of this century have not seriously raised the androgynous theme but rather have emphasized the need of gender complementarity. Karl Barth is typical.[14] He believes that our humanity, created in the image of God, is "fellow-humanity." We are incomplete by ourselves. Men and women come into their fullness only in intimate relation to persons of the opposite sex. Barth's position rests on the assumption that by nature the personalities and qualities of the two sexes are essentially different and that each needs the other for completion. There is no androgyny. Barth draws a clear conclusion from this concerning homosexuality: it is perversion and idolatry. One who seeks same-sex union is narcissistically seeking the self. It is a quest for self-satisfaction and self-sufficiency, but such aims can never be realized because the two sexes are fundamentally necessary for each other. While I find Barth's emphasis on the *social* nature of our true humanity commendable, his notion of gender complementarity is deeply flawed. It rests on the uncritical use of gender stereotypes, and it particularly oppresses gays and lesbians, all who are female (because those stereotypes do), and all who are single (among the latter, Jesus included). The notion of gender complementarity is a giant step backward from androgyny.

Androgyny is an ancient theme, prevalent in classical mythology. In Christian thought it was present far earlier than Berdyaev. Yet I believe his was the first clear statement of the essential androgyny of *both* sexes. Earlier versions, blatantly patriarchal, found only the male androgynous. Woman was made necessary as a differentiated sexual being only because man had lost his state of perfection and needed her feminine principle for his human completion. She, however, remained half human.

Nevertheless, androgyny as a theological concept, even in Berdyaev's promising way, runs into some of the same problems as are present in current social psychology. One problem is both definitional and practical. Does the concept mean that both "feminine" and "masculine" characteristics somehow essentially (by nature or by God's design) exist together in every individual, and thus they should be developed and expressed? This seems to be the most common understanding. In the psychological literature sometimes it is labeled "monoandrogynism," to distinguish it from variations of the theme. But this can be oppressive in its own way. Now each person has two sets of gender traits to learn and incorporate instead of one. Now everyone is expected to acquire thoroughly both "instrumental/agentic" ("masculine") and "expressive/nurturant" ("feminine") characteristics in equal amounts, a standard that would seem to double the pressure that people traditionally have felt.

Even more basically, another problem is that androgyny is based on the assumption that there are, indeed, two distinct and primordial sets of personality characteristics — one "masculine," the other "feminine." Even if we assume that each sex is capable of developing both sets of traits, the definition itself perpetuates the very problem it had hoped to overcome. It still locates one constellation of qualities essentially and dominantly in men and the other constellation essentially and dominantly in women. Jung's psychological thought exemplifies this, as do those who draw upon him, for example, in speaking of the male's need to develop "his latent feminine side." In fact, there is a built-in obsolescence to this concept. For if each sex stopped adhering only to its primary characteristics, and if the two gender stereotypes subsequently became less distinct from each other, androgyny in the current sense would lose its meaning.

One way out of the conceptual difficulty is simply to envision the complete transcendence of gender-role traits (sometimes called the "polyandrous" possibility). Here, personality traits are seen as having no connection at all with biological sex. Each individual is viewed as different from every other individual, for each has unique interests and capacities. In many ways this vision is promising. It frees individuals to be who they uniquely are. However, there remains a problem. The notion of gender-role transcendence, while it honors uniqueness, does not hold up any vision of inclusiveness or relative balance in personal qualities. A given individual could still be as one-sided, even though the rigid linkage between certain traits and one's biological sex had been severed.

Nevertheless, an important question still remains. Is there anything *distinctive* to the experience of one's own biological sex that grounds us in the development of a more whole personality, a personhood richer than its specific gender stereotype? More particularly, is there anything in the male body experience that enables him to transcend the traditional cultural images of masculinity?

If that *is* the case, it is difficult to see why the call to more inclusive personhood would be fundamentally oppressive. If as a man I were called upon to acquire feminine qualities *in addition to my natural masculinity,* that would be one thing. I might be capable of doing that, but it would feel much like learning a second language as an adult, adding another linguistic capability to my native tongue. Even if through years of study and practice I become somewhat proficient, my second language would always be that — a second language, added on, requiring additional effort. My strong inclination would always be to see the world primarily through the images of the language of my birth. On the other hand, were I "naturally bilingual" — born into a bilingual family and society, schooled in the images of both from my earliest days — the inclusiveness of languages would not feel like a burden. It would feel natural.

My illustration admittedly suffers, because languages are thoroughly social inventions and learnings. Our bodies are not. While they have many social, learned meanings attached to them, they also have a biological givenness. My point, however, is this: We have been given "bilingual bodies." Even if one language has been developed more than the other, the second language is not foreign to us. It is not something we need to add on. It is just as originally part of us as the language with which, by accident of circumstances, we have become more familiar.

It is time to move beyond the usual meanings of androgyny. The vision for men is not to develop "feminine" energies (or for women to develop "masculine" energies). Rather, the vision for men is the fullest development of our *masculine* energies. But the issue is *fullness*. We are not talking only of phallic qualities. Penis is vulnerable, soft, receptive. Penis represents and invites the spirituality of the Via Negativa. But a penis is not "feminine" — it is as authentically masculine as is phallus. It bears qualities rooted in the fullness of the male's sexual experience, in the fullness of his body affirmation. So we who are men are simply invited to develop the masculine more richly. To speak this way is not to play word games. Linguistic sleight-of-hand tricks are abstractions. Incarnational reflection does not thrive on abstractions, but tries to represent bodily realities honestly.

Finally, it is important to recognize that each dimension of the male genital experience involves the other. Each of us experiences only one body, though in our experience there is the conjunction of apparent opposites. Paradoxically, the opposites are only apparently so. Each is implied by and contained within the other. Penis is always potentially phallus. The soft receptivity of penis implies relationality. But phallus is aroused as the genital aspects of relationship are anticipated or fantasized. So, also, the hard energy of phallus literally bears the signs of gentleness. The lover is amazed at the velvety texture and softness of the head of the man's rock-hard erection. Men know the vulnerability of their testicles and shield them from harm even during arousal and lovemaking. Indeed, male vulnerability is most present exactly at the spot where colloquial language locates male courage: "He has balls."[15]

Such is the marvelous conjunction of apparent opposites in the male's sexual body, a wholeness inviting him to richness of personhood. It is at the same time the bodily experienced invitation to richness of spirituality through the apparent opposites of Via Positiva and Via Negativa. Such is the golden ball of legend, representing connectedness and radiant energy.

POWER AND SIZE

One of the central issues in spirituality is *power*.[16] It is evident whenever personal beings are present to each other. Men's lives — and the lives of all those affected by patriarchy — have been dominated by one particular perception of power. It is *unilateral* power. It is also called zero-sum power, or the power of a closed energy system, inasmuch as it carries with it the assumption that there is only a limited quantity of power available, so that the more one person gets the less is available to the other. Unilateral power is nonmutual and nonrelational. Its purpose is to produce the largest possible effect on another, while being least affected by the other. Its ideal is control.

"In this view," writes Bernard Loomer, "Our size or stature is measured by the strength of our unilateral power. Our sense of self-value is correlative to our place on the scale of inequality."[17] But the sense of self one has in this understanding is nonrelational, self-contained. It is the traditional masculine ideal of the Lone Ranger. The aim is to move toward maximum self-sufficiency. Dependency on others is weakness. But this kind of power, in reducing mutuality, produces estrangement among people. We are deadened to our interdependence and to the mystery of each other. This is unmodified phallic power.

Christianity has often embraced this view of power in its views of God. At such times it has seen God as omniscient, omnipotent, and controlling the world by divine fiat. This theology was built upon the same sexual dualism that split spirit from body. Spirit was seen as eternal, complete, and changeless, while body was temporal, incomplete, and changeable. God had unilateral power. "He" was perfect in his completeness and unaffected by those "below."

At the same time Christian theology embraced this unilateral understanding of power as applied to God, it had problems. The gospel message was quite clear that among people this was "worldly" power. Because such power was one-way and controlling, it seemed to be the antithesis of love. When Jesus renounced the power of the world, it was this kind of power he forsook. Thus, in Christianity a view of love as similarly one-way arose. It was the traditional interpretation of agape — a one-way divine love, a concern for the other with no concern for oneself. It was this kind of love that Christians were told to emulate. A one-sided love became the compensation for a one-sided power. One extreme was designed to offset a contrary extreme. The loss of eros and the goodness of the erotic, the confusion of selfishness with self-love — such were the prices exacted by unilateral power and unilateral love.

There is, however, another understanding of power. "This is the ability both to produce and to undergo an effect. It is the capacity both to influence others and to be influenced by others."[18] This is *relational* power. It is generative power, the power of an open energy system. Instead of [power being] a fixed, limited amount, the assumption is that shared power can generate more power. People are enhanced by this kind of power, mystery is affirmed, interdependence is celebrated. This, however, is not the power represented by the penis, but by the whole of the genitals and the whole of the body.

These distinctions concerning power bear on the problem of androgyny. Traditional androgyny begins with a combinationist assumption. It takes a fixed notion of the masculine (the active agent) and a fixed notion of the feminine (the receiving, nurturing one) and tries to combine them in one person. However, in regard to power, both understandings of gender roles are deficient. The "feminine" principle has been under attack because it suggests a neurotic dependence on others and lack of sufficient autonomy. The "masculine" has been under attack because it suggests the urge to dominate others without being at the same time influenced by them. The point is that both are faulty. Adding one to another to achieve a balance is not the solution. Rather, the solution is understanding that both are definitions marred by fear and insecurity. The "feminine" fears self-dependence, while the "masculine" fears interdependence. Such fear is born of insecurity. It is the absence of authentic power.

Just as wholeness for either a man or a woman is not some combination of the masculine and the feminine, so also authentic relational power is not a neat combination of the active and the receptive. Relational power understands that the capacity to absorb the influence of another without losing the self's own center is as truly a quality of power as is the strength of exerting influence on another.

Loomer calls this kind of strength "size," the capacity to become large enough to make room for another within the self without losing the self's own integrity or freedom.

The world of the individual who can be influenced by another without losing his or her identity or freedom is larger than the world of
the individual who fears being influenced.... The stature of the individual who can let another exist in his or her own creative freedom
is larger than the size of the individual who insists that others must
conform to his own purposes and understandings."[19]

Sexual experience always involves power. The experience of phallus
without penis is unilateral power. The colloquial male ideal of the phallus
is "two feet long, made of steel, and lasts all night." Phallus can handle
multiple orgasms (or partners) without being reduced to flaccidity. The
phallic perception of woman is as the receptacle for phallic power and
emission. The ideal: affect without being affected.

In contrast, the man who affirms his whole sexuality knows that both
phallus and penis are one. They are different but interdependent qualities of one male reality. Each at the same time is the other. In spite of
the myth of phallic unaffectedness, men know that they are not made
of steel, nor do they last all night. Phallus not only delivers effect but is
also very much affected. In intercourse it is changed, transformed into
penis. "Transformed" is a good word. Sometimes we use the language of
death and resurrection about the male genital experience, but it is time
to reassess that imagery. It can be highly misleading, even destructive.
Yet I fear that the image is fairly common in the male psyche. It suggests
that phallus is alive and then, when spent, dies. Penis, then, is the death
from which phallus is raised once again. But this interpretation implies a
very unilateral understanding of power. Only the phallus has power, the
penis does not. Further, the suggestion is that, at least in the heterosexual experience, the woman is somehow associated with "reducing" the
phallus to flaccidity. Thus once again we make, even if unconsciously, the
connection between woman and passivity. Now the woman somehow is
responsible for the man's passivity, his loss of power and agency. But with
the language of death and resurrection the psychic connections become
more vicious. Now the phallus dies, and the connection is established
between the woman and death. And death is assumed to be the enemy.

But when the phallus becomes penis it does not die. There is simply
a change to another form of its life. When the phallus becomes penis it
does not lose its power, except when that power is understood unilater-
ally. Rather, the penis has a different kind of power. It is now the man's
genital sexuality expressing its capacity to absorb change. What was once
hard and imperious is now soft and gentle. In both dimensions the man
is experiencing his masculine power, and both are aspects of relational
power. True power is mutuality, making claims and absorbing influence.
It is different from the "mutuality" of external relatedness, which trades

in force, compromise, and accommodation. It understands the paradox that the greatest influence often consists in being influenced, in enabling another to make the largest impact on oneself.

When a man so understands his sexuality he better understands true power, and when he understands power he better understands his sexuality. The same is true of size, for size and power are intimately related. However, "the wisdom of the world" about male genital size measures quality precisely in terms of quantity. Bigger is better. The masculinist fantasy says not only "made of steel" but also "two feet long." It does not matter that sexologists and sexual therapists tell us that the actual size of the male organ is quite irrelevant to effectual sexual functioning and the quality of lovemaking — irrelevant except for one thing: too large an organ causes problems. Still, myth and fantasy persist. Pubescent boys still measure themselves and each other. The record holders are honored in the neighborhood gang. And, as noted earlier, Freud continues to be debunked in his contention that penis envy is a persistent phenomenon of the woman's unconscious; rather, it persists in the surreptitious, glancing comparisons made in the men's locker room.

In contrast to such worldly wisdom about size as quantitative, consider Loomer's description:

> By *size* I mean the stature of a person's soul, the range and depth of his [or her] love, his [or her] capacity for relationships. I mean the volume of life you can take into your being and still maintain your integrity and individuality, the intensity and variety of outlook you can entertain in the unity of your being without feeling defensive or insecure. I mean the strength of your spirit to encourage others to become freer in the development of their diversity and uniqueness. I mean the power to sustain more complex and enriching tensions. I mean the magnanimity of concern to provide conditions that enable others to increase in stature.[20]

When a man understands this meaning of size, his genital sexuality is less anxiously, more graciously celebrated. And when that is true, he also better understands the true meaning of size as a criterion of genuine power.

If the themes of death and resurrection can be misleading when applied to penis and phallus, surely they have valid and profound meanings for our sexual and bodily lives more generally. The resurrection of the body in our experience means that mind and body no longer make war on each other, each trying to control or dominate the other. Now I can feel that I *am* my body, and that does not in any way contradict the fact that I am my mind or spirit. Death separates. Resurrection and life reunite. To be raised to life is to discover that I am one person. Body and mind are no longer felt to be distinct.

We usually have such an experience now and then. Most likely it is temporary, soon forgotten, for we have lived much of our lives with dualistic self-understandings and dualistic perceptions of reality at large. So body and mind fall apart again, each competing with the other for the prize of being me. Death sets in once more. But resurrections occur, and in those moments I know myself to be one. When that happens, the experience of oneness with myself brings with it the strong sense of connectedness with the rest of the world. I feel connected to — more than separated from — the people, creatures, and things among whom I live. They have their own identities, yet they also become part of me and I of them. My resurrection is that world's resurrection as I know that world.[21] The same applies to a man's genital perception. Resurrection occurs when penis and phallus are one, neither competing for the honor of being the man. When that happens there is true power — and authentic size.

JESUS AS SEXUAL MAN AND MAN OF POWER

Jesus as the Christ has been desexualized by most Christian piety throughout the ages. Sexual dualism has kept its sturdy grip, and incarnation, the real presence of God in human flesh, has been a scandal too great for most of the church to believe. A spiritualized God, acting in proper taste, simply would not do that sort of thing. Docetism, the belief that, in Jesus, God was not really humanly enfleshed but only appeared to be, was early declared a heresy by the church, but it still is very much alive. And about the most effective way of denying Jesus' full humanity has been to deny (outright or by embarrassed silence) his sexuality. Some of the early Christian Gnostics (who abhorred the flesh) represent the extreme. They could not even bring themselves to believe that Jesus needed to eat; he took food with his followers from time to time so as not to alarm them. The thought of Jesus engaged in digestion, defecation, and urination would have appalled them. To the present-day Gnostics of whatever stripe, of course, the thought of Jesus' sexual arousal, erection, and orgasm is at best exceedingly poor taste and at worst blasphemous.

Just as popular piety has been aghast at the thought, theologians for the most part have simply avoided the issue of Jesus' sexuality other than to affirm his celibacy. Only rarely have they faced the question directly. William Phipps, one of the rare ones, has come to the conclusion that Jesus was probably married at one time.[22] Phipps finds no biblical evidence for Jesus' virginity, but rather finds a picture of Jesus as fully immersed in sexuality-affirming Jewish culture, a culture which in fact rejected celibacy in both theory and practice. Jesus, who was hardly pictured as an ascetic by the Gospels, probably married sometime during those years about which we have no information (between ages twelve and thirty). Before his public ministry began, something — we do not know what — happened to his wife. The idea of a celibate savior, Phipps concludes, is not the product of the apostolic age but rather grew out of Christianity's later contact with the dualism of Hellenistic Greece.

I believe the case for Jesus' marriage is highly debatable. Had it happened, surely there would have been some apostolic mention of it. But whether or not Jesus married is not really the crux of the issue. His sexuality is, and investigations like that of Phipps help us to take the issue with greater seriousness. The question is not an esoteric one. If we who call ourselves Christian are unsure of the full humanity of him whom we call Truly Human, we shall be unsure of what full humanity means for us. If our image of authentic personhood in Jesus denigrates sexuality, we will do the same within ourselves.

Actually, some of the "secular theologians" have most effectively pressed the question of Jesus' sexuality. Nikos Kazantzakis and D. H. Lawrence have done so in literature. A particularly interesting inquiry is provided by a distinguished art historian, Leo Steinberg, in *The Sexuality of Christ in Renaissance Art and in Modern Oblivion*.[23] Steinberg observes that for a millennium of Christian history Jesus' sexuality was disregarded by theology and art, which focused virtually all attention on his divinity. Then came the Renaissance and the rediscovery of the glories of humanity.

Now devout Christian painters from Flanders to Florence removed the drapery from the figure of Jesus and purposely exposed his genitals.

> In many hundreds of pious religious works, from before 1400 to past the mid-16th century, the ostensive unveiling of the Child's sex, or the touching, protecting or presentation of it, is the main action. . . . And the emphasis recurs in images of the dead Christ, or of the mystical Man of Sorrows. . . . All of which has been tactfully overlooked for half a millennium.[24]

In the great cathedrals hung paintings of the Holy Family in which Mary herself deliberately spreads the infant's thighs so that the pious might gaze at his genitals in wonder. In other paintings the Magi are depicted gazing intently at Jesus' uncovered loins as if expecting revelation. In still others Jesus' genitals are being touched and fondled by his mother, by St. Anne, and by himself. So also in the paintings of the passion and crucifixion, the adult Jesus is depicted as thoroughly sexual. In some, his hand cups his genitals in death. In others the loincloth of the suffering Christ is protruding with an unmistakable erection.

Steinberg gives several interpretations of this Renaissance art. For one thing, it proved to the believer that Jesus' chastity was real and valid. Sexual abstinence without potency is an empty lesson. Abstinence is meaningful only if it is in combination with a vigorous sexuality. "Virginity, after all, constitutes a victory over concupiscence only where the susceptibility to its power is at least possible."[25] Further, the shamelessness of exposing the infant Jesus' genitals for the admiration of others points back to our original innocence and points forward to our redemption from sin and shame, as the incarnation promises. His open adult sexuality depicted in the passion art promises our redemption.

> Delivered from sin and shame, the freedom of Christ's sexual member bespeaks that aboriginal innocence which in Adam was lost. We may say that Michelangelo's naked Christs — on the cross, dead, or risen — are, like the naked Christ Child, not shameful, but literally and profoundly "shame-less."[26]

And, most fundamentally, the focus on the bodily sexuality of Jesus demonstrated the thoroughness, the completeness of the incarnation, God's choice to embody divinity in humanity. "Therefore, to profess that God once embodied [God]self in human nature is to confess that the eternal, there and then, became mortal and sexual. Thus understood, the evidence of Christ's sexual member serves as the pledge of God's humanation."[27]

We have long known how deeply the Renaissance was committed to the goodness and beauty of the human body. Now we know how radically incarnational its theology was, at least as depicted through the world of art. A half millennium has elapsed since the Renaissance artists made their bold statements about the Christ's sexuality, and most people have chosen not to notice the obvious in their art. Such is the "modern oblivion" about the issue. We continue in that oblivion to our profound deprivation.

Nevertheless, the affirmation of Jesus' sexuality raises difficult problems of another sort, precisely because he was male. The maleness of that one believed to be Christ has been used in countless ways as an instrument of patriarchal oppression. It has been used to "prove" the maleness of God, to outlaw women from ministry, to keep men in control. I agree fully with the protest against this oppressive theological misuse of Jesus' maleness, and I stand with those feminist women and men who despair over the church's tortured slowness in being redeemed on this matter. The central issue at stake is not Jesus' maleness but his *humanity,* to which his full human sexuality is crucial testimony. Indeed, Jesus' life, teachings, and the circumstances of his death all were remarkable protests against patriarchy.[28]

My concern at this point, however, is a different one: How can Jesus help men deal creatively with their own male sexuality? I believe that the ways are manifold, and what I have tried to suggest in this chapter are only a few of them. He stands as teacher, embodiment, and releaser of relational power — a judgment on our phallic unilateral power, but also an invitation to a full-bodied life-giving mutuality. His sexuality was present in his power, and his power was present in his healing sexuality.

Jesus stands as central symbol of the sexuality-spirituality dialectic. Renaissance artists saw in him the full and unified genitality of both phallus and penis, and portrayed him (to repeat Steinberg's words) "profoundly shame-less." Correspondingly, he strikingly embodied and taught the spirituality of both the Via Positiva and the Via Negativa, as is evident from the Gospel accounts. He stands for us as symbol of our sexual-spiritual hope and possibility.

For human beings Jesus stands as clue to our authentic humanity in ways that far transcend the categories of sex and gender. In a less patriarchal age and culture than his, the person recognized as the paradigmatic Christ might well have been female. Yet Jesus was a first-century Jew, and he was male. This does not mean that through him maleness was certified as normative humanity. It does mean, however, that we who also happen to be male can find clues in him toward a richer and more authentic masculinity for ourselves. As a male I see this in the symbolism of Jesus' genital sexuality and the phallus-penis dialectic portrayed by Renaissance artists. I see in Jesus a compelling picture of male sexual wholeness, of creative masculinity, and of the redemption of manhood from both oppressiveness and superficiality. Yet countless women who are Christian also find in Jesus the intimate connection between their own female sexuality and spirituality. I suspect this is the case because Jesus embodies a sexual-spiritual reality that moves beyond our current understandings of androgyny.

I have argued that the notion of androgyny typically operates with a "combinationist" assumption. It begins with a fixed notion of masculine traits and a fixed notion of feminine traits. Then it moves to the contention that these fundamentally different qualities can and should be combined in any one individual regardless of biological sex. We have seen several problems with this concept. One of the major ones is the claim that we are called upon to develop a side of our personalities different from the one that seems rooted in our own particular bodies. The combinationist problem (in whatever form it occurs) is always grounded in an underlying dualism. Regarding androgyny, the dualism lies in the belief that the two sets of gender qualities are *essentially* different from each other, the assumption that authentic masculinity and authentic fem-

ininity are mutual opposites. From this assumption it follows that, in
developing "the feminine" in himself, a man will add a different "something" on to that which is essentially himself. For example, he must
acquire vulnerability and receptivity, qualities supposedly not natural to
one with a male organ, to one equipped biologically to penetrate rather
than to receive. I have suggested that men have encouraged this gender
dualism through a one-sided definition of the masculine, a definition
that magnifies the meanings of the phallus and neglects the reality of
the penis.

Now the connection to be named is that between Christology and
these gender issues. Like our struggle in recent decades to understand
gender issues through the concept of androgyny, the Christological concepts that have dominated the centuries of Christian thought and piety
have also been combinationist and dualistic. They have largely maintained that divinity and humanity are two essentially opposite realities
somehow brought into perfect combination in one unique person. And
when that occurred in Jesus it was a miracle and was not to be repeated.

But at least two major problems resulted from these prevailing
Christologies. First, divinity dominated humanity to the point that
Jesus' humanity became an illusion. Countless Christians believed that
Jesus Christ was actually God disguised as a human being. It was the
Superman/Clark Kent image. Jesus was the celestial visitor from outer
space who lived for a time on earth disguised as one of us, did feats
of superhuman power, and then returned to his glorious home in the
skies.[29]

The second problem stemmed from the first. The ordinary believer
found it difficult to understand and internalize such a meaning. Since
this Christ event was defined by the church as unique, by definition
it was also out of the range of daily human experience. It was utterly
removed from the humanity people knew to be their own. Hence, the
Christic miracle became a formula, to be accepted by faith and mediated
by churchly sacraments for the believer's salvation.

Both of these Christological problems have significant connections to
the gender issues before us. The divinity that seemed to dominate and
squeeze out Jesus' humanity was largely a phallic definition of the divine. It was an understanding of God's power that was heavily unilateral
and one-directional. It was a zero-sum perception that magnified divine
power at the expense of human power. Suspicious of the relational mutuality of a human Jesus and a divine God, tradition perceived both power
and love as one-way streets. So also the masculine side of the androgyny
formula has been equally phallic and one-sided. Just as divine and human
were seen as opposites, likewise the masculine qualities and the feminine.

The Christological formula became abstract and confusing because it was removed from ordinary human experience. The same has been true with the androgyny formula. When a man is called to develop "his feminine side" but at the same time has been taught that this feminine side is foreign to his own male bodily experience — defined as phallus — a man finds himself striving to develop qualities that seem strange to his own biological sexuality. Some sort of miracle seems necessary if the two opposites are to be combined.

But what if the realities — both Christological and sexual — are significantly different from these accepted formulas? What if the connections are essentially more intimate than we have supposed? How might that look?

I believe that Jesus did not understand himself to be ontologically different from other human beings. Nor did he intend to monopolize the Christic reality (the intimate communion of divine and human). His self-understanding and his mission were precisely the opposite. He did not aim to control and hoard the Christic possibility, but rather to release and share it among and with everyone. His uniqueness lay not in having two natures, one divine and one human, miraculously combined. Rather, he possessed the same human nature we all have, but remarkably and fully open in mutuality with God's loving power. We might recall that even John's Gospel, which contains an exalted view of Jesus as the Christ, maintains that all who believe in him (all who are open to his message of the presence of God) are given the power to become the sons and daughters of God. The authentically human and the presence of the truly divine are, indeed, closer than we had imagined. When we embrace God we embrace that which is not foreign to our own human essence but that which makes us more truly human.

The same principle holds for our sexuality. Women are tracing for themselves the meanings of the richly conjunctive sexual-spiritual reality in Christ. No man can do that for women, nor should he try. We who are male have plenty to do for ourselves in this regard. But now the connections seem to be clearer than before.

Jesus remains the paradigmatic Christ-bearer of Christian faith and life. He embodied the divine-human communion with a fullness that awes, compels, judges, challenges, comforts, and attracts us. He is also the Christ-*barer*, the one who lays bare and open that Christic possibility for us all.

And now it seems clearer that this Christic possibility is intimately connected with our sexual wholeness. What is it to be a man? To be fully masculine is one of the two ways given to humanity of being fully human. To be fully masculine does not mean embracing something of gender foreignness, strange to our own male bodily experience. Rather, it means embracing the fullness of the revelation that comes through our male bodies. There is good phallic energy in us which we can claim and celebrate. It is the earthy phallus: deep, moist, and sensuous, primitive and powerful. The phallic energy in us is also solar: penetrating, thrusting, achieving, and with the desire for self-transcendence. Equally important *and equally male,* there is good penile energy is us. It is soft, vulnerable, and receptive. It is a peaceful power. It knows that size is not merely quantitative; more truly it is that strength of mutuality which can be enriched by other life without losing its own center.

The orgasmic sexual experience brings its own revelation. The hard and explosive phallic achievement becomes in an instant the soft, vulnerable tears of the penis. Both are fully male. Both are deeply grounded in a man's bodily reality. Both dimensions of life are fully present when a man is most human. And to be fully human is to know the Christ — not as supernatural invader but as that reality truest to our own natures, and as that reality which intimately connects us with everyone and everything else.

Tribute for Patricia Woodward

Lucy V. Hitchcock

My lover's bones lie scattered
on a hillside
in Mendocino County.
It is a place made sacred
by the pilgrimages
of her friends.
The sun rarely breaks through.
Clouds press down upon the chaparral,
caress the pounding sea.
Delicate, gray-green plants struggle
to survive. Tiny flowers grace
her grave, their colors changing
with the season. Two narcissus, planted
at the scattering, rose the next spring,
but never bloomed. Only wild things
can flourish in such a place.

I return when I can. My home
is on another coast. Alone,
or with a companion, I climb
the long ridge from the campground.
The hills roll out in unison,
endlessly to the eye.
I come here to remember
eternity; that death is as natural
as the curve of ocean against the land
and as cold.
The skeleton of a small animal

catches my eye. I bend down
to extricate it from the sandy soil.
Cradled in my palm, I carry it
toward memory, carry it gently,
as if it mattered if the bones shattered.

Each time, anxious that I may
no longer recognize the spot, that
the ground will shift, I am relieved
when my feet pick out the hollow
in the final rise.
I see her ashes, fraying lace
along the gray-green bodice of the hill
and I am thankful.
In my lifetime, I could not bear
to come and find her broken body
missing. I long to touch
these remnants of her substance.
I stoop and place
the fine mammalian frame
amidst her bones. I finger a piece
of ash and breathe out, sighing.

I fondle this remnant
between forefinger and thumb,
crouched down against the wind.
I hug my arms around my knees
and remember our beginnings.
It was on Roger and Jane's sheepskin
rug before the fire. I was drawn,
a cluster of iron filings,
to her vulnerability and
her strength. Five foot two,
she could fill a room with pathos
or with laughter. She would carry on
her fist splitting the air,
the crowd in stitches,
raising her power.

. . . .

She helped us to laugh at ourselves.
No aspect of our humanity was verboten.

Or, the protagonist in a psychodrama,
she would reveal her injuries, her face
creased by misery and loss.
I could not leave her pain alone.
I gave her my telephone number.
Two days later she called.
Then, housesitting in the Berkeley Hills,
it all began. We faced each other,
chatting on the couch. We were specific
about our lives, our dreams.
She kept asking if she should leave.
I kept asking her to stay. She stayed.
There is something essentially natural
about coming to love a woman. And warm.

Sappho had pulled at my bridle
for years. Here, unchecked, safe
with my own sex, I felt released
to give. Trembling fingers, membranes,
throat poured out auras, juices, sound.
She was the competent one. I responded
in kind. We were wild, joyful. And then,
so that she could not be left, she ran.
It was all there. I should have known.
But Love, bit between the teeth,
cannot be recalled. I would not let her go;
I would not harm her. Those were my gifts
to her. And she, gentle lover,
taught me how to suffer and to laugh.
She would say, "Let yourself be little."
And I was.

Human strength arises through
our vulnerability. It's a queer concept,
rarely learned by men. Some lessons
come harder to one body than another.
Women, less endowed with musculature,
have better access to this.
Perhaps, women can be teachers,
if there are pupils in the room.
My lioness lover was the recipient
of aggression, as a child.

I learned of it from her nightmares.
Asleep, she would begin whimpering,
"no, no, don't!" and end screaming
in fear. Nights in sequence,
men would pursue her, beat her,
chase her to the wall.

I suppose we could blame her father
who beat her with a belt and lashed her
with sarcasm at her mother's urging.
Tired, drunk, it is not hard
to abuse one more demanding child.
I met them in their sober years.
He, a small, tough, retired plumber,
would dress up like a clown
for his grandchildren. She, crippled
by a stroke, spewed hatred of her lot
on all who listened; and yet she loved
to laugh. Together, they had reared
ten children in the Church.
Parental humility was a gift
not received in time for this
middle daughter, born with a caul.

Blessed, cursed, she struggled
with the terrors of the night.
Touching her arm as she slept,
I would urge her, "Don't run!
Turn and tell them to let you be."
She would fight them and me
as well. "Leave me alone. Leave me —
alone." We would both end quivering
for our own reasons. Once, I almost
lost her. She told me she was leaving me,
went home, drank three tumblers of cognac
and called for help. I came. Enraged
by terror, she destroyed her room and tried
to climb out a high window. Heavier and
desperate, I wrestled her to the floor
and pinned her until she passed out.

We wrestled most of our demons
to the floor, yet lost each other
in the end. We were lovers and partners
for four dramatic years before she died.
Now, sometimes, I am glad she is dead.
I would not want her to see our friends
living with AIDS as we lived with leukemia.
I would not want her to know
the body's failure to fight infection
has spread to the world.
I would not want her to read that
the abuse of children has reached
the point where Guatemalan *niños*
are sold for 20,000 dollars US for/their/
internal/organs. I would not want her
to witness the spread of suffering.

The year before her last,
Pat became a carpenter.
She lifted weights in preparation,
ran extra laps around the track,
practiced yoga to center.
She joined the union as an apprentice.
She enjoyed "going in drag,"
in a green hard hat, a tool belt,
work boots. She started right off
in heavy construction.
She looked tough enough, smoking
a cigarette, being one of the guys.
High up on a scaffolding,
strapped to a beam,
healthy, beloved, even serene,
she climbed close to heaven.

When I think of her now, I miss her life.
When friends make me laugh, my body remembers.
Having learned from her of suffering,
I am less attracted to pain. I prefer joy:
deep, visceral, determinative joy.
. . . .
My friend Meg and I, in a hollow
on this Mendocino highland,

attempt to light a candle.
Backs to the wind, hands shivering,
we use up thirteen matches, but it is done.
Giggling at what she would think,
kneeling steadily, we watch the beeswax drip
and burn. Even the wooden base catches fire.
Anywhere two women can light a candle
in the wind, Pat's spirit will live.

Toward a New Theology of Sexuality

Judith Plaskow

Jewish attitudes toward sexuality are complex and often confusing and conflicting. Both historical changes and developments and contradictions within particular historical movements and periods yield an array of views on sexuality from the freest to the most inhibited.[1]

THREE PATRIARCHAL ATTITUDES*

From a feminist standpoint, there are three aspects of Jewish attitudes toward sexuality particularly in need of exploration and change: the centrality of an "energy/control" paradigm of sexuality; the assumption that all sexuality is the same, namely marital and exclusively heterosexual; and the special place of women in the economy of sexual control. While each of these topics might be the subject of a separate article, I will consider them only briefly as background for setting out an alternative feminist perspective on sexuality.

The Centrality of Control

An emphasis on control is central to Jewish understandings of sexuality. From the viewpoint of the tradition's "energy/control" model, sexuality is an independent and sometimes alien energy that must be held in check through personal discipline and religious constraints.[2] While the sexual impulse is given by God and thus is a normal and healthy part of human life, sanctified within its proper framework, sexuality also requires careful, sometimes rigorous control in order that it not violate

---

* Heads added.

"Toward a New Theology of Sexuality" by Judith Plaskow is reprinted from *Standing Again at Sinai* by Judith Plaskow (San Francisco: Harper & Row, 1991). Copyright © 1990 by Judith Plaskow. Reprinted by permission of HarperCollins Publishers Inc.

the boundaries assigned it. Conflicts between affirming sexuality and enforcing restraint emerge in the tradition in a number of forms, in part
through the very naming of the sexual impulse. The rabbis called this
impulse the *yetzer-hara,* the evil impulse, and yet at the same time acknowledged its necessity to the creation and sustenance of the world.
"Were it not for the evil impulse," said Rabbi Nahman b. Samuel, "man
would not build a house, or take a wife, or beget a child, or engage in
business."[3]

Sexuality as Marital

Assuming that sexuality must be controlled, the tradition understands
heterosexual marriage as the proper framework for taming and enjoying the sexual impulse. Even within marriage, sex is forbidden during
menstruation and for seven days thereafter. Outside the boundaries of
marriage lies a whole realm of licentiousness and transgression that must
be carefully guarded against with well-defined restraints. Legal prohibitions, moral standards, and social expectations all serve to delineate
certain periods within a marriage as the sole realm of the sexually permitted. So pervasive is the assumption that sex is properly marital and
heterosexual that homosexuality gets short shrift, even by way of inter-
diction. Male homosexuality is a major offense (*to'evah,* an abomination),
but it is assumed by the rabbis to be so rare in Israel that there is little
need for safeguards against it.

The Special Place of Women

While moral norms concerning sexuality generally apply both to men
and women, women play a special role in the Jewish understanding of
sexuality. They are the ubiquitous temptations, the sources and symbols
of illicit desire, the ones whose sexuality threatens even their husbands/
possessors with the possibility of illegal action. To speak of control is necessarily to speak of women — of the need to cover them, avoid them, and
contain them in proper (patriarchal) families where their threat is mini-
mized if it cannot be overcome. Laws concerning marriage and divorce
decrease the danger of women's sexuality by providing for the acquisition and relinquishment of male rights to that sexuality. Marriage brings
the "wild and unruly potentialities of female sexuality" under control
by designating a woman's sexuality as a particular man's possession.[4]

The control of women's sexuality and its role in the institution of
the family, the normativeness of heterosexuality, and the energy/control
paradigm of sexuality are all connected pieces of a patriarchal understanding of sexuality. Where women's sexuality is seen as an object to
be possessed, and sexuality itself is perceived as solely heterosexual and

as an impulse that can take possession of the self, the central issues surrounding sexuality will necessarily be issues of control. The question then becomes how a positive Jewish feminist discourse about sexuality can move beyond this patriarchal framework, not only rejecting its ethical implications but also defining sexuality in fundamentally different terms.

A FEMINIST VIEW

In the past twenty years, feminists have reconceptualized the nature and functions of human sexuality, generating alternatives to the energy/control model that potentially establish our thinking about sexuality on new foundations. Rather than seeing sexuality as a separate and alien energy that can engulf the self, feminists have described it as part of a continuum of embodied self-expression or as part of a spectrum of erotic energy that ideally suffuses all activities in our lives.[5]

Audre Lorde, in her brilliant essay "Uses of the Erotic: The Erotic as Power," describes the erotic as the lifeforce, the capacity for feeling, the capacity for joy, a power we are taught to fear and ignore by a society that "defines the good in terms of profit rather than in terms of human need." The erotic is a source of empowerment, a "lens through which we [can] scrutinize all aspects of our existence," evaluating them "honestly in terms of their relative meaning within our lives."[6]

Ethicist Beverly Harrison similarly interprets sexuality as a reality rooted in "our bodies, our selves." Setting out the base points for a feminist moral theology, Harrison argues that "all our knowledge, including our moral knowledge, is body-mediated knowledge." Our sensuality, or our capacity for feeling, is the foundation stone of our connection to the world, the prerequisite without which we would lose all ability to act or to value. Our sexuality, as an aspect of our embodiedness and inherent in it, is one especially intense dimension of our body-mediated power, of the body space that is "literally the ground of our personhood."[7]

This view of sexuality as part of a spectrum of body/life energy rather than a special force or evil inclination has at least two important implications for understanding the place of sexuality in human life. First of all, it challenges the value of control by suggesting that we cannot suppress sexual feelings without suppressing our capacity for feeling more generally. If sexuality is one dimension of our ability to live passionately in the world, then in cutting off our sexuality, we diminish our overall power to feel, know, and value deeply. While the connection between sexuality and feeling does not compel us to act out all our sexual feelings, it does mean we must honor and make room for feelings — including sexual ones — as "the basic ingredient in our relational transaction with the world."[8] Second, insofar as sexuality is an element in the embodiment that mediates our relation to reality, an aspect of the life energy that enables us to connect with others in creativity and joy, sexuality is profoundly connected to spirituality, indeed is inseparable from it. Sexuality is that part of us through which we reach out to other persons and to God, expressing the need for relationship, for the sharing of self and of meaning.[9] When we touch that place in our lives where sexuality and spirituality come together, we touch our wholeness and the fullness of our power, and at the same time our connection with a power larger than ourselves.[10]

RETHINKING AMBIVALENT ATTITUDES

Feminist reconceptualizations of the energy/control model of sexuality and affirmation of the profound connection between sexuality and spirituality provide directions for rethinking the ambivalent attitudes toward sexuality within Judaism.

Sexuality and Spirituality

Acceptance and avowal of a link between sex and spirit is by no means foreign to Jewish experience. In the mysteries of the marriage bed on Sabbath night; in the sanctity of the Song of Songs; for mysticism, in the very nature and dynamics of the Godhead, sexual expression is an image of and path to the holy.[11] Yet again and again in theology and practice, Judaism turns away from and undermines this acknowledged connection by defining sexuality in terms of patriarchal possession and control. Since such categories are inimical to the mutuality, openness, and vulnerability in sexual relations that tie sexuality to the sacred, a feminist approach to sexuality must reconstruct both the institutional and conceptual bases for linking sexuality with the spiritual.

It is striking that one of the profoundest images of freedom and mutuality in sexual relations that the Jewish tradition has to offer is at the same time its central image of the connection between sexuality and spirituality. Unlike the Garden of Eden, where Eve and Adam are ashamed of their nakedness and women's subordination is the punishment for sin, the Garden of the Song of Songs is a place of sensual delight and sexual equality. Unabashed by their desire, the man and woman of these poems delight in their own embodiment and the beauty surrounding them, each seeking the other out to inaugurate their meetings, each rejoicing in the love without dominion that is also the love of God.[12] Since this book offers a vision of delight that is easier to achieve in a sacred garden than in the midst of daily demands, it is perhaps no criticism of the institution of marriage that the couple in the Song of

Songs is not married. Yet the picture of mutuality and the sacredness of mutuality offered by this book stand in fundamental tension with the structures of marriage as Judaism defines them. When the central rituals of marriage and divorce celebrate or enact the male possession and release of female sexuality and exclude the possibility of loving same-sex relationships, what are the supports and resources for the true reciprocity of intimate exchange that marks the holiness of Song of Songs? The achievement of mutuality in the marriage bed is extremely difficult in the absence of justice in those institutions that legitimate and surround it.

Transformation of the Legal Framework of Marriage

A first concrete task, then, of the feminist reconstruction of Jewish attitudes towards sexuality is the radical transformation of the institutional legal framework within which sexual relations are supposed to take place. Insofar as Judaism maintains its interest in the establishment of enduring relationships outside a patriarchal framework, these relationships will be entered into and dissolved by mutual initiative and consent. "Marriage" will not be about the transfer of women or the sanctification of potential disorder through the firm establishment of women in the patriarchal family, but [about the] the decision of two adults — any two adults — to make their lives together, lives which include the sharing of sexuality. Although in the modern West, it is generally assumed that such a commitment constitutes a central meaning of marriage, this assumption is contradicted by a religious (and secular) legal system that outlaws homosexual marriage and institutionalizes inequality in its basic definitions of marriage and divorce.

This redefinition of the legal framework of marriage is based both on rejection of the institutionalization of heterosexuality and on the important principle that sexuality is not something we can acquire or possess in another. We are each the possessor of our own sexuality — in Adrienne Rich's phrase, the "presiding genius" of our own bodies.[13] The sharing of sexuality with another is something that should happen only by mutual consent, a consent that is not a blanket permission, but that is continually renewed in the actual rhythms of particular relationships. This principle, simple as it seems, challenges both the fundamental assumptions of Jewish marriage law and the Jewish understanding of what women's sexuality is "about." It defines as immoral legal regulations concerning the possession, control, and exchange of women's sexuality, and [it] disputes the perspective that a woman's sexuality is her contribution to the family rather than the expression of her own embodiment.

Moving Beyond Ourselves

If one firm principle for feminist thinking about sexuality is that no one can possess the sexuality of another, a second principle is that sexuality is not something that pertains only or primarily to the self. Indeed, our sexuality is fundamentally about moving out beyond ourselves. The connecting, communicative nature of sexuality is not something we can experience or look for only in sexual encounters narrowly defined, but in all real relationships in our lives. We live in the world as sexual beings. As Audre Lorde argues, our sexuality is a current that flows through all activities that are important to us, in which we invest our selves. True intellectual exchange, common work, shared experience, are laced with sexual energy that animates and enlivens them. The bonds of community are erotic bonds. The power that is generated by real community, that gives us access to a greater power that grounds and embraces us, is in part the power of our own sexual life energy that flows through community and enlarges and seals it. We are all, women and men, embodied sexual persons who respond sexually to the women and men among whom we live.

This erotic nature of community is by no means lost on Judaism; indeed, it is the subject of profound ambivalence in both the midrash and law. Extensive rabbinic legislation enforcing the separation of the sexes tries to protect against the feelings it recognizes, even as it acknowledges the sexual power of community. If the energy of community is erotic, there are no guarantees that eroticism will stay within prescribed legal boundaries rather than breaking out and disrupting communal sanctity. The strict "fence around the law" that is necessary when it comes to sexual behavior is itself testimony to the power of sexuality.

It is tempting for a feminist account of sexuality to deny the power of the erotic, depicting the rabbinic fear of it as simply misplaced. But it is truer to experience to acknowledge the power of sexuality to overturn rules and threaten boundaries. Then feminists can embrace this power as a significant ally. There is no question that the empowerment that comes from owning the erotic in our lives can disturb community and undermine familiar structures. On the level of sexual behavior, if we allow ourselves to perceive and acknowledge sexual feelings, there is always the danger we may act on them, and they may not correspond to group consensus about whom we may desire and when. And when we understand the erotic not simply as sexual feeling in the narrow sense but as our fundamental life energy, owning this power in our lives is even more threatening to established structure.

In Audre Lorde's terms, if we allow the erotic to become a lens through which we evaluate all aspects of our existence, we can no longer "settle for the convenient, the shoddy, the conventionally expected, nor the merely safe."[14] Having glimpsed the possibility of genuine satisfaction in work well done, we are less likely to settle for work that is alienating and meaningless. Having experienced the power and legitimacy of our own sexual desire, we are less likely to subscribe to a system that closely and absolutely prescribes and proscribes the channels of that desire. Having experienced our capacity for creative and joyful action, we are less likely to accept hierarchical power relationships that deny or restrict our ability to bring that creativity and joy to other aspects of our lives. It may be that the ability of women to live within the patriarchal family and the larger patriarchal structures that govern Jewish life depends on our suppression of the erotic, on our numbing ourselves to the sources of vision and power that fuel meaningful resistance. Obviously, from a patriarchal perspective, then, erotic empowerment is dangerous. That is why, in Lorde's words, "we are taught to separate the erotic demand from most vital areas of our lives other than sex," and that is why we are also taught to restrain our sexuality, so that it too fits the parameters of hierarchical control that govern the rest of our lives.[15]

NURTURING THE EROTIC

From a feminist perspective, however, the power and danger of the erotic are not reasons to fear and suppress it but to nurture it as a profound personal and communal resource in the struggle for change. When "we begin to demand from ourselves and from our life-pursuits that they feel in accordance with that joy which we know ourselves to be capable of," we carry with us an inner knowledge of the kind of world we are seeking to create.[16] If we repress this knowledge because it also makes us sexually alive, then we repress the clarity and creative energy that is the basis of our capacity to envision and work toward a more just social order.

This understanding of the power of the erotic is a particularly crucial corrective to rabbinic attitudes toward sexual control. The rabbis recognized the connection between the sexual impulse and human creativity. "The bigger the man, the bigger the *yetzer,*" they said, and advised, "Hold him [the *yetzer hara*] off with the left hand and draw him nigh with the right."[17] Yet at the same time they acknowledged the role of sexuality as an ingredient in all activity, they apparently believed one could constantly guard against sexuality without damaging the larger capacity to act and to feel. To love God with all the heart meant to love God with the good *and evil* impulses, and yet it was imagined one could rein in the evil impulse without diminishing the love of God.[18] If we take sexuality seriously, however, as an expression of our embodiment that cannot be disconnected from our wider ability to interact feelingly with the world, then to learn fear and shame of our own bodies and those of others — even when these feelings are intermixed with other conflicting attitudes — is to learn suspicion of feeling as a basic way of valuing and knowing. We should not expect, then, to be able to block out our sexual feelings without blocking out the longing for social relations rooted in mutuality rather than hierarchy, without blocking out the anger that warns us that something is amiss in our present social arrangements, without blocking and distorting the fullness of our love for God.[19]

Living Dangerously

I am not arguing here for free sex or for more sexual expression, quantitatively speaking. I am arguing for living dangerously, for choosing to take responsibility for working through the possible consequences of sexual feeling rather than repressing sexual feeling and thus feeling more generally. I am arguing that our capacity to transform Judaism and the world is rooted in our capacity to be alive to the pain and anger that is caused by relationships of domination and to the joy that awaits us on the other side. I am arguing that to be alive is to be sexually alive and that in suppressing one sort of vitality we suppress the other. The question becomes then: Can we affirm our sexuality as the gift it is, making it sacred not by cordoning off pieces of it, but by increasing our awareness of the ways in which it connects us to all things? Can we stop evicting our sexuality from the synagogue, hiding it behind a *mechitzah* or praying with our heads, and instead bring it in, offering it to God in the experience of full spiritual/physical connection? Dare we trust our capacity for joy — knowing it is related to our sexuality — to point the direction toward new and different ways of structuring communal life?

Obviously, I am suggesting that the implications of a changed conception of sexuality go well beyond the sexual sphere, and yet it is also the case, of course, that they shape that sphere as well. The ability to feel deeply in the whole of our lives affects what we want and are willing to accept in the bedroom, just as what we experience in the bedroom prepares us for mutuality or domination in the rest of our lives. A new understanding of sexuality and a transformed institutional context for sexual relationships will have significant impact on personal sexual norms. If the traditional models and categories for understanding sexuality are no longer morally acceptable from a feminist perspective, but sexuality is fundamentally about relationships with others, what values might govern sexual behavior for modern Jews?

Mutuality, Respect, and Empowerment

To see sexuality as an aspect of our life energy, as part of a continuum with other ways of relating to the world and other persons, is to insist that the norms of mutuality, respect for difference, and joint empowerment that characterize the larger feminist .vision of community apply also — indeed especially — to the area of sexuality. If in our general communal life we seek to be present with each other in such a way that we can touch the greater power of being in which all communities dwell, how much more should this be true in those relationships that are potentially the most open, intimate, and vulnerable in our lives?

The unification of sexuality and spirituality provides an ideal of what a sexual relationship can be, an ideal that is more a measure of the possible than the continuing reality of everyday. What keeps this ideal alive as a recurring possibility is the exercise of respect, responsibility, and honesty — commensurate with the nature and depth of the particular relationship — as basic values in any sexual connection. In terms of concrete life choices, I believe that radical mutuality is most fully possible in the context of an ongoing committed relationship in which sexual expression is one dimension of a shared life. Long-term partnerships may be the richest setting for negotiating and living out the meanings of mutuality, responsibility, and honesty amidst the distractions, problems, and pleasures of every day.

Such partnerships are not, however, a choice for all adults who want them and not all adults would choose them, given the possibility. To respond within a feminist framework to the realities of different life decisions and at the same time affirm the importance of sexual well-being as an aspect of our total well-being, we need to apply certain fundamental values to a range of sexual styles and choices. While honesty, responsibility, and respect are goods that pertain to any relationship, the concrete meaning of these values will vary considerably depending on the duration and significance of the connection involved. In one relationship, honesty may mean complete and open sharing of feelings and experiences; in another, clarity about intent for that encounter. In the context of a committed partnership, responsibility may signify lifelong presence, trust, and exchange; in a brief encounter, discussion of birth control, condoms, and AIDS. At its fullest, respect may mean regard for another as a total person; at a minimum, absence of pressure or coercion and a commitment, in Lorde's words, not to "look away" as we come together.[20] If we need to look away, then we should walk away: the same choices about whether and how to act on our feelings that pertain to any area of moral decision making are open to us in relation to our sexuality.

Gay and Lesbian Relationships

The same norms that apply to heterosexual relationships also apply to gay and lesbian relationships. While many aspects of the traditional Jewish rejection of homosexuality need to be rethought, a feminist reconceptualization of sexuality must view homosexual choice in light of the continuity between sexual energy and embodied life energy. If we see sexuality as part of what enables us to reach out beyond ourselves, and thus as a fundamental ingredient in our spirituality, then the issue of homosexuality must be framed differently from the ways in which it is most often discussed. The question of the morality of homosexuality becomes one not of Jewish law, or the right to privacy, or freedom of choice, but the affirmation of the value to the individual and society of each of us being able to find that place within ourselves where sexuality and spirituality come together.[21] It is possible that some or many of us for whom the connections between sexuality and personal and spiritual power emerge most richly, or only, with those of the same sex could choose to lead heterosexual lives for the sake of conformity to Jewish law or wider social pressures and values. But this choice would then represent both a renunciation of the full power of the erotic within our lives and a violation of the deeper vision offered by the Jewish tradition that sexuality can be a medium for the experience and reunification of God. Although historically this Jewish vision has been expressed entirely in heterosexual terms, the reality is that for some Jews it has been realized in relationships with both men and women, while for others it is realized only in relationships between two men or two women. Thus what calls itself the Jewish path to holiness in sexual relations is for some a cutting off of holiness — a sacrifice that comes at high cost for both the individual and community.

Potential acceptance of gays and lesbians by the Jewish community raises the issue of children — for Judaism a primary warrant for sexual relations and the facade that prejudice often stands behind in rejecting homosexuality as a Jewish choice. Again to place this issue in the context of a feminist paradigm for understanding sexuality, procreation is a dimension of our sexuality, just as sexuality itself is a dimension of our embodied personhood. If sexuality allows us to reach out to others, having children is a way of reaching out beyond our own generation, affirming the biological continuity of life and the continuity of Jewish community and communal values. Insofar as Jewish communities have an important stake in the rearing of Jewish children, it is in their interest to structure communal institutions to support in concrete ways all Jews who choose to raise children, including increasing numbers of lesbians and gay men.[22] But just as Judaism has always recognized that procreation does not exhaust the meaning of sexuality, so having children does not exhaust the ways in which Jews can contribute to future generations.[23] Recognition of the continuities between sexuality and personal empowerment strengthens the conviction of the inherent value of sexuality as an expression of our personhood and of our connection with and love for others. The sense of integrity and self-worth that a loving sexual relationship can foster enhances the capacity to make commitments to the future, whether this takes the form of bearing and raising children or nurturing communal continuity in other ways.

A Connection with God

Lastly, but underlying all that I have said, sexuality as an aspect of our life energy and power connects us with God as the sustaining source of energy and power in the universe. In [our] reaching out to another sexually with the total self, the boundaries between self and other can dissolve and we may feel ourselves united with larger currents of energy and sustenance. It is also the case, however, that even in ordinary daily reachings out to others, we reach toward the God who is present in connection, in the web of relation with a wider world. On the one hand, the wholeness, the "all-embracing quality of sexual expression" that includes body, mind, and feeling, is for many people the closest we can come in this life to experiencing the embracing wholeness of God.[24] On the other hand, the everyday bonds of community are also erotic bonds through which we touch the God of community. In recognizing the continuity between our own sexual energy and the greater currents that nourish and renew it, we affirm our sexuality as a source of energy and power that, schooled in the values of respect and mutuality, can lead us to the related and therefore sexual God.

Eudora

Audre Lorde

At the compound, Easter Saturday, she was just coming out of a week's drinking binge which started with the firing of Robert Oppenheimer, the atomic scientist, in the states. I was full of the Good Friday festivities in Mexico City, which I had attended with Frieda and Tammy the day before. They had gone to Tepotzlán. I was sunning myself on my front lawn.

"Hello, down there! Aren't you overdoing it?" I looked up at the woman whom I had noticed observing me from an upper window in the two-story dwelling at the edge of the compound. She was the only woman I'd seen wearing pants in Mexico except at the pool.

I was pleased that she had spoken. The two women who lived separately in the double house at that end of the compound never appeared at tables in the Plaza. They never spoke as they passed my house on their way to the cars or the pool. I knew one of them had a shop in town called La Señora, which had the most interesting clothes on the Square.

"Haven't you heard, only mad dogs and englishmen go out in the noonday sun?" I shaded my eyes so I could see her better. I was more curious than I had realized.

"I don't burn that easily," I called back. She was framed in the large casement window, a crooked smile on her half-shaded face. Her voice was strong and pleasant, but with a crack in it that sounded like a cold, or too many cigarettes.

"I'm just going to have some coffee. Would you like some?"

I stood, picked up the blanket upon which I'd been lying, and accepted her invitation.

"Eudora" by Audre Lorde is reprinted from *Zami: A New Spelling of My Name* by Audre Lorde (Freedom, Calif.: Crossing Press, 1983). Used by permission.

She was waiting in her doorway. I recognized her as the tall grey-haired woman called La Periodista.

"My name's Eudora," she said, extending her hand and holding mine firmly for a moment. "And they call you La Chica, you're here from New York, and you go to the new university."

"Where did you find all that out?" I asked, taken aback. We stepped inside.

"It's my business to find out what goes on," she laughed easily. "That's what reporters do. Legitimate gossip."

Eudora's bright spacious room was comfortable and disheveled. A large easy chair faced the bed upon which she now perched cross-legged, in shorts and polo shirt, smoking, and surrounded by books and newspapers.

Maybe it was her direct manner. Maybe it was the openness with which she appraised me as she motioned me towards the chair. Maybe it was the pants, or the informed freedom and authority with which she moved. But from the moment I walked into her house, I knew Eudora was gay, and that was an unexpected and welcome surprise. It made me feel much more at home and relaxed, even though I was still feeling sore and guilty from my fiasco with Bea, but it was refreshing to know I wasn't alone.

"I've been drinking for a week," she said, "and I'm still a little hung-over, so you'll have to excuse the mess."

I didn't know what to say.

Eudora wanted to know what I was doing in Mexico, young, Black, and with an eye for the ladies, as she put it. That was the second surprise. We shared a good laugh over the elusive cues for mutual recognition among lesbians. Eudora was the first woman I'd met who spoke about herself as a lesbian rather than as "gay," which was a word she hated. Eudora said it was a north american east-coast term that didn't mean anything to her, and what's more most of the lesbians she had known were anything but gay.

When I went to the market that afternoon, I brought back milk and eggs and fruit for her. I invited her to dinner, but she wasn't feeling much like eating, she said, so I fixed my dinner and brought it over and ate with her. Eudora was an insomniac, and we sat talking late late into the night.

She was the most fascinating woman I had ever met.

Born in Texas forty-eight years before, Eudora was the youngest child in an oil-worker's family. She had seven older brothers. Polio as a child had kept her in bed for three years, "so I had a lot of catchin' up to do, and I never knew when to stop."

In 1925, she became the first woman to attend the University of Texas, integrating it by camping out on the university grounds for four years in a tent with her rifle and a dog. Her brothers had studied there, and she was determined to also. "They said they didn't have living accommodations for women," Eudora said, "and I couldn't afford a place in town."

She'd worked in news all her life, both print and radio, and had followed her lover, Franz, to Chicago, where they both worked for the same paper. "She and I were quite a team, all right. Had a lot of high times together, did a lot of foolishness, believed a lot of things.

Then Franz married a foreign correspondent in Istanbul," Eudora continued, drily, "and I lost my job over a byline on the Scottsboro case." She worked for a while in Texas for a Mexican paper, then moved into Mexico City for them.

When she and Karen, who owned La Señora, were lovers, they had started a bookstore together in Cuernavaca in the more liberal forties. For a while it was a rallying place for disaffected americans. This was how she knew Frieda.

"It was where people came to find out what was really going on in the states. Everybody passed through." She paused. "But it got to be a little too radical for Karen's tastes," Eudora said carefully. "The dress shop suits her better. But that's a whole other mess, and she still owes me money."

"What happened to the bookstore?" I asked, not wanting to pry, but fascinated by her story.

"Oh, lots of things, in very short order. I've always been a hard drinker, and she never liked that. Then when I had to speak my mind in the column about the whole Sobell business, and the newspaper started getting itchy, Karen thought I was going to lose that job. I didn't, but my immigration status was changed, which meant I could still work in Mexico, but after all those years I could no longer own property. That's the one way of getting uppity americans to keep their mouths shut. Don't rock big brother's boat, and we'll let you stay. That was right up Karen's alley. She bought me out and opened the dress shop."

"Is that why you broke up?"

Eudora laughed. "That sounds like New York talk." She was silent for a minute, busying herself with the overflowing ashtray.

"Actually, no," she said finally. "I had an operation, and it was pretty rough for both of us. Radical surgery, for cancer. I lost a breast." Eudora's head was bent over the ashtray, hair falling forward, and I could not see her face. I reached out and touched her hand.

"I'm so sorry," I said.

"Yeah, so am I," she said, matter-of-factly, placing the polished ashtray carefully back on the table beside her bed. She looked up, smiled, and pushed the hair back from her face with the heels of her hands. "There's never enough time to begin with, and still so damn much I want to do."

"How are you feeling now, Eudora?" I remembered my nights on the female surgery floor at Beth David. "Did you have radiation?"

"Yes, I did. It's almost two years since the last one, and I'm fine now. The scars are hard to take, though. Not dashing or romantic. I don't much like to look at them myself." She got up, took down her guitar from the wall, and started to tune it. "What folksongs are they teaching you in that fine new university up the mountain?"

Eudora had translated a number of texts on the history and ethnology of Mexico, one of which was a textbook assigned for my history class. She was witty and funny and sharp and insightful, and knew a lot about an enormous number of things. She had written poetry when she was younger, and Walt Whitman was her favorite poet. She showed me some clippings of articles she had written for a memorial-documentary of Whitman. One sentence in particular caught my eye.

> I met a man who'd spent his life in thinking, and could understand me no matter what I said. And I followed him to Harleigh in the snow.

The next week was Easter holidays, and I spent part of each afternoon or evening at Eudora's house, reading poetry, learning to play the guitar, talking. I told her about Ginger, and about Bea, and she talked about her and Franz's life together. We even had a game of dirty-word Scrabble, and although I warned her I was a declared champion, Eudora won, thereby increasing my vocabulary no end. She showed me the column she was finishing about the Olmec stone heads, and we talked about the research she was planning to do on African and Asian influences in Mexican art. Her eyes twinkled and her long graceful hands flashed as she talked, and by midweek, when we were not together, I could feel the curves of her cheekbone under my lips as I gave her a quick goodbye kiss. I thought about making love to her, and ruined a whole pot of curry in my confusion. This was not what I had come to Mexico to do.

There was an air about Eudora when she moved that was both delicate and sturdy, fragile and tough, like the snapdragon she resembled when she stood up, flung back her head, and brushed her hair back with the palms of her hands. I was besotted.

Eudora often made fun of what she called my prudishness, and there was nothing she wouldn't talk about. But there was a reserve about her own person, a force-field around her that I did not know how to pass, a sadness surrounding her that I could not breach. And besides, a woman of her years and experience — how presumptuous of me!

We sat talking in her house later and later, over endless cups of coffee, half my mind on our conversation and half of it hunting for some opening, some graceful, safe way of getting closer to this woman whose smell made my earlobes burn. Who, despite her openness about everything else, turned away from me when she changed her shirt.

On Thursday night we rehung some of her bark paintings from Tehuantepec. The overhead fan hummed faintly; there was a little pool of sweat sitting in one wing of her collarbone. I almost reached over to kiss it.

"Goddammit!" Eudora had narrowly missed her finger with the hammer.

"You're very beautiful," I said suddenly, embarrassed at my own daring. There was a moment of silence as Eudora put down her hammer.

"So are you, Chica," she said, quietly, "more beautiful than you know." Her eyes held mine for a minute so I could not turn away.

No one had ever said that to me before.

It was after 2:00 A.M. when I left Eudora's house, walking across the grass to my place in the clear moonlight. Once inside I could not sleep. I tried to read. Visions of Eudora's dear one-sided grin kept coming between me and the page. I wanted to be with her, to be close to her, laughing.

I sat on the edge of my bed, wanting to put my arms around Eudora, to let the tenderness and love I felt burn away the sad casing around her and speak to her need through the touch of my hands and my mouth and my body that defined my own.

"It's getting late," she had said. "You look tired. Do you want to stretch out?" She gestured to the bed beside her. I came out of my chair like a shot.

"Oh, no, that's all right," I stammered. All I could think of was that I had not had a bath since morning. "I — I need to take a shower, anyway."

Eudora had already picked up a book. "Goodnight, Chica," she said without looking up.

I jumped up from the edge of my bed and put a light under the water-heater. I was going back.

"What is it, Chica? I thought you were going to bed." Eudora was reclining exactly as I had left her an hour before, propped up on a pillow against the wall, the half-filled ashtray next to her hand and books littering the rest of the three-quarter studio bed. A bright towel hung around her neck against the loose, short-sleeved beige nightshirt.

My hair was still damp from the shower, and my bare feet itched from the dew-wet grass between our houses. I was suddenly aware that it was 3:30 in the morning.

"Would you like some more coffee?" I offered.

She regarded me at length, unsmiling, almost wearily.

"Is that what you came back for, more coffee?"

All through waiting for the *calentador* to heat, all through showering and washing my hair and brushing my teeth, until that very moment, I had thought of nothing else but wanting to hold Eudora in my arms, so much that I didn't care that I was also terrified. Somehow, if I could manage to get myself back up those steps in the moonlight, and if Eudora was not already asleep, then I would have done my utmost. That would be my piece of the bargain, and then what I wanted would somehow magically fall into my lap.

Eudora's grey head moved against the bright serape-covered wall behind her, still regarding me as I stood over her. Her eyes wrinkled and she slowly smiled her lopsided smile, and I could feel the warm night air between us collapse as if to draw us together.

I knew then that she had been hoping I would return. Out of wisdom or fear, Eudora waited for me to speak.

Night after night we had talked until dawn in this room about language and poetry and love and the good conduct of living. Yet we were strangers. As I stood there looking at Eudora, the impossible became easier, almost simple. Desire gave me courage, where it had once made me speechless. With almost no thought I heard myself saying,

"I want to sleep with you."

Eudora straightened slowly, pushed the books from her bed with a sweep of her arm, and held out her hand to me.

"Come."

I sat down on the edge of the bed, facing her, our thighs touching. Our eyes were on a level now, looking deeply into each other. I could feel my heart pounding in my ears, and the high steady sound of the crickets.

"Do you know what you're saying?" Eudora asked softly, searching my face. I could smell her like the sharp breath of wildflowers.

"I know," I said, not understanding her question. Did she think I was a child?

"I don't know if I can," she said, still softly, touching the sunken place on her nightshirt where her left breast should have been. "And you don't mind this?"

I had wondered so often how it would feel under my hands, my lips, this different part of her. Mind? I felt my love spread like a shower of light surrounding me and this woman before me. I reached over and touched Eudora's face with my hands.

"Are you sure?" Her eyes were still on my face.

"Yes, Eudora." My breath caught in my throat as if I'd been running. "I'm very sure." If I did not put my mouth upon hers and inhale the spicy smell of her breath my lungs would burst.

As I spoke the words, I felt them touch and give life to a new reality within me, some half-known self come of age, moving out to meet her.

I stood, and in two quick movements slid out of my dress and underclothes. I held my hand down to Eudora. Delight. Anticipation. A slow smile mirroring my own softened her face. Eudora reached over and passed the back of her hand along my thigh. Goose-flesh followed in the path of her fingers.

"How beautiful and brown you are."

She rose slowly. I unbuttoned her shirt and she shrugged it off her shoulders till it lay heaped at our feet. In the circle of lamplight I looked from her round firm breast with its rosy nipple erect to her scarred chest. The pale keloids of radiation burn lay in the hollow under her shoulder and arm down across her ribs. I raised my eyes and found hers again, speaking a tenderness my mouth had no words yet for. She took my hand and placed it there, squarely, lightly, upon her chest. Our hands fell. I bent and kissed her softly upon the scar where our hands had rested. I felt her heart strong and fast against my lips. We fell back together upon her bed. My lungs expanded and my breath deepened with the touch of her warm dry skin. My mouth finally against hers, quick-breathed, fragrant, searching, her hand entwined in my hair. My body took charge from her flesh. Shifting slightly, Eudora reached past my head toward the lamp above us. I caught her wrist. Her bones felt like velvet and quicksilver between my tingling fingers.

"No," I whispered against the hollow of her ear. "In the light."

Sun poured through the jacarandas outside Eudora's window. I heard the faint and rhythmical whirr-whoosh of Tomás's scythe as he cut back the wild banana bushes from the walk down by the pool.

I came fully awake with a start, seeing the impossible. The junebug I had squashed with a newspaper at twilight, so long before, seemed to be moving slowly up the white-painted wall. It would move a few feet up from the floor, fall back, and then start up again. I grabbed for my glasses from the floor where I had dropped them the night before. With my glasses on, I could see that there was a feather-thin line of ants descending from the adobe ceiling down the wall to the floor where the junebug was lying. The ants, in concert, were trying to hoist the carcass straight up the vertical wall on their backs, up to their hole on the ceiling. I watched in fascination as the tiny ants lifted their huge load, moved, lost it, then lifted again.

I half-turned and reached over to touch Eudora lying against my back, one arm curved over our shared pillow. The pleasure of our night flushed over me like sun on the walls of the light-washed colorful room. Her light brown eyes opened, studying me as she came slowly out of sleep, her sculptured lips smiling, a little bit open, revealing the gap beside her front teeth. I traced her mouth with my finger. For a moment I felt exposed, unsure, suddenly wanting reassurance that I had not been found wanting. The morning air was still dew-damp, and the smell of our loving lay upon us.

As if reading my thoughts, Eudora's arm came down around my shoulders, drawing me around and to her, tightly, and we lay holding each other in the Mexican morning sunlight that flooded through her uncovered casement windows. Tomás, the caretaker, sang in soft Spanish, keeping time with his scythe, and the sounds drifted in to us from the compound below.

"What an ungodly hour," Eudora laughed, kissing the top of my head and jumping over me with a long stride. "Aren't you hungry?" With her towel around her neck, Eudora made *huevos,* scrambled eggs Mexican-style, and real *café con leche* for our breakfast. We ate at the gaily painted orange table between the tiny kitchen and her bedroom, smiling and talking and feeding each other from our common plate.

There was room for only one of us at the square shallow sink in the kitchen. As I washed dishes to insure an ant-free afternoon, Eudora leaned on the doorpost, smoking lazily. Her hipbones flared like wings over her long legs. I could feel her quick breath on the side of my neck as she watched me. She dried the dishes, and hung the towel over a tin mask on the kitchen cabinet.

"Now let's go back to bed," she muttered, reaching for me through the Mexican shirt I had borrowed to throw over myself. "There's more."

By this time the sun was passing overhead. The room was full of reflected light and the heat from the flat adobe over us, but the wide windows and the lazy ceiling fan above kept the sweet air moving. We sat in bed sipping iced coffee from a pewter mug.

When I told Eudora I didn't like to be made love to, she raised her eyebrows. "How do you know?" she said, and smiled as she reached out and put down our coffee cup. "That's probably because no one has ever really made love to you before," she said softly, her eyes wrinkling at the corners, intense, desiring.

Eudora knew many things about loving women that I had not yet learned. Day into dusk. A brief shower. Freshness. The comfort and delight of her body against mine. The ways my body came to life in the curve of her arms, her tender mouth, her sure body — gentle, persistent, complete.

We run up the steep outside steps to her roof, and the almost full moon flickers in the dark center wells of her eyes. Kneeling, I pass my hands over her body, along the now-familiar place below her left shoulder, down along her ribs. A part of her. The mark of the Amazon. For a woman who seems spare, almost lean, in her clothing, her body is ripe and smooth to the touch. Beloved. Warm to my coolness, cool to my heat. I bend, moving my lips over her flat stomach to the firm rising mound beneath.

On Monday, I went back to school. In the next month, Eudora and I spent many afternoons together, but her life held complications about which she would say little.

Eudora had been all over Mexico. She regaled me with tales of her adventures. She seemed always to have lived her life as if it were a story, a little grander than ordinary. Her love of Mexico, her adopted land, was deep and compelling, like an answer to my grade-school fantasies. She knew a great deal about the folkways and beliefs of the different peoples who had swept across the country in waves long ago, leaving their languages and a small group of descendants to carry on the old ways.

We went for long rides through the mountains in her Hudson convertible. We went to the Brincas, the traditional Moorish dances in Tepotzlán. She told me about the Olmec stone heads of African people that were being found in Tabasco, and the ancient contacts between Mexico and Africa and Asia that were just now coming to light. We talked about the legend of the China Poblana, the Asian-looking patron saint of Puebla. Eudora could savor what was Zapotec, Toltec, Mixtec, Aztec in the culture, and how much had been so terribly destroyed by Europeans.

"That genocide rivals the Holocaust of World War II," she asserted.

She talked about the nomadic Lacondonian Indians, who were slowly disappearing from the land near Comitán in Chiapas, because the forests were going. She told me how the women in San Cristóbal de las Casas give the names of catholic saints to their goddesses, so that they and their daughters can pray and make offerings in peace at the forest shrines without offending the catholic church.

She helped me plan a trip south, to Oaxaca and beyond, through San Cristóbal to Guatemala, and gave me the names of people with whom I could stay right through to the border. I planned to leave when school was over, and secretly, more and more, hoped she could come with me.

Despite all the sightseeing I had done, and all the museums and ruins I had visited, and the books I had read, it was Eudora who opened those doors for me leading to the heart of this country and its people. It was Eudora who showed me the way to the Mexico I had come looking for, that nourishing land of light and color where I was somehow at home.

"I'd like to come back here and work for a while," I said, as Eudora and I watched women dying wool in great vats around the market. "If I can get papers."

"Chica, you can't run away to this country or it will never let you go. It's too beautiful. That's what the *café con leche* crowd can never admit to themselves. I thought it'd be easier here, myself, to live like I wanted to, say what I wanted to say, but it isn't. It's just easier not to, that's all. Sometimes I think I should have stayed and fought it out in Chicago. But the winters were too damned cold. And gin was too damned expensive." She laughed and pushed back her hair.

As we got back into the car to drive home, Eudora was unusually quiet. Finally, as we came over the tip of Morelos, she said, as if we'd continued our earlier conversation, "But it would be good if you came back here to work. Just don't plan on staying too long."

Eudora and I only went to the Plaza once together. Although she knew the people who hung out there, she disliked most of them. She said it was because they had sided with Karen. "Frieda's all right," she said, "but the rest of them don't deserve a pit to hiss in."

We sat at a small table for two, and Jeroméo ambled over with his bird cages to show his wares to the newcomers. The ever-present *chamaquitos* came to beg *centavos* and errands. Even the strolling mariachi players passed by to see if we were a likely prospect for serenading. But only Tammy, irrepressible and pre-adolescent, bounded over to our table and leaned possessively against it, eager for conversation.

"Are you coming shopping with me tomorrow?" she inquired. We were going to buy a turtle to keep her duck company.

I told her yes, hugged her, and then patted her fanny. "See you tomorrow," I said.

"Now the tongues can wag again," Eudora said, bitterly. I looked at her questioningly.

"Nobody knows anything about us," I said, lightly. "And besides, everybody minds their own business around here."

Eudora looked at me for a moment as if she was wondering who I was.

The sun went down and Jeroméo covered his birds. The lights on the bandstand came on, and Maria went around, lighting candles on the tables. Eudora and I paid our bill and left, walking around the closed market and down Guerrero hill toward Humboldt No. 24. The air was heavy with the smell of flowers and woodfire, and the crackle of frying grasshoppers from the vendors' carts lining Guerrero hill.

The next afternoon when Tammy and I came from the market, we joined Frieda and her friends at their table. Ellen was there, with her cat, and Agnes with her young husband Sam, who was always having to go to the border for something or other.

"Did we interrupt something?" I asked, since they had stopped talking.

"No, dear, just old gossip," Frieda said, drily.

"I see you're getting to know everybody in town," Agnes said brightly, sitting forward with a preliminary smile. I looked up to see Frieda frowning at her.

"We were just saying how much better Eudora looks these days," Frieda said, with finality, and changed the subject. "Do you kids want *café* or *helada*?"

It bothered me that Frieda sometimes treated me like her peer and confidante, and at other times like Tammy's contemporary.

Later, I walked Frieda and Tammy home, and just before I turned off, Frieda said off-handedly, "Don't let them razz you about Eudora, she's a good woman. But she can be trouble."

I pondered her words all the way up to the compound.

That spring, McCarthy was censured. The Supreme Court decision on the desegregation of schools was announced in the english newspaper, and for a while all of us seemed to go crazy with hope for another kind of america. Some of the *café con leche* crowd even talked about going home.

SUPREME COURT OF U.S. DECIDES AGAINST SEPARATE EDUCATION FOR NEGROES. I clutched the Saturday paper and read again. It wasn't even a headline. Just a box on the lower front page.

I hurried down the hill towards the compound. It all felt monumental and confusing. The Rosenbergs were dead. But this case which I had only been dimly aware of through the NAACP's *Crisis,* could alter the whole racial climate in the states. The supreme court had spoken. For me. It had spoken in the last century, and I had learned its "separate but equal" decision in school. Now something had actually changed, might actually change. Eating ice cream in Washington, D.C., was not the point; kids in the south being able to go to school was.

Could there possibly, after all, be some real and fruitful relationship between me and that malevolent force to the north of this place?

The court decision in the paper in my hand felt like a private promise, some message of vindication particular to me. Yet everybody in the Plaza this morning had also been talking about it, and the change this could make in american life.

For me, walking hurriedly back to my own little house in this land of color and dark people who said *negro* and meant something beautiful, who noticed me as I moved among them — this decision felt like a promise of some kind that I half-believed in, in spite of myself, a possible validation.

Hope. It was not that I expected it to alter radically the nature of my living, but rather that it put me actively into a context that felt like progress, and seemed part and parcel of the wakening that I called *Mexico*.

It was in Mexico that I stopped feeling invisible. In the streets, in the buses, in the markets, in the Plaza, in the particular attention within Eudora's eyes. Sometimes, half-smiling, she would scan my face without speaking. It made me feel like she was the first person who had ever looked at me, ever seen who I was. And not only did she see me, she loved me, thought me beautiful. This was no accidental collision.

I never saw Eudora actually drinking, and it was easy for me to forget that she was an alcoholic. The word itself meant very little to me besides derelicts on the Bowery. I had never known anyone with a drinking problem before. We never discussed it, and for weeks she would be fine while we went exploring together.

Then something, I never knew what, would set her off. Sometimes she'd disappear for a few days, and the carport would be empty when I came from school.

I hung around the compound in those afternoons, waiting to see her car drive in the back gate. Once I asked her afterwards where she'd been.

"In every *cantina* in Tepotzlán," she said matter-of-factly. "They know me." Her eyes narrowed as she waited for me to speak.

I did not dare to question her further.

She would be sad and quiet for a few days. And then we would make love.

Wildly. Beautifully. But it only happened three times.

Classes at the university ended. I made my plans to go south — Guatemala. I soon realized that Eudora was not coming with me. She had developed bursitis, and was often in a lot of pain. Sometimes in the early morning I heard furious voices coming through Eudora's open windows. Hers and La Señora's.

I gave up my little house with its simple, cheerful long-windowed room, and stored my typewriter and extra suitcase at Frieda's house. I was going to spend my last evening with Eudora, then take the second-class bus at dawn south to Oaxaca. It was a fifteen-hour trip.

Tomás's burro at the gate. Loud voices beneath the birdsong in the compound. La Señora almost knocking me over as she swept past me down Eudora's steps. Tomás standing in Eudora's entryway. On the orange table an unopened bottle of pale liquor with no label.

"Eudora! What happened?" I cried. She ignored me, speaking to Tomás in spanish. "And don't give La Señora anything of mine again, understand? Here!" She handed him two pesos from the wallet on the table.

"Con su permiso," he said with relief, and left quickly.

"Eudora, what's wrong?" I moved toward her, and she caught me at arm's length.

"Go home, Chica. Don't get involved in this."

"Involved in what? What's going on?" I shrugged off her hands.

"She thinks she can steal my bookstore, ruin my life, and still have me around whenever she wants me. But she's not going to get away with it anymore. I'm going to get my money!" Eudora hugged me tightly for a moment, then pushed me away. There was a strange acrid smell upon her.

"Goodbye, Chica. Go on back to Frieda's house. This doesn't concern you. And have a good trip. When you come back next time we'll go to Jalisco, to Guadalajara, or maybe up to Yucatán. They're starting a new dig there I'm going to cover..."

"Eudora, I can't leave you like this. Please. Let me stay!" If only I could hold her. I reached out to touch her again, and Eudora whirled away, almost tripping over the table.

"No, I said." Her voice was nasty, harsh, like gravel. "Get out! What makes you think you can come into someone's life on a visa and expect..."

I flinched in horror at her tone. Then I recognized the smell as tequila, and I realized she had been drinking already. Maybe it was the look on my face that stopped her. Eudora's voice changed. Slowly, carefully — almost gently — she said, "You can't handle this, Chica. I'll be all right. But I want you to leave, right now, because it's going to get worse, and I do not want you around to see it. Please. Go."

It was as clear and as direct as anything Eudora had ever said to me. There was anger and sadness beneath the surface of her words that I still did not understand. She picked up the bottle from the table and flopped into the armchair heavily, her back to me. I had been dismissed.

I wanted to burst into tears. Instead, I picked up my suitcase. I stood there, feeling like I'd been kicked in the stomach, feeling afraid, feeling useless.

Almost as if I'd spoken, Eudora's voice came muffled through the back of the armchair.

"I said I'll be all right. Now go."

I moved forward and kissed the top of her tousled head, her spice-flower smells now mixed with the acrid smell of tequila.

"All right, Eudora, I'm going. Goodbye. But I'm coming back. In three weeks, I'll be back."

It was not only a cry of pain, but a new determination to finish something I had begun, to stick with — what? A commitment my body had made? or with the tenderness which flooded through me at the curve of her head over the back of the chair?

To stick with something that had passed between us, and not lose myself. And not lose myself.

Eudora had not ignored me. Eudora had not made me invisible. Eudora had acted directly towards me.

She had sent me away.

I was hurt, but not lost. And in that moment, as in the first night when I held her, I felt myself pass beyond childhood, a woman connecting with other women in an intricate, complex, and ever-widening network of exchanging strengths.

"Goodbye, Eudora."

When I arrived back in Cuernavaca just before the rains — tired, dirty, and exhilarated — I headed for Frieda's house and my clean clothes. She and Tammy had just come in from the farm in Tepotzlán.

"How's Eudora?" I asked Frieda, as Tammy fetched us cool drinks from the kitchen.

"She's left town, moved up to the District, finally. I hear she's reporting for a new daily up there."

Gone. "Where's she living?" I asked dully.

"Nobody has her address," Frieda said quickly. "I understand there was one hell of a brawl up at the compound between her and La Señora. But evidently they must have gotten their business settled, because Eudora left soon afterwards. It all happened right after you left." Frieda sipped her *fresca* slowly. Glancing at me, she took some change from her pocket and sent Tammy to the market for bread.

I carefully kept what I hoped was an impassive expression on my face as I toyed with my fruit drink, screaming inside. But Frieda put her drink down, leaned forward, and patted me on the arm reassuringly.

"Now don't worry about her," she said kindly. "That was the best thing in the world Eudora could have done for herself, getting out of this fishbowl. If I wasn't afraid of losing Tammy to her father in the states, I think I'd leave tomorrow." She settled back in her chair, and fixed me with her level, open gaze.

"Anyway, you're going back home next week, aren't you?"

"Yes," I said, knowing what she was saying and that she was quite right.

"But I hope to come back some day." I thought of the ruins at Chichen-Itzá, of the Olmec heads in Tabasco, and Eudora's excited running commentaries.

"I'm sure you will, then," Frieda said, encouragingly.

I returned to New York on the night of July 4th. The humid heat was oppressive after the dry hot climate of Mexico. As I got out of the taxi on Seventh Street, the sound of firecrackers was everywhere. They sounded thinner and higher than the fireworks in Mexico.

The Tidal Dance

Redwing Wilderbrook

Your deep brown wells
    pierce my sea-green eyes
stirring subdued tidal pools
    to rising waves
that strain toward the rocky shore
like the incoming tide...
    each wave stretching to cover
and caress every hardened muscle,
    which in turn rises upward
ever so fiercely to taste the salty spray,
    the sea sucks the barnacles
from their homes to let them
    dance upon the foam...

The sea recedes, freshened, calm,
    eyes wide and satisfied,
rejoicing with the gray gulls' cries...
    moving out to dance with dolphins
the waves stretch wide in delight
    to receive their silver tails,
soothing their slick bodies,
    they circle around,
they circle around
    head to tail
they circle around,
    and suddenly they turn
to center, converge their heads,
    torsos tightly pressed upward

they leap as one
    fifty feet high
sending squeals of joy
    to the stars in the
darkened sky...

Their calls carried to the heavens
    cause fires to ignite
the starry coals to brilliant flames,
    which flee familiar spots
to shoot across vast stretches
    of empty time and place,
raining wishes as ashes
    upon the waiting sea,
salted drops taking each one gently down
    with a contented sigh
to rest upon the sandy floor...

The thick ash layers lie,
    building like bricks
waters rising up and over
    moving new curls ever onward
the white froth bubbles back
    to lick again the rocky shore,
to fill anew the tidal pool.

For the Classroom

Susan E. Davies

This book works from the present to the future, from personal experiences to the structure of society, from oppression to vision. Inherent in the choice of selections is an awareness of the multiplicity of visions, the variety of experiences, and the importance of critical thinking about both the present and the future. It is a hope-filled book that presumes that in the naming and the struggle there may come justice, and that freedom and strength are possible on the journey as well as at the goal.

In song and poetry, story, essay, and ritual, the writers in this volume have raised fundamental questions about who we are as sexual beings. They have challenged centuries of assumptions and conclusions, offered alternative possibilities, and even reaffirmed some traditional wisdom. The selections provide a wide range of analyses, visions, and suggestions for constructing a normative sexual ethics. In this section, I explore some possible ways of using these materials in a classroom setting. I also offer some questions for further research by class members.

The issues raised in this volume go to the root of who we know ourselves to be as embodied persons, persons composed of body and spirit. Thus exploration of the issues calls for a pedagogy that engages the whole self, not simply our minds. Further, since exploration of sexual experience and sexual ethics can be frightening and painful, it must occur in a context that is respectful and accepting of different points of view. Principles of this pedagogy are described first, followed by questions and activities to use in teaching.

PRINCIPLES OF A FEMINIST PEDAGOGY

Form and content are intrinsically related. *How* we teach and learn affects *what* we teach and learn. Therefore, the following principles are important in determining *how* we teach and learn.

Respect for Contexts

Respect and appreciation for all individuals in their emotional, sociological, and cultural contexts include respect for the views and experiences, the opinions, feelings, and positions of people in the learning environment — including both participants and those persons represented by the selections in this volume. Such respect does not mean believing that everyone's ideas are equally true. It does mean recognizing that everyone has arrived at her or his "present" with a history growing out of her or his life experiences. Further, such respect recognizes that human beings are whole people, with emotions, bodies, and minds, and that learning and teaching are activities of whole human beings, not simply minds. Our experiences and socialization, and our feelings about them, are intrinsically connected with our cognition, and they contribute to or inhibit learning. As we learn from and teach one another, we should each recognize and own our individual condition. Our condition shapes who we are and where we begin in our learning and teaching and in understanding our own sexuality.

The assumption of the editors is that generic "right" or "true" answers have never existed and do not exist now. There is no single "right" description of what it means to be female or male, what it means to be a sexual human being, what it means to be gay, straight, or bisexual. Individuals and groups of people may have similar lives and yet experience great differences in the living of those lives. Thus, students should be encouraged to ask questions of themselves and of one another — questions that help to raise their awareness of other views, not primarily to sharpen their cognitive skills.

Respect for the Learning Process

Respect for and excitement about the learning and teaching processes require that we remember that none of us will ever know another person completely, nor we will ever be known completely by another. The process of learning can often lead us to change fundamental self-understandings and even our awareness of our situation in the world. Depending on our personal security and strength, such change can be an adventure or can hasten retreat into protective stances. Learning and teaching need to be both challenging and gentle, direct and supportive.

Inclusiveness

Inclusiveness in the classroom means recognizing a multiplicity of realities for both students and teacher(s). Such inclusiveness may demand something as simple as moving student desks and the instructor's desk into a circle, rather than lining up the desks in rows facing the instructor. It means at least checking with the students at the outset of the course to see if materials or issues that are of concern to them have been omitted. It may mean planning the course together with the students. Inclusiveness will mean careful monitoring of materials to ensure that many viewpoints are included in the conversation. It may mean expecting students to work with one another in small groups or pairs. It may mean working out learning contracts at the beginning of the course, so that the instructor is not in role of judge but is a co-learner and facilitator of learning.

Recognizing Structures of Oppression

The inhabitants of the United States live in a culture that oppresses many groups within it. We all need to recognize the structures of oppression that have placed some groups of people in positions of privilege and others in situations of less than full humanity. One of the purposes of this book is to help students in institutions of higher learning to listen to the ways in which oppression has affected the lives of the contributors who share their experiences and feelings in this volume. In addition, the students should be encouraged to name the ways in which they all have participated, at one time or another, in those structures of oppression, whether they have been in an advantaged or a disadvantaged position.

Further, when oppressed people begin to speak honestly about their experiences in an oppressive culture, they may often reveal their anger and rage, which may evoke anger and resistance in others. Some students may say things that will strike others as prejudiced, oppressive, ignorant, or stupid. It is important to allow anger to be expressed and to establish a class contract that does not silence others because they fear disapproval or rejection.

The Relation of Understanding and Action

A fundamental assumption of this book is that as members of society we are all called to work actively for change in the conditions and situations of individuals, small groups, and larger units in order to move toward the vision of wholeness. We cannot change what we do not recognize. We can only be bound by it. As our awareness increases and as we connect with one another in the struggle, we are empowered to move toward *strength* that is mutual, *respect* that is deeply rooted, and *liberation* for all people.

APPLICATION TO TEACHING STYLE

These feminist principles may be applied to teaching style in a number of ways.

1. Identify your experience. For instance, I speak as a white North American woman from the Midwest, with a public school education, a degree from an Eastern women's college, and two graduate degrees. As a woman, I experience oppression and victimization. As a white woman with considerable educational and professional status, I participate in victimizing others. As a woman of my time, I am infected with racism, sexism, ageism, homophobia, classism, ablebodiedism, and all the other oppressive, divisive means by which people are classified in United States society. When I teach, these and other factors are part of the teaching and learning environment. Explore the significance of who you are for your role as an instructor. Reread "The Logic of Interstructured Oppression" by Marcia Riggs and relate it to your stance in the classroom.

2. Move out of the position of dominance in the conveying of knowledge. Provide models of truths and realities that are different from yours by having people of different experiences speak from their particular life and knowledge. Encourage students to offer their insights and expertise not only in areas specific to the course but in the one area in which they are certain to be the expert — their own life.

3. Seek out and use media other than books as means of learning. Try not only films and videotapes, but music, dance, poetry, and the visual arts as well. An individual or group project might be to find ways to express freedom and mutuality in nonverbal ways. Class projects might be designed for two or three students, rather than for individuals, as a way of modeling the connections we have with one another. The class might decide to divide the learning materials into sections. Groups of students can prepare ways in which to present it, thus involving both students and teachers in the ownership of learning.

4. Ask questions of the students and encourage their questions, not to attack others but to deepen self-understanding.

QUESTIONS AND ACTIVITIES FOR THE CLASSROOM

Part One: The Ground We Walk On

Days of Our Lives

The book begins with personal experience as a declaration of the particularity of lived experience and as a model for classroom work. These selections reflect the profound conflicts and joys that fill everyday life. They contain struggle and humor, loss and triumph, uprootings and dissonance. One way of beginning the class is by inviting the students to tell stories of their social, emotional, and spiritual histories, including any absurdity, anger, affection, and despair that these entailed. Then as they read the various selections in this volume, ask specific questions related to the material.

Look at the different kinds of love expressed in this section.

- Does the traditional triad of eros, agape, and *philia* fit the kinds of love, the images, the richness of relationships, described in these selections?

- How do these traditional categories relate to Deborah Carney's essay "Sexuality and the Eucharist" in Part Two?

- Can the new kinds of love in these selections all fit in the carefully delineated categories we have inherited? Should they?

- To what extent do categories function to exclude? To require conformity? To limit our capacity to conceive new ideas?

- Does love function as an ethical principle?

- If love functions as an ethical principle, how does it do that? When we think of love as an ethical principle, what meaning do we give to it?

- Is love a spontaneous emotion or a conscious act of the will?

- If we say "love" is the reason for an action, what do we mean?

VICKI SEARS uses affectionate, wry humor to reflect on adolescent sexuality and her struggle toward the socially constructed roles of womanhood. Humor requires distance between the subject and the speaker and also the willingness to suspend commitment. Pornography, rape, abortion, sexual identity, sexual ethics, doctrines of God, humanity, and nature have rarely been treated with humor, except as part of a denigration or rejection of the subject.

- How does Sears see womanhood as a social construction?

- How has that construction affected your life as a woman?

- Does humor function in sexuality and in theology? If so, how?

- Is there a role or should there be a role in our thinking, our living, and our common struggle for justice for acknowledging absurdities in sexuality and spirituality?

GINA MASUR'S imagery connects the natural world and sexuality.

- Is this connection liberating? If so, in what ways?
- How has the church used that connection?
- How has the connection permitted and encouraged the abuse of both human sexuality and the natural world?
- Should such a connection be maintained?
- What would a healthy connection look like?
- Considering Merchant's essay, "Production, Reproduction, and Dominion over Nature," in light of Masur's poetry, what similarities or differences do you find?

ROBERTO MENDOZA delineates the oppressive effects of white macho violence, homophobia, and sexism on the Black Power movement and the American Indian Movement. His writing connects the oppression of women with the oppression of black and indigenous peoples and all oppression with the dominant ideology of sex, violence, and power described in later sections by Stoltenberg, Ellison, and Heyward.

- Trace the effects of that dominant ideology, in privilege for some and debilitation for all, in aspects of your life experience.
- Analyze a community group or campus organization using Mendoza's work as a paradigm.
- How has internalized oppression affected your life?

SHARON HASHIMOTO and NELLIE WONG both write of their loving connections with an older woman.

- What are the qualities of the love being described here?
- How does love of an older woman fit the inherited three categories?
- Should there be only one category, love?
- How would you distinguish between acts of the will and of the emotions, sexual attraction and commitment, unselfish love and possessiveness?
- How do the younger and older women connect with each other? Is this connection valuable? Should it be a norm for all loving relationships?
- Do you think there is a unique connection between Asian cultural contexts and these images of love? If so, explain.
- What visions of hope and endurance arise from the stories? How do these visions connect with questions of race and class, of heterosexism and ageism and ableism?

SUSAN SAVELL has written a song about internalized oppression and a woman's refusal to accept it any longer.

- How is singing an experience different from speaking it?
- If you have a copy of "The Power of My Love for You" (cassette by Heartlight Records, 1986. P.O. Box 253, Biddeford Pool, ME 04006), listen to the music and the rhythm, the expression of words and music.
- What is the difference in the content between reading the words and hearing them in their intended context?
- How has the model of the "good girl" shaped the socially acceptable presence of women in class interactions, in "Take Back the Night" marches, in women soldiers going off to war?

ADA MARÍA ISASI-DÍAZ and, later in this volume, ELIZABETH BOUNDS address the difficulty white North American feminists have in taking seriously the experience and words of people of color. White women and men, including white feminists, must struggle to see and own the fact of their privilege, their easy assumption that their experience is the norm. This task is especially difficult for white, heterosexual, ablebodied young men, but it is essential in the view of this book and of the whole feminist enterprise.

- Explore your difficulty or ease in hearing other students' stories.
- Identify barriers that keep you from accepting other people's experience as valid.
- In what ways is another's experience applicable to you?
- Isasi-Díaz speaks of the flowers and the weeds she received from her mother. What kind of garden have you received from your mother and father as sexual beings, as members of particular racial, class, and ethnic groups?

PAULA LORRAINE ROPER combines Golgotha, the altar of sacrifice and hope, sensuous imagery, and the life of a woman.

- What is Roper saying about love and suffering? About the role of Jesus and the lives of women? About what happens at the eucharistic celebration?
- Can hair be stroked with thorns, wrists kissed with nails? If so, give examples.
- Does the poem evoke any images from your life as a woman? From your religious background?
- How would the poem be different if Jesus were leading, charming, and lulling a man to Golgotha?

Here are some further questions to help the class reflect on Days of Our Lives.

- How have race, class, gender, sexual choice, privilege, and physical condition shaped your sexuality?

- As a white member of the class, name five ways in which your white skin gives you privilege. As a straight person? As an ablebodied person? As a man? As a member of the middle class? As a young person?

- How does possession of at least one of these favored characteristics affect your life? Your relation to the divine? Your relation to the dominant culture? Your relation to your cultural group? Your relation to your family of origin?

- How has your self-image been shaped by television and the cultures it reflects?

- Compare the experience of those who grew up with Ginger Rogers and Fred Astaire to those who knew the musical *South Pacific* and the films *The Graduate* or *Rambo*.

Religious Community, Theology, and Sexuality

North American white culture has been built on a single model of the fullness of humanity, that of the ablebodied, straight, light-skinned, male individual who controls nature. The person who fits this mold is regarded as having the inherent right to dominate others who fit it only partially or not at all and is also required to establish dominance over them.

- A consequence of the model is that it is unsafe for most of North American society to be out alone at night — unsafe because of their gender, their color, their age, their physical abilities, their economic status.

- What is the ethical content of constructed North American white society?

- How have you adjusted to or challenged this society?

- How have you experienced marginalization? How have you experienced the need to search out roots or to put down new roots?

- How have these experiences shaped your understanding of yourself as a female or male person composed of both body and spirit?

- What price have you paid for being who you are, for coming from a particular place?

- Who has been part of your journey from despair toward freedom?

- How have you as a student who is part of the dominant culture — white or male or straight or ablebodied or young or all five — found it necessary to learn and adapt to other cultural worlds?

ROBIN GORSLINE claims that personal experience has primary authority, that scripture, which upholds straight men, cannot and does not have a previous authoritative claim on individuals or groups.

- Do you agree or disagree with Gorsline's view? Why?

- What values are inherent in using experience as the primary norm as distinguished from considering it as only one of four dominant influences in life — scripture, tradition, reason, and experience?

- Gorsline, like Heyward later in the volume, draws connections between the oppression of gay men and that of women as a group. Where can you see such oppression functioning?

- How is Gorsline's claim that gay liberation interprets scripture, and not the other way around, different from, or the same as, the churchly or rabbinic claim to make authoritative pronouncements on the meaning of scripture?

SUSAN E. DAVIES connects her experiences of incest and sexual abuse with the dominant white, patriarchal ideology and theology addressed by Gorsline and Heyward. She muses on the need for a controlling divine power to enforce limits on abusers.

- What connections can you see in your social and personal life between the hierarchical religious and theological structures and abusive behavior?

- Is pyramidal structure inherently abusive? What values are contained in such a structure?

EMILIE M. TOWNES urges us to reexamine everything, to go back to where we started and examine it all. Racism, sexism, and heterosexism have existed in a silence that must be shattered, and all three affect both cultural and religious responses to AIDS.

- What religious roots of sexual oppression can you identify? How has the church come to neglect, ignore and devalue the human body?

- How do you participate in such devaluing?

- How do you respond to AIDS from your sexual, cultural, and religious perspectives?

- What does Townes mean when she says that the dynamic that allows a child to exist in poverty is the same one that allows us to fear our bodies and treat ourselves as pieces of a puzzle rather than a magnificent design?

- Use her article as a paradigm for investigating what the churches and synagogues in your community are doing and could do regarding AIDS.

DEBORAH H. CARNEY and SUSAN E. DAVIES report from their survey of women who have been marginalized by homophobia in North American culture and in the church. The lesbian and bisexual clergywomen who responded to their questionnaire have committed themselves to a church that denies or hides their existence.

- What are the ethical issues for women clergy? What are they for the churches that rely on internal and external homophobia to control lesbian and gay clergy?

- How is the status of clergy tied to the options available to lesbians within the church?

- How does Gorsline's reclaiming of the Sodom story connect with the experiences reported by the lesbian and bisexual clergywomen?

- What norms for biblical interpretation are the women using? Do they differ from Gorsline's?

Social Structures and Sexuality

Throughout this section, violence and pain are connected with sexuality. It may be helpful to give students time to acknowledge these connections both intellectually and emotionally. Help and encourage them but do not insist.

- Explore how different the reality described in these selections is from the more romantic myths that may have formed part of your growing up.

- Share with the class as you can some of your stories — of pain and violence, love and joy.

- Trace the sources of the pain and violence in light of the images, beliefs, and expectations dominant in American culture. Consider structures that connect sex with domination and power over, which most of the authors describe.

Try some nonverbal activities here. For instance, ask members of the class to pair off, men with men and women with women, to give each other foot massage. Each pair brings a basin, towel, and, if they wish, some fragrant oil. They take turns massaging their partner's feet, one at a time, beginning with toes and working backward to the ankles. They should massage hard enough to avoid tickling. Allow about ten minutes a foot. *Be sure no one is forced into this exercise*. After the massage, ask members to share their feelings.

CAROLYN MERCHANT describes the new man of science, who must not think that the "inquisition of nature is in any part interdicted or forbidden." Nature must be "bound into service" and made a "slave," put "in constraint" and molded by the mechanical arts. The "searchers and spies of nature" are to discover her plots and secrets.

- Take this statement as a paradigm for the ways white European males treated Africans, Asians, European women, Native Americans, and the natural world. Examine your science and history texts and your theology and philosophy books for examples of this position.

- Merchant connects nature, women, and animals as objects to be controlled and exploited. Gorsline includes gay men in the list. Analyze a conflict within your community that shows the interconnected oppression of gay men, nature, animals, and women.

MARCIA RIGGS develops an analytical paradigm for understanding the connections and complexities of human relationships.

- Describe Riggs's paradigm. Analyze your own life in light of it.

- Riggs recommends that white women renounce their privilege, in certain contexts, with respect to women of color. Where, if at all, might that principle be applicable in your life?

- If you are straight, for instance, should you avoid marriage so that you can stand in solidarity with gay and bisexual people?

- Examine the other essays in this section for the ways in which the writers explain dimensions of what Riggs calls "interstructured oppression."

- What is the understanding of human sexuality that holds that men must have outlets for their sexual tension? How does this view affect one's conception of the fundamental nature of women and men as human beings? How does that understanding affect the socioeconomic status of men and women of different races and classes? What are the theological and sociological implications of the idea that sexual acts are the penetration of the female by the male?

- When even electrical and plumbing supplies are distinguished as male and female, where do lesbian and gay male sexual activities find a place?

- How have you yourself imbibed these cultural definitions?

CARTER HEYWARD says that "among the economically privileged, freedom is more important than justice."

- How is Heyward's statement connected to decisions you, your family, your religious group, and your ethnic community have made and are making?

- Can you trace the line between your relative economic privilege, disadvantage, or oppression and the choices you have made regarding freedom and justice?

- How are those choices connected with your race, gender, sexual orientation, and mental and physical condition?

- What does Heyward mean by saying that "abuse dynamics are basic, even sacred, to traditional modes of parenting, religious leadership, physical, emotional and spiritual healing, and teaching?" How is this statement connected with Davies' experiences?

- Heyward, Stoltenberg, and Ellison challenge those traditional views and look at joint empowerment as a core value for sexuality and sexual activity. How is their understanding of power different from or similar to your views? To the views of American culture?

MARY E. HOBGOOD and, in the next section, MARY E. HUNT and ELEANOR H. HANEY all challenge the normativeness of marriage and monogamy.

- Do you agree with that challenge? Why?

- Describe an integrated, nondualistic sexuality.

- Several authors in this volume speak of a liberated sexuality, but unless individuals and social groups are liberated in other aspects of life, can one speak of liberated sexuality?

- How can we talk about right and wrong sexualities when we don't know yet what sexual liberation is?

- Within Christian tradition, there has been a specific ethic of sexuality, with its own rules and values. Central to the ethic has been the rule, for instance, that only the heterosexual expression of sexuality is right. Do you agree that there should be a specific sexual ethic? If so, what should its content be? Who should decide it and on what basis?

- Hobgood connects economic and sexual ethics in capitalist societies. Both are based on individual ownership and possession, and both are alienating and destructive. She notes that the fear of being considered promiscuous and debauched is a mask for our fear of choice. Do you agree? How is this connected with Davies' fear of chaos if there is no omnipotent God to keep evil in check?

CHRYSTOS speaks of the interconnectedness of human beings and other natural things such as rocks and water.

- What does Chrystos mean by love?

- How is her concept of love connected with the love expressed in "The Death of Long Steam Lady?"

ELIZABETH M. BOUNDS examines the impact of economic, racist, and military policies of the United States on Asian societies, particularly on women.

- How is Bounds's analysis different from or similar to yours?

- To what extent do you agree with her conclusions?

JOHN STOLTENBERG invites men to become erotic traitors to male supremacy, to reject the sex-class system into which those with penises and vaginas are born.

- How would such rejection affect you, as a man, as a woman? Would you lose or gain social status? How? Why?

- Both Haney and Stoltenberg reject the idea of two genders, arguing that gender is a social construction. How has your gender been socially constructed by your family, your religious community, the media, by your racial or ethnic community?

- How do you collaborate in that construction?

- What are the enforcement mechanisms — dress codes, behavioral mannerisms, occupational and social roles, speech patterns, sexual connections — that keep you in your gendered position?

- How is the sex-class system reproduced in each generation?

- How is your relationship with the divine affected by your gender? Do you have religious privileges because of your gender?

NILDA RIMONTE addresses domestic violence in the Asian American communities on the West Coast of the United States.

- Are there cross-cultural ethical norms that allow Rimonte and others to evaluate domestic violence? Should there be?

DEBRA CONNORS identifies economic elements in the model of full humanity as straight, white, male, and ablebodied and names the pain of those who are not economically viable members of the society.

- Can you locate similar pain in your life or in the history of your family or community?

- Has falling short of the fullness of humanity as defined by the model been oppressive in developing your sexual identity? If so, how?

- If you have an overt or hidden "disability," has Connors given words to some of your experience? Has reading her essay given you any power? Name that empowerment.

GLORIA ANZALDÚA offers sexual images of swollen feet, buzzing mosquitoes digging and sucking, and a woman on her back.

- What other sexual images are there in this volume, negative and positive?

- Write a nonlinear, imagistic piece regarding your sexuality.

- Write a piece on the sexuality of God.

PAULA LORRAINE ROPER links the earth, human labor, the sacrifice of the cross, impotence, and divine impatience.

- How does Roper envision old people?

- What is the old woman doing at the cross? Why is the earth an unforgiving womb?

- How do you respond to the old men's tools and the young men's sowed impotency?

- What are the choices made by human beings? How are women envisioned? How are men envisioned?

MARVIN M. ELLISON speaks of violent images of God.

- How are Ellison's images connected with Davies' understanding of the theological roots of abusive behavior?

- As a man, recall the way you feel about how you connect with other men and then talk about it.

- As a man, do you agree with Ellison regarding distancing?

- What do you as a man think are the ethical implications of reimaging God? What are the ethical implications of male bonding?

- As a woman, how do you respond to Ellison's owning of male violence and the responsibility of silence?

- As a woman, have you experienced violence promoted by silence? If so, how?

- By what faith, in Ellison's terms, do you live?

- Does your faith promote mutual well-being of bodies and spirits together? If so, how?

- Does your faith promote violence? If so, how?

Part Two: The Land We Seek

Personal Statements

As Part One, "The Ground We Walk On," began with personal experience, so the visions of "The Land We Seek" begin in personal statements. The lyricist, composer, and writer each offer opportunities to ground theological reflection in intimate, immediate experience. Classroom consideration of this brief section might well begin with expressions of personal visions by both instructor and students of how their lives would look if they embodied justice and mercy. The individual visions might then be considered in small or large groups for class presentation.

GLORIA ANZALDÚA, in "*Cihuatlyotl,* Woman Alone," creates a new form, using neither accepted poetic presentation nor standard prose format.

- What is accomplished by Anzaldúa's new form for feminist revisioning?
- Try expressing one experience in two or three literary, visual, or musical forms. How does the form shape the expression of the experience?

RUTH C. DUCK'S and ANN MACKENZIE'S hymn is meant to be sung not by an individual but by a community.

- What difference does community participation in the hymn make for the experience of the words and the music?
- The hymn is a prayer to God. What sorts of images of the divine does Duck offer? What sorts of images of human relationships with the divine?
- Haney, Townes, Ellison, and Evans all speak of community. How are their images similar to or different from the one assumed by this hymn? What values are inherent in each one's understanding of community?

New Theologies and Ethics

This concluding section offers visions of how we can live with one another in justice, wholeness, and truth. Each of the writers addresses part of the larger whole, in which all individuals and groups live, and speaks of what the world might be if mutual respect and passionate abundance formed the basis for human community. As you read and respond to the essays, ask yourself who benefits from the particular vision.

- Who has the capacity to bring this vision into being?
- Who is excluded from decision making in the author's new world?
- Who would pay and what would be the price if this new ethic were to be embodied in our social connections?
- Can there be fundamental theological and ethical change without someone paying the price of the ticket?

GLORIA ANZALDÚA ushers us into a new land with a new form. She places herself and the reader on the borderlands, in the tension between the need for particularity, for rootedness, for somewhereness and some-oneness, and the need for a new land, where each person is connected with everyone and becomes something new. She offers another image of the combination of race, earth, gender, and sexuality and finds liberation through moving out, not belonging, and then returning to claim and reclaim. She moves out on a pilgrimage to discover who she is and returns to her roots.

Anzaldúa describes the *mestiza* as one who makes a conscious rupture with all oppressive traditions of culture and religion. She communicates that rupture, documents the struggle. She reinterprets history, and using new symbols, she shapes new myths. She adopts new perspectives toward the dark skinned, women, and queers. She strengthens her tolerance (and intolerance) for ambiguity. She is willing to share, to make herself vulnerable to foreign ways of seeing and thinking. She surrenders all notions of safety, of the familiar.

- What would it be like to be a *mestiza*? To be a *mestizo*?

- As a person who speaks only English, what was your experience of having portions of the text in Spanish? Did you skip them? Did you struggle for a while to read them?

- As a person who speaks English and Spanish, what was your reaction to the mixing of the languages, sometimes with English translation, but always using Spanish words with their independent integrity?

- If you live in a primarily English-speaking area of the country, how do you experience descriptions of bilingual society? Do these descriptions affect your identity? Your sexuality? If your first language is neither Spanish nor English, how do your experiences of moving between two language communities affect your theology? Your identity?

- Anzaldúa speaks from the border between two linguistic and cultural worlds, and her use of language reflects that positioning. Border towns are places of mixed languages and mixed races. They raise fundamental questions about one's own heritage and place in the world. Can you, as an inhabitant of an English-speaking area, imagine yourself as a member of a border town? If you live in a border town or move regularly between language communities, can you imagine a multicultural community with an identity and cohesiveness of its own which includes two or more languages? What should such a culture look like? What kind of sexual ethic might emerge?

- Should white North Americans go back and claim their white European heritage? If so, how can they do so in a nonoppressive way?

PAULA GUNN ALLEN shifts the focus of Native American history from the men to the women.

- How does Allen's shift change your understanding of Native Americans?

- Would the same shift change your relationship to your family history? Your ethnic history? Your bodily self-awareness?

ELEANOR H. HANEY describes a dominant Western attitude toward sexuality as a problem of control and locates the chief means of that control in the monogamous, heterosexual family.

- How has your family of origin or of choice functioned to control sexuality — between the parents, between other family members and parents, in the sexual identity and activity of individual family members?

- Do you agree that sexuality must be controlled? If not, how should it be treated?

- Do you agree with the alternatives offered by Haney? Why or why not?

- Haney, Hunt, and Hobgood all propose a paradigm of friendship as the norm by which to develop human relationships. How does that paradigm differ from the norms by which you presently act?

- How would your life be changed if the norm for relationships between human beings and relationships between human beings and the divine were changed to friendship?

- Haney names justice, healing, survival, power, life abundant, nurture, and respect as critical values for living. She spells out some ways these values could operate. How would you challenge or supplement her vision? Are any values missing from her vision?

- Haney and Ellison both declare that no one has clean hands, that no choice is merely good or right, that all of us are the products of an oppressive structure and have developed our ethical constructs within that world. Do you find those declarations freeing or paralyzing? Do you agree that no one is innocent? Is this another version of the Christian doctrine of original sin?

Both MARY E. HUNT and, in an earlier section, MARY E. HOBGOOD offer paradigms for sexual relationships.

- What is the difference between Hunt's and Hobgood's paradigms and that of your cultural or religious tradition?

- What are the dangers in breaking down the norm of heterosexual monogamous coupling?

- What ethical issues are raised? For whom?

- How would taking up Hunt's challenge alter your sexual ethic? How would it change your images of God, your connections with your body, your relationship to your community?

VICKI HOLLANDER, Hunt, and Haney all suggest that we should create new ceremonies that reflect our ethics and theologies. Hollander both reclaims and creates a divorce ceremony.

- Consider creating ceremonies of your own around the sexual passages of your life — commitments and separations, the beginning and end of menstruation, for instance. Have you a religious or cultural tradition to draw on in creating such rituals?
- Many books of rituals are now available, primarily for women but also some for men. You may wish to explore some of these and share your findings with the class.

DEBORAH H. CARNEY speaks from her experiences with sexual and spiritual union and makes some connections between them. She finds God in the arms of her beloved and her beloved at the communion table. Living between the present and the future, she speaks of sexual union as a means of grace that is as valid as the eucharist.

- How does Carney's vision differ from the mind-body dualism inherent in most Christian and Jewish theology?
- Is her experience dependent upon class or race or gender or privilege? If so, in what ways?
- Is she experiencing what Haney and Plaskow envision?
- What values are involved in her position?

JAMES H. EVANS JR. insists that the oppression experienced by the whole black community, both male and female, must be the starting point for black theology. In addition, he says that "Black men do not experience sexism directly."

- Do you agree with Evans' statement?
- How is sexism understood here?
- How can we use Evans' critical principle to examine our own contexts, both personal and institutional?
- If neither blackness nor humanness is as important as white maleness in white theology, what is the paradigm Evans rejects?
- Is that paradigm connected with Stoltenberg's and Nelson's presentations of maleness?
- How should black theology change, if it is to respond to Evans' argument?
- Evans speaks of the adoption by black men of white male attitudes toward black women. What can you learn from this about the life of oppressed groups?
- What is "black love?" How is it different from "white love?"
- Why should black male liberation theologians listen to and work with black female liberation theologians?

- How would fidelity to Jesus Christ as presented by Evans serve to change the norms of the black community?

- What are the criteria by which individuals and groups should accept or reject specific positions within scripture, tradition, and experience?

- What values are embodied in those criteria, and how do they compare with Gorsline's principle of authority?

JAMES B. NELSON speaks of both the penis and the phallus as two essential modes of male genital experience.

- How do you feel about talking about the penis as Nelson does?

- Explore the impact of having a penis on your identity as a man.

- What is the significance of having a clitoris for a woman?

- Nelson connects the sexual and the spiritual. How does such a connection affect your understanding of self as sexual, as spiritual? Does it offer normative possibilities for action?

- Nelson takes male sexuality as a paradigm for understanding the relationship between human and divine and the nature of Jesus as the Christ. "To be fully masculine...means embracing the fullness of the revelation that comes through our male bodies." What does such a claim mean for your life as a man? What does it mean for your life as a woman?

LUCY V. HITCHCOCK'S poem sings of pain and deep, visceral, determinative joy. She celebrates life and death and connections of friendship and sexuality and spirituality. She mourns for Guatemalan *niños* who are sold for their internal organs.

- Are there depths in your life that could be plumbed by a poem, a short story, or a song? Can you make these connections?

JUDITH PLASKOW, like Eleanor Haney, identifies the importance of control in sexuality. Plaskow goes on to note that control of women's sexuality is central in Jewish tradition. Carney, Ellison, Nelson, and Plaskow all agree on the crucial nature of the connections between sexuality and spirituality and point to elements within the Jewish and Christian traditions that contain those connections.

- Are there similar connections within the black churches?

- How would Western white worship be altered if such connections were affirmed?

- How would your relation to your body and your sexuality change if those connections were part of your fundamental self-understanding?

- Plaskow cites the power of the erotic for communication, for breaking barriers. She sees sexuality as an aspect of our life energy. How does such an understanding change your concept of Judaism?

- Should the erotic be a value, an ethical norm?

- Can you reconstruct sexuality into a construct that is nonsexist, nonracist? Based on Riggs's article, do you think it is possible? Whose experiences and perspectives should be a part of reconstructing sexuality?

- Write your own sexual ethic and share it with the class.

AUDRE LORDE's autobiographical statement reflects joy and pain and learning to let go. It also celebrates the power of the erotic in a lesbian relationship and in a relationship with a woman who has been "disabled" by surgery for breast cancer.

- Lorde says, "It was in Mexico that I stopped feeling invisible." What are the interactions in the story between sexism, racism, homophobia, and the Anglo sense of superiority in relation to Mexico?

- How does Eudora's scarred body and Lorde's response to it affect your attitude toward your relationships to others, toward your body, and toward the bodies of others?

- Go back to the early discussions of love in the first section of the book. Does Lorde's story illumine your understanding of love? If so, how?

REDWING WILDERBROOK writes of power, erotic power in the straining of waves toward the rocky shore. Like Masur, she embeds her sexual experience in the world of nature, in the ocean and its surging, sucking dance.

- How is Wilderbrook's vision different from the world described by Merchant?

- Are there ethical norms to be developed from such a vision?

- Is sexuality inherently tied to the spiritual and the natural worlds? Should it be?

- How can you celebrate your sexuality?

Notes

A HISPANIC GARDEN IN A FOREIGN LAND

1. My understandings of culture are greatly influenced by Geertz and Scannone. See Clifford Geertz, *The Interpretations of Culture* (New York: Basic Books, 1973), and Juan Carlos Scannone, "Teología, Cultura Popular y Discernimiento," in *Cultura Popular y Filosofía de la Liberación* (Buenos Aires: Fernando García Cambeiro, 1975), 241–70.
2. As I type in my apartment I face a poster that reads, I AM A WOMAN BRINGING BIRTH TO MYSELF.
3. *Building Feminist Theory: Essays from QUEST* (Harlow, England: Longman's Group, 1981).
4. Marcia Ann Gillespie, "My Gloves Are Off, Sisters," *MS Magazine,* April 1987, 19–20.
5. Ibid.
6. Three books that have been very important for me in the area of friendship are Margaret Farley, *Personal Commitments* (New York: Harper & Row, 1986); Isabel C. Heyward, *The Redemption of God* (Lanham, Md.: University Press of America, 1982); and Janice Raymond, *A Passion for Friends* (Boston: Beacon Press, 1986).
7. See Sonia Johnson, *Going Out of Our Minds: The Metaphysics of Liberation* (Freedom, Calif.: Crossing Press, 1987).

LET US BLESS OUR ANGELS

1. This project was begun in a class on biblical ethics at Union Theological Seminary, New York City, taught by Norman Gottwald. I am in Professor Gottwald's debt for providing me a forum for finding my voice as a feminist gay man in relation to the Bible, and I am also indebted to several other colleagues at Union for their help and support: Victoria Rue, Sharon Moe, Carol Chambers, and especially the lesbian feminist theologian Anne E. Gilson.
2. The feminist liberation ethicist Marvin M. Ellison Jr., of Bangor Theological Seminary, suggested the inclusion of the fifth principle.
3. Early gay liberation history from Stonewall forward is best captured in Karla Jay and Allen Young, eds., *Out of the Closets: Voices of Gay Liberation* (New York: Quick Fox, 1972). Observations about later years are my own, based on my involvement in the movement and my reading of publications such as Boston's *Gay Community News* and the national gay men's newsmagazine, the

Advocate, as well as history-sharing over the gay grapevine. Good sources for pre-Stonewall history include Jonathan Katz's *Gay American History: Lesbians and Gay Men in the U.S.A., A Documentary* (New York: Avon Books, 1976) and Andrea Weiss and Greta Schiller's *Before Stonewall: The Making of a Gay and Lesbian Community* (Tallahassee, Fla.: Naiad Press, 1988), an illustrated guide to the film of the same name.

4. See Eva C. Keuls, *The Reign of the Phallus: Sexual Politics in Ancient Athens* (New York: Harper & Row, 1985) and Paul Veyne, "Homosexuality in Ancient Rome" in *Western Sexuality: Practice and Precept in Past and Present Times,* ed. Philippe Aries and Andre Bejin (Oxford, England: Basil Blackwell, 1985) for important material on prohibitions against "passive" sexual behavior among males with high social status in these two cultures.

5. The work of Elisabeth Schüssler Fiorenza is particularly helpful in revealing the moral agency of biblical women. See her *In Memory of Her: A Feminist Theological Reconstruction of Christian Origins* (New York: Crossroad, 1984) and *Bread Not Stone: The Challenge of Feminist Biblical Interpretation* (Boston: Beacon Press, 1984).

6. Kenneth Dover, *Greek Homosexuality* (Cambridge, Mass.: Harvard University Press, 1978), 105. Of course, anal violation as a method of maintaining masculinist hierarchies occurs in various all-male settings today, most notably in prisons.

7. I am indebted to Katie Geneva Cannon for teaching me, at the Episcopal Divinity School, about the power of naming, and to Margaret Cerullo, of Hampshire College, for suggesting we "interrupt the monologue."

8. Carter Heyward, "Heterosexism: Enforcing Male Supremacy," *The Witness* 69 (April 1986): 18. Heyward is the feminist theologian whose work most closely examines and challenges structural heterosexism.

9. An important examination of penalties for "sodomy" appears in Louis Compton, *Byron and Greek Love: Homophobia in 19th Century England* (Berkeley: University of California Press, 1985). England hanged scores of men, and countless others died in the infamous pillories of that land in the nineteenth century. Mass murder of homosexual men reached its apex in Nazi Germany. More recently, the United States Supreme Court cited the Genesis text and historical attitudes toward sodomy in its 1986 ruling in *Bowers* vs. *Hardwick* upholding the Georgia state statute outlawing sodomy.

10. See the following for discussions of Genesis 19: Derrick Sherwin Bailey, *Homosexuality and the Western Christian Tradition* (London: Longmans Green & Co., 1955); John Boswell, *Christianity, Social Tolerance and Homosexuality: Gay People in Western Europe from the Beginning of the Christian Era to the Fourteenth Century* (Chicago: University of Chicago Press, 1980); and George Edwards, *Gay/Lesbian Liberation: A Biblical Perspective* (New York: Pilgrim Press, 1984).

REFLECTIONS ON THE THEOLOGICAL ROOTS OF ABUSIVE BEHAVIOR

1. Parenthetical numbers indicate hymns in *The Pilgrim Hymnal* (New York: The Pilgrim Press, 1958).

2. From "That Cause Can Neither Be Lost," words by Kr. Ostergaard, translated by J. C. Aaberg, music by J. Nellemann in *A World of Song,* copyright 1941, by D.A.Y.D.L. in *Connecticut Sings,* edited by Connecticut Pilgrim Fellowship, 125 Sherman Street, Hartford, Conn.

3. Augustine, *De Trinitate* 7.7.10.

4. Susan Savell.

5. Jim Manley.

6. Alice Hildebrand Rudiger. Used by permission.

THE PRICE OF THE TICKET

1. James Baldwin, *The Price of the Ticket* (New York: St. Martin's Press, 1985), "Introduction," xix.

PRODUCTION, REPRODUCTION, AND THE FEMALE

1. On women in Renaissance Italy, see Joan Kelly-Gadol, "Did Women Have a Renaissance?" in *Becoming Visible: Women in European History,* ed. Renate Bridenthal and Claudia Koonz (Boston: Houghton Mifflin, 1977), 137–64. The discussion of England is based on Alice Clark, *Working Life of Women in the Seventeenth Century* (1919; New York: Augustus M. Kelly, 1968), 6–13, 38–39, 42–46, 64–68, 86–92, 103–4, 146–49, 209–11, 216–29; Richard T. Vann, "Toward a New Lifestyle: Women in Preindustrial Capitalism," in *Becoming Visible,* 192–216, esp. 200–205; G. E. Fussell and K. R. Fussell, *The English Countrywoman: A Farmhouse Social History, A.D. 1500–1900* (London: Melrose, 1953); Christina Hole, *The English Housewife in the Seventeenth Century* (London: Chatto & Windus, 1953).

2. Clark, *Working Life,* 265–69; Barbara Ehrenreich and Deirdre English, *Witches, Midwives, and Nurses* (Old Westbury, N.Y.: Feminist Press, n.d.); Jean Donnison, *Midwives and Medical Men* (New York: Schocken, 1977), 1–41; Irving S. Cutter and Henry R. Viets, *A Short History of Midwifery* (Philadelphia: Saunders, 1964), 46–50; Hilda Smith, "Gynecology and Ideology," in *Liberating Women's History,* ed. Berenice A. Carroll (Urbana: University of Illinois Press, 1976), 110; and H. Smith, "Reason's Disciples: Seventeenth-Century English Feminists," (Ph.D. diss., University of Chicago, 1975), 179–92. On the controversy over the licensing of midwives, see James H. Aveling, *English Midwives, Their History and Prospects* (1872; reprint London: Elliott, 1967), 22–46, and J. Aveling, *The Camberlens and the Midwifery Forceps* (1882; reprint, New York: AMS Press, 1977), 34–48; Thomas R. Forbes, *The Midwife and the Witch* (New Haven, Conn.: Yale University Press, 1966), 112–55; Kate Campbell Hurd Mead, *A History of Women in Medicine* (Haddam, Conn.: Haddam Press, 1938); Herbert R. Spencer, *The History of British Midwifery from 1650 to 1800* (London: Bale, 1927), introduction and chap. 1, especially 3–6.

3. Quoted in Cutter and Viets, *Midwifery,* 49.

4. William Harvey, *Exercitationes de Generatione Animalium* (1651; trans. Robert Willis, London: Sydenham Society, 1847), 533–34.

5. Treatments of Francis Bacon's contributions to science include Paolo Rossi, *Francis Bacon: From Magic to Science* (London: Routledge & Kegan Paul, 1968); Lisa Jardine, *Francis Bacon: Discovery and the Art of Discourse* (Cambridge: Cambridge University Press, 1974); Benjamin Farrington, *Francis Bacon: Philosopher of Industrial Science* (New York: Schumann, 1949); Margery Purver, *The Royal Society: Concept and Creation* (London: Routledge & Kegan Paul, 1967).

6. James I, *Daemonologie* (1597; New York: Barnes & Noble, 1966); Keith Thomas, *Religion and the Decline of Magic* (New York: Charles Scribner's Sons, 1971), 520; Wallace Notestein, *A History of Witchcraft in England from 1558 to 1718* (New York: Apollo Books, 1968), 101; Ronald Seth, *Stories of Great Witch Trials* (London: Baker, 1967), 83.

7. Bacon, "De Dignitate et Augmentis Scientiarum," (written 1623) in *Works,* ed. James Spedding, Robert Leslie Ellis, Douglas Devon Heath, 14 vols. (London: Longmans Green, 1870), 4:296. The ensuing discussion was stimulated by William Leiss's, *The Domination of Nature* (New York: Braziller, 1972), chap. 3, 45–71.

8. Bacon, "Preparative Towards a Natural and Experimental History," *Works* 4:263. Italics added.

9. Bacon, "De Dignitate," *Works* 4:298. Italics added.
10. Bacon, "The Great Instauration" (written 1620), *Works* 4:20; "The Masculine Birth of Time," in *The Philosophy of Francis Bacon* ed. and trans. Benjamin Farrington (Liverpool: Liverpool University Press, 1964), 62; "De Dignitate," *Works* 4:287, 294.
11. Quoted in Moddy E. Prior, "Bacon's Man of Science," in *The Rise Of Modern Science in Relation to Society* ed. Leonard M. Marsak (London: Collier-Macmillan, 1964), 45.
12. Rossi, *Bacon,* 21; Leiss, *Domination of Nature,* 56; Bacon, *Works* 4:294; Henry Cornelius Agrippa, *De Occulta Philosophia Libri Tres* (Antwerp, 1531): "No one has such powers but he who has cohabited with the elements, vanquished nature, mounted higher than the heavens, elevating himself above the angels to the archetype itself, with whom he then becomes cooperator and can do all things," as quoted in Frances A. Yates, *Giordano Bruno and the Hermetic Tradition* (New York: Vintage Books, 1964), 136.
13. Bacon, "Novum Organum," pt. 2, in *Works* 4:247; "Valerius Terminus," in *Works* 3:217, 219; "The Masculine Birth of Time," in *The Philosophy of Francis Bacon,* 62.
14. Bacon, "The Masculine Birth of Time," and "The Refutation of Philosophies," in *The Philosophy of Francis Bacon,* 62, 129, 130.
15. Bacon, "Novum Organum," in *Works* 4:246; "The Great Instauration," in *Works* 4:29; "Novum Organum," pt. 2, in *Works* 4:247.
16. Alain of Lille, *De Planctu Naturae,* in *The Anglo-Latin Satirical Poets and Epigrammatists,* ed. T. Wright (Wiesbaden: Kraus Reprint, 1964), 2:441, 467; Thomas Kuhn, "Mathematical vs. Experimental Traditions in the Development of Physical Science," *Journal of Interdisciplinary History* 7, no. 1 (Summer 1976): 1–31, see 13. On the Accademia del Cimento's experiments see Martha Ornstein [Bronfenbrenner], *The Role of Scientific Societies in the Seventeenth Century* (reprint, New York: Arno Press, 1975), 86.
17. Bacon, "Thoughts and Conclusions on the Interpretation of Nature or A Science of Productive Works," in *Philosophy of Francis Bacon,* 96, 93, 99.
18. Bacon, "The New Atlantis," in *Works* 3:129–66. Quotes in order on 147, 148–49, 150, 148.

THE LOGIC OF INTERSTRUCTURED OPPRESSION

1. I think that Walker's term "womanist" aligns well with Bell Hooks's understanding of feminism as a political commitment as expressed in *Feminist Theory: From Margin to Center* (Boston: South End Press, 1984, chap. 2). The point that Hooks makes is that focusing on feminism as a political commitment moves us beyond an emphasis on individual identity and lifestyle. At the same time, this move makes it possible for black women and other women of color to speak of sexist oppression as one of the political issues about which they are concerned rather than putting it in opposition to other political issues, such as racist oppression. In Hooks's words, "The shift in expression from 'I am a feminist' to 'I advocate feminism' could serve as a useful strategy for eliminating the focus on identity and lifestyle. It could serve as a way women who are concerned about feminism as well as other political movements could express their support while avoiding linguistic structures that give primacy to one particular group," p. 30.
2. See Alice Walker, *In Search of Our Mothers' Gardens: Womanist Prose* (New York: Harcourt Brace Jovanovich, 1983), xi–xii for her definitions of womanist.
3. Katie G. Cannon, " 'Hitting a Straight Lick with a Crooked Stick': The Womanist Dilemma in the Development of a Black Liberation Ethic," *The Annual of the Society of Christian Ethics* (1987), 165–77.

4. I emphasize that this gender connection actually refers to the biological fact of being female in light of the sociological clarification that gender designates the sociocultural significance we attach to the biological fact. For it is the biological fact that is central to this idea of relationality; if gender (understood sociologically) were the crux of the idea, then the sociohistoric dimension of oppression would not be ignored. See Richard T. Shaefer, *Racial and Ethnic Groups* (Boston: Little, Brown and Co., 1979), 395–98, for a sociological discussion of sex and gender, and Arthur Brittan and Mary Maynard, *Sexism, Racism and Oppression* (New York: Blackwell, 1984), 8–15, for a discussion of biological essentialism as an explanation of sexist and racist oppression.

5. See Ruth L. Smith, "Feminism and the Moral Subject" in *Women's Consciousness, Women's Conscience,* ed. Barbara Hilkert Andolsen, Christine E. Gudorf, and Mary D. Pellauer (New York: Winston Press, 1985), 235–50 and Ruth Smith, "Moral Transcendence and Moral Space in the Historical Experiences of Women," *Journal of Feminist Studies in Religion* 4, no. 2 (Fall 1988): 21–37; Beverly Harrison, "Theological Reflection in the Struggle for Liberation" in *Making the Connections,* ed. Carol S. Robb (Boston: Beacon Press, 1985), 249–59 for discussions by white feminist ethicists that I think do contribute theoretically to a strong ethical stance premised upon relationality.

6. I am adopting this term from, and basing my proposal of a womanist logic primarily on, Althea Smith and Abigail J. Steward, "Approaches to Studying Racism and Sexism in Black Women's Lives," *Journal of Social Issues* 39, no. 3 (1983): 1–15, where a theoretical discussion of a contextual interactive model for understanding the dynamic relationship between sexism and racism is presented.

7. Hooks, *Feminist Theory,* 31.

8. I realize that the implications of a logic of interstructured oppression presented here do not fully offer a way to make ethical decisions in relation to black men and other men of color. However, my aim has been to focus upon women and women's self-understanding of their interrelatedness as a precondition for feminist/womanist morality and action that would require fuller analysis of the relationship between the macro societal context and micro communal contexts in which women and men interact.

HETEROSEXISM: ENFORCING MALE SUPREMACY

1. Adrienne Rich, "Compulsory Heterosexuality and Lesbian Existence," in her *Blood, Bread and Poetry: Selected Prose, 1979 — 1985* (New York: W. W. Norton, 1986), 63–64.

2. Mario Mieli, *Homosexuality and Liberation: Elements of a Gay Critique,* trans. David Fernbach (London: Gay Men's Press, 1980), 30–31.

3. I first used this analogy, in detail, in my essay "Can Anglicans Be Feminist Liberation Theologians and Still Be Anglicans?" in *The Trial of Faith: Theology and the Church Today,* ed. Peter Eaton (West Sussex, England: Churchman Publishing, 1988), 30–31.

4. Charlie Howard, a twenty-three-year-old gay man, drowned after being beaten and thrown from a bridge by three teenage men in Bangor, Maine, on July 7, 1984. The three men — Shawn Mabry, James Baines, and Daniel Ness — were released without bail to their parents' custody. They were charged as juveniles and pleaded guilty to manslaughter. They were sentenced to indeterminate terms at the Maine Youth Center.

5. For more on Marx and alienation, see Erich Fromm, *Marx's Concept of Man,* with a translation from Marx's *Economic and Philosophical Manuscripts* by T. B. Bottomore (New York: Frederick Ungar, 1961). In his chapter "Alienation," Fromm states:

Alienation (or "estrangement") means, for Marx, that man [sic] does *not* experience himself as the acting agent in his grasp of the world, but that the world (nature, others, and he himself) remains alien to him. They stand above and against him as objects, even though they may be objects of his own creation. Alienation is essentially experiencing the world and oneself passively, receptively, as the subject separated from the object. (44)

6. Audre Lorde, "Uses of the Erotic: The Erotic as Power," in her *Sister Outsider: Essays and Speeches* (Trumansburg, N.Y.: Crossing Press, 1984), 57.
7. James B. Nelson, *Between Two Gardens: Reflections on Sexuality and Religious Experience* (New York: Pilgrim Press, 1983), 5–6.
8. Beverly Wildung Harrison, *Making the Connections: Essays in Feminist Social Ethics,* ed. Carol S. Robb (Boston: Beacon Press, 1985), 149.
9. See Marie M. Fortune, *Sexual Violence: The Unmentionable Sin* (New York: Pilgrim Press, 1983), 16–26.
10. Ibid., 27–30.
11. Ibid., 77–79.
12. Harrison, "Misogyny and Homophobia: The Unexplored Connections," in *Making the Connections,* 135–51.
13. Rennie Golden and Sheila Collins, *Struggle Is a Name for Hope* (London: West End Press, 1972).

MARRIAGE, MARKET VALUES, AND SOCIAL JUSTICE

1. Marvin M. Ellison, "Common Decency: A New Christian Sexual Ethics," *Christianity and Crisis* 50, no. 16 (November 1990): 352–56.
2. Compulsory heterosexuality has been well defined in Adrienne Rich's essay "Compulsory Heterosexuality and Lesbian Existence," *Signs* 5, no. 41 (1980): 631–60.
3. Whites need to appreciate more fully how traditional marriage has developed historically as a white, middle-income structure. In the black community, for example, strong permanent ties have always been valued. But in a situation where unemployed men could not pay for sexual activity with wives, sexuality has had different social significance, has been more multiple, improvisational, and interdependent than in the white community. Whites also need to appreciate how accusations of sexual depravity toward those who exercised greater personal choice in sexuality have served to maintain race and class hierarchies. See John Scanzoni, Karen Polonko, Jay Teachman, and Linda Thompson, *The Sexual Bond: Rethinking Familial and Close Relationships* (Newberry Park, N.Y.: Sage Publications, 1989), 266. See also John D'Emilio and Estelle B. Friedman, *Intimate Matters: A History of Sexuality in America* (New York: Harper & Row, 1988), 187, 273.
4. Raymond J. Lawrence, "Toward a More Flexible Monogamy," in *The Future of Sexual Relations,* ed. Robert T. Francoeur and Anna K. Francoeur (Englewood Cliffs, N.J.: Prentice-Hall, 1974), 72.
5. I am grateful to Bonnie Kreps for this basic insight. See her *Subversive Thoughts, Authentic Passion* (San Francisco: Harper & Row, 1990), 34–35.
6. For example, celibacy in singleness and monogamy in marriage are opposed to practices of our most ancient tribal ancestors. Tribal peoples saw children as the responsibility of the whole community. They greatly honored women and did not value virginity or monogamy. Conventional sexual ethics is fairly recent to the human scene and is rooted in the rise of monotheism, kingship, and patriarchal control of land and property, including women and their children. See Mary Condren, *The Serpent and the Goddess* (New York: Harper & Row,

1989), 3–43, and Paula Gunn Allen, *The Sacred Hoop* (Boston: Beacon Press, 1986), 31–42. For data on more recent communities, see C. S. Ford and F. A. Beach, *Patterns of Sexual Behavior* (New York: Ace, 1959), esp. 115–19; and D. Marshall and R. Suggs, eds., *Human Sexual Behavior* (Englewood Cliffs, N.J.: Prentice-Hall, 1972).

7. Ruth Sidel, *Women and Children Last: The Plight of Poor Women in Affluent America* (New York: Penguin Books, 1986), 17.

8. Scanzoni, et al., *The Sexual Bond,* 130; and Susan Crain Bakos, "Why Do Happily Marrieds So Often Have Secret Lovers?," *Cosmopolitan* (March 1990), 176. See also Jessie Bernard, *The Future of Marriage* (New Haven, Conn.: Yale University Press, 1982); and James R. Smith and Lynn G. Smith, *Beyond Monogamy* (Baltimore: Johns Hopkins University Press, 1974).

9. See Lawrence Stone, *Road to Divorce: England 1530–1987* (New York: Oxford University Press, 1990).

10. See Frank Mort, "Sexuality: Regulation and Contestation" in *Homosexuality: Power and Politic,* ed. Gay Left Collective (New York: Allison & Busby, 1980), 38–51.

11. William Julius Wilson, *The Truly Disadvantaged* (Chicago: University of Chicago Press, 1987); and Eloise Thomas, "Myths and Facts of Women and Work," *Probe* 14 (January- February 1986): 7.

12. For insight into this connection, I am indebted to Smith and Smith, *Beyond Monogamy,* 33–35.

13. The use of such terms as "affair," "adultery," "premarital," and "extramarital" assumes compulsory monogamy as the norm.

14. For an award-winning study that argues that friendship, especially the friendship dynamic exhibited between women, is a more adequate model for human bonding and relational ethics than traditional marriage, see Mary E. Hunt, *Fierce Tenderness: A Feminist Theology of Friendship* (New York, Crossroads, 1991).

15. Silvia Federici, "The Great Witch Hunt," *The Maine Scholar* 1 (Autumn 1988): 31–52.

16. Mariana Valverde, *Sex, Power and Pleasure* (Philadelphia: New Society Publishers, 1987), 35.

17. See Richard J. Gelles and Claire Pedrick Cornell, *Intimate Violence in Families* (Beverly Hills, Calif.: Sage, 1985), who find, for example, that in the United States one in five children grows up in poverty, one in every three women will be raped as an adult, one in every four daughters and one in every eight sons is molested by the age of eighteen, and every thirty-nine seconds a woman is battered in her own home. For the connection between sexual repression and violence, see Marvin Ellison, "Refusing to Be Good Soldiers," in this volume; and James B. Nelson, *The Intimate Connection* (Philadelphia: Westminster Press, 1988), 71–75.

18. See Audre Lorde, "Uses of the Erotic: The Erotic as Power" in her *Sister Outsider* (New York: Crossing Press, 1984), 53–59.

19. See Isabel Carter Heyward, *The Redemption of God* (Lanham, Md.: University Press of America, 1982); Carter Heyward, *Touching Our Strength: The Erotic as Power and Love of God* (San Francisco: Harper & Row, 1989), 109, 75; and James B. Nelson, *Embodiment: An Approach to Sexuality and Christian Theology* (Minneapolis: Augsburg Press, 1978), esp. 34.

20. I am not arguing against the goodness of *chosen* monogamy either on a permanent or temporary basis. For example, in the beginning of a relationship, during childbearing years, as a health measure against what are presently life-threatening sexually transmitted diseases, sexual monogamy that is negotiated and chosen can be good. I am arguing that insofar as monogamy is assumed

to be compulsory, it retards human growth in freedom and responsibility to ourselves and others.

21. Margaret Nichols, "Lesbian Sexuality: Issues and Developing Theory" in *Lesbian Psychologies,* ed. Boston Lesbian Psychologies Collective (Chicago: University of Illinois Press, 1987), 117–19.

22. Eleanor H. Haney, *Vision and Struggle* (Portland, Me.: Astarte Shell Press, 1989), 98.

23. I owe this insight to my partner of almost two decades, Tom Chittick.

24. See Beverly W. Harrison, *Making the Connections* (Boston: Beacon Press, 1985), 87, 93.

25. Indeed, I believe the traditional marriage ethic is part of what Sharon Welch calls "the Western ethic of control." This ethic is based on the Enlightenment notion that the human condition can be improved by rationalization and social control and that responsible action is action that is likely to succeed. The only type of action that is sure of success, however, is coercive action, for we can never guarantee love and cooperation. Love and cooperation demand a willingness to share power. They demand an ethic of risk, a willingness to become vulnerable to the other. Welch says that Western ethics has bolstered monopoly capitalism, the arms race, and the national-security state. I add it has provided the foundation for traditional marriage. Western ethics sees responsibility only in the establishment of security through the defeat of competition and the control of the other. See Sharon D. Welch, *A Feminist Ethic of Risk* (Minneapolis: Fortress Press, 1990).

26. Hunt, *Fierce Tenderness,* 28.

27. Bernard Haring, "Dynamism and Continuity in a Personalist Approach to Natural Law" in *Norm and Context in Christian Ethics,* ed. Gene H. Outka and Paul Ramsey (New York: Charles Scribner's Sons, 1968), 202–3. Haring goes on to say that "we have to face new and undreamed of possibilities of changing our own heritage, of interfering in biological and psychological processes. Historicity belongs to the constitutive structure of man [sic], to his human vocation as well as his power of thinking, his freedom, his sexual determination, his faculties of joy and laughter." Within contemporary Catholic moral theology, Haring's insights about the historically conditioned character of moral reasoning should be applied to the area of sexual ethics, just as they are being applied to the ethics of war and peace and economics.

SEXUALITY AND ECONOMIC REALITY

1. Alison Wynne, *No Time for Crying: Stories of Philippine Women* (Hong King: Resource Center for Philippine Concerns, 1980), 51–52.

2. Throughout this essay I will use "prostitutes" to refer to women and young girls. However, it is important to note the increasing numbers of boy prostitutes reported in the Philippines and Thailand, who also service men.

3. Sharon Welch describes two aspects of solidarity: "(1) granting each group sufficient respect to listen to their ideas and to be challenged by them and (2) recognizing that the lives of the various groups are so intertwined that each is accountable to the other." Sharon Welch, *A Feminist Ethic of Risk* (Minneapolis: Fortress Press, 1990), 133.

4. A wealth of epistemological discussion on this point exists in contemporary feminist, social, and philosophical work. The work of Michel Foucault on the relations of truth and power is one excellent example in philosophy. Other examples are Dorothy E. Smith, "A Sociology for Women" and Bell Hooks, *Feminist Theory: From Margin to Center* (Boston: South End Press, 1984) in feminist theory.

5. As Beverly Harrison writes, "We live in a world historical situation where one geopolitical economy controls all people.... since the global capitalist mode of production pervades and controls all our social relations, we can no longer afford to analyze any of the patterns of exploitation shaping our own community's reality in discrete isolation," from "Theological Reflection in the Struggle for Liberation," in her *Making the Connections* (Boston: Beacon Press, 1985), 245–46.

6. Often theoretical discussion arises from a conflict in organizing and tactics. An example is the "dual systems" debate in recent feminist economic theory over the relation between capitalist economies and patriarchy, which arose from tensions over the question of whether European and U.S. women should organize separately or as part of a broad socialist movement. See Lydia Sargent, ed., *Women and Revolution* (Boston: South End Press, 1981); Michele Barrett, *Women's Oppression Today* (London: New Left Books, 1980); Johanna Brenner and Maria Ramas, "Rethinking Women's Oppression," *New Left Review,* March/April 1984, 144.

7. Personal conversations. See also P. Holden, J. Horlemann, and G. F. Pfafflin, eds., *Tourism/Prostitution/Development* (Bangkok: Ecumenical Coalition on Third World Tourism, 1983), 20.

8. Ibid., 40.

9. Pasuk Phongpaichit, *From Peasant Girls to Bangkok Masseuses* (Geneva: International Labor Organization, 1982), 7. See also Holden, Horlemann, and Pfafflin, *Tourism*.

10. Cited in "The Sexual Revolution," *Far Eastern Economic Review,* 6 January 1976, 21.

11. Special issue on prostitution, *Women's Links: An Occasional Publication,* Women's Concerns Desk, Christian Conference of Asia, Singapore, September 1986, 9–12. It is interesting to see how the shift from local women to foreign women as army prostitutes occurred in both Europe and Japan. Partly, of course, the problem is practical — imperialist armies spend much their time outside of their own country. Yet the shift is also ideological as it is accompanied by the "heightening" of women's status through the symbol of "our" women (vs. "their" women) protecting "our" hearth and home values.

12. Holden, Horlemann, and Pfafflin, *Tourism,* 14, 60.

13. All the new roads, for example, were built by the United States to run from Bangkok to the R & R areas, not to the agricultural sectors, which made them useless for developing farm production.

14. The Marcos government spent many more millions on tourist development than on housing and employment for Filipinos, a pattern followed by the Aquino government. The Korean government, with the help of Japanese capital, has developed an enormous tourist complex on Cheju Island. Since 1985, tourism has been promoted as the top income-producing sector of the Thai economy (see Holden, Horlemann, and Pfafflin, *Tourism,* 41–42, 44; EMPOWER pamphlet, Bangkok, undated).

15. Holden, Horlemann, and Pfafflin, *Tourism,* 89–90.

16. Quoted in talk by Nina Christiansen, First U.S. Conference on Global Trafficking in Women, October 1988, New York.

17. Holden, Horlemann, and Pfafflin, *Tourism,* 13.

18. "Forced" may go beyond structural pressures, as rural families may sell their daughters into prostitution (sometimes disguised as labor contracts), or brothel owners, reacting to the high demand of the tourist/military trade, may kidnap young girls.

19. Noeleen Heyzer, *Working Women in South-East Asia: Development, Subordination and Emancipation* (Philadelphia: Open University Press, 1986), 65.

20. As Diane Elson and Ruth Pearson state, "The capitalist exploitation of women as wage workers is parasitic upon their subordination as a gender." Elson and Pierson, "The Subordination of Women and the Internationalization of Factory Production," in *Of Marriage and the Market,* ed. K. Young, C. Wolkowitz, and R. McCullagh (London: RKP, 1981), 31.

21. Heyzer, *Working Women,* 57.

22. Priscilla Alexander, "Prostitution: A Difficult Issue for Feminists," in *Sex Work: Writings by Women in the Sex Industry,* ed. F. Delacoste and P. Alexander (Pittsburgh: Cleis Press, 1987), 187.

23. See *Plight of Asian Workers in the Electronics Industry* (Hong Kong: CCA-URM, 1982), 27.

24. Quoted in talk by Aurora Xavate de Dios, First U.S. Conference on Global Trafficking in Women. A U.S. soldier remembers Vietnamese women as "of another culture, another color, another race.... You've got an M-16. What do you need to pay for...?" Mark Baker, *Nam* (New York: William Morrow & Co., 1981), 321.

25. Talk by Yayori Matsui, First U.S. Conference on Global Trafficking in Women. Although Japan is, of course, an Asian country, I follow non-Japanese Asian women and progressive Japanese women such as Matsui in grouping its impact with that of First World countries.

26. Talk, First U.S. Conference on Global Trafficking in Women.

27. For discussion of the implications of these views for sexual ethics, see Beverly Harrison and Carter Heyward, "Pain and Pleasure: Avoiding the Confusion of Christian Tradition in Feminist Theory," in *Christianity, Patriarchy, and Abuse: A Feminist Critique,* ed. J. Brown and C. Bohn (New York: Pilgrim Press, 1989).

28. See Michel Foucault, *The History of Sexuality. Volume 1: An Introduction,* trans. Robert Hurley (New York: Vintage Books, 1980).

29. Julia O'Faolain and Lauro Martinez, eds., *Not in God's Image: Women in History* (London: Fontana/Collins, 1973), 307–9. As Michel Foucault writes, "Sex was not something one simply judged, it was a thing one administered," Foucault, *History of Sexuality,* 24.

30. Frances Finnegan, *Poverty and Prostitution: A Study of Victorian Prostitutes in York* (New York: Cambridge University Press, 1979), 8.

31. Judith Walkowitz, "Male Vice and Female Virtue: Feminism and the Politics of Prostitution in Nineteenth-Century Britain," in *Powers of Desire: The Politics of Sexuality,* ed. A. Snitow, C. Stansell, and S. Thompson (New York: Monthly Review Press, 1983), 425, 424.

32. Statement of the 1983 Global Feminist Workshop to Organize Against Traffic in Women, in *International Feminism: Network Against Female Sexual Slavery, Report of the Global Feminist Workshop to Organize Against Traffic in Women,* ed. K. Barry, C. Bunch, and S. Castley (New York: International Women's Tribune Center, 1984), 53, 26.

33. Dworkin and Russell, talk, First U.S. Conference on Global Trafficking in Women. Barry has written that economic analysis can mystify the analysis of the root causes of prostitution (Kathleen Barry, *Female Sexual Slavery* [New York: Avon Books, 1979], 9).

34. Barry, Bunch, and Castley, *International Feminism,* 53.

35. Ibid., 26, 28.

36. Catherine MacKinnon, *Toward a Feminist Theory of the State* (Cambridge, Mass.: Harvard University Press, 1989), 243.

37. Talk by Lisa Go, First U.S. Conference on Global Trafficking in Women.

38. Ibid.

39. *Proceedings,* GABRIELA 4th National Congress, March 1987, Davao City, Philippines.

40. EMPOWER literature, Bangkok.
41. Harrison, *Making the Connections,* xviii. Angela Davis writes, "If we do not attempt to understand the nature of sexual violence as it relates to racial, class, and government violence and power, we cannot even begin to develop strategies which will allow us to eventually purge our society" in *Violence Against Women and the Ongoing Challenge to Racism,* Freedom Organizing Series no. 5 (Latham, N.Y.: Kitchen Table: Women of Color Press, 1985), 10.
42. See, for example, the work of Katie Cannon, Audre Lord, Toni Morrison, Alice Walker, G. Hull, P. Scott, B. Smith, eds., *All the Women Are White, All the Blacks Are Men, But Some of Us Are Brave* (New York: Feminist Press, 1982); C. Moraga and G. Anzaldúa, eds., *This Bridge Called My Back* (New York: Kitchen Table: Women of Color Press, 1983); and G. Anzaldúa, *Making Face, Making Soul: Haciendo Caras* (San Francisco: Aunt Lute Foundation, 1990).
43. Hooks, *Feminist Theory,* 14.

DOMESTIC VIOLENCE AMONG PACIFIC ASIANS

1. "Pacific Asian" is defined here as those persons from the Asian and Pacific regions who retain their native languages and whose worldview remains essentially Asian despite varying levels of Western acculturation.
2. The main languages, however, are Chinese, Japanese, Tagalog, Korean, Vietnamese, Cambodian, Hindustani, Thai, and less often Samoan.
3. This essay is based on my observations as executive director of the Los Angeles-based, nonprofit Center for the Pacific Asian Family, which I founded in 1978. It began with a rape-victim-assistance hotline and has grown to a four-pronged program including a battered-women's shelter, a child-abuse treatment and prevention program and a self-employment program called "Women Entrepreneurs." Some of my conclusions are also drawn from tentative studies I conducted to determine the concrete needs of our clients.
4. Pacific Asians now represent 85 percent of the caseload at the center. From 1982 to 1985, 90 percent of the resident clients were battered women and their children; the remaining 10 percent were rape victims or childhood sexual-assault cases.
5. There has always been a direct correlation between the presence of ethnic workers and the number of clients from that particular ethnic group. One reason for this includes the traditional help-seeking behavior of Pacific Asians starting with the immediate family, relatives, community resources, and then to agencies such as the center. Another has to do with the center's policy of doing outreach only to those communities that are represented by either paid or volunteer staff.
6. *Los Angeles Times,* 1983
7. Manocchio and Petit, *Families Under Stress* (London: Routledge & Kegan Paul, 1975), 103.
8. One consequence of this extended family configuration is that a Pacific Asian woman may be abused by her husband as well as by other relatives, male and female, including brother, uncles, cousins, and mother-in-law. The traditional power structure does not necessarily apply in families where older parents are brought to America by adult children; these parents become dependents of their grown children.
9. Manocchio and Petit, *Families Under Stress.*
10. Leonore Walker, *The Battered Women,* 1978.
11. Walker, *The Battered Women;* and Fleming, *Stopping Wife Abuse.*
12. In 1982 a counselor at the center reported that 80 percent of the women she interviewed mentioned the need for sexual companionship as a reason for returning to an abusive partner when she introduced the subject.

13. The residents at the center can stay for fourteen days as a general rule, but when language and resources are at issue, a longer stay (sometimes considerably longer) is possible.
14. Many battered women stay in abusive relationships because of the very real fear that they will lose immigration status if they are divorced. If her husband wants to get rid of her because he has become involved with another woman or for the price of a green card, as we see more and more at the shelter, she may be forced to endure the humiliation and the difficulties of being discarded without resources and without status.
15. Totman, *Social Causes of Illness* (London, 1979).
16. Wolfe, 1974.
17. Totman, *Social Causes of Illness*.
18. Figures in Los Angeles Country indicate that child abuse is 129 percent more prevalent in homes with spousal abuse (Statement by Lt. Richard Willey, Los Angeles County Sheriff's Department, 2 March 1983).
19. Alessio and Hearns, "Group Treatment of Children in Shelters for Battered Women," in *Battered Women and Their Families,* ed. Roberts (New York: Springer Series, 1984).
20. Myers and Wright, 1980; Pizzey, 1977.
21. Del Martin.

DISABILITY, SEXISM, AND THE SOCIAL ORDER

1. Richard H. Woodfall Burn and W. Strahan, *The History of the Poor Laws* (London: Law Printers to the King's Most Highest Majesty), 1764.
2. Mary Rotha Clay, *The Medieval Hospitals of England* (London: Frank Cass & Co., 1909), ch. 1.
3. Joseph Heffernan, *Introduction to Social Welfare: Power, Scarcity and Common Human Needs* (Itasca, Ill.: P. E. Peacock Publishers, 1981), 189.
4. Ibid., 188–206.
5. Clay, *Medieval Hospitals,* 51–55.
6. Richard French, *From Homer to Helen Keller: A Social and Educational History of the Blind* (New York: American Foundation for the Blind, 1932).
7. Karl Marx, *Capital: A Critique of Political Economy* (New York: Vintage Books, 1977), vol. 1, chs. 9 & 10, 346.
8. Harry Braverman, *Labor and Monopoly Capital: The Degradation of Work in the Twentieth Century* (New York: Monthly Review Press, 1977), 83.
9. Robert Ruffner, "DuPont Has the Answer," *Mainstream,* May 1983.
10. Frances Fox Piven and Richard Cloward, *Regulating the Poor: The Functions of Social Welfare* (New York: Vintage Books, 1976), 3–38.
11. Irving Goffman, *Stigma: Notes on the Management of Spoiled Identity* (Englewood Cliffs, N.J.: Prentice-Hall, 1963), 2–40.
12. Stephen Jay Gould, *Ever Since Darwin: Reflections in Natural History* (New York: Norton, 1977) 63–69.
13. Richard Hofstadter, *Social Darwinism in American Thought* (Boston: Beacon Press, 1955).
14. Joan Smith, *Social Issues and the Social Order: The Contradiction of Capitalism* Cambridge, Mass.: Winthrop Publishers, 1981) 6–11.
15. Frances Koestler, *The Unseen Minority: A Social History of Blindness in the United States* (New York: David McKay Co., 1976), 209–30.
16. "Section 504 of the Rehabilitation Act of 1973: Briefing Guide," Washington, D.C.: Office for Civil Rights, November 8, 1979.
17. Mina Caulfield, "Equality, Sex and Mode of Production," in *Social Inequalities: Anthropological and Developmental Approaches,* ed. Gerald Berraman (New York: Academic Press, 1981), 203.

Catherine G. Nelson, Maria Stecenko, Deborah Lieberman, and Carol Park have all provided me with greatly appreciated editorial assistance at various stages in the development of this essay. Deborah also typed several rather unwieldy versions of it, always on short notice. My dear friend, Carol, has been of tremendous support. Her warmth, advice, and humor have made all the difference. I wish to thank each of you for your generosity, patience, and encouragement.

REFUSING TO BE "GOOD SOLDIERS"

1. Bell Hooks, *Feminist Theory: From Margin to Center* (Boston: South End Press, 1984), 72.
2. Tony Eardley, "Violence and Sexuality" in *The Sexuality of Men*, ed. Andy Metcalf and Martin Humphries (London: Pluto Press, 1985), 87.
3. Wayne Eisenhart, USMC, quoted by Rick Ritter, "Bringing War Home: Vets Who Have Battered" in *Battered Women's Directory*, ed. Betsy Warrior, 9th ed. (Richmond, Ind.: Earlham College, 1985), 254.
4. J. Glenn Gray, *The Warriors: Reflections on Men in Battle* (New York: Harper & Row, 1970), xviii.
5. Joseph H. Pleck, "Men's Power with Women, Other Men, and Society: A Men's Movement Analysis," in *The American Man*, ed. Elizabeth H. Pleck and Joseph H. Pleck (Englewood Cliffs, N.J.: Prentice-Hall, 1980), 428.
6. Audre Lorde, "Uses of the Erotic: The Erotic as Power" in *Take Back the Night: Women on Pornography*, ed. Laura Lederer (New York: William Morrow & Company, 1980), 299.
7. James B. Nelson, *The Intimate Connection: Male Sexuality, Masculine Spirituality* (Philadelphia: Westminster Press, 1988), 80.
8. Eardley, "Violence and Sexuality," 86.
9. Sally Miller Gearhart, "The Future — If There Is One — Is Female" in *Reweaving the Web of Life: Feminism and Nonviolence*, ed. Pam McAllister (Philadelphia: New Society Publishers, 1982), 281.
10. Gray, *The Warriors*, 175.
11. John Sabini and Maury Silver, *Moralities of Everyday Life* (New York: Oxford University Press, 1982), 83, 51.
12. Barbara Smith, "Between a Rock and a Hard Place: Relationships Between Black and Jewish Women" in *Yours in Struggle: Three Feminist Perspectives on Anti-Semitism and Racism*, ed. Elly Bulkin, Minnie Bruce Pratt, and Barbara Smith (Brooklyn: Long Haul Press, 1984), 71.
13. Denise Levertov, "A Speech: For Antidraft Rally, D.C., March 22, 1980" in her *Candles in Babylon* (New York: New Directions Publishing Corp., 1982), 96.

LA CONCIENCIA DE LA MESTIZA

1. This is my own "take off" on José Vasconcelos' idea. José Vasconcelos, *La Raza Cósmica: Misión de la Raza Ibero-Americana* (Mexico: Aguilar S.A. de Ediciones, 1961).
2. Ibid.
3. Arthur Koestler termed this "bisociation." Albert Rothenberg, *The Creative Process in Art, Science, and Other Fields* (Chicago: University of Chicago Press, 1979), 12.
4. In part, I derive my definitions for "convergent" and "divergent" thinking from Rothenberg, *Creative Process*, 12–13.
5. To borrow chemist Ilya Prigogine's theory of "dissipative structures." Prigogine discovered that substances interact not in predictable ways, as it was taught in science, but in different and fluctuating ways to produce new and more complex structures, a kind of birth he called "morphogenesis," which created

unpredictable innovations. Harold Gilliam, "Searching for a New World View," *This World,* January 1981, 23.

6. *Tortillas de masa harina:* corn tortillas are of two types, the smooth uniform ones made in a tortilla press and usually bought at a tortilla factory or super-market, and *gorditas,* made by mixing *masa* with lard or shortening or butter (my mother sometimes puts in bits of bacon or *chicharrones*).

7. Gina Valdés, *Puentes y Fronteras: Coplas Chicanas* (Los Angeles: Castle Litho-graph, 1982), 2.

8. Richard Wilhelm, *The I Ching or Book of Changes,* trans. Cary F. Baynes (Princeton, N.J.: Princeton University Press, 1950), 98.

9. *"Soledad "* is sung by the group Haciendo Punto en Otro Son.

10. Out of the twenty-two border counties in the four border states, Hidalgo County (named for Father Hidalgo, who was shot in 1810 after instigating Mexico's revolt against Spanish rule under the banner of *la Virgen de Guadalupe*) is the most poverty-stricken county in the nation as well as the largest home base (along with Imperial Valley in California) for migrant farmworkers. It was here that I was born and raised. I am amazed that both it and I have survived.

SEXUAL BEING

1. Margaret Miles, *Augustine on the Body* (Missoula, Mont.: Scholars Press, 1979), 97.

2. Ibid., 68.

3. Augustine, *The City of God: The Basic Writings of St. Augustine,* vol. 2, ed. Whitney J. Oates (New York: Random House, 1948), bk. 14, ch. 26, 272.

4. F. Van der Meer, *Augustine the Bishop: Religion and Society at the Dawn of the Middle Ages,* trans. Battershaw and Lamb (New York: Harper Torchbooks, 1961), 183.

5. Augustine, *On the Good of Marriage, St. Augustine: Treatises on Marriage and Other Subjects,* ed. Roy J. Deferrari (Washington, D.C.: Catholic University of America Press, 1955), 9.

6. Quoted in John Boswell, *Christianity, Social Tolerance, and Homosexuality: Gay People in Western Europe from the Beginning of the Christian Era to the Fourteenth Century* (Chicago: University of Chicago Press, 1980), 157.

7. Ibid., 74–75.

8. To trace the influence of a philosophical legacy on the present ethos and insti-tutionalization of sexuality is not to deny that many other forces were also at work, including economic ones.

9. James B. Nelson, *Embodiment* (Minneapolis: Augsburg Publishing House, 1978), 117.

10. James B. Nelson, *Between Two Gardens: Reflections on Sexuality and Religious Experience* (New York: Pilgrim Press, 1983), 4.

SEXUALITY AND THE EUCHARIST

1. Felice Rhiannon, "If They Had Told Us This Our Lives Would Be Very Different," *Woman of Power* no. 2 (Cambridge, Mass.: Summer 1985), 15.

2. James B. Nelson, *Between Two Gardens: Reflections on Sexuality and Theology* (New York: Pilgrim Press, 1985), 5.

3. James F. White, *Sacraments as God's Self-Giving* (Nashville: Abingdon Press, 1983), 13.

4. Gerald F. May, M.D., *Will and Spirit: A Contemplative Psychology* (San Francisco: Harper & Row, 1982), 149.

5. Julian of Norwich, *Revelations of Divine Love,* trans. M. L. Del Mastro (Garden City, N.Y.: Doubleday & Co., 1977), 121, 98.

6. May, *Will and Spirit,* 151.
7. Cited in James B. Nelson, *Embodiment* (Minneapolis: Augsburg Publishing House, 1978), 253.
8. Ibid., 254.

WOMEN, MEN, AND BLACK THEOLOGY

1. Michele Wallace, *Black Macho and the Myth of the Superwoman* (New York: Dial Press, 1979), 13.
2. Jeanne Noble, *Beautiful, Also, Are the Souls of My Black Sisters* (Englewood Cliffs, N.J.: Prentice-Hall, 1978), 301.
3. Julia Mayo, "The New Black Feminism: A Minority Report" in *Contemporary Sexual Behavior: Critical Issues in the 70's,* ed. Joseph Zubin and John Money (Baltimore: Johns Hopkins University Press, 1973), 182.
4. James H. Cone, *A Black Theology of Liberation* (Philadelphia: Lippincott Publishing Co., 1970), 53.
5. James Cone, *God of the Oppressed* (New York: Seabury Press, 1975), 15.
6. Frances Beale, "Double Jeopardy: To Be Black and Female" in *Black Theology: A Documentary History, 1966–1979,* ed. Gayraud Wilmore and James Cone (Maryknoll, N.Y.: Orbis, 1979), 368–76.
7. Cone, *Black Theology of Liberation,* 66.
8. Ibid.
9. Ibid., 67.
10. Jacquelyn Grant, "Black Theology and the Black Woman" in *Black Theology: A Documentary History 1966–1979,* ed. Gayraud Wilmore and James Cone (Maryknoll, N.Y.: Orbis, 1979), 421.
11. Cone, *A Black Theology of Liberation,* 73.
12. Grant, "Black Theology and the Black Woman," 424.
13. Ibid., 426.
14. Cone, *God of the Oppressed,* 17.
15. Noble, *Beautiful, Also, Are the Souls,* 315.
16. Wallace, *Black Macho and the Myth,* 7.
17. Cone, *Black Theology of Liberation,* 32.
18. Ibid., 140, 219.
19. Wallace, *Black Macho and the Myth,* 79.
20. Noble, *Beautiful, Also, Are the Souls,* 336.
21. Ibid., 343.
22. Delores S. Williams, "Black Women's Literature and The Task of Feminist Theology," in *Immaculate and Powerful,* ed. C. W. Atkinson, C. H. Buchanan, and M. R. Miles (Boston: Beacon Press, 1985), 88–110.
23. Katie Geneva Cannon, "The Emergence of Black Feminist Consciousness," in *Feminist Interpretation of the Bible,* ed. Letty M. Russell (Philadelphia: Westminster Press, 1985), 30–40.
24. Toinette Eugene, "While Love Is Unfashionable" in *Women's Consciousness, Women's Conscience,* ed. B. H. Andolsen (New York: Winston-Seabury Press, 1985), 121–41.

EMBRACING MASCULINITY

1. Eugene Monick, *Phallos: Sacred Image of the Masculine* (Toronto: Inner City Books, 1987), 34.
2. Mark Strage, *The Durable Fig Leaf* (New York: William Morrow & Co., 1980), chs. 1 and 5; also Monick, *Phallos,* ch. 2.
3. Rudolf Otto, *The Idea of the Holy,* trans. John W. Harvey (London: Oxford University Press, 1923), cf. Monick, *Phallos,* 26.

4. Monick calls this the "clithonic phallos," see 94–96.
5. Cf. Monick, *Phallos*, 48–49
6. I am indebted to the Rev. Kenneth W. Taylor for these projection insights and also for pressing me to reflect more about the affirmation of genital softness.
7. See Matthew Fox, *Western Spirituality: Historical Roots, Ecumenical Routes* (Notre Dame, Ind.: Fides/Claretian, 1979); also Fox's *Original Blessing*.
8. Quotations from Eckhart are taken from Fox, *Original Blessing*, 132–33, 137, 139.
9. See Robert A. Raines's beautiful meditation on sinking, in *A Faithing Oak: Meditations from the Mountain* (New York: Crossroad, 1982), 9–10.
10. *Selected Poems of Rainer Maria Rilke*, trans. Robert Bly (New York: Harper & Row, 1981), 21.
11. Starhawk, *Dreaming the Dark: Magic, Sex, and Politics* (Boston: Beacon Press, 1982), xiv.
12. See my fuller discussion of androgyny in *Embodiment* (Minneapolis: Augsburg Publishing House, 1978), 98–101. While I still endorse much of that discussion, I am now inclined to move beyond the concept. A useful summary of the social-psychological literature on androgyny is found in Susan A. Basow, chs. 1 and 13.
13. Nicolas Berdyaev's thought on androgyny is found mainly in his *The Meaning of Creativeness* (1914). I am quoting the summary by Philip Sherrard in *Christianity and Eros* (London: SPCK, 1976), 61–62.
14. See Karl Barth, *Church Dogmatics* (Edinburgh: T. & T. Clark, 1961), 3/4, esp. 166.
15. Monick, *Phallos*, 50.
16. In these reflections on power I have been particularly influenced by Bernard Loomer, "Two Kinds of Power," *Criterion* 15, no. 1 (Winter 1976).
17. Ibid., 14.
18. Ibid., 19.
19. Ibid., 21.
20. Bernard Loomer, "S-I-Z-E," *Criterion* 13, no. 3 (Spring 1974): 21.
21. See Williams, *True Resurrection*, 33.
22. Leo Steinberg, *The Sexuality of Christ in Renaissance Art and in Modern Oblivion* (New York: Pantheon Books, 1983).
23. Ibid., 1.
24. Ibid., 17
25. Ibid., 23.
26. Ibid., 13.
27. Patricia Wilson-Kastner's *Faith, Feminism and the Christ* (Philadelphia: Fortress Press, 1983) is a helpful treatment of this issue.
28. The Superman image is from Tom Harpur, *For Christ's Sake* (Boston: Beacon Press, 1987), 32.
29. Ibid., 118–19.

TOWARD A NEW THEOLOGY OF SEXUALITY

1. Samuel Glasner, "Judaism and Sex," in *The Encyclopedia of Sexual Behavior*, ed. Albert Ellis and Albert Abarbanel (New York: Hawthorn Books, 1967), 2:575–84. Cited in Joan Scherer Brewer, *Sex and the Modern Jewish Woman: An Annotated Bibliography* (Fresh Meadows, N.Y.: Biblio Press, 1986), 8–10.
2. Martha Vicinus, "Sexuality and Power: A Review of Current Work in the History of Sexuality," *Feminist Studies* 8, no. 1 (Spring 1982): 136.
3. Seymour Siegel, "Some Aspects of the Jewish Tradition's View of Sex," in *Jews and Divorce*, ed. Jacob Freid (New York: KTAV Publishing House, 1968), 168–69.

4. Jacob Neusner, *A History of the Mishnaic Law of Women,* 5 vols. (Leiden: E. J. Brill, 1980), 5:271–72.
5. Audre Lorde, "Uses of the Erotic: The Erotic as Power," in her *Sister Outsider* (Trumansburg, N.Y.: Crossing Press, 1984), 53–59. Cf. Vicinus, "Sexuality and Power," 136.
6. Lorde, "Uses of the Erotic," 57.
7. Beverly Wildung Harrison, "The Power of Anger in the Work of Love: Christian Ethics for Women and Other Strangers," "Sexuality and Social Policy," and "Misogyny and Homophobia: the Unexplored Connections," all in her *Making the Connections: Essays in Feminist Social Ethics* (Boston: Beacon Press, 1985), 13, 87, 149.
8. Harrison, "The Power of Anger," 14.
9. James B. Nelson, *Between Two Gardens: Reflections on Sexuality and Religious Experience* (New York: Pilgrim Press, 1983), 6; Harrison, "Misogyny and Homophobia," 149.
10. For this insight, and for all I will say in the rest of this essay, I am profoundly indebted to four years of discussion of sexuality and spirituality with my sisters in B'not Esh. See Martha Ackelsberg, "Spirituality, Community, and Politics: B'not Esh and the Feminist Reconstruction of Judaism," *Journal of Feminist Studies in Religion* 2, no. 2 (Fall 1986): 115.
11. Arthur Green, "A Contemporary Approach to Jewish Sexuality," in *The Second Jewish Catalog,* ed. Sharon Strassfeld and Michael Strassfeld (Philadelphia: The Jewish Publication Society, 1976), 98.
12. Nelson, *Between Two Gardens,* 7.
13. Adrienne Rich, *Of Woman Born: Motherhood as Experience and Institution* (New York: W. W. Norton, 1976), 285.
14. Lorde, "Uses of the Erotic," 57.
15. Ibid., 55.
16. Ibid., 57.
17. Epstein, *Sex Laws and Customs in Judaism* (New York: KTAV, 1967), 14.
18. Gordis, *Love and Sex: A Modern Jewish Perspective* (New York: Farrar Straus Giroux, 1978), 106.
19. Harrison, "The Power of Anger," 13–14.
20. Lorde, "Uses of the Erotic," 59.
21. I am grateful to Denni Liebowitz for putting the issue in this way. Conversation, Fall 1983.
22. Martha Ackelsberg, "Families and the Jewish Community: A Feminist Perspective," *Response* 14, no. 4 (Spring 1985): 15–16.
23. David M. Feldman, *Marital Relations, Birth Control, and Abortion in Jewish Law* (New York: Schocken Books, 1974), chaps. 2, 4, 5; Martha Ackelsberg, "Family or Community?" *Sh'ma,* 20 March 1987, 76–78.
24. Green, "A Contemporary approach," 98.

About the Contributors

Paula Gunn Allen, a Laguna Pueblo-Sioux, is a scholar, activist, novelist, poet, and professor of Native American studies at the University of California, Berkeley. Recent publications include *The Sacred Hoop: Recovering the Feminine in American Indian Traditions* and *Spider Woman's Granddaughters*.

Gloria Anzaldúa, a Chicana *tejana* lesbian, feminist activist, poet, teacher, and essayist, has been active in the migrant-workers movement. She is coeditor of *This Bridge Called My Back: Writings by Radical Women of Color* and author of *Borderlands/La Frontera: The New Mestiza*.

Elizabeth M. Bounds is a doctoral candidate in social ethics at Union Theological Seminary, New York. Her essay is based on her experiences and research while she was working for the Office for East Asia and the Pacific of the National Council of Churches of Christ in the U.S.A.

Deborah H. Carney's family heritage is rooted in the church and academia. While she cherishes her ancestors, she seeks to explore their theories by grounding herself in experience. She holds a master of divinity degree from Bangor Theological Seminary. Her life work is among the mentally retarded, whom she teaches and guides and from whom she is constantly learning.

Chrystos, a Menominee, is an artist, writer, and political activist. She is the recent author of *Not Vanishing*.

Debra Connors has a degree from San Francisco State University in interdisciplinary Social Science and has taught women's studies there. Her research interests include the history of science and technology and the social history of disability. Despite almost lifelong diabetes, which has rendered her partially sighted and arthritic, she continues to be a political activist, beach comber, and urban gardener.

Susan E. Davies is a white feminist activist and an associate professor of pastoral studies at Bangor Theological Seminary in Bangor, Maine. A minister in the United Church of Christ, she leads workshops and Bible studies and is pursuing additional studies in religion and education.

Ruth C. Duck is a United Church of Christ clergywoman, hymn writer, and assistant professor of worship at Garrett-Evangelical Theological Seminary in Evanston, Illinois. She has edited several books of worship resources, including *Touch Holiness*, with coeditor Maren Tirabassi.

Marvin M. Ellison is professor of Christian social ethics at Bangor Theological Seminary in Bangor, Maine. He lectures nationally on justice issues and is the primary author of the new Presbyterian Church (U.S.A.) position paper on sexuality, "Keeping Body and Soul Together."

James H. Evans Jr. is president and Robert K. Davies Professor of Systematic Theology at Colgate Rochester Divinity School, Bexley Hall, and Crozer Theological Seminary.

Robin Gorsline writes, works for justice and feminist-gay liberation, and dances at Radical Faerie gatherings. He is a doctoral candidate at Union Theological Seminary.

Eleanor H. Haney, a scholar and activist of English background, is a partner in Astarte Shell Press, a feminist publishing company, and author of *Vision and Struggle: Meditations on Feminist Spirituality and Politics*.

Sharon Hashimoto is a poet whose work has been included in *The Gathering Ground* and many poetry journals.

Carter Heyward is a theologian, activist, and writer, who teaches at the Episcopal Divinity School, Cambridge, Massachusetts. Her most recent book is *Touching Our Strength: The Erotic as Power and the Love of God*.

Lucy V. Hitchcock brings poetry, narrative theology, and a commitment to the creation of a just economic community to the practice of Unitarian Universalist ministry. Formerly new congregations program director at the Unitarian Universalist Association in Boston, she now serves a new congregation in Aloha, Oregon. She is completing a doctor of ministry program at Hartford Seminary with an emphasis on congregational studies and ministry for social transformation.

Mary E. Hobgood holds a Ph.D. in religious studies from Temple University. Her dissertation, *Catholic Social Teaching and Economic Theory*, is a 1991 publication of Temple University Press. She has taught at several colleges and universities on the East Coast and lives with her husband and children in Allentown, Pennsylvania.

Vicki Hollander is a rabbi and maker of rituals who has served in Conservative, Reform, and Havurah congregations and is now guiding a new Jewish community in Seattle. In addition, she is currently working as a marriage and family therapist. She is also a coordinator of volunteers and bereavement services at Hospice of Seattle.

Mary E. Hunt, an activist and feminist theologian, is cofounder and codirector of WATER (Women's Alliance for Theology, Ethics, and Ritual) in Silver Spring, Maryland. She is the author of *Fierce Tenderness: A Feminist Theology of Friendship*.

Ada María Isasi-Díaz is a Hispanic, feminist activist and theologian committed to the liberation of Hispanic women. Her most recent book, written with Yolanda Tarango, is *Hispanic Women: Prophetic Voice in the Church*.

Audre Lorde, a black poet, essayist, and activist, has inspired and challenged feminists throughout the world with her speaking and writing. She is the author of many books, including *Sister Outsider: Essays and Speeches, The Cancer Journals,* and *Zami: A New Spelling of My Name*.

Ann MacKenzie holds a bachelor's degree from Albion College, Albion, Michigan, and a master's degree in scared music from Boston University School of Theology. She studied composition with internationally renowned German composer Heinz Werner Zimmermann. After the untimely death of the English theologian and hymnologist Erik Routley in 1982, she took over the editing of the hymnal *Rejoice in the Lord* for the Reformed Church in America. She composes sacred choral music, setting original texts to music as well as using scriptural material. She has served as organist-choir director in several Massachusetts churches, leads workshops in music, and teaches privately.

Gina Masur is a Jewish feminist and poet. A recent graduate of Goddard College, Plainfield, Vermont, she is currently at the Kripalu Center in western Massachusetts.

Roberto Mendoza, a Creek-Chicano activist and writer, is the author of *Look! A Nation Is Coming*.

Carolyn Merchant is professor of environmental history and ethics at the University of California, Berkeley. She is the author of *The Death* *of Nature: Women, Ecology, and the Scientific Revolution* and *Ecological Revolutions: Nature, Gender, and Science in New England*.

James B. Nelson is professor of Christian Ethics at United Theological Seminary in the Twin Cities, Minneapolis, Minnesota. He is the author of many books, including *Embodiment* and *Between Two Gardens*.

Judith Plaskow is associate professor of religious studies at Manhattan College, New York. She is the editor of *Standing Again at Sinai: Rethinking Judaism from a Feminist Perspective* and cofounder and coeditor of *The Journal of Feminist Studies in Religion*.

Marcia Riggs teaches ethics in the graduate and theological schools at Drew University, Madison, New Jersey. Her teaching, research, and writing address such subjects as racism, the socioreligious-ethical traditions of black women, womanist and feminist ethics, affirmative action, justice and social policy, and the black women's club movement of the nineteenth century. She lectures and leads workshops on the interconnections of race, gender, and class oppression.

Nilda Rimonte, born and reared in the Philippines, founded the first child-abuse-and-treatment program for Pacific Asians in Los Angeles. She is also the founder of the Center for the Pacific-Asian Family and Women Entrepreneurs, a self-employment and business program for women.

Paula Lorraine Roper received a bachelor's degree in English from Fisk University and a master's degree from Northwestern. She has taught literature and writing at several colleges, including Fisk and the University of Tennessee, where she is currently pursuing a doctorate in English.

Susan Savell is a minister of the Peace Church of Southern Maine. She also travels nationally as a recording and performing artist and composer.

Vickie Sears, a Cherokee-Anglo, is a writer, teacher, and feminist therapist. Her poetry has been published in *Gathering Ground* and *Sinister Wisdom*.

John Stoltenberg holds a master of divinity degree from Union Theological Seminary and a master of fine arts degree in theater from Columbia University. A writer and editor, he chairs the task force on pornography of the National Organization of Men Against Sexism and is co-founder of Men Against Pornography. He helped create Brother-Peace: An International Day of Actions to End Men's Violence.

Emilie M. Townes is assistant professor of Christian social ethics at Saint Paul School of Theology, Kansas City, Missouri. She is an ordained American Baptist minister and editor of a forthcoming collection of essays, *Womanist Perspectives on Evil and Suffering*.

Redwing Wilderbrook, a third-generation Scandinavian, is an eco-feminist minister, poet, environmental educator, and mother.

Nellie Wong, a socialist feminist writer, has been active in unions and the Freedom Socialist Party. She has also taught writing and women's studies at several colleges and universities.